DOMINIQUE OSUCH
WRITER

SANDRINE MARTIN
ART

# Niki
## DE SAINT PHALLE

*THE GARDEN OF SECRETS*

**nbm** GRAPHIC NOVELS
Nantier · Beall · Minoustchine
NEW YORK

ISBN 9781681121581
Library of Congress Control Number 2018933161
© 2014 Casterman
© 2018 NBM for the English translation
Translation by Joe Johnson
Lettering by Big Bird Zatryb
Printed in China
1st printing May 2018

# CHAPTER 1

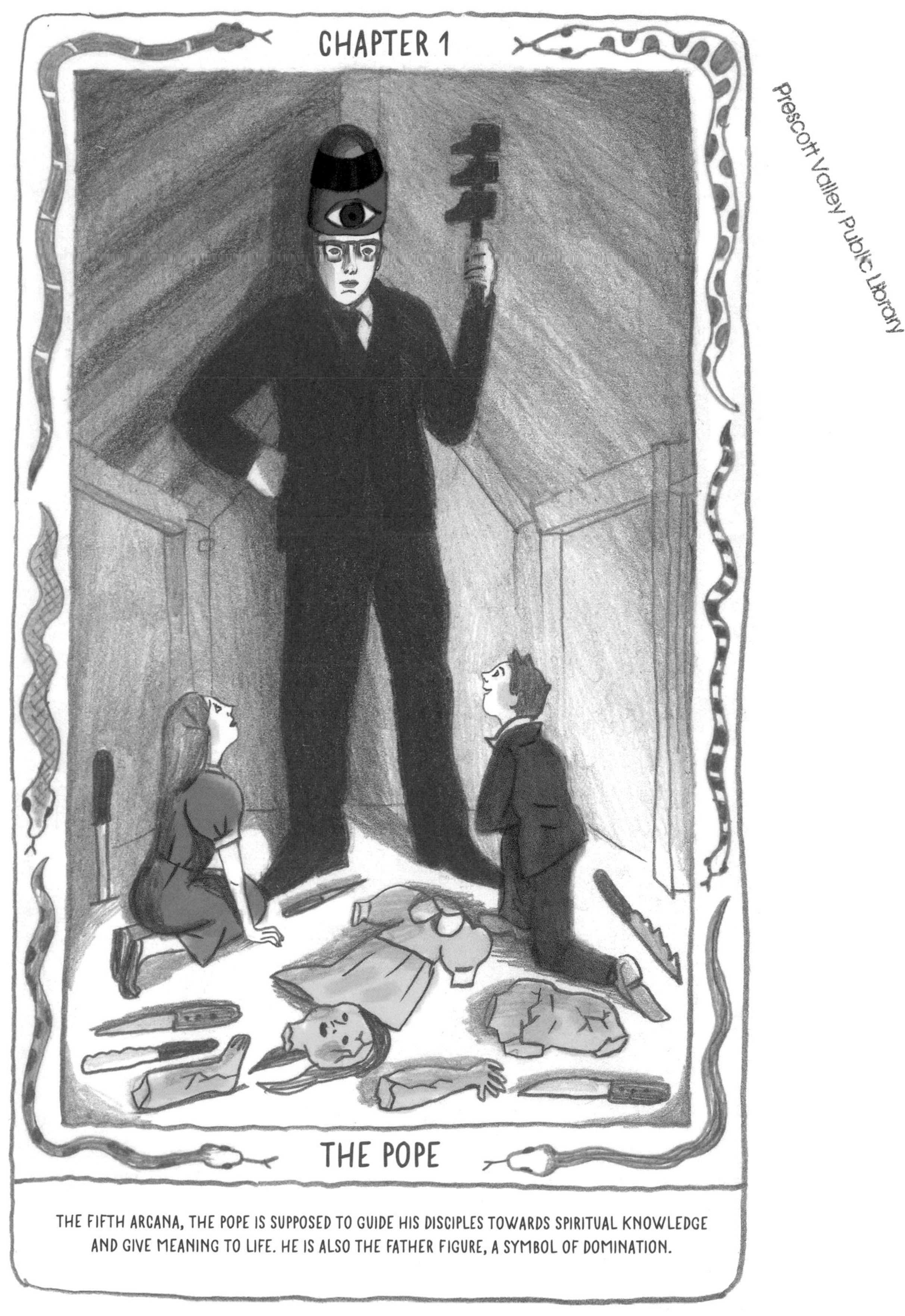

## THE POPE

THE FIFTH ARCANA, THE POPE IS SUPPOSED TO GUIDE HIS DISCIPLES TOWARDS SPIRITUAL KNOWLEDGE AND GIVE MEANING TO LIFE. HE IS ALSO THE FATHER FIGURE, A SYMBOL OF DOMINATION.

OCTOBER 29, 1930, 6:40AM, NEUILLY-SUR-SEINE, FRANCE

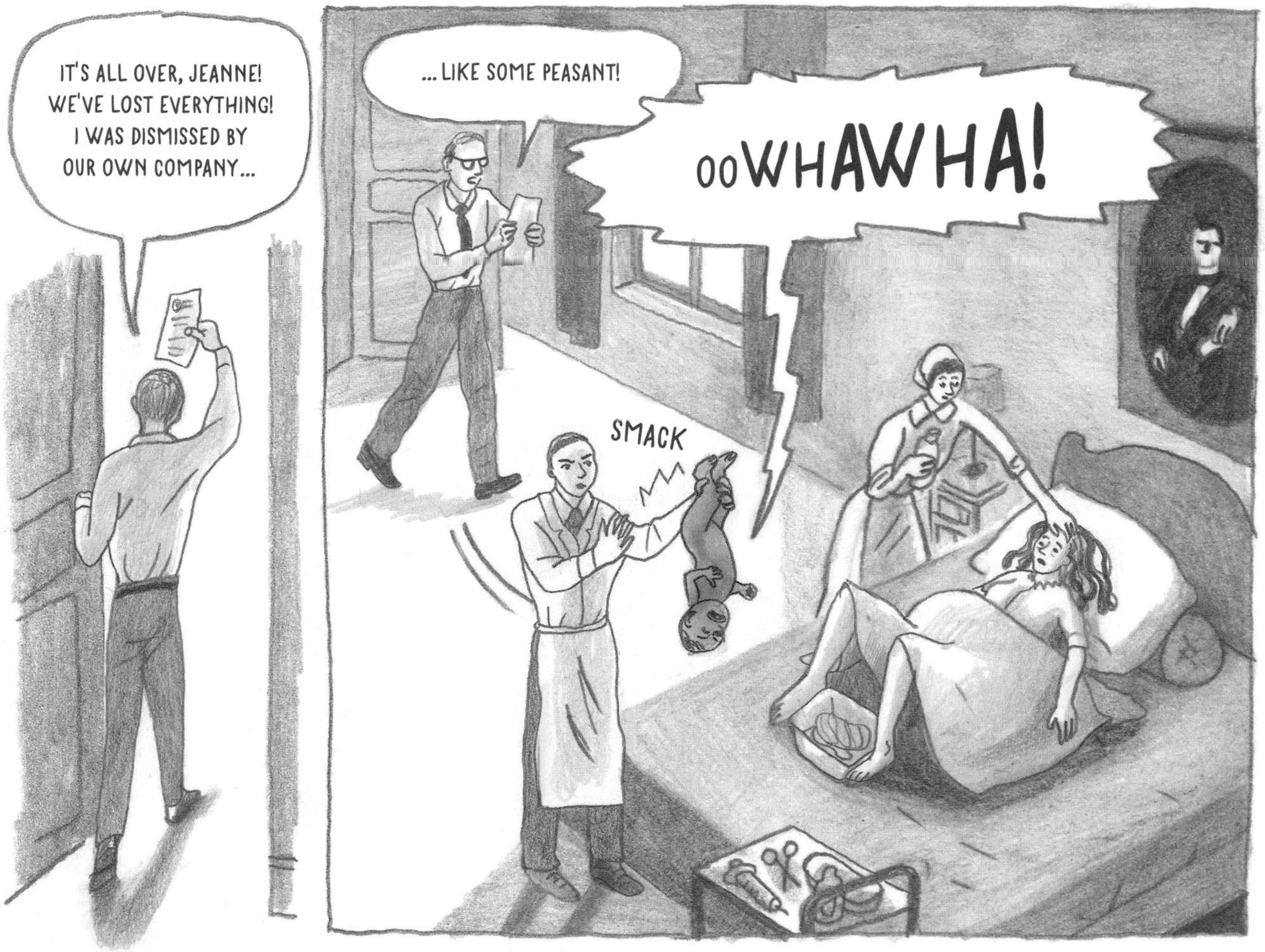
IT'S ALL OVER, JEANNE! WE'VE LOST EVERYTHING! I WAS DISMISSED BY OUR OWN COMPANY...
...LIKE SOME PEASANT!
OOWHAWHA!
SMACK

*The ancestry of this man seemingly so unconcerned by the surge of new life was: Phillipe de Saint Phalle, lord of Cudot, deceased circa 1480, and also Richard, his grandson, baron of Cudot. And others, too, lords, counts, and even a bishop...a very ancient aristocracy going back generations, which had to maintain its status!*

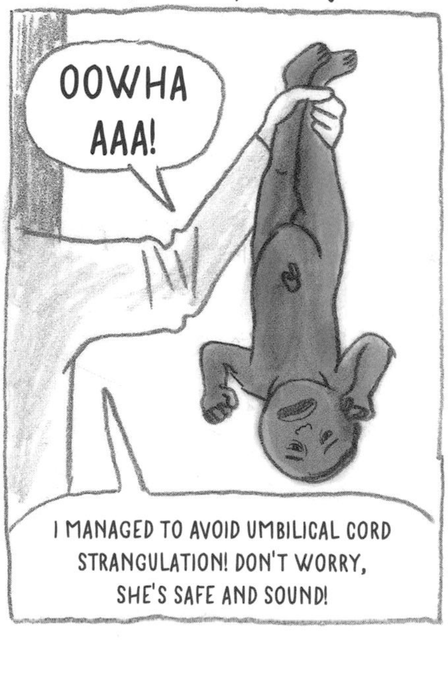
OOWHA AAA!
I MANAGED TO AVOID UMBILICAL CORD STRANGULATION! DON'T WORRY, SHE'S SAFE AND SOUND!

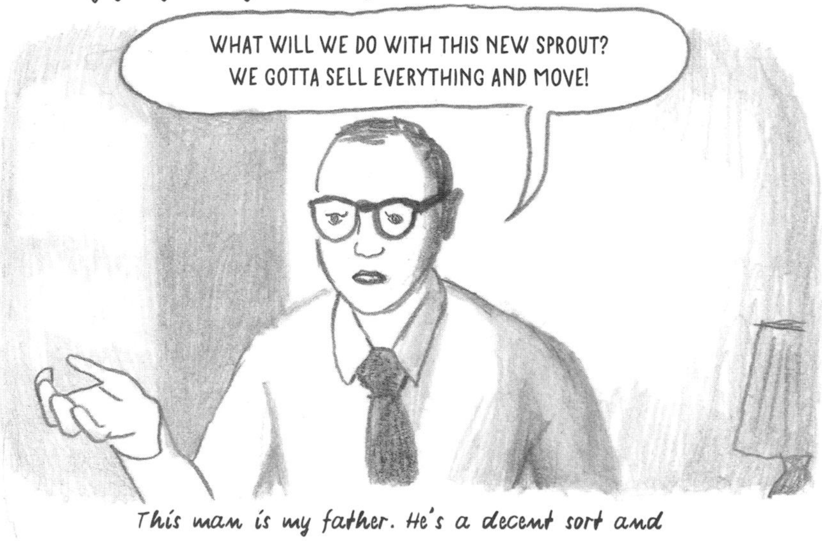
WHAT WILL WE DO WITH THIS NEW SPROUT? WE GOTTA SELL EVERYTHING AND MOVE!

*This man is my father. He's a decent sort and libertarian, even revolutionary, too! It's simply that no one ever taught him how to show his love...*

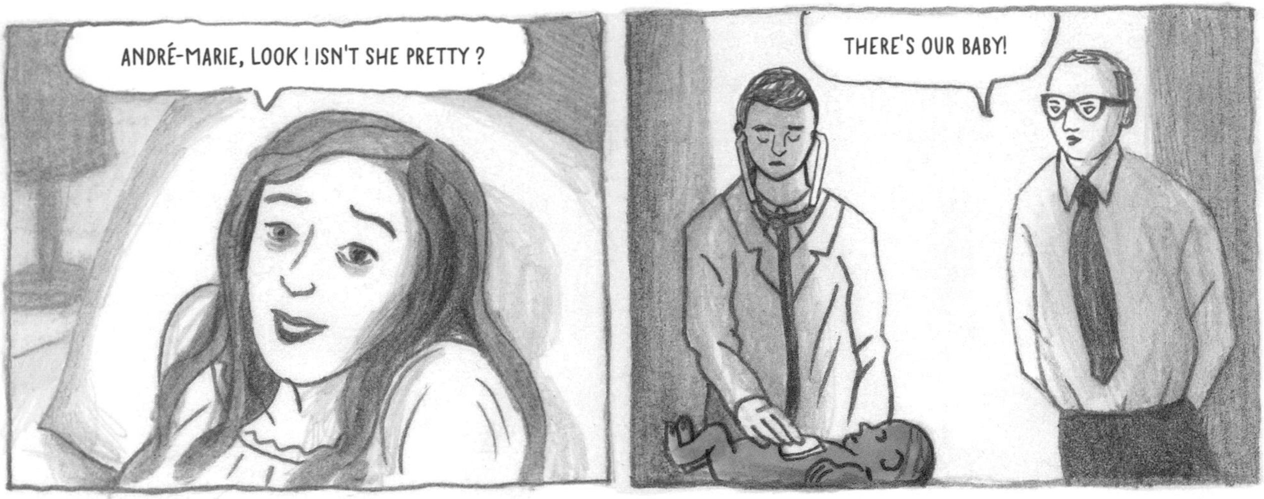
ANDRÉ-MARIE, LOOK! ISN'T SHE PRETTY?
THERE'S OUR BABY!

*Nobody ever taught her how to love either. She, however, was making such an effort, while her husband was cheating on her in the meantime.*

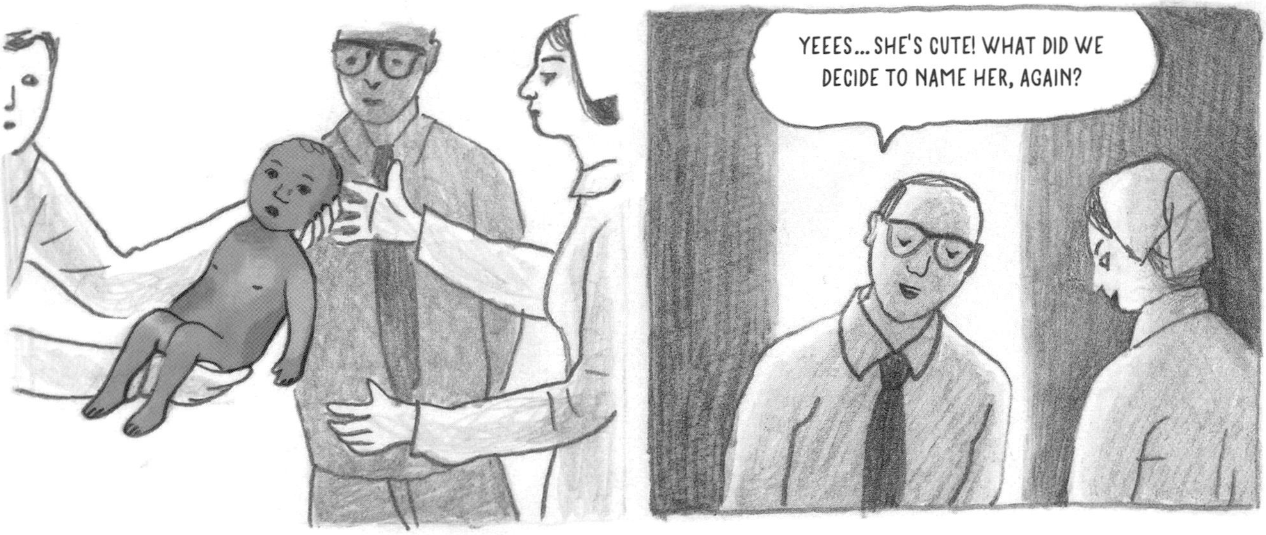
YEEES... SHE'S CUTE! WHAT DID WE DECIDE TO NAME HER, AGAIN?

*...I remember her tears while I was still sheltered in the cavern of her womb!*

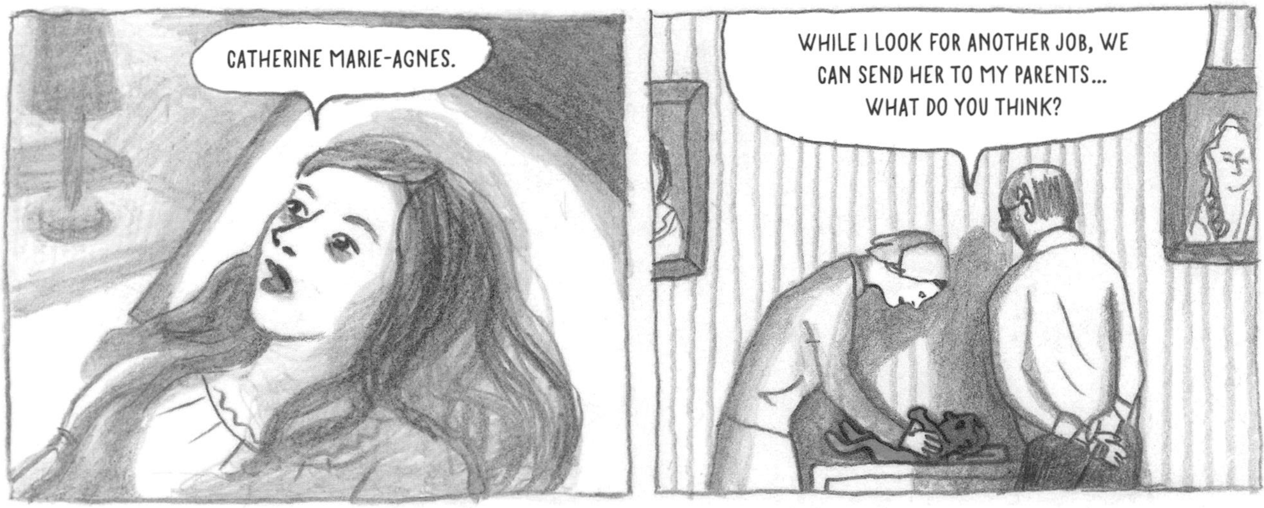
CATHERINE MARIE-AGNES.
WHILE I LOOK FOR ANOTHER JOB, WE CAN SEND HER TO MY PARENTS... WHAT DO YOU THINK?

*Mama, why did you abandon me? What did I do wrong? Your love shimmers around me despite your absence, like the petals of a rose scattered over your dress of silvery satin...*

1935, THE CHÂTEAU DE FILLERVAL, OISE, FRANCE.

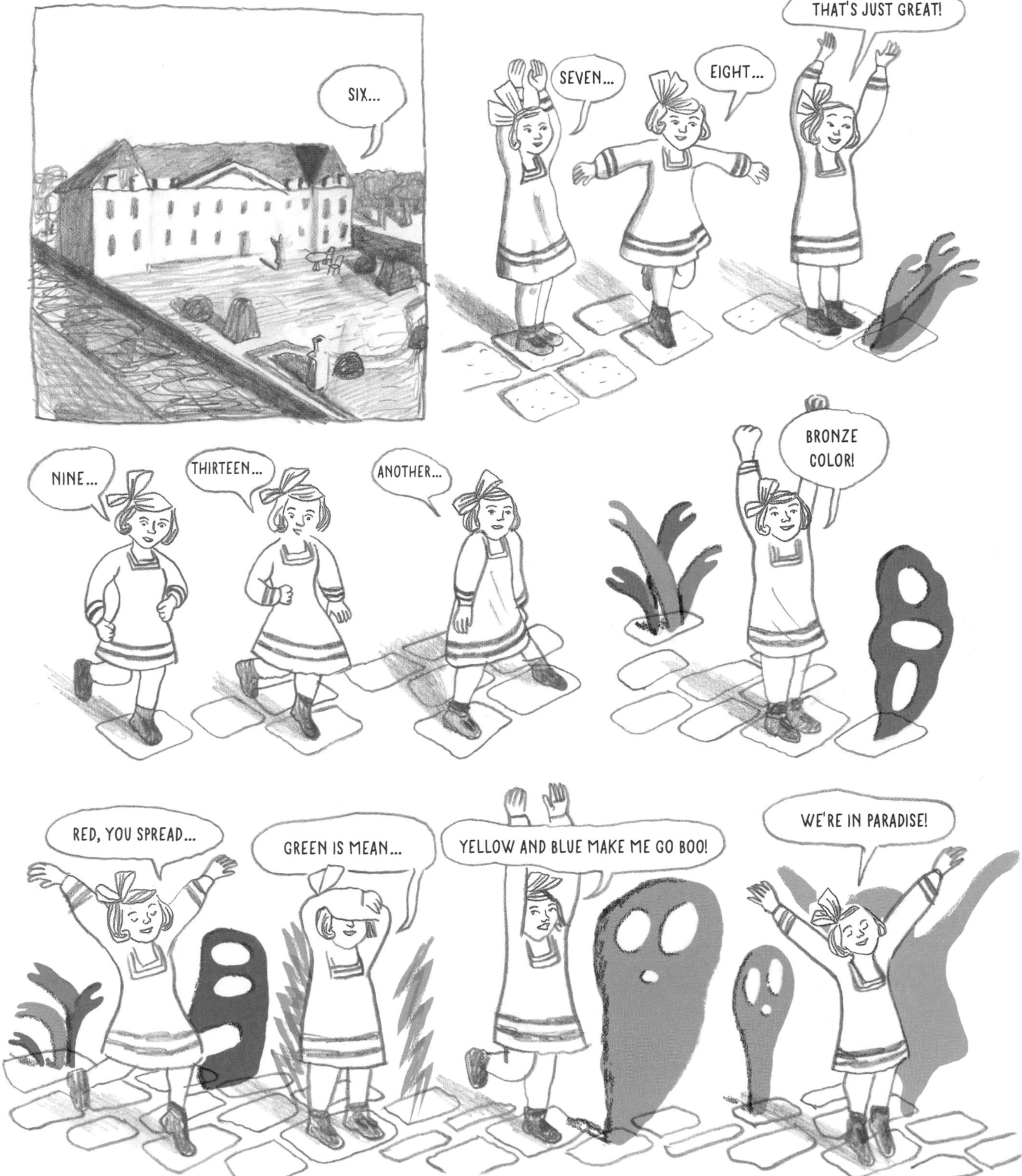
SIX...
SEVEN...
EIGHT...
THAT'S JUST GREAT!
NINE...
THIRTEEN...
ANOTHER...
BRONZE COLOR!
RED, YOU SPREAD...
GREEN IS MEAN...
YELLOW AND BLUE MAKE ME GO BOO!
WE'RE IN PARADISE!

*I don't need you, Mother!*
*Your poor opinion of me was so painful and, in the end, so useful!*

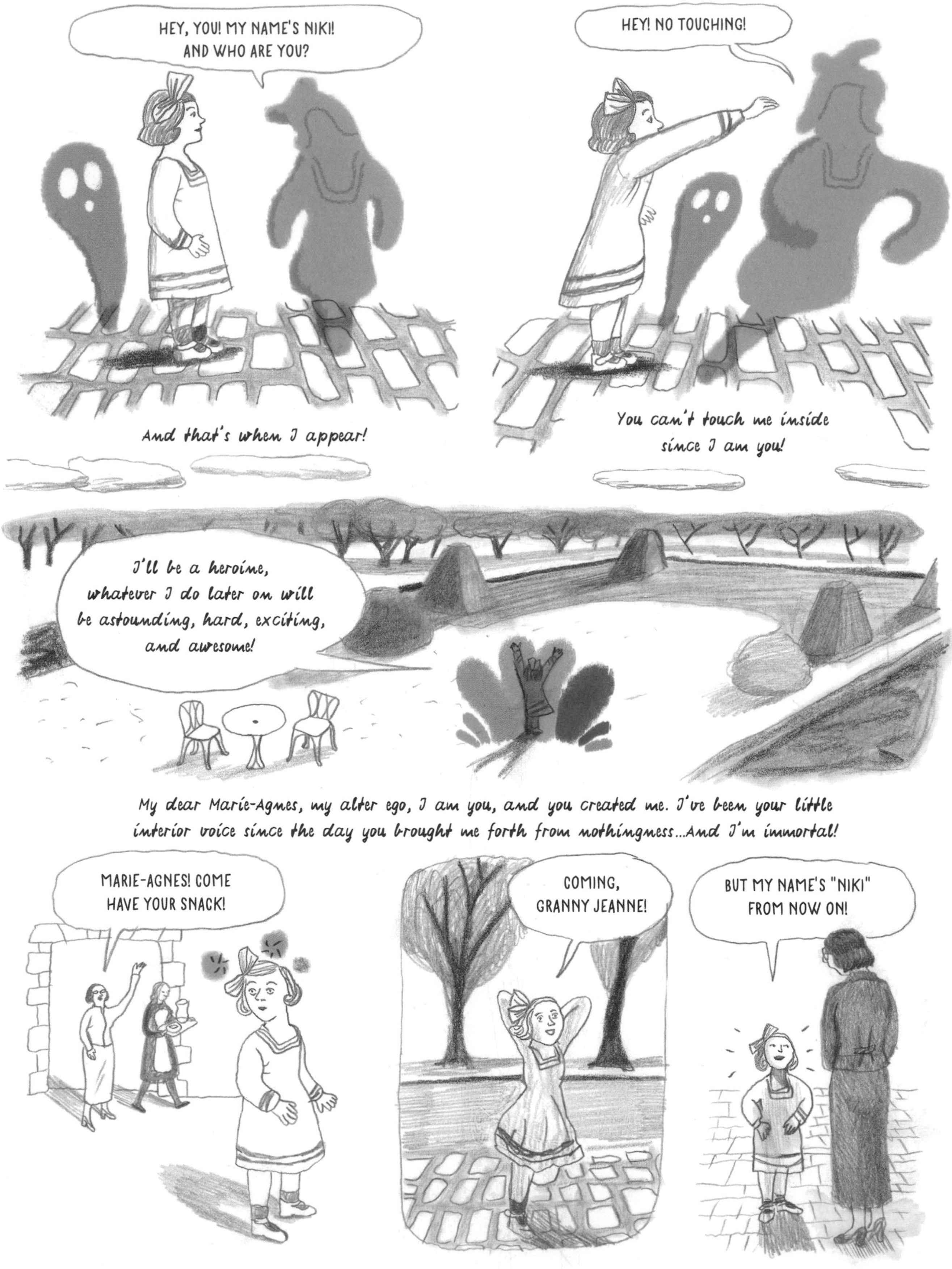
HEY, YOU! MY NAME'S NIKI! AND WHO ARE YOU?
And that's when I appear!
HEY! NO TOUCHING!
You can't touch me inside since I am you!
I'll be a heroine, whatever I do later on will be astounding, hard, exciting, and awesome!
My dear Marie-Agnes, my alter ego, I am you, and you created me. I've been your little interior voice since the day you brought me forth from nothingness...And I'm immortal!
MARIE-AGNES! COME HAVE YOUR SNACK!
COMING, GRANNY JEANNE!
BUT MY NAME'S "NIKI" FROM NOW ON!

1939, NOROTON POINT, CONNECTICUT.

*I was fierce...fierce and instinctive like a scorpion...*

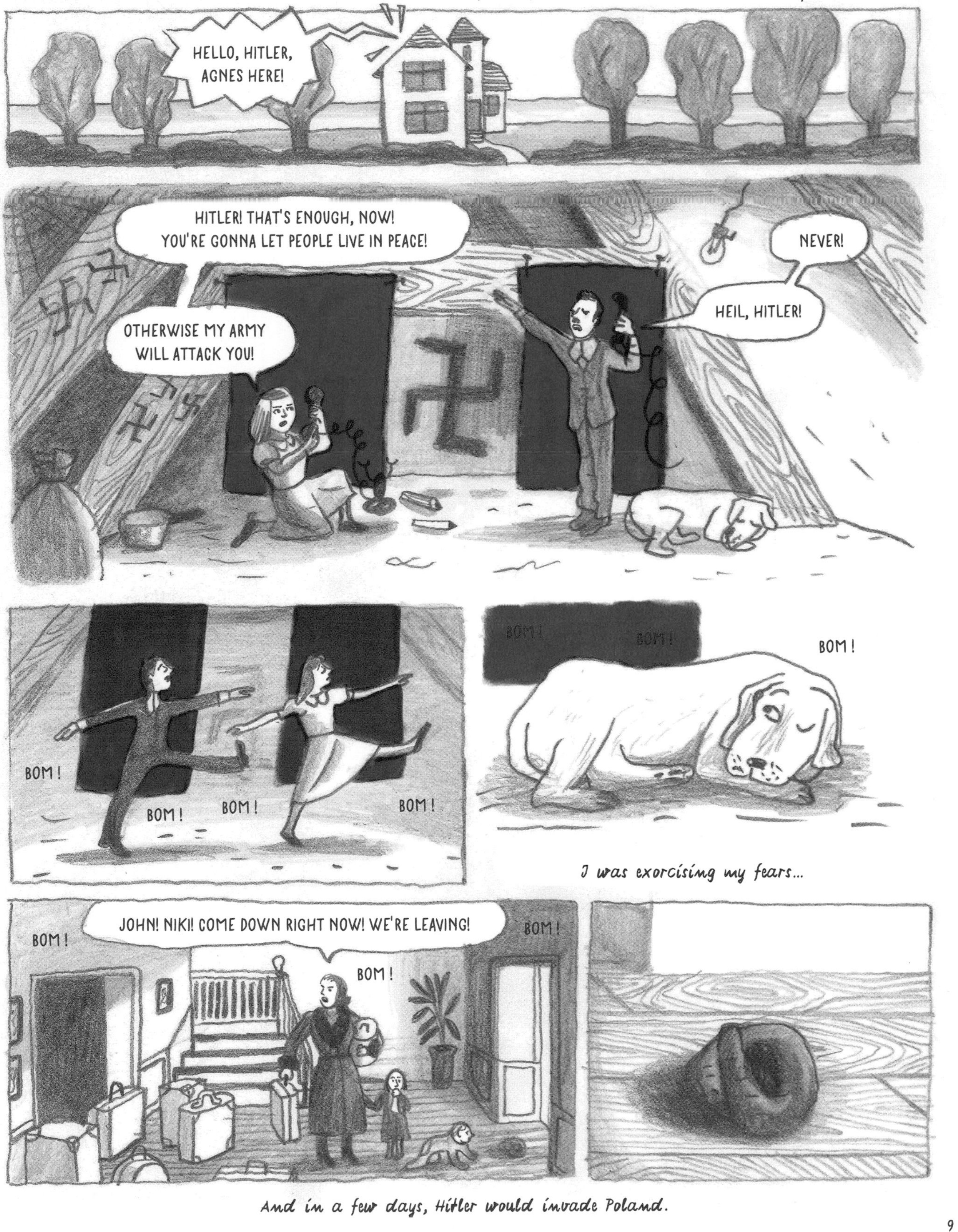
HELLO, HITLER, AGNES HERE!
HITLER! THAT'S ENOUGH, NOW! YOU'RE GONNA LET PEOPLE LIVE IN PEACE!
OTHERWISE MY ARMY WILL ATTACK YOU!
NEVER!
HEIL, HITLER!
BOM!
BOM!
BOM!
BOM!
BOM!
BOM!
BOM!
BOM!
JOHN! NIKI! COME DOWN RIGHT NOW! WE'RE LEAVING!
BOM!
BOM!

*I was exorcising my fears...*

*And in a few days, Hitler would invade Poland.*

1941, DARIEN, CONNECTICUT.

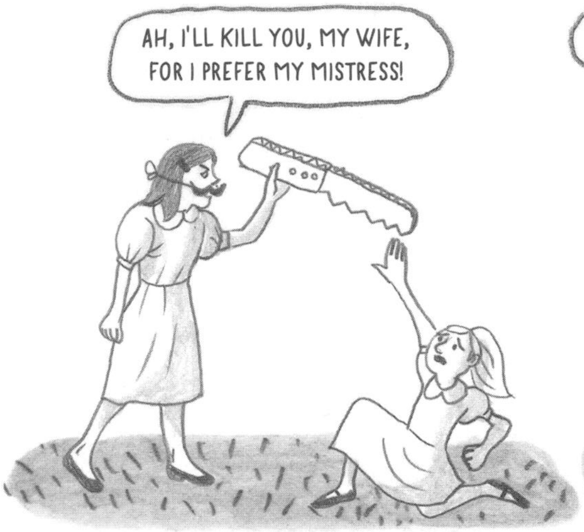
AH, I'LL KILL YOU, MY WIFE, FOR I PREFER MY MISTRESS!

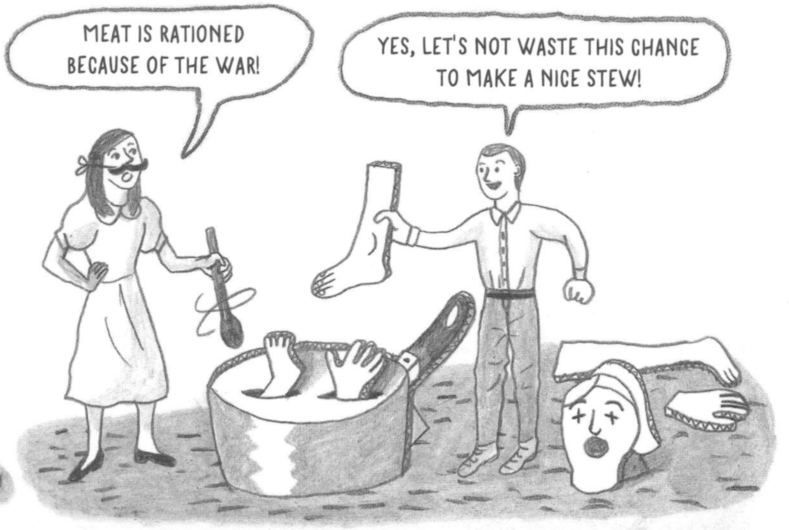
MEAT IS RATIONED BECAUSE OF THE WAR!
YES, LET'S NOT WASTE THIS CHANCE TO MAKE A NICE STEW!

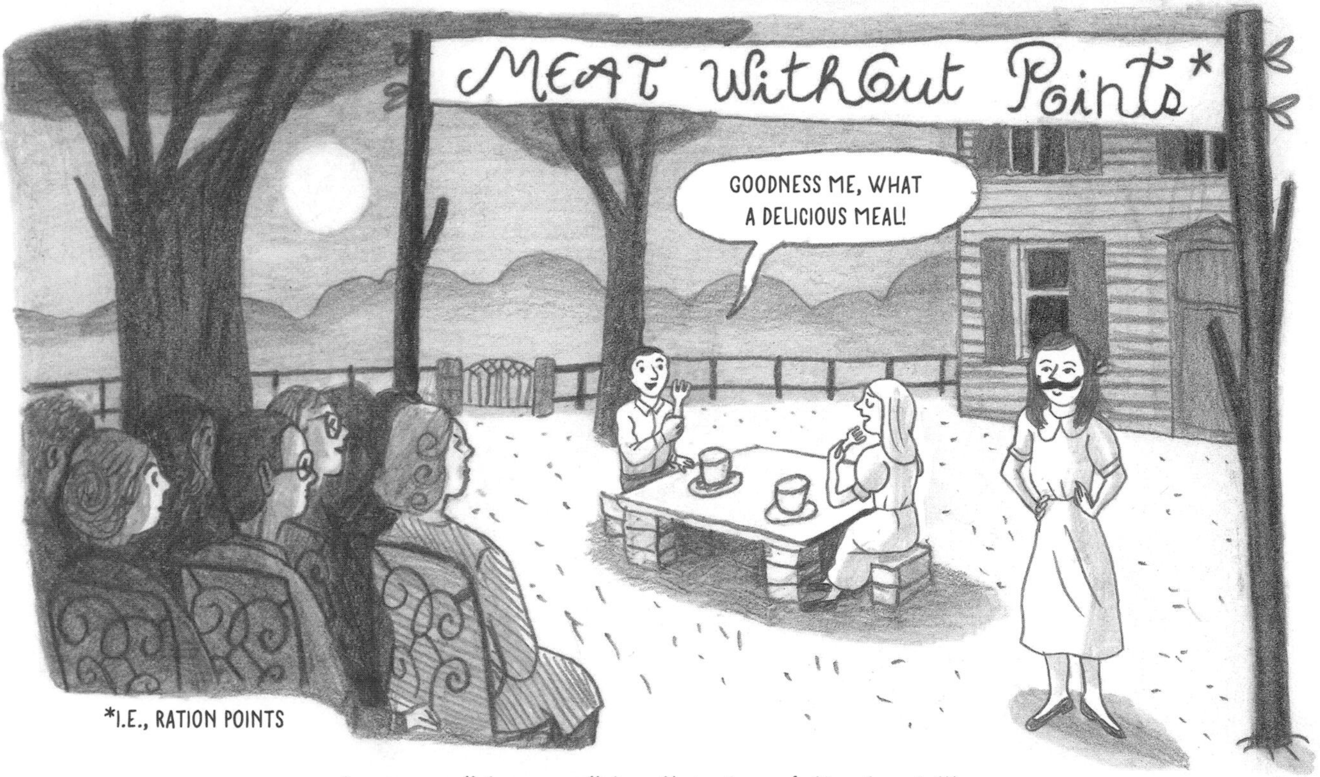
MEAT WithOut Points*
GOODNESS ME, WHAT A DELICIOUS MEAL!

*I.E., RATION POINTS

*I was a wild, very wild soul! And my father loved it!*

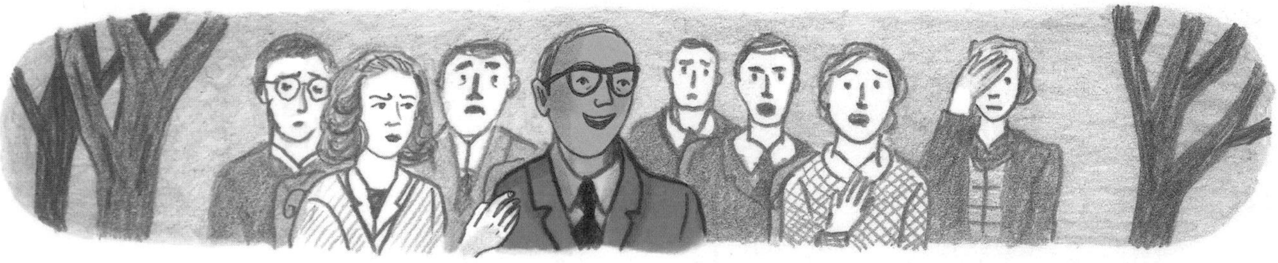

*Later, I preferred to bring happiness...*

1947, PRINCETON, NEW JERSEY.

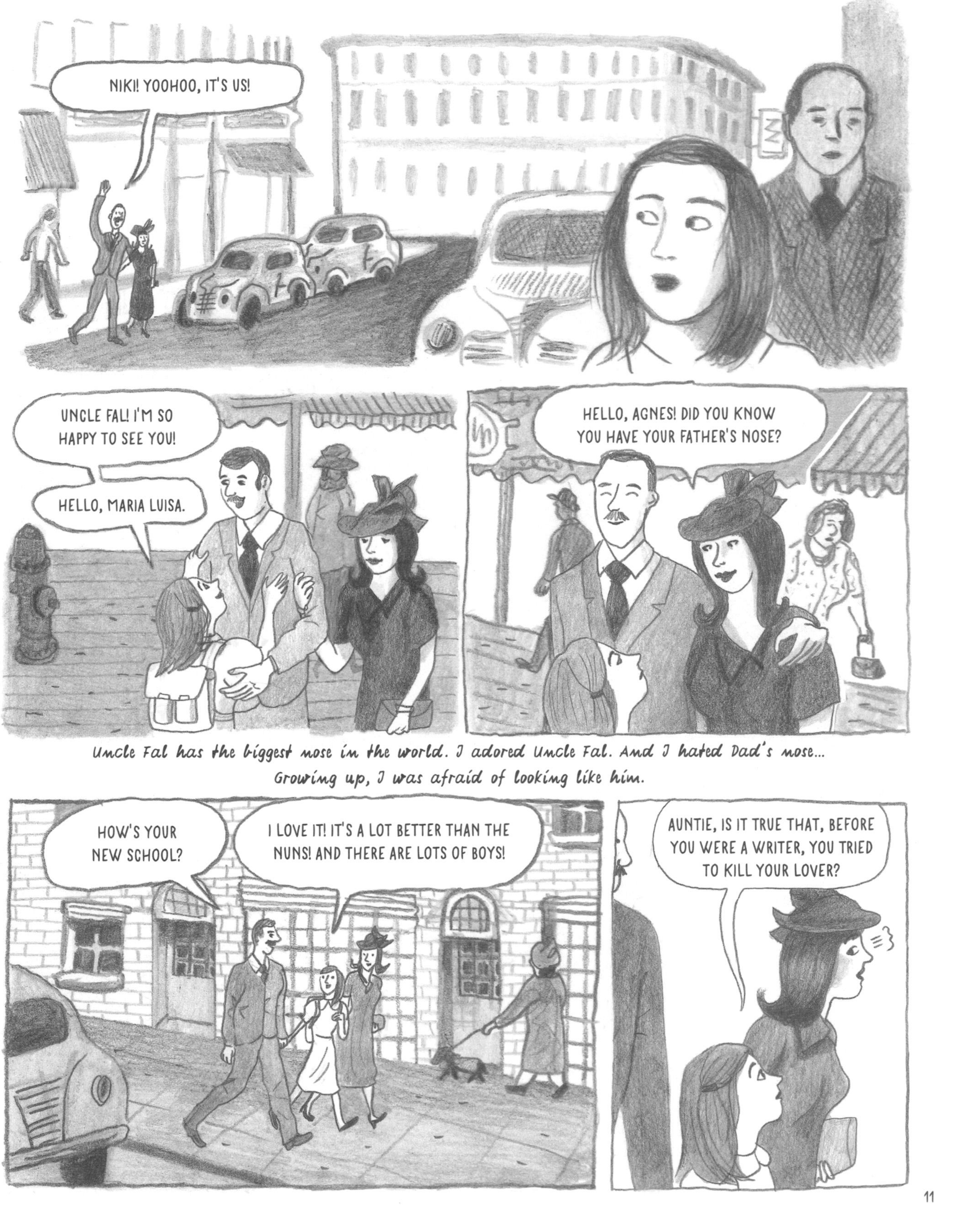
NIKI! YOOHOO, IT'S US!
UNCLE FAL! I'M SO HAPPY TO SEE YOU!
HELLO, MARIA LUISA.
HELLO, AGNES! DID YOU KNOW YOU HAVE YOUR FATHER'S NOSE?
Uncle Fal has the biggest nose in the world. I adored Uncle Fal. And I hated Dad's nose... Growing up, I was afraid of looking like him.
HOW'S YOUR NEW SCHOOL?
I LOVE IT! IT'S A LOT BETTER THAN THE NUNS! AND THERE ARE LOTS OF BOYS!
AUNTIE, IS IT TRUE THAT, BEFORE YOU WERE A WRITER, YOU TRIED TO KILL YOUR LOVER?

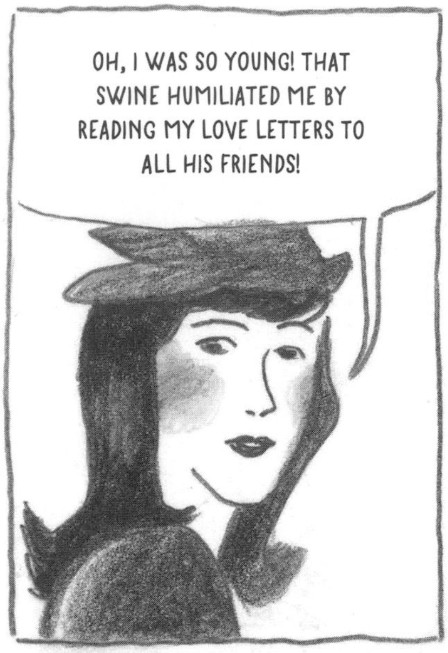
OH, I WAS SO YOUNG! THAT SWINE HUMILIATED ME BY READING MY LOVE LETTERS TO ALL HIS FRIENDS!

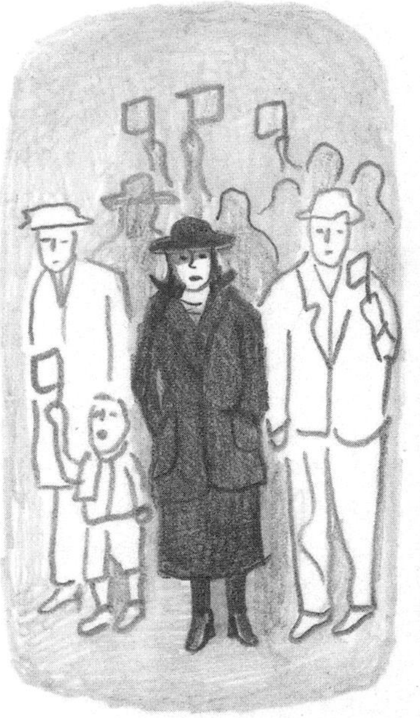

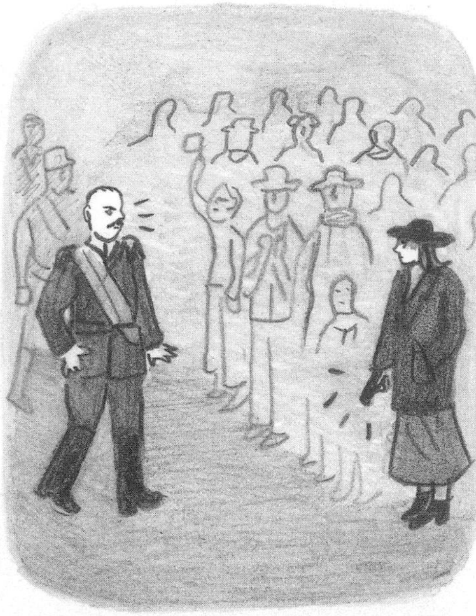

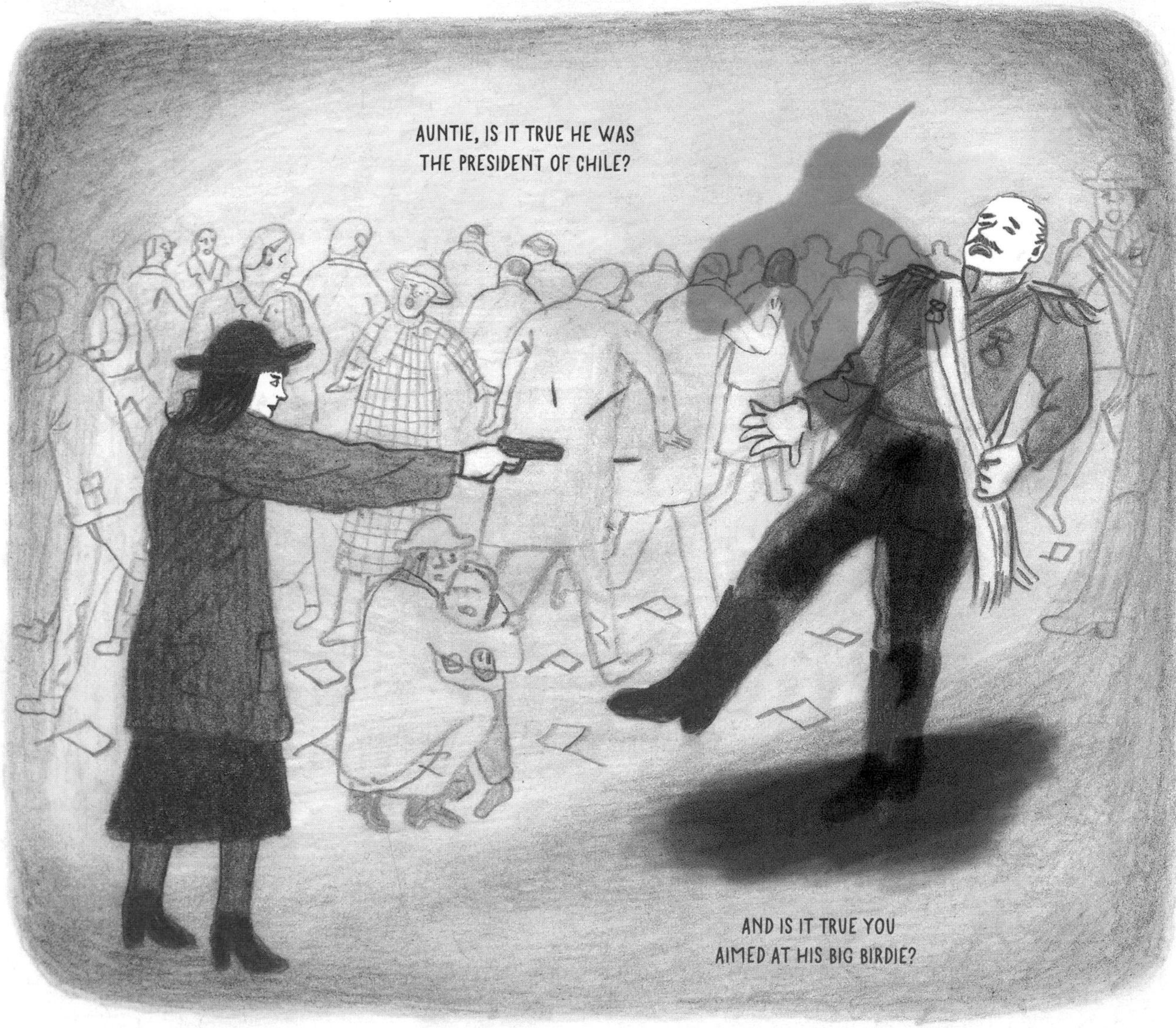
AUNTIE, IS IT TRUE HE WAS THE PRESIDENT OF CHILE?
AND IS IT TRUE YOU AIMED AT HIS BIG BIRDIE?

1942, NEW ENGLAND: THE SUMMER OF SNAKES

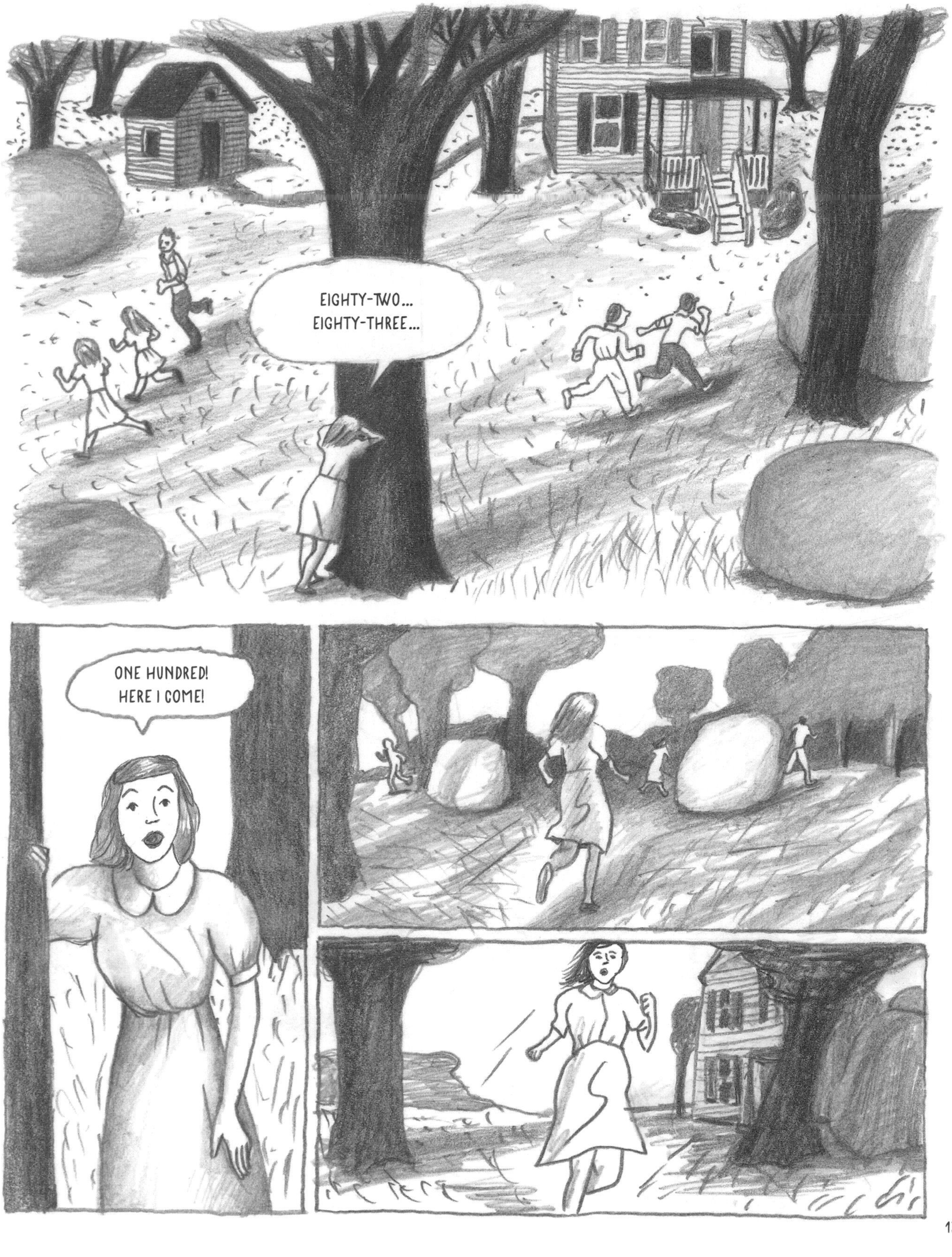
EIGHTY-TWO...
EIGHTY-THREE...
ONE HUNDRED!
HERE I COME!

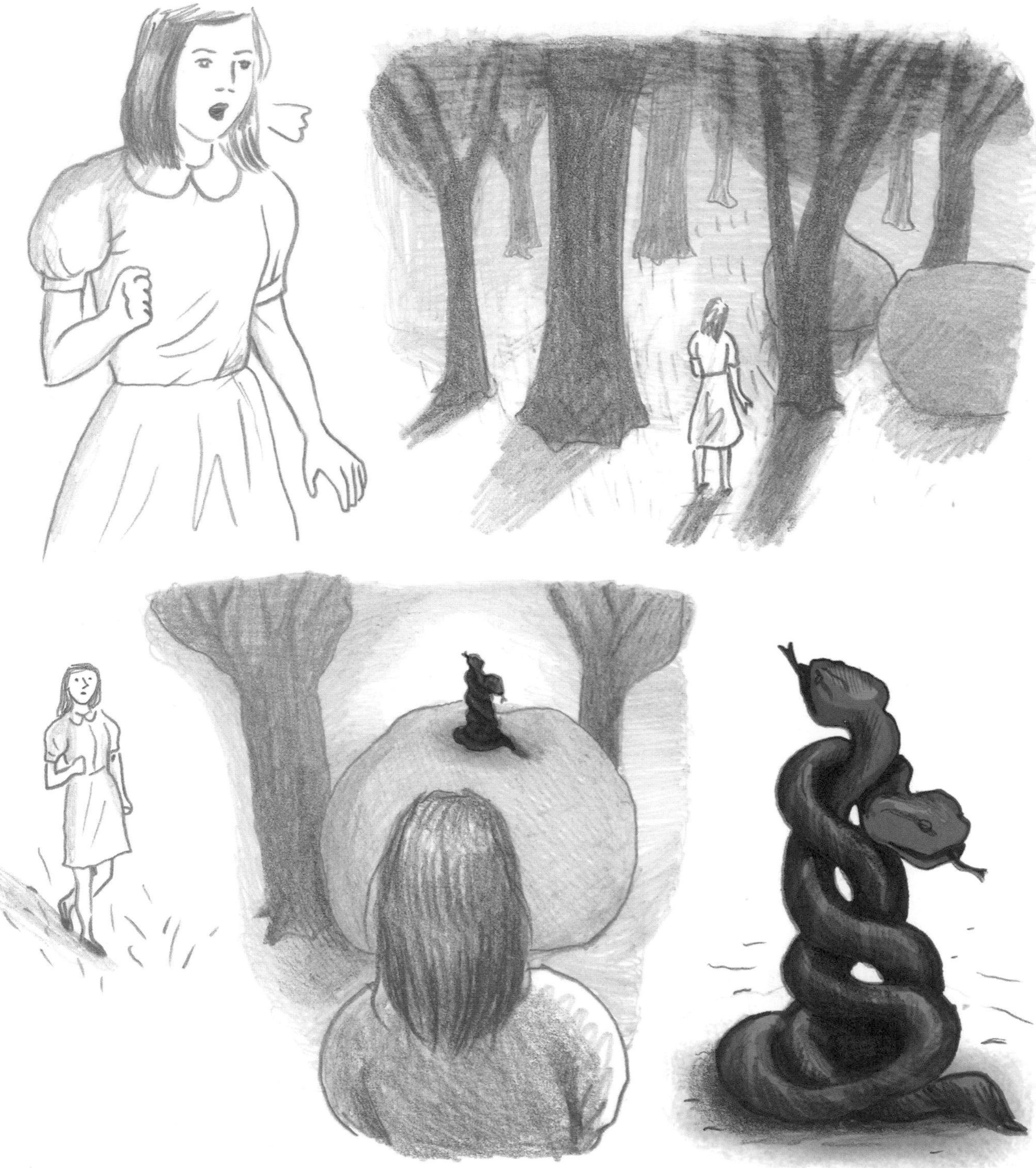

*I'd looked death in the eyes! But other reptiles would soon slither against me...*

Once he'd found about it, my father had all the serpents living nearby poisoned.

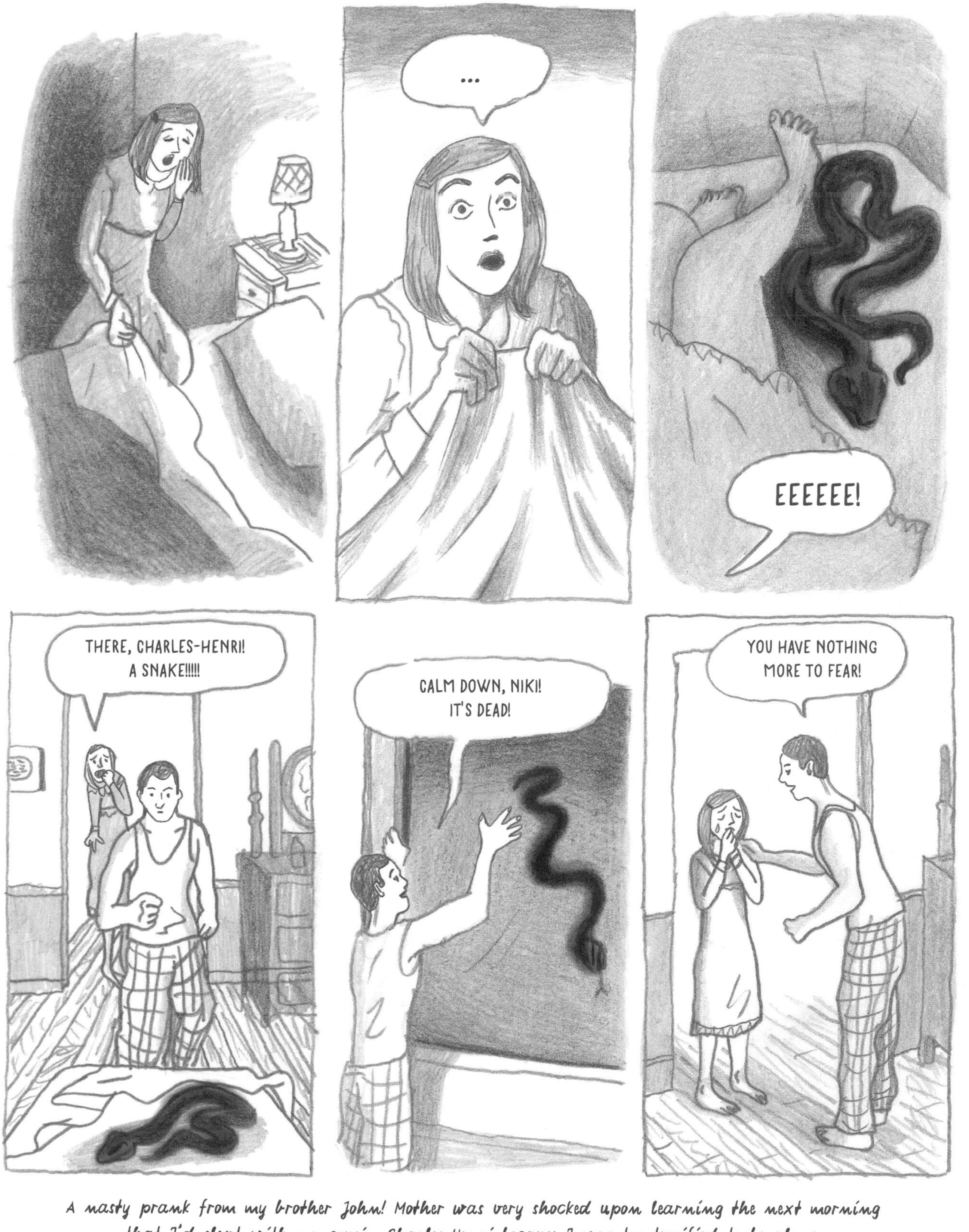
...
EEEEEE!
THERE, CHARLES-HENRI! A SNAKE!!!!!
CALM DOWN, NIKI! IT'S DEAD!
YOU HAVE NOTHING MORE TO FEAR!

A nasty prank from my brother John! Mother was very shocked upon learning the next morning that I'd slept with my cousin Charles-Henri because I was too terrified to be alone.

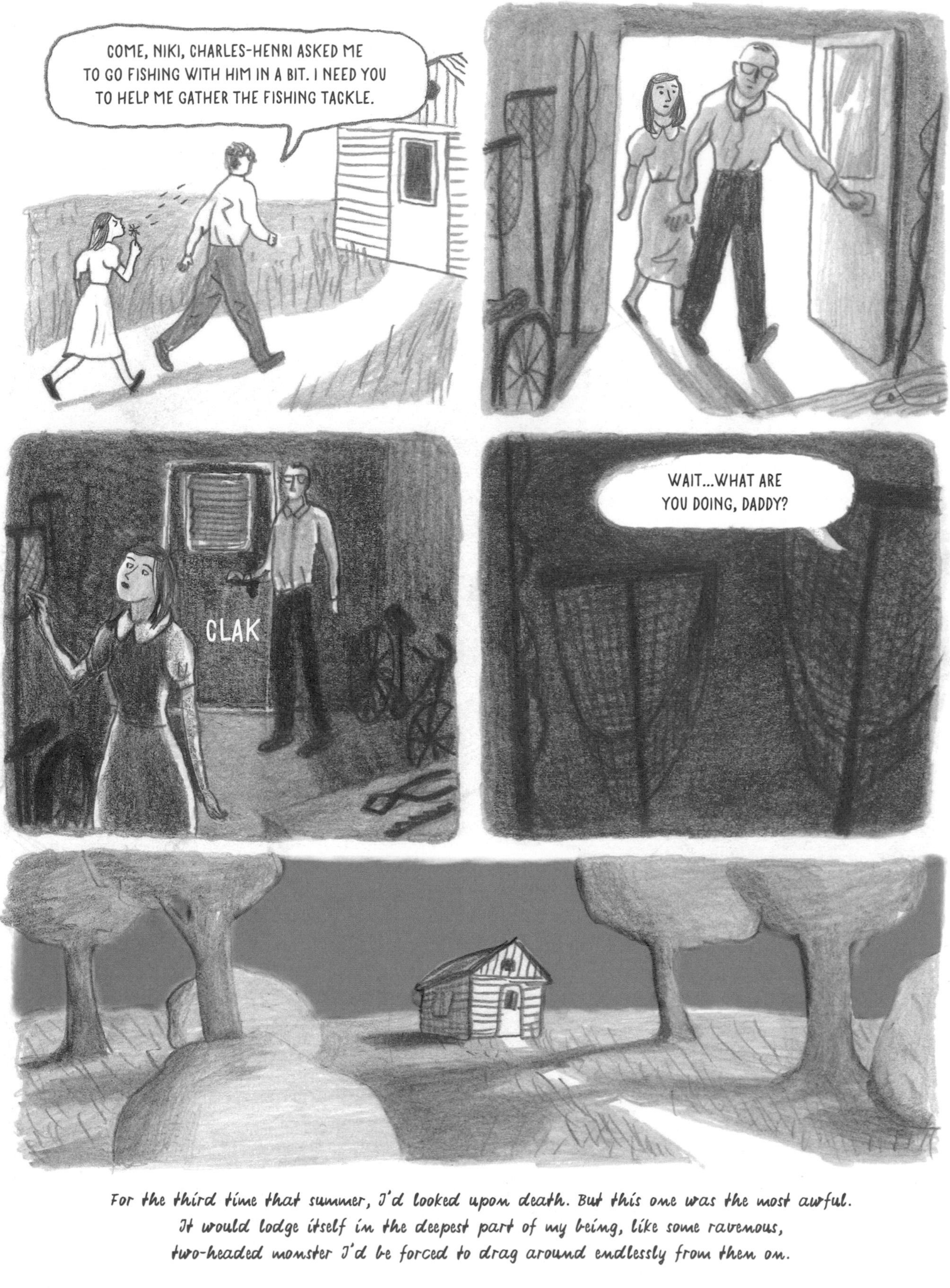
COME, NIKI, CHARLES-HENRI ASKED ME TO GO FISHING WITH HIM IN A BIT. I NEED YOU TO HELP ME GATHER THE FISHING TACKLE.
CLAK
WAIT...WHAT ARE YOU DOING, DADDY?

*For the third time that summer, I'd looked upon death. But this one was the most awful. It would lodge itself in the deepest part of my being, like some ravenous, two-headed monster I'd be forced to drag around endlessly from then on.*

# CHAPTER 2

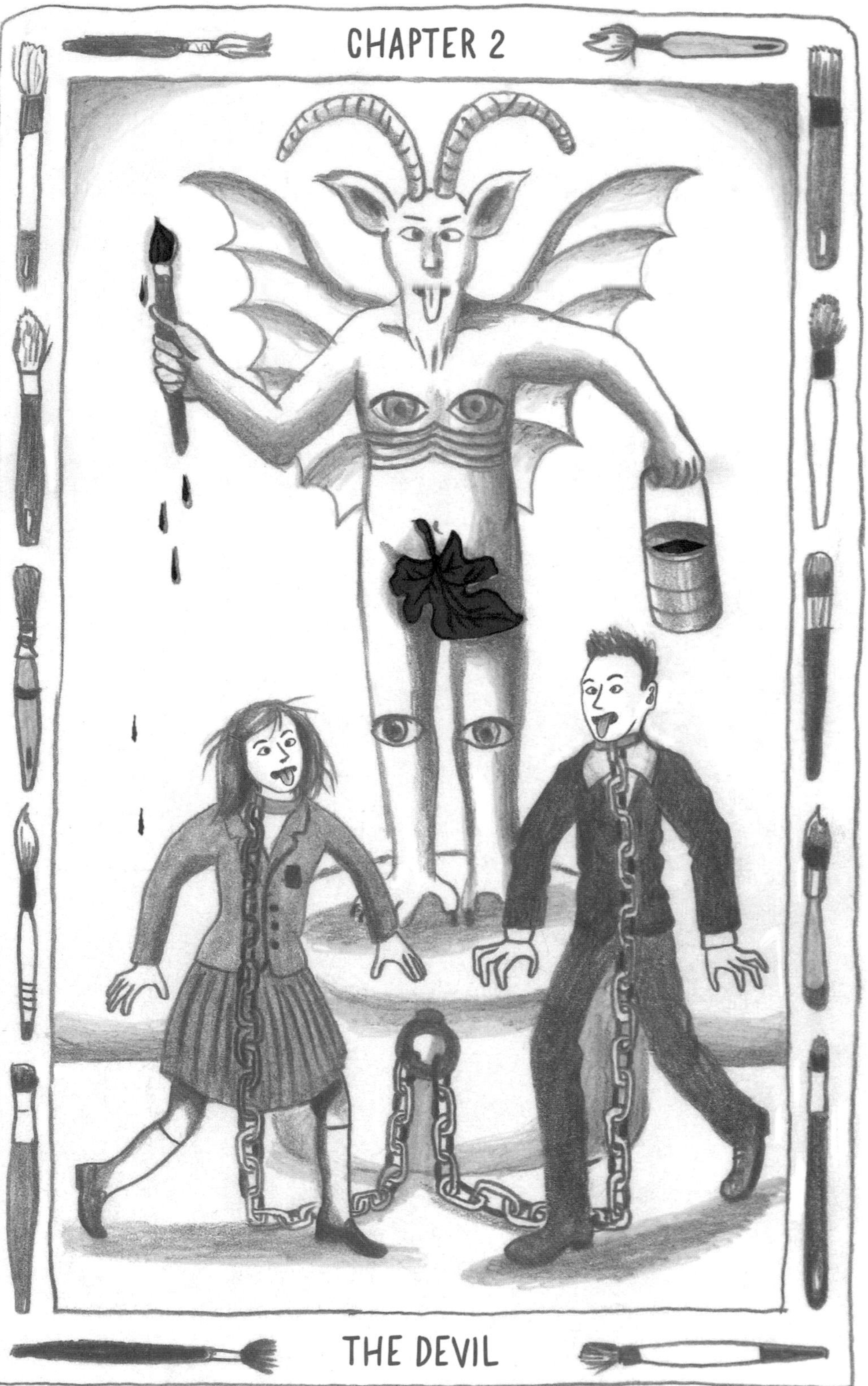

## THE DEVIL

FIFTEENTH ARCANA, THE DEVIL IS SCIENCE WITHOUT A CONSCIENCE.
IT REVEALS THE TRUTH WITH NO TABOOS, BUT KEEPS ITS SECRET GARDEN.
IT KNOWS HOW TO SEDUCE, ITS GOAL IS TO UNBRIDLE SEXUAL URGES.

*Do you remember, Noelle Love? It was so exciting!*

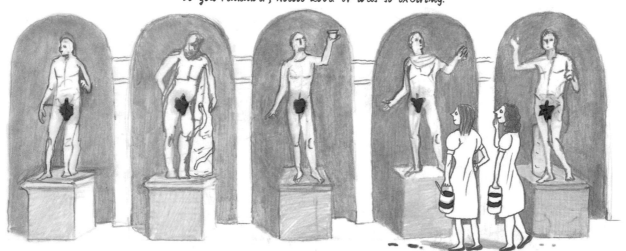

*I, Niki, affirm that Art will take control!*

EEEEE! JESUS AND MARY! WHAT HAVE YOU DONE, GIRLS?

*...The proof.*

*I haven't been able to cry in a long time.*

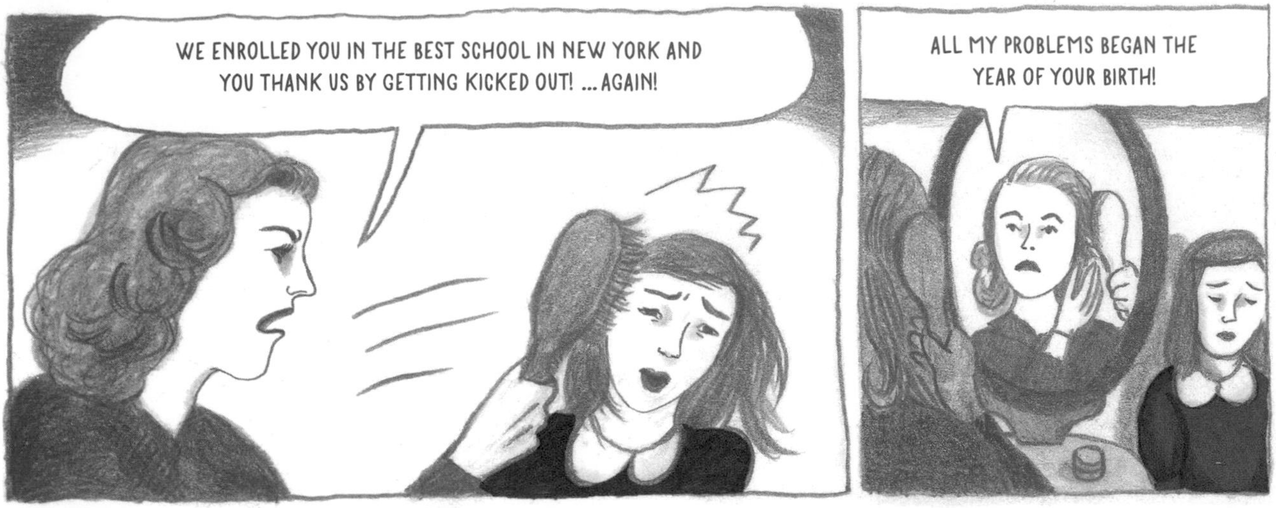
WE ENROLLED YOU IN THE BEST SCHOOL IN NEW YORK AND YOU THANK US BY GETTING KICKED OUT! ... AGAIN!
ALL MY PROBLEMS BEGAN THE YEAR OF YOUR BIRTH!

*My tears changed into stones, ever so heavy, deep in my chest...*

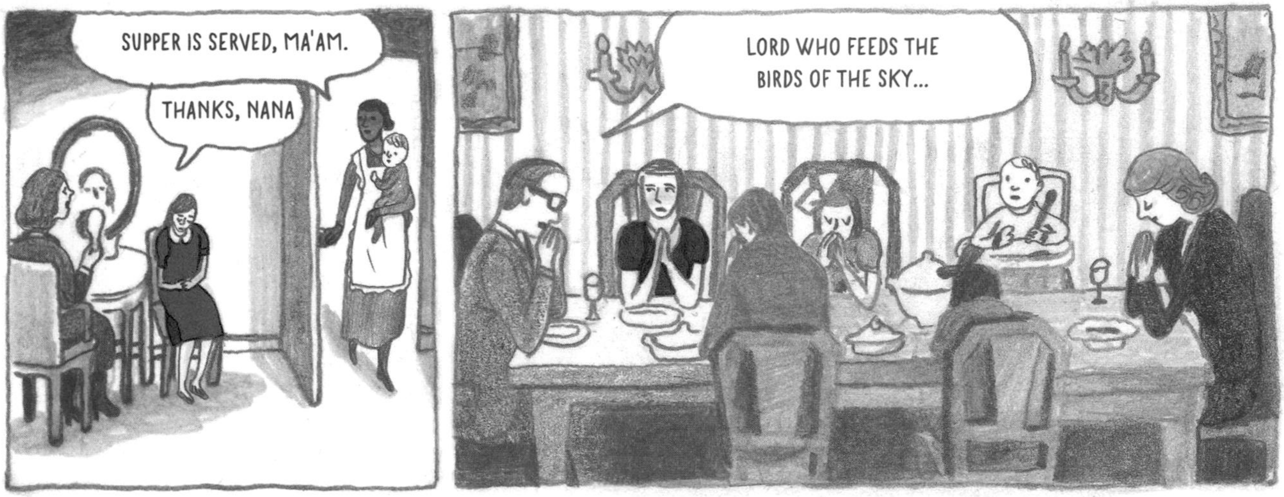
SUPPER IS SERVED, MA'AM.
THANKS, NANA
LORD WHO FEEDS THE BIRDS OF THE SKY...

*I've always adored birds. I'd love to be a bird! Tearing myself away from the soil, forgetting the weight of my body...*

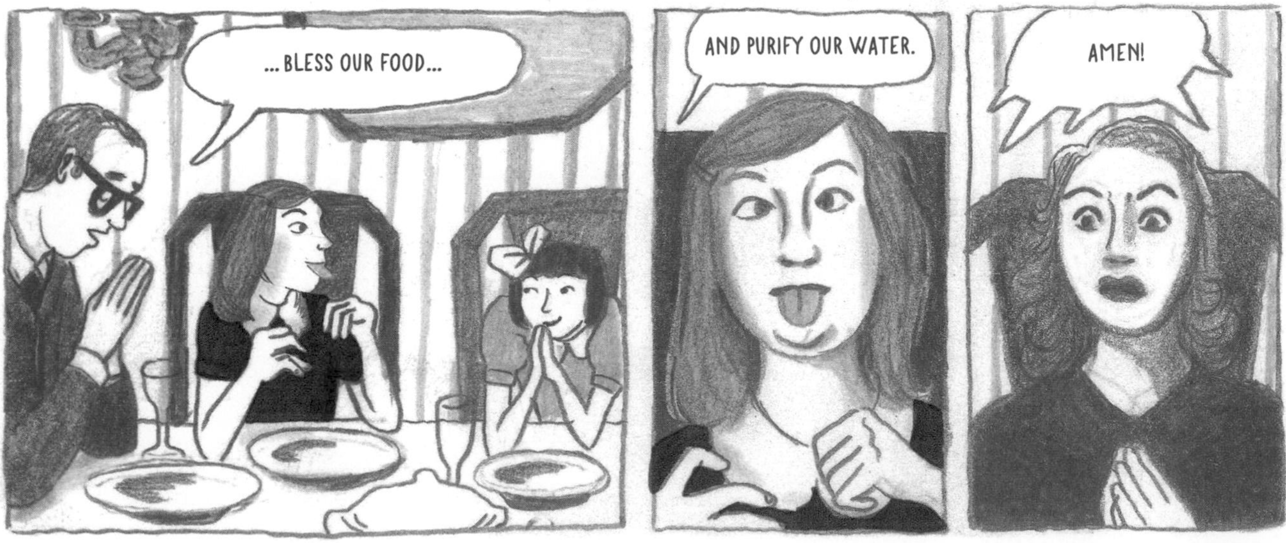
... BLESS OUR FOOD...
AND PURIFY OUR WATER.
AMEN!

After that, Mother restricted me to the kitchen. I'd eat alone and didn't have to put up with saying grace anymore. It was the only place I felt good.

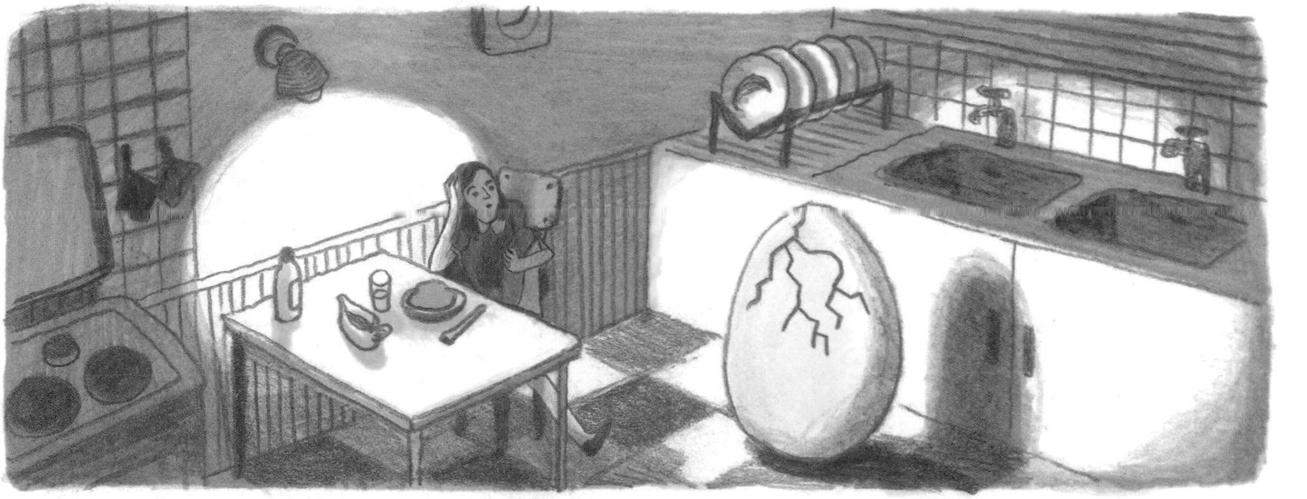

I think I hatched from an enormous egg set in the kitchen.

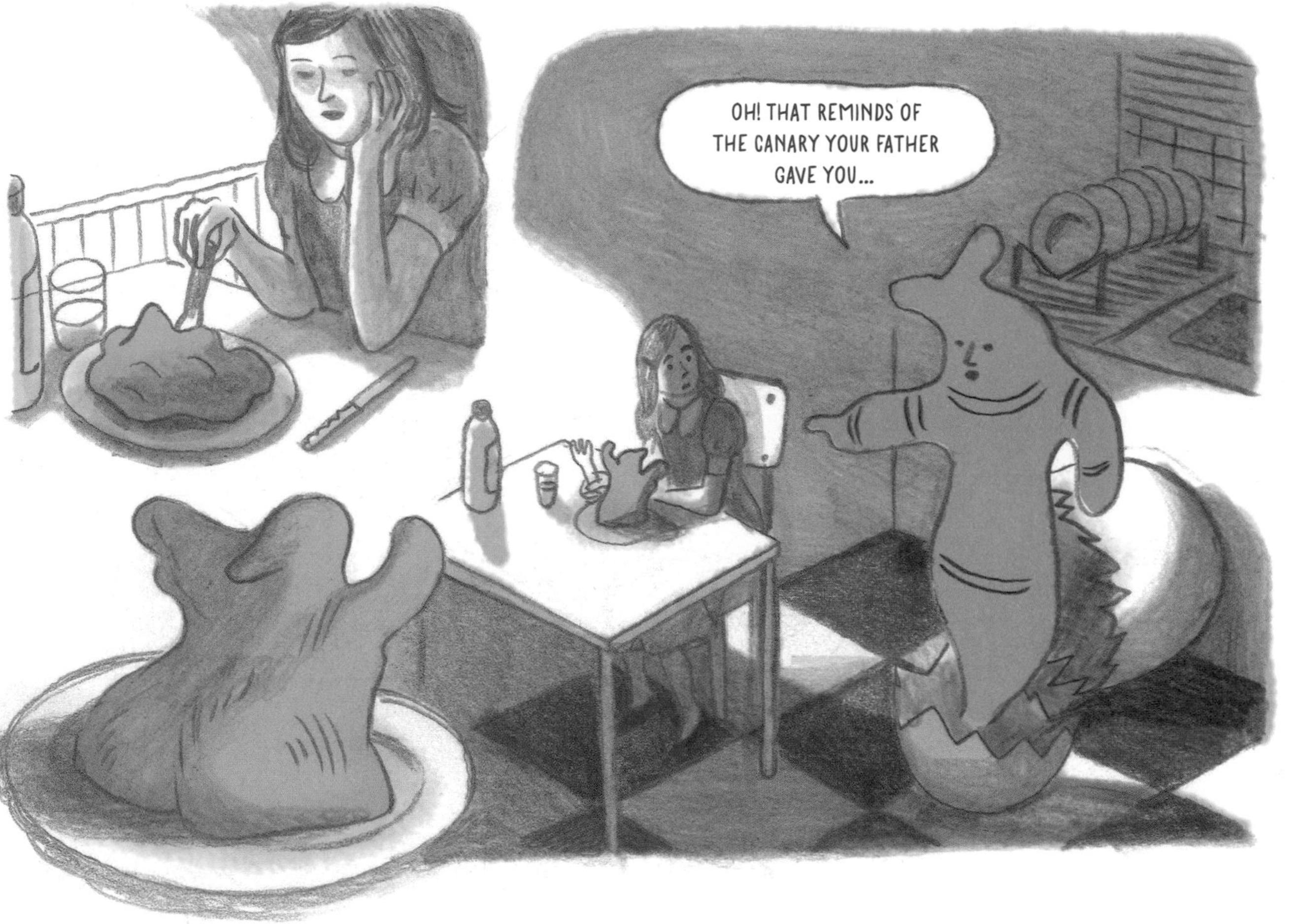
OH! THAT REMINDS OF THE CANARY YOUR FATHER GAVE YOU...

I'd left it out in the yard, a little ball of feathers, all alone, all night long, a string on its foot so it wouldn't fly away...I loved it so much! I carried it around all the time! Once I remembered about it the next morning, I ran to fetch it...the only thing left were some tiny bones at the end of the string...

1945, A PAROCHIAL SCHOOL, SUFFERN, NY.

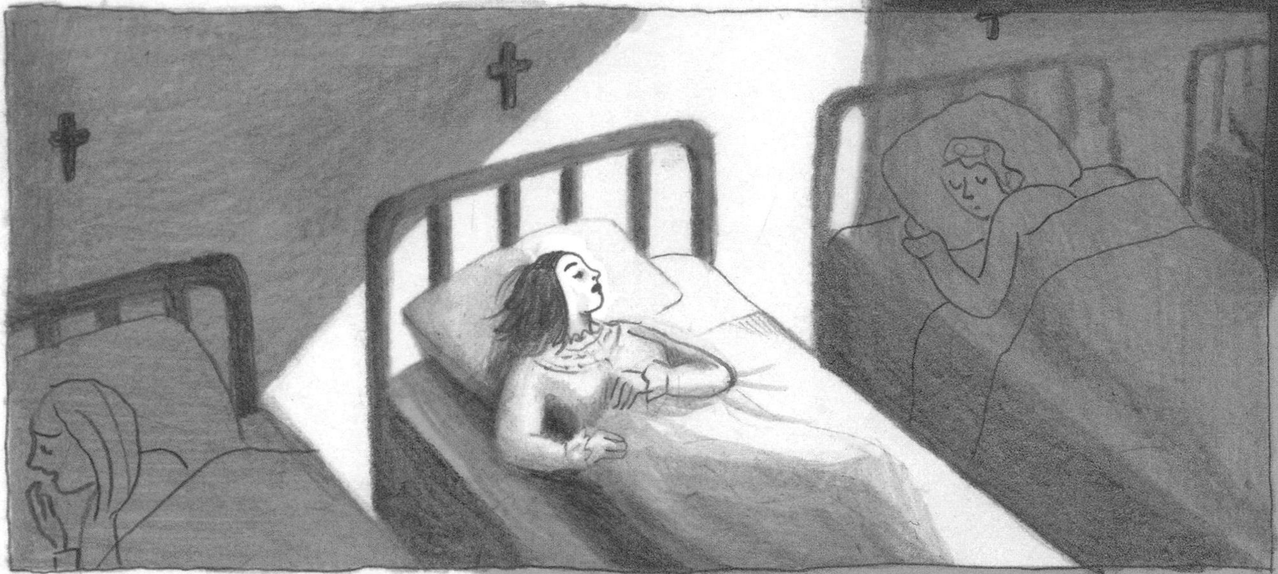

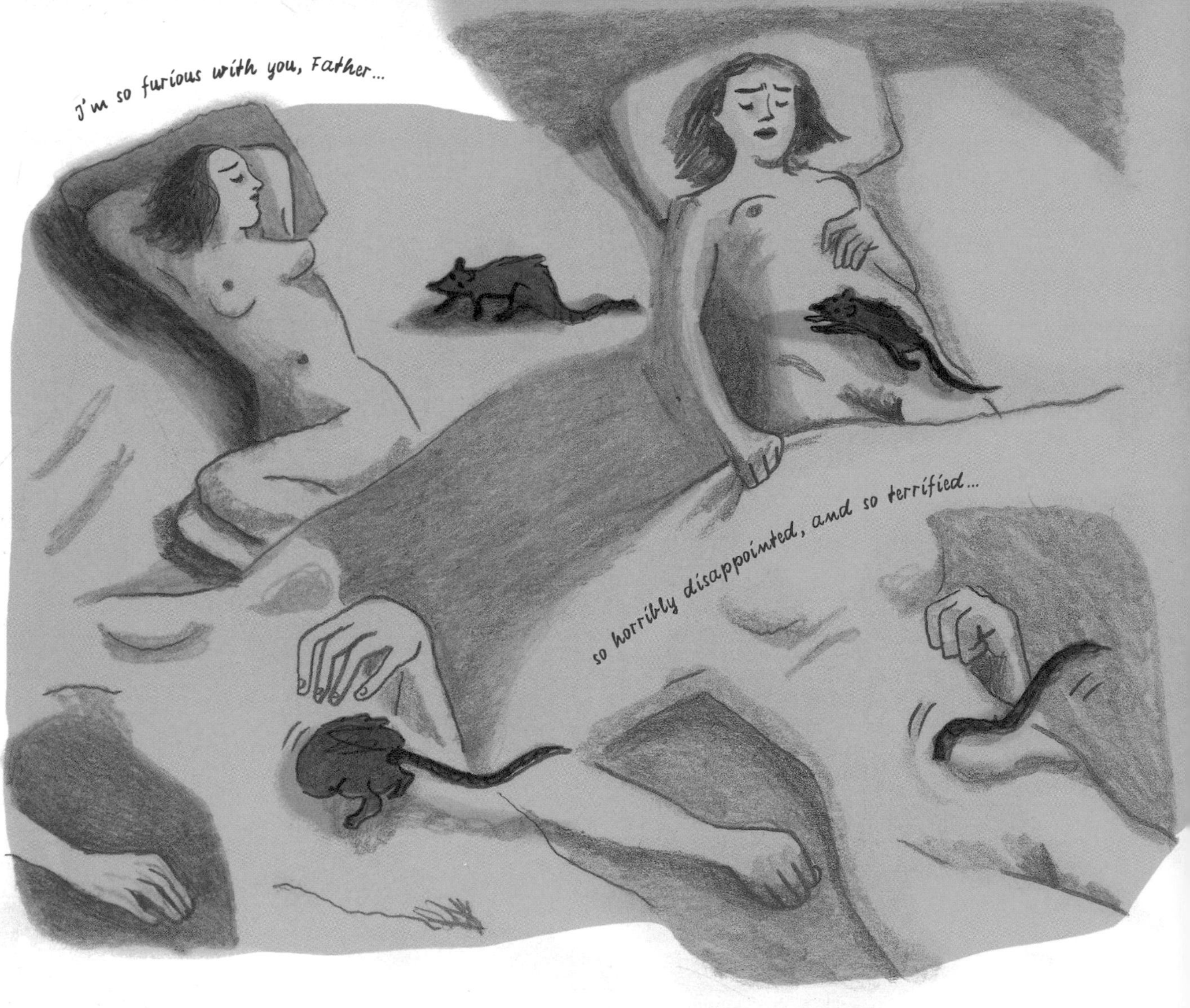
I'm so furious with you, Father...
so horribly disappointed, and so terrified...

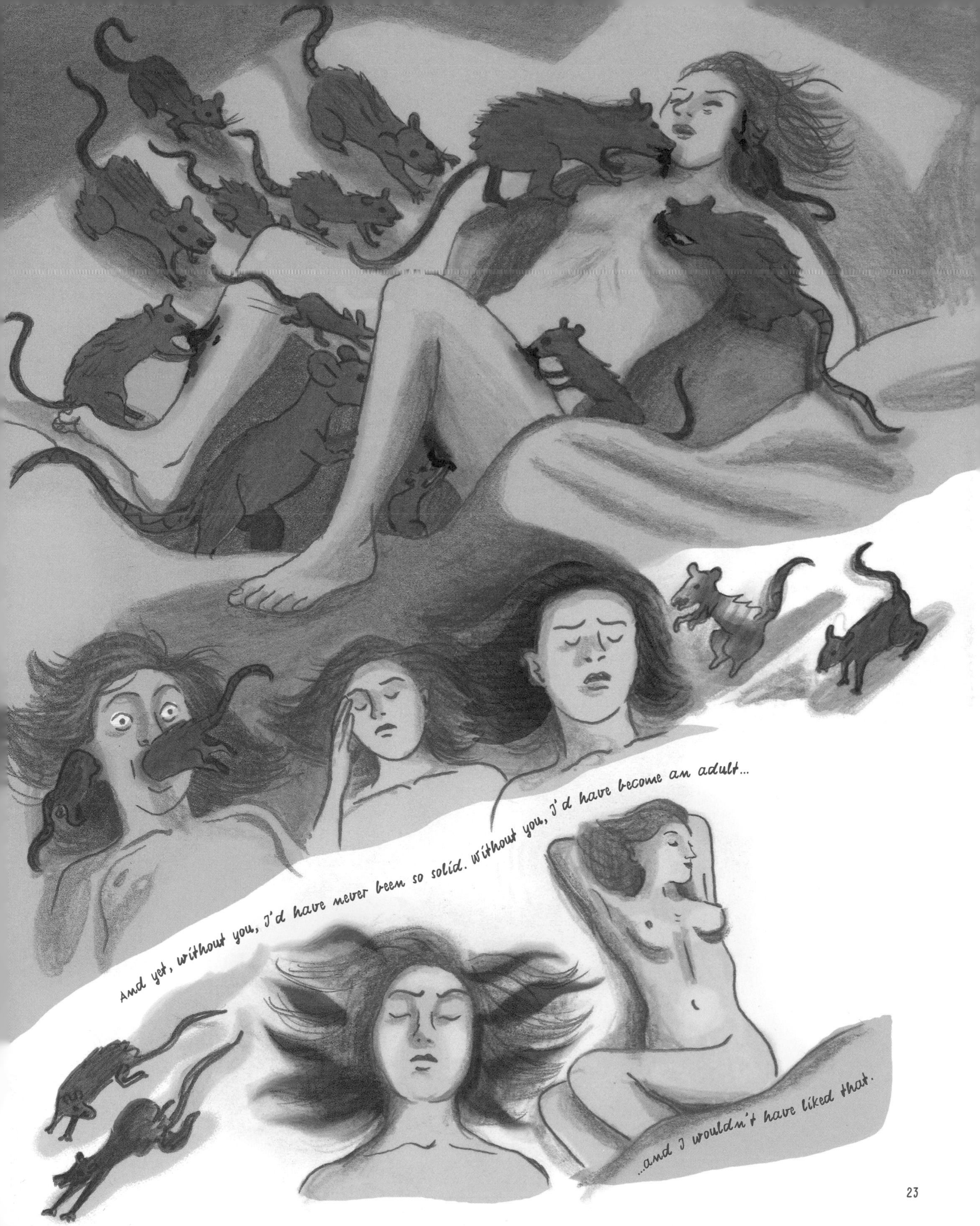
And yet, without you, I'd have never been so solid. Without you, I'd have become an adult...
...and I wouldn't have liked that.

1947, BROADWAY, NYC.

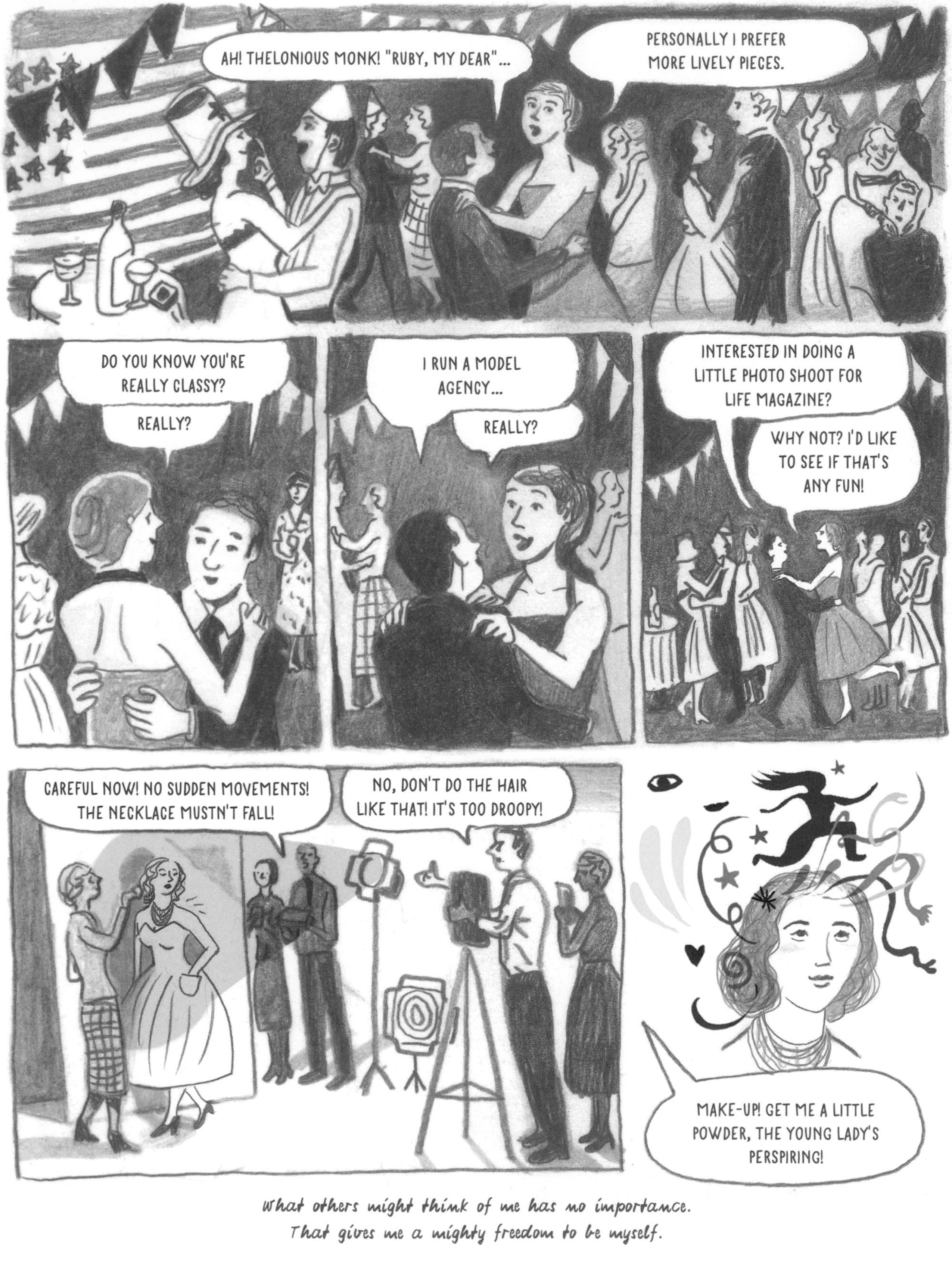
AH! THELONIOUS MONK! "RUBY, MY DEAR"...
PERSONALLY I PREFER MORE LIVELY PIECES.
DO YOU KNOW YOU'RE REALLY CLASSY?
REALLY?
I RUN A MODEL AGENCY...
REALLY?
INTERESTED IN DOING A LITTLE PHOTO SHOOT FOR LIFE MAGAZINE?
WHY NOT? I'D LIKE TO SEE IF THAT'S ANY FUN!
CAREFUL NOW! NO SUDDEN MOVEMENTS! THE NECKLACE MUSTN'T FALL!
NO, DON'T DO THE HAIR LIKE THAT! IT'S TOO DROOPY!
MAKE-UP! GET ME A LITTLE POWDER, THE YOUNG LADY'S PERSPIRING!

*What others might think of me has no importance.*
*That gives me a mighty freedom to be myself.*

1948. BETWEEN NYC AND PRINCETON.

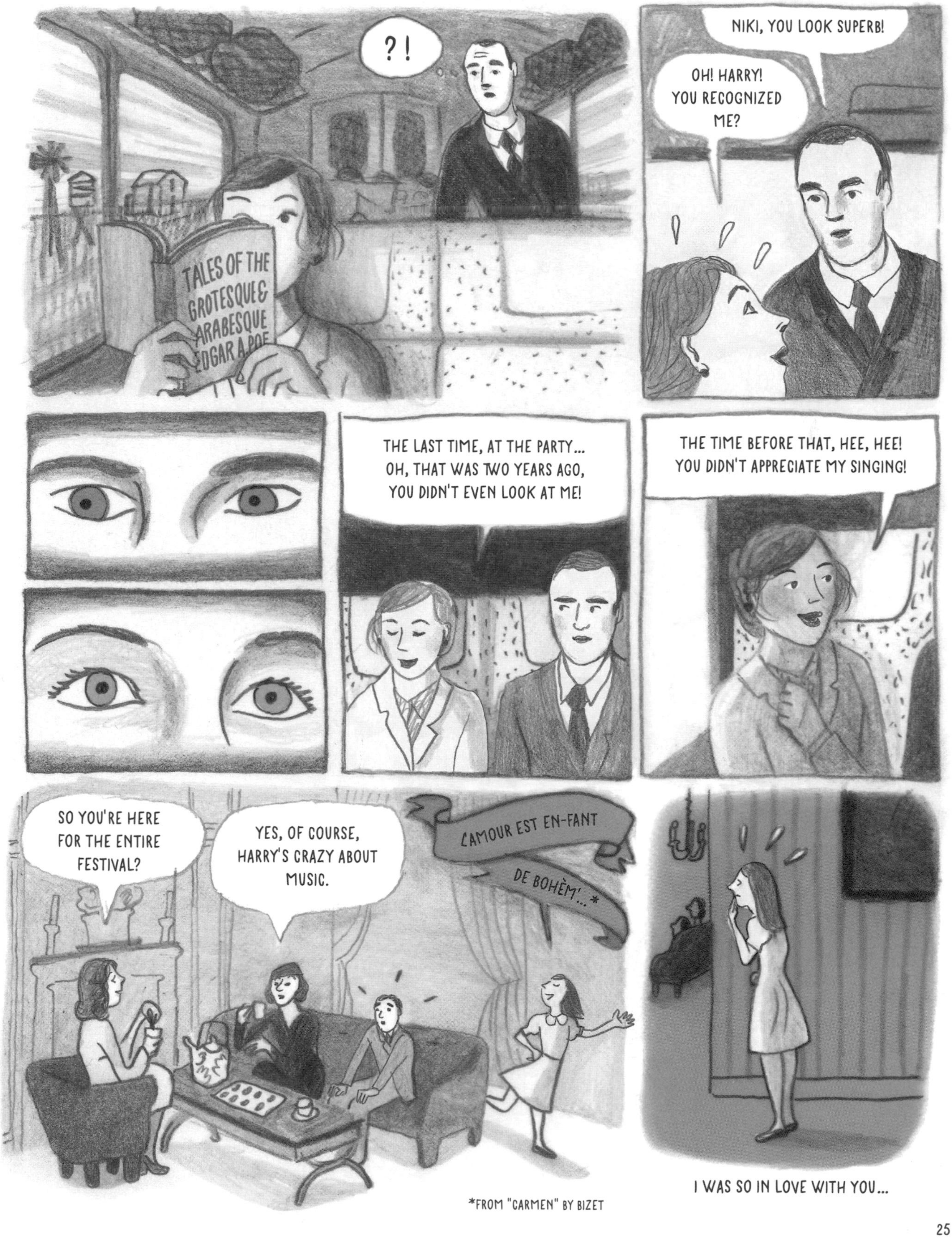
?!
TALES OF THE GROTESQUE & ARABESQUE EDGAR A. POE
NIKI, YOU LOOK SUPERB!
OH! HARRY! YOU RECOGNIZED ME?
THE LAST TIME, AT THE PARTY... OH, THAT WAS TWO YEARS AGO, YOU DIDN'T EVEN LOOK AT ME!
THE TIME BEFORE THAT, HEE, HEE! YOU DIDN'T APPRECIATE MY SINGING!
SO YOU'RE HERE FOR THE ENTIRE FESTIVAL?
YES, OF COURSE, HARRY'S CRAZY ABOUT MUSIC.
L'AMOUR EST EN-FANT
DE BOHÈM'...*
I WAS SO IN LOVE WITH YOU...

*FROM "CARMEN" BY BIZET

We were minors...back then, two people who are so young can't love one another openly.
Love is forbidden. So anything is fine for having time alone...

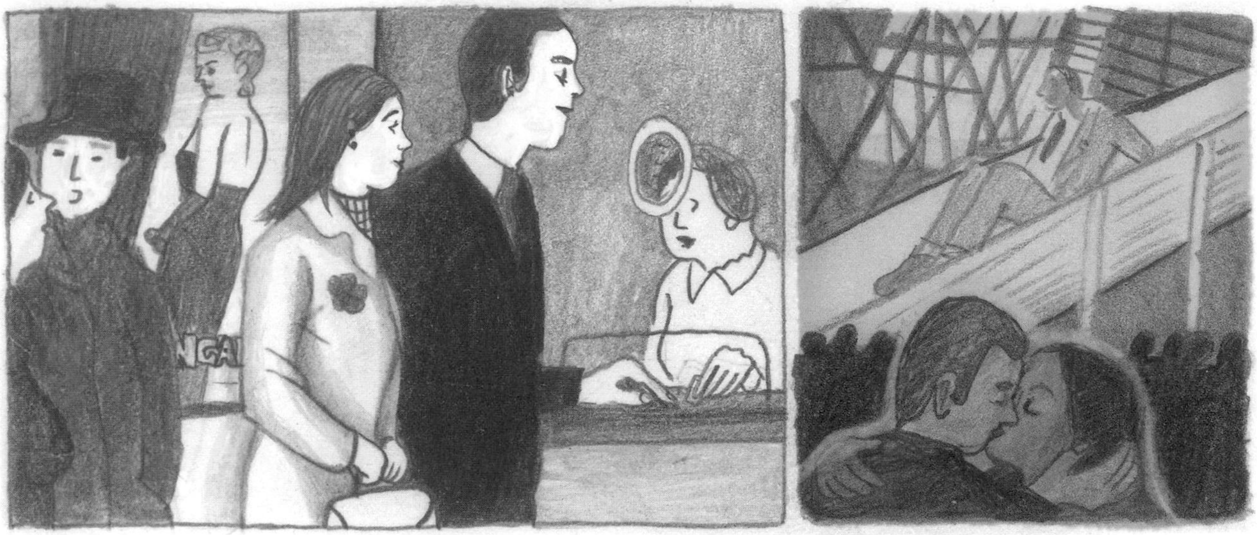

We liked The Lady from Shanghai a lot...we badly wanted to make love!
If only we had a fairy godmother who'd transform us into
joyous squirrels to frolic atop the trees of Central Park!

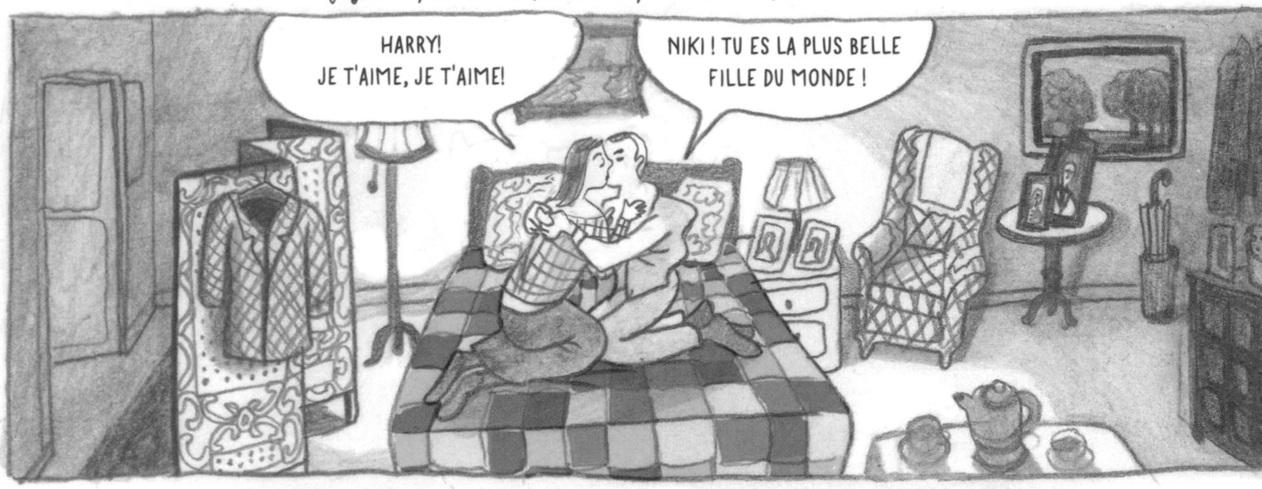
HARRY!
JE T'AIME, JE T'AIME!
NIKI ! TU ES LA PLUS BELLE
FILLE DU MONDE !

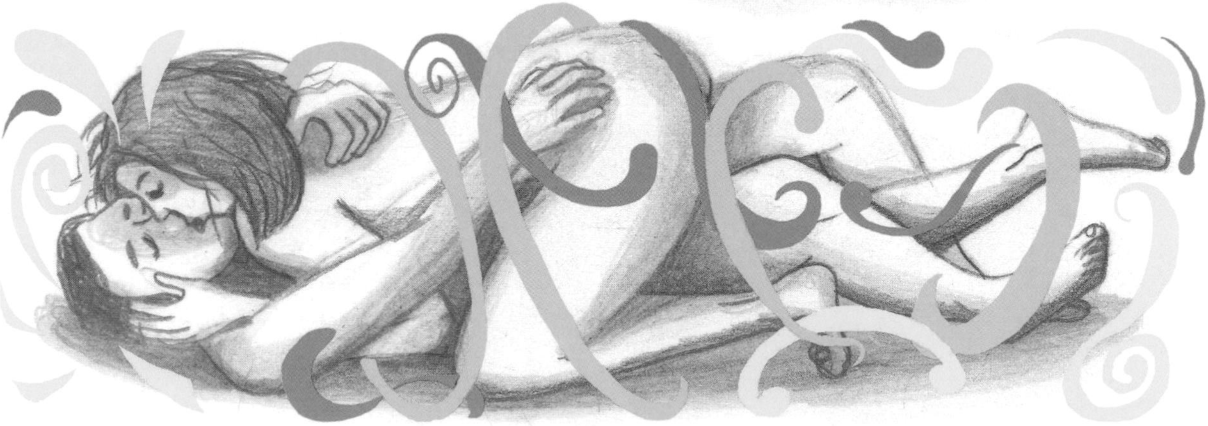

My heart, my emotions...it was all so sparkling! How I love love!

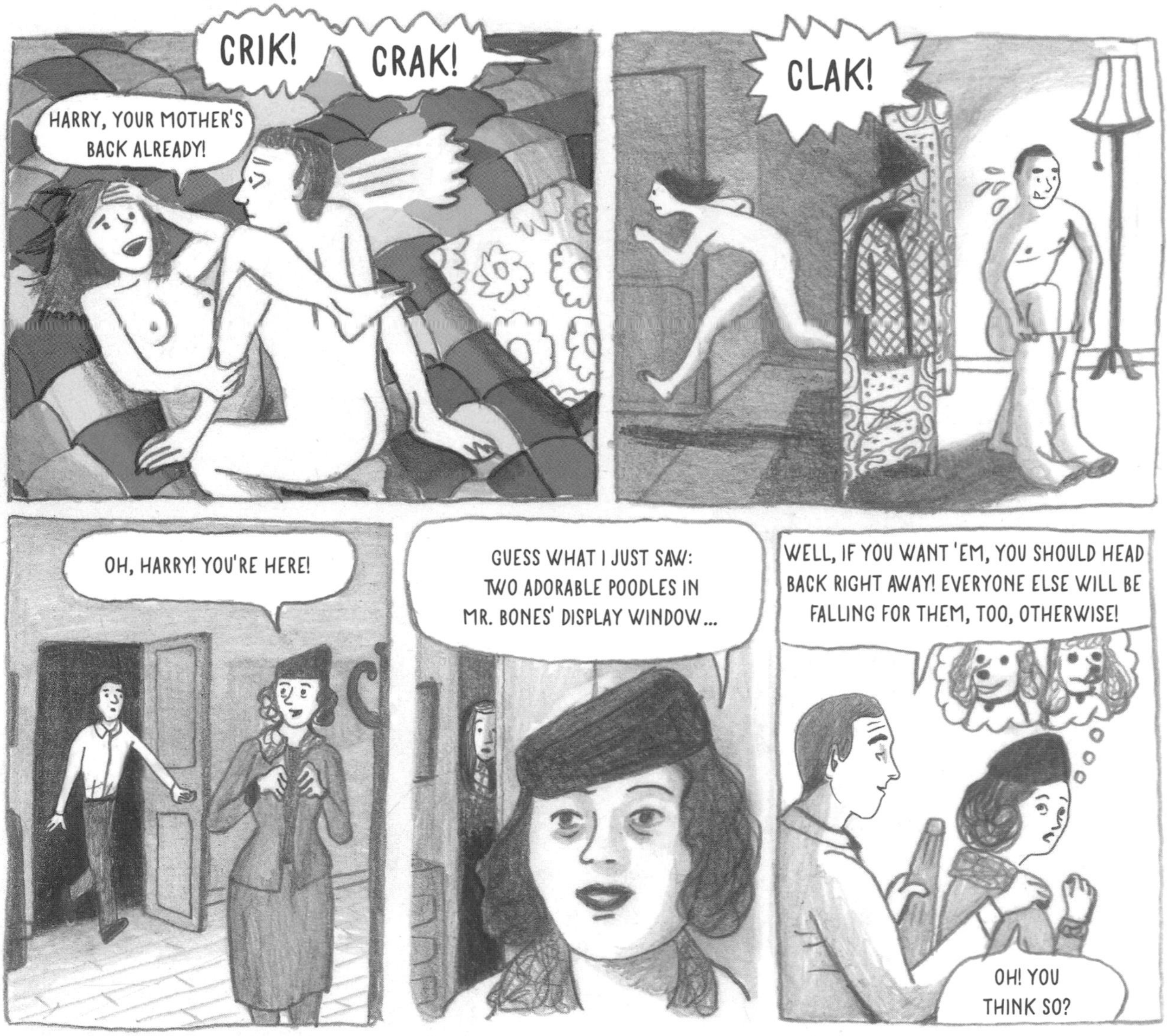
CRIK!
CRAK!
HARRY, YOUR MOTHER'S BACK ALREADY!
CLAK!
OH, HARRY! YOU'RE HERE!
GUESS WHAT I JUST SAW: TWO ADORABLE POODLES IN MR. BONES' DISPLAY WINDOW...
WELL, IF YOU WANT 'EM, YOU SHOULD HEAD BACK RIGHT AWAY! EVERYONE ELSE WILL BE FALLING FOR THEM, TOO, OTHERWISE!
OH! YOU THINK SO?

*After a few months of a dangerous life, we made the decision to "run away," meaning...*

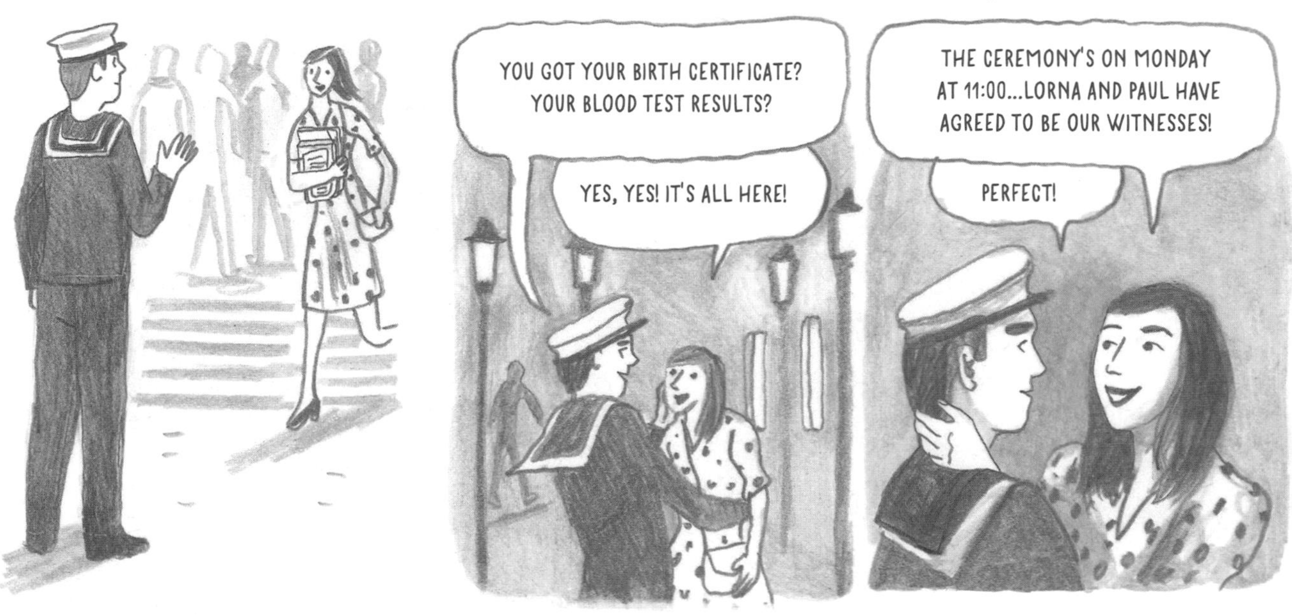
YOU GOT YOUR BIRTH CERTIFICATE? YOUR BLOOD TEST RESULTS?
YES, YES! IT'S ALL HERE!
THE CEREMONY'S ON MONDAY AT 11:00...LORNA AND PAUL HAVE AGREED TO BE OUR WITNESSES!
PERFECT!

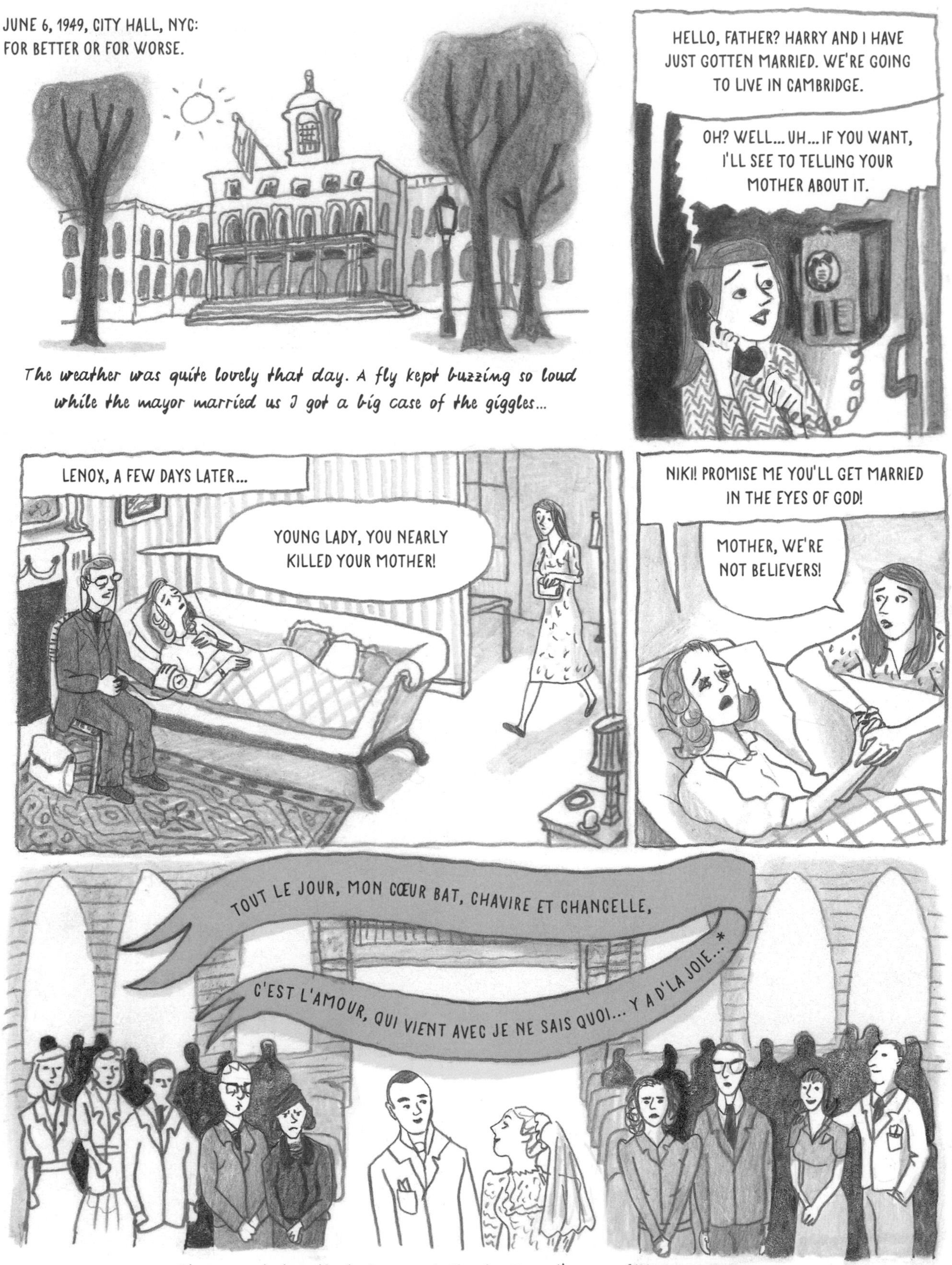
JUNE 6, 1949, CITY HALL, NYC:
FOR BETTER OR FOR WORSE.
The weather was quite lovely that day. A fly kept buzzing so loud while the mayor married us I got a big case of the giggles...
HELLO, FATHER? HARRY AND I HAVE JUST GOTTEN MARRIED. WE'RE GOING TO LIVE IN CAMBRIDGE.
OH? WELL... UH... IF YOU WANT, I'LL SEE TO TELLING YOUR MOTHER ABOUT IT.
LENOX, A FEW DAYS LATER...
YOUNG LADY, YOU NEARLY KILLED YOUR MOTHER!
NIKI! PROMISE ME YOU'LL GET MARRIED IN THE EYES OF GOD!
MOTHER, WE'RE NOT BELIEVERS!
TOUT LE JOUR, MON CŒUR BAT, CHAVIRE ET CHANCELLE,
C'EST L'AMOUR, QUI VIENT AVEC JE NE SAIS QUOI... Y A D'LA JOIE...*
It was raining that day and Charles Trenet's song filled our heads...

*ALL DAY LONG, MY HEART THROBBED, WAVERED, AND FALTERED, IT'S LOVE, WHICH COMES ALONG WITH I DON'T KNOW WHAT... IT'S JOY...

# CHAPTER 3

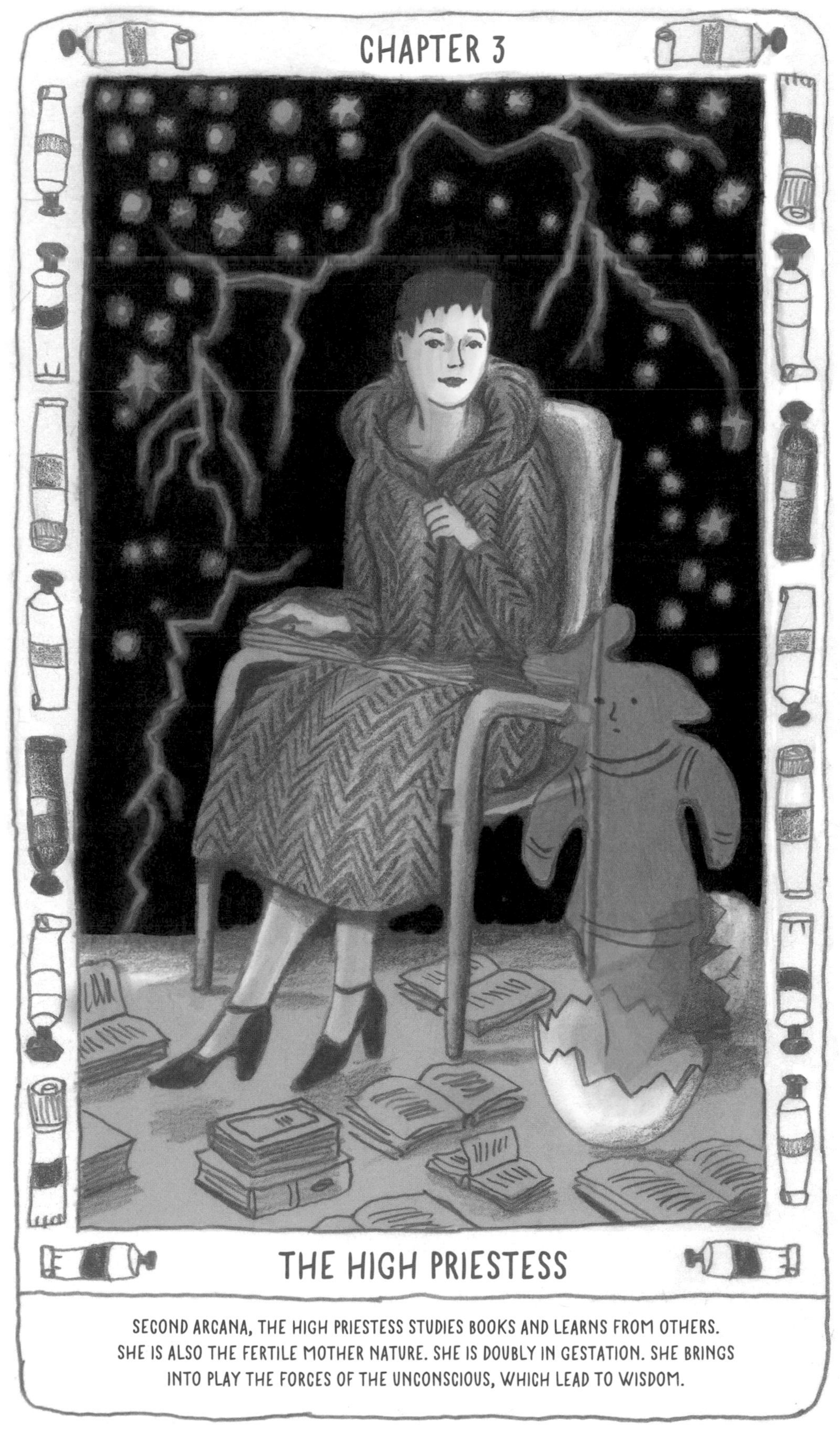

## THE HIGH PRIESTESS

SECOND ARCANA, THE HIGH PRIESTESS STUDIES BOOKS AND LEARNS FROM OTHERS. SHE IS ALSO THE FERTILE MOTHER NATURE. SHE IS DOUBLY IN GESTATION. SHE BRINGS INTO PLAY THE FORCES OF THE UNCONSCIOUS, WHICH LEAD TO WISDOM.

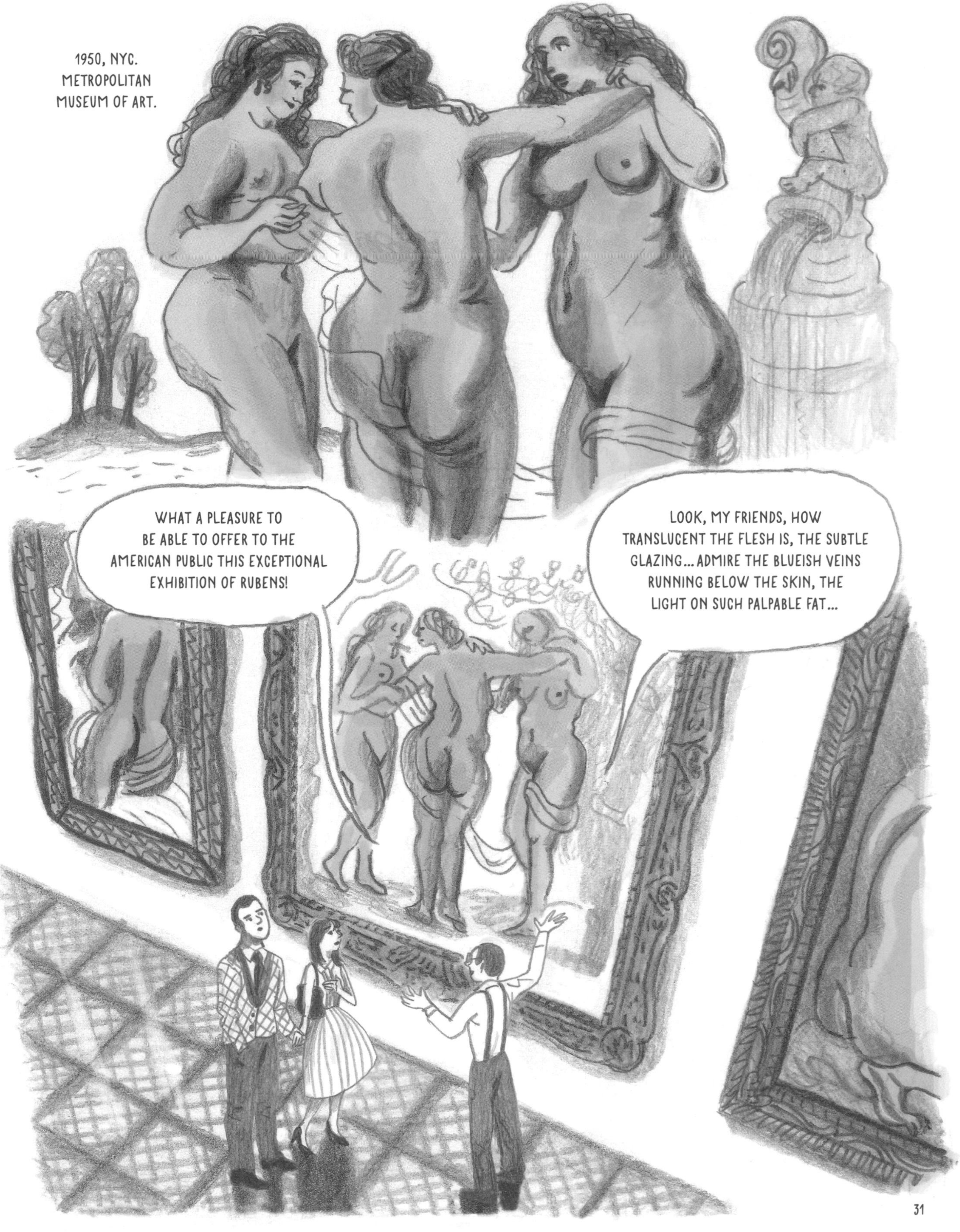
1950, NYC. METROPOLITAN MUSEUM OF ART.
WHAT A PLEASURE TO BE ABLE TO OFFER TO THE AMERICAN PUBLIC THIS EXCEPTIONAL EXHIBITION OF RUBENS!
LOOK, MY FRIENDS, HOW TRANSLUCENT THE FLESH IS, THE SUBTLE GLAZING... ADMIRE THE BLUEISH VEINS RUNNING BELOW THE SKIN, THE LIGHT ON SUCH PALPABLE FAT...

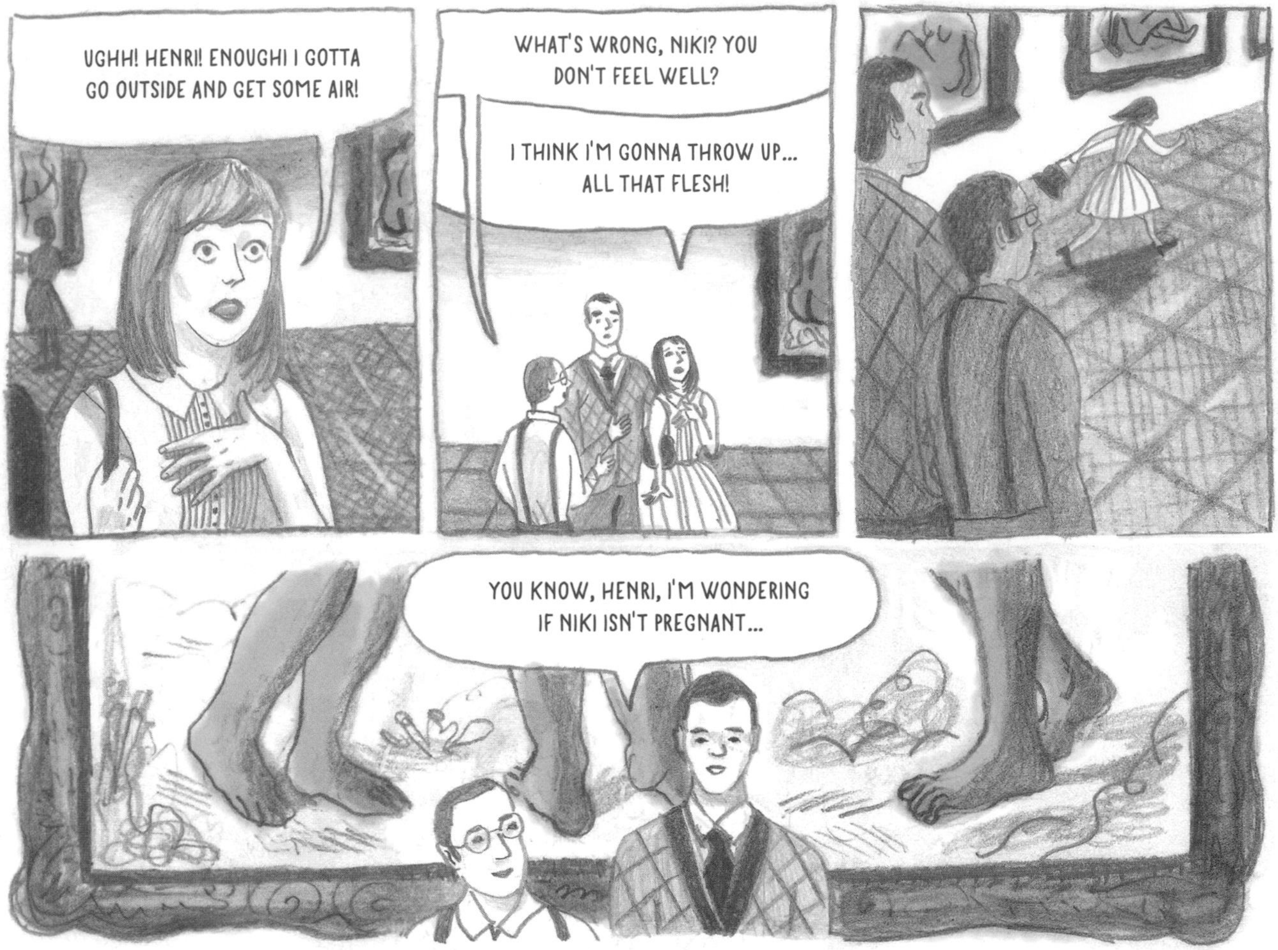
UGHH! HENRI! ENOUGH! I GOTTA GO OUTSIDE AND GET SOME AIR!
WHAT'S WRONG, NIKI? YOU DON'T FEEL WELL?
I THINK I'M GONNA THROW UP... ALL THAT FLESH!
YOU KNOW, HENRI, I'M WONDERING IF NIKI ISN'T PREGNANT...

*Upon learning this news, Harry's mother didn't speak a word to him anymore, and mine introduced me to some toad-faced abortionist!*

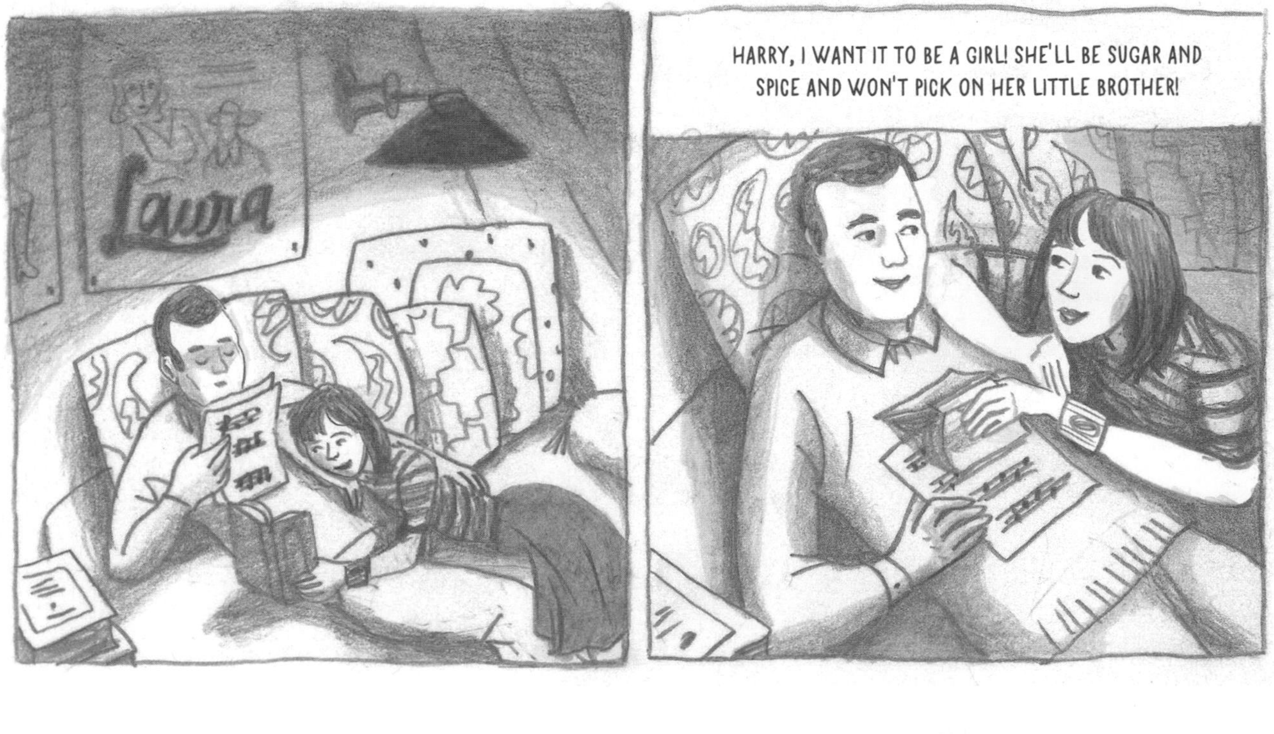
Laura
HARRY, I WANT IT TO BE A GIRL! SHE'LL BE SUGAR AND SPICE AND WON'T PICK ON HER LITTLE BROTHER!

APRIL 23, 1951, BOSTON HOSPITAL.

*The birthing methods in the Fifties were almost medieval... The future mother was nothing but meat, and the only thing expected of her was complete passivity!*

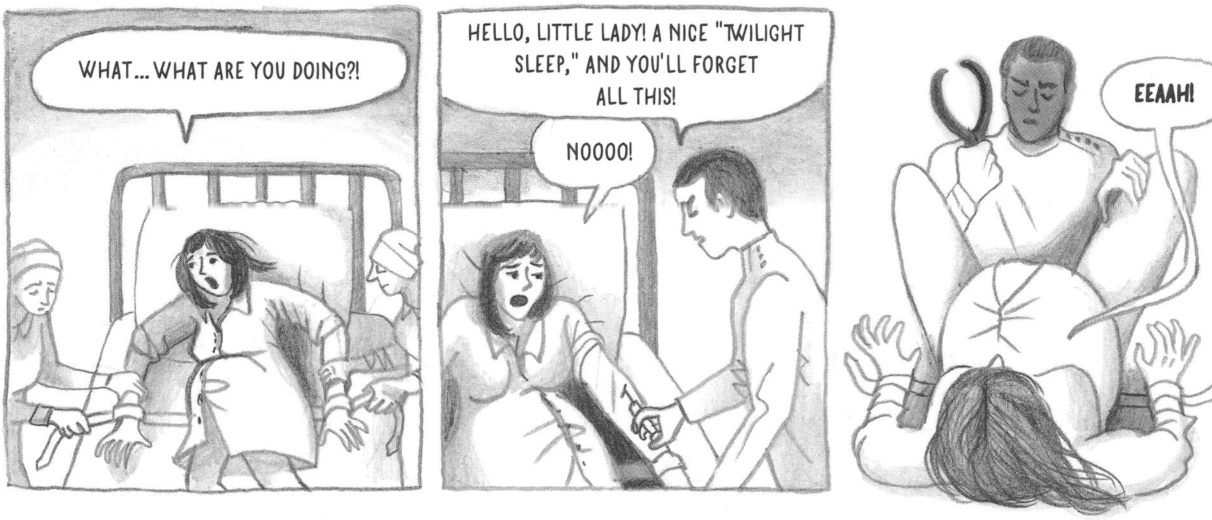

WHAT... WHAT ARE YOU DOING?!
HELLO, LITTLE LADY! A NICE "TWILIGHT SLEEP," AND YOU'LL FORGET ALL THIS!
NOOOO!
EEAAH!


*I saw the forceps approaching my belly like the pinchers of a giant scorpion that was going to devour me and destroy my baby.*

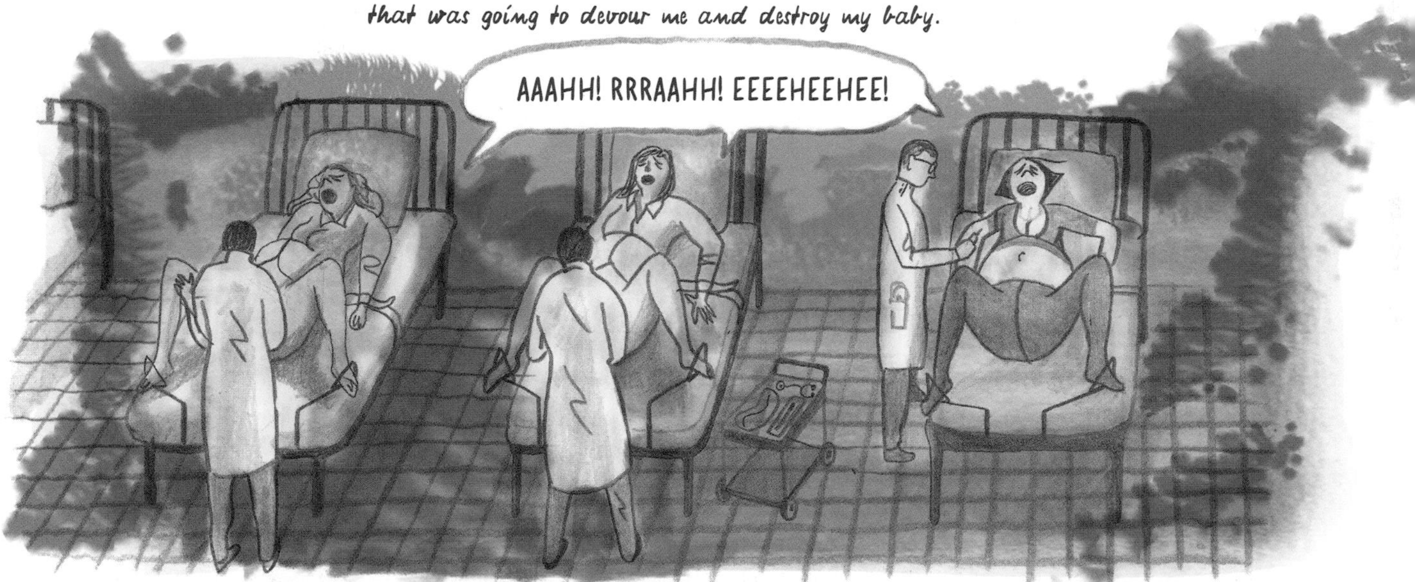

AAAHH! RRRAAHH! EEEEHEEHEE!


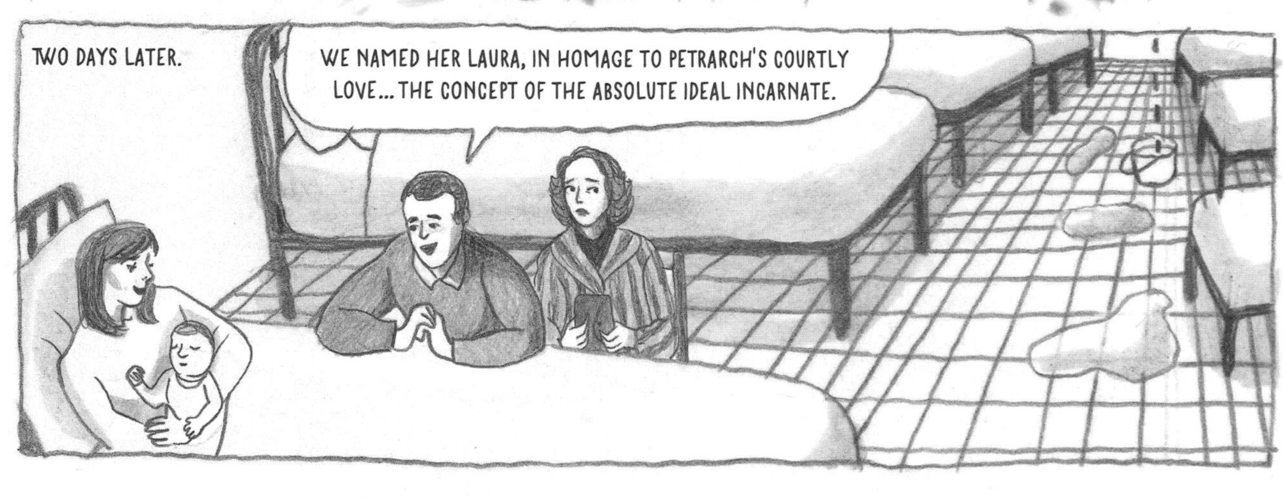

TWO DAYS LATER.
WE NAMED HER LAURA, IN HOMAGE TO PETRARCH'S COURTLY LOVE... THE CONCEPT OF THE ABSOLUTE IDEAL INCARNATE.

AUGUST 1951. *Mother had been scandalized when, after leaving the hospital, I'd wanted to leave the sleeping baby in the car while we stopped at a restaurant...I thought her reaction was a bit much!*

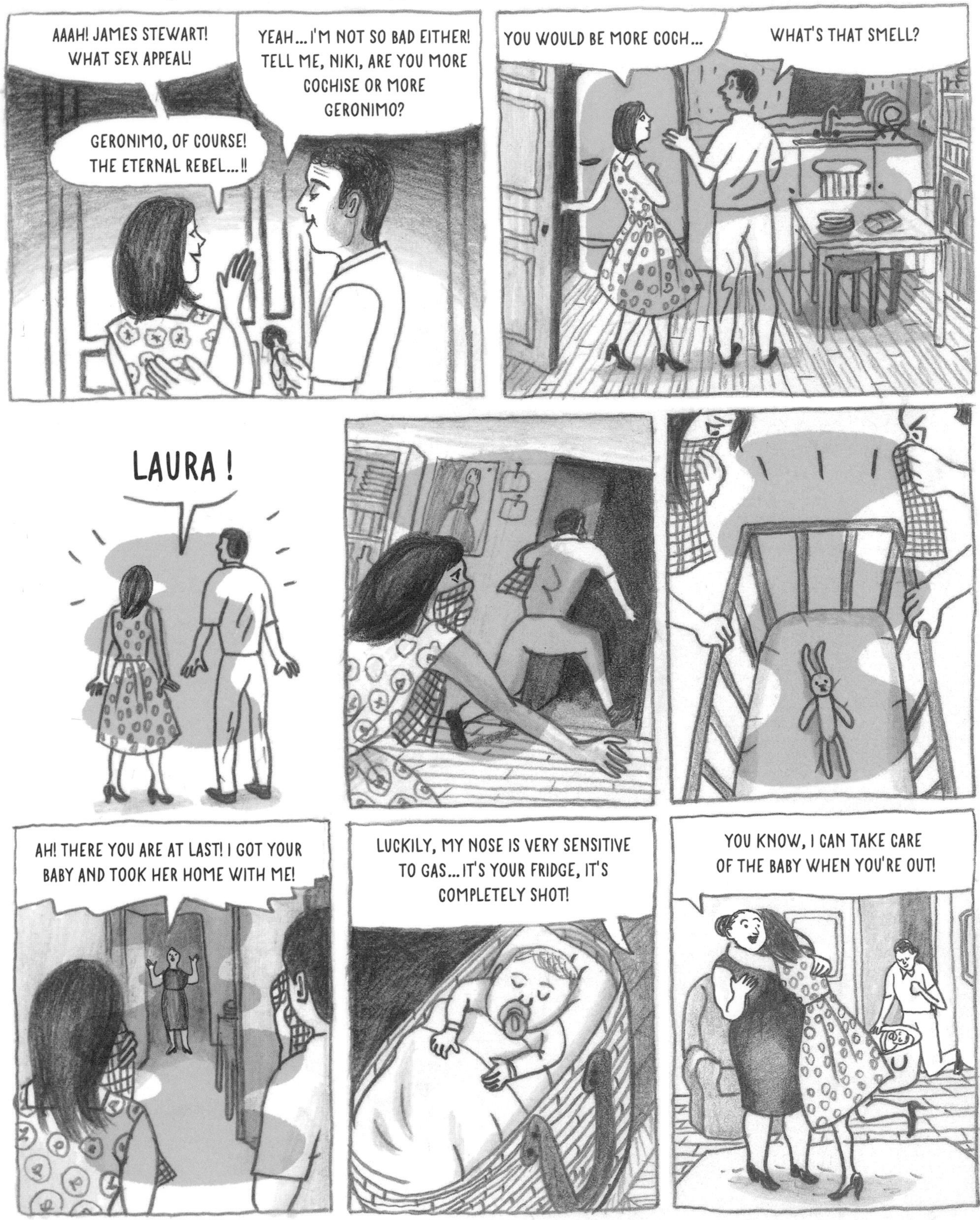

AAAH! JAMES STEWART! WHAT SEX APPEAL!
YEAH... I'M NOT SO BAD EITHER! TELL ME, NIKI, ARE YOU MORE COCHISE OR MORE GERONIMO?
GERONIMO, OF COURSE! THE ETERNAL REBEL...!!
YOU WOULD BE MORE COCH...
WHAT'S THAT SMELL?
LAURA !
AH! THERE YOU ARE AT LAST! I GOT YOUR BABY AND TOOK HER HOME WITH ME!
LUCKILY, MY NOSE IS VERY SENSITIVE TO GAS... IT'S YOUR FRIDGE, IT'S COMPLETELY SHOT!
YOU KNOW, I CAN TAKE CARE OF THE BABY WHEN YOU'RE OUT!


*Mother was right: I wasn't ready for my turn at being a responsible mother*

FALL 1951.

I knew Harry was having an affair with a much older woman...
And I felt out of place in a traditional American household.
My malaise grew at the same time as my health began to falter.

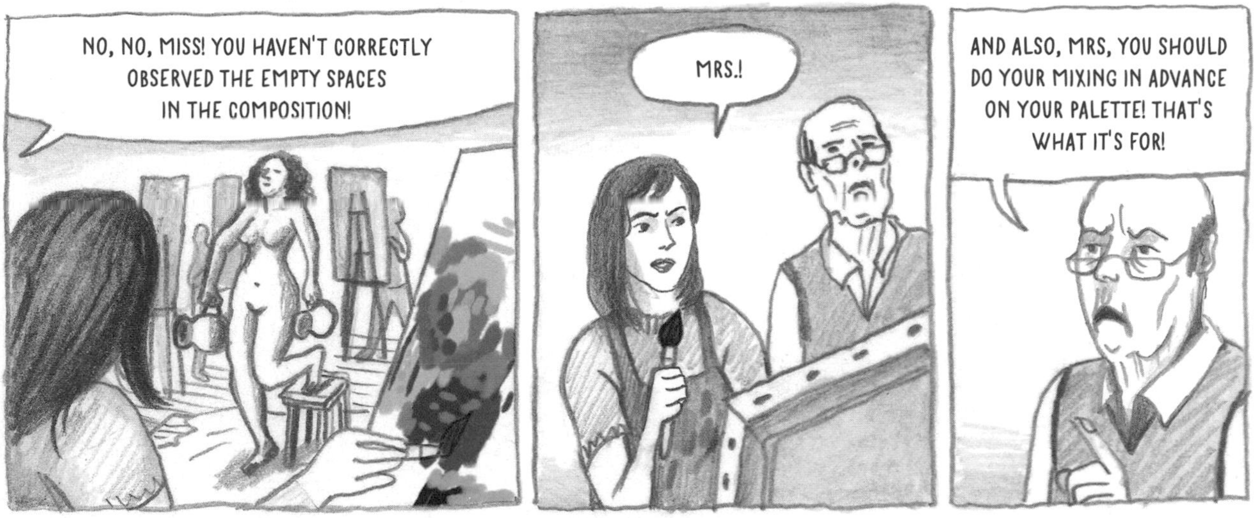

NO, NO, MISS! YOU HAVEN'T CORRECTLY OBSERVED THE EMPTY SPACES IN THE COMPOSITION!
MRS.!
AND ALSO, MRS, YOU SHOULD DO YOUR MIXING IN ADVANCE ON YOUR PALETTE! THAT'S WHAT IT'S FOR!


I'm incapable of conforming to any such model. I don't see things in three dimensions.
Once they're transcribed on canvas or paper, they become "flat"!
I understood almost immediately that I should rely only on my own experience.

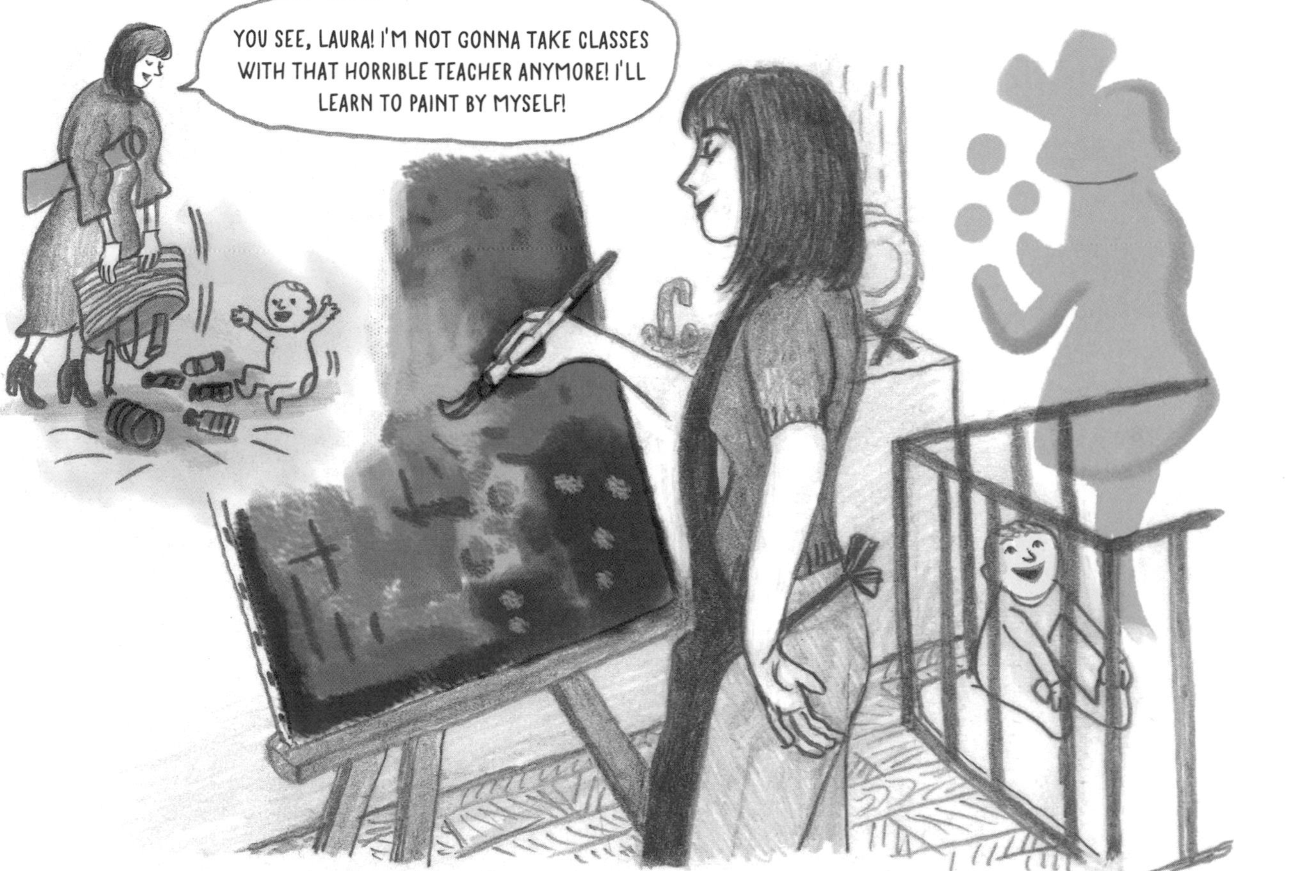

YOU SEE, LAURA! I'M NOT GONNA TAKE CLASSES WITH THAT HORRIBLE TEACHER ANYMORE! I'LL LEARN TO PAINT BY MYSELF!


Suddenly, it's as if time stops...It becomes magic! Harry's infidelities,
my bouts of hyperthyroidism, it all seems so futile!

1952, PARIS. *Paris, the place where EVERYTHING was happening! Avant-garde plays, the possibility of meeting the personalities of the moment, and among the best theater courses in the world...*

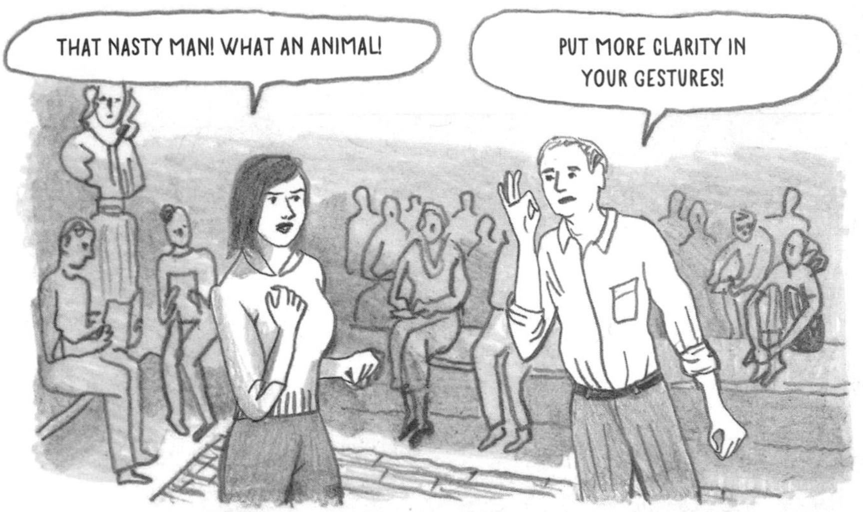
THAT NASTY MAN! WHAT AN ANIMAL!
PUT MORE CLARITY IN YOUR GESTURES!

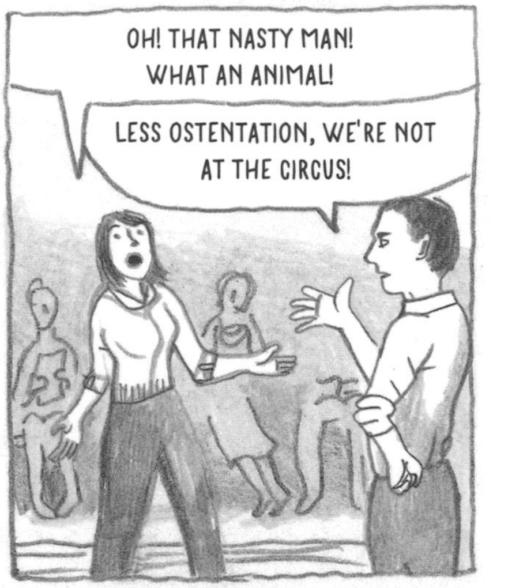
OH! THAT NASTY MAN! WHAT AN ANIMAL!
LESS OSTENTATION, WE'RE NOT AT THE CIRCUS!

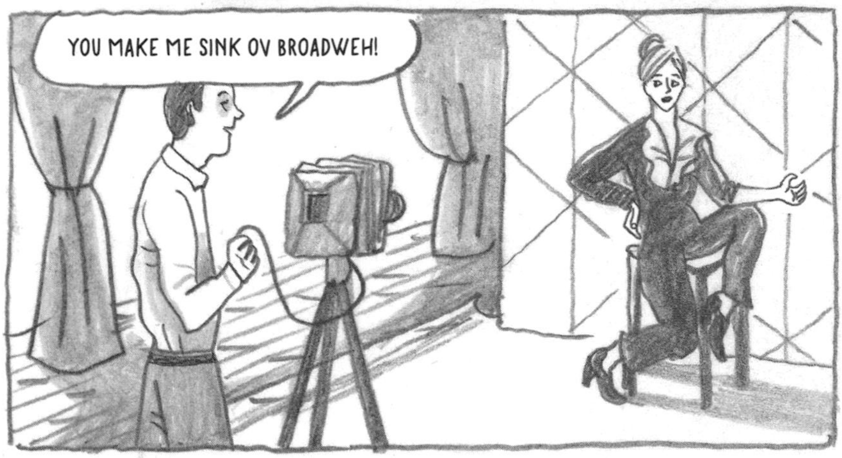
YOU MAKE ME SINK OV BROADWEH!

*Henry Clarke loved to make use of me...I get back into fashion photography for Elle and Vogue. Luckily, babysitters were cheap in Paris, and Laura was never alone...*

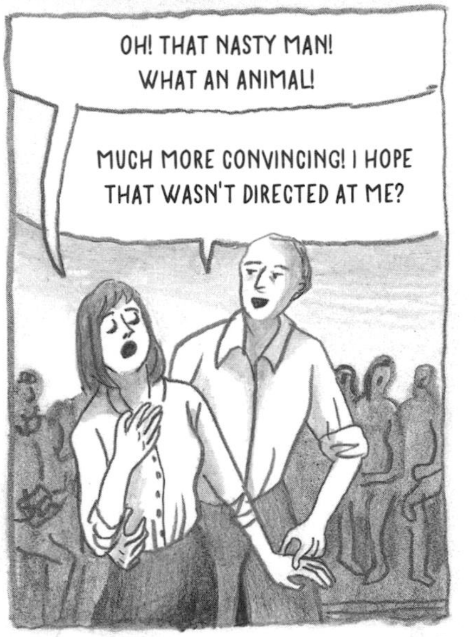
OH! THAT NASTY MAN! WHAT AN ANIMAL!
MUCH MORE CONVINCING! I HOPE THAT WASN'T DIRECTED AT ME?

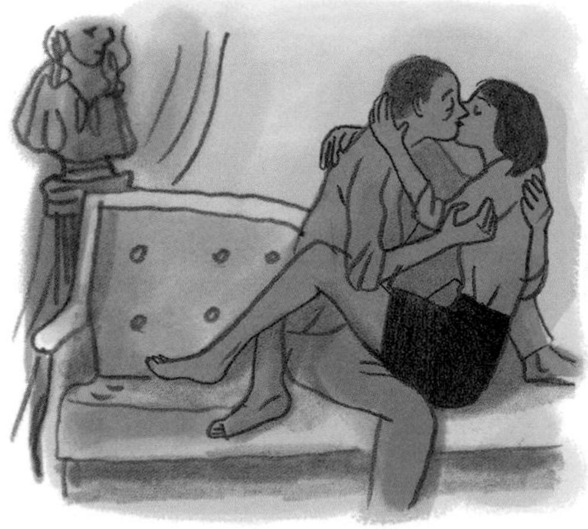

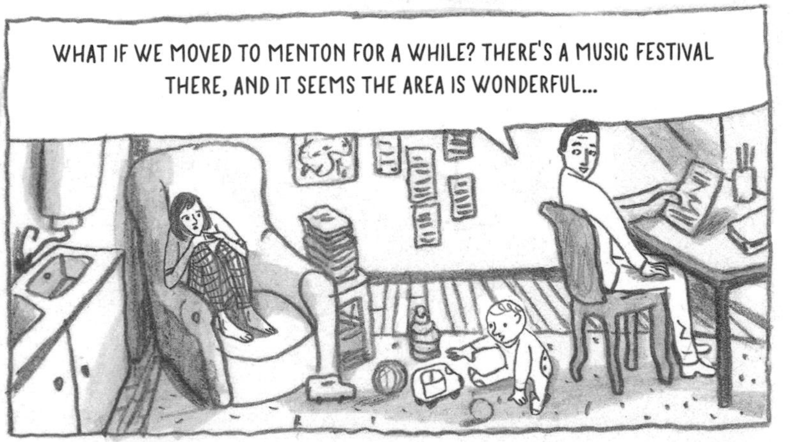
WHAT IF WE MOVED TO MENTON FOR A WHILE? THERE'S A MUSIC FESTIVAL THERE, AND IT SEEMS THE AREA IS WONDERFUL...

*This very short-lived adventure accentuated Harry's and my shared estrangement... I felt myself slowly flowing into a swamp......*

# CHAPTER 4

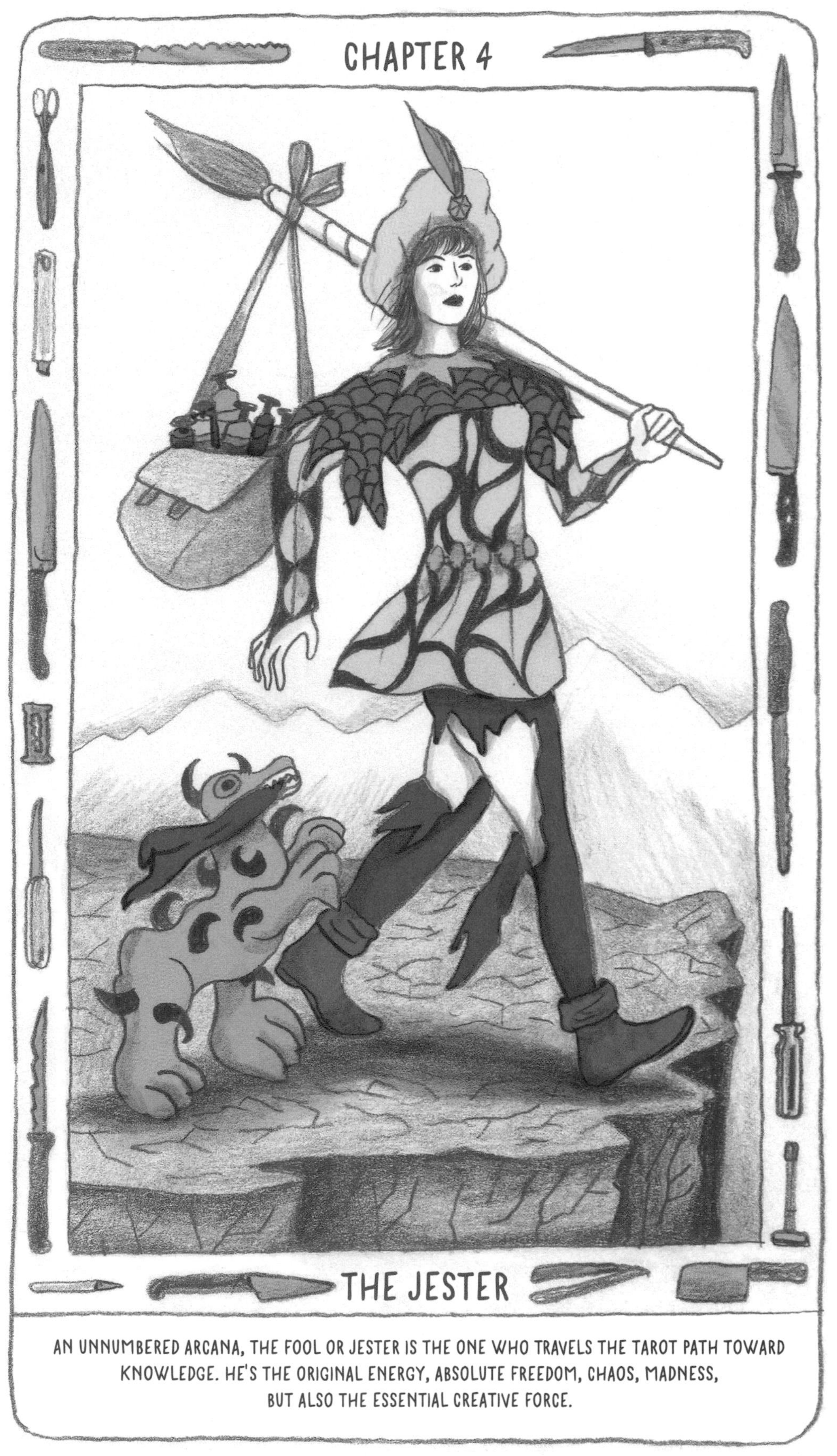

## THE JESTER

AN UNNUMBERED ARCANA, THE FOOL OR JESTER IS THE ONE WHO TRAVELS THE TAROT PATH TOWARD KNOWLEDGE. HE'S THE ORIGINAL ENERGY, ABSOLUTE FREEDOM, CHAOS, MADNESS, BUT ALSO THE ESSENTIAL CREATIVE FORCE.

AUTUMN 1953, MENTON, FRANCE.

*Lord George Gordon was passionate about botany and English literature. A survivor of the last war, he was obsessed with shortening his life as soon as possible, but couldn't bring himself to take the plunge... I was infatuated with this very noble figure and myself aspired to a carefully staged end.*

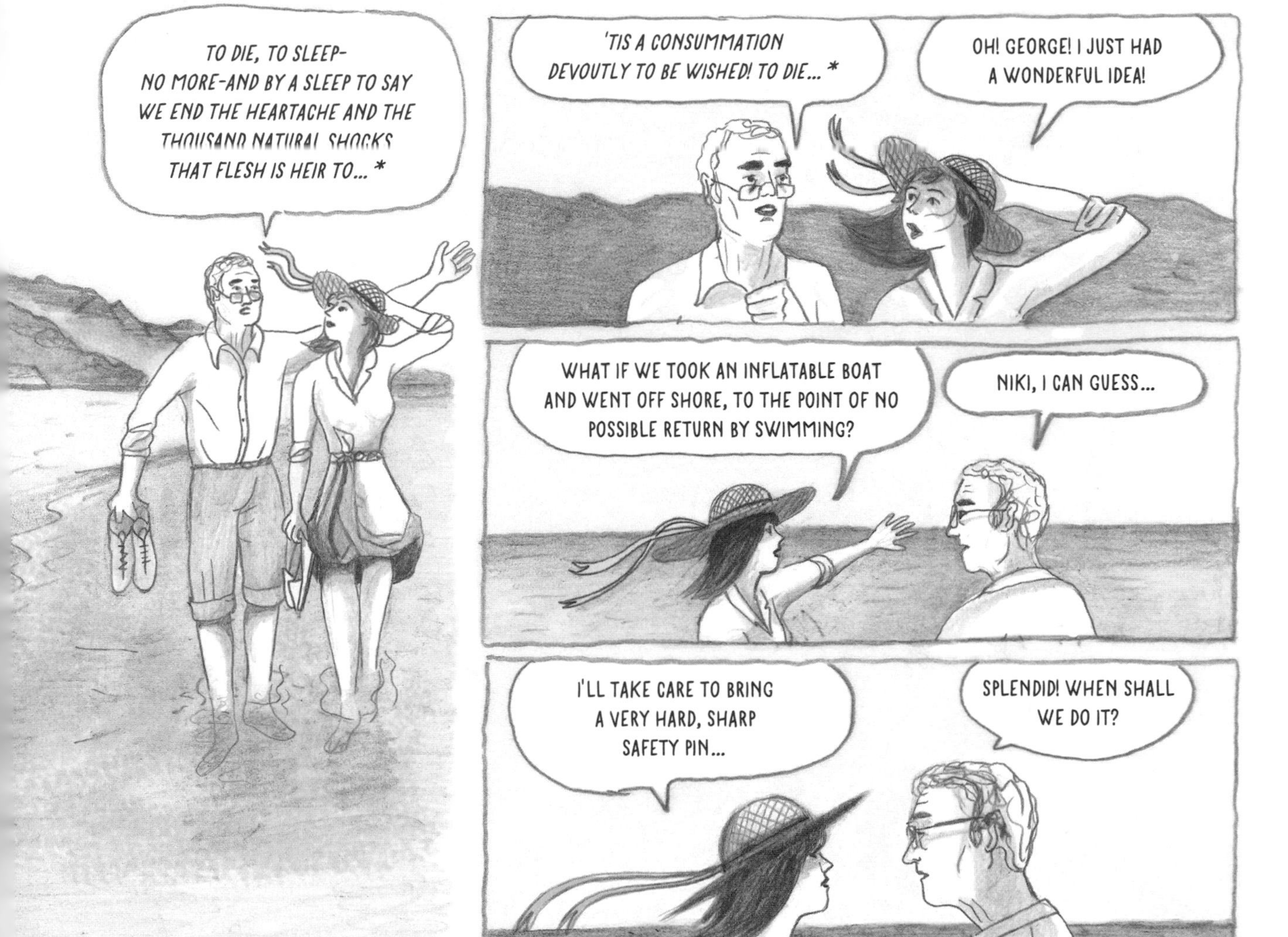

TO DIE, TO SLEEP- NO MORE-AND BY A SLEEP TO SAY WE END THE HEARTACHE AND THE THOUSAND NATURAL SHOCKS THAT FLESH IS HEIR TO... *
'TIS A CONSUMMATION DEVOUTLY TO BE WISHED! TO DIE... *
OH! GEORGE! I JUST HAD A WONDERFUL IDEA!
WHAT IF WE TOOK AN INFLATABLE BOAT AND WENT OFF SHORE, TO THE POINT OF NO POSSIBLE RETURN BY SWIMMING?
NIKI, I CAN GUESS...
I'LL TAKE CARE TO BRING A VERY HARD, SHARP SAFETY PIN...
SPLENDID! WHEN SHALL WE DO IT?


*WILLIAM SHAKESPEARE, HAMLET, ACT 3, SCENE 1.

*My interior demons were in the process of engulfing me...all the more so because some do-gooder had reported Harry's infidelity with milord's younger wife!*

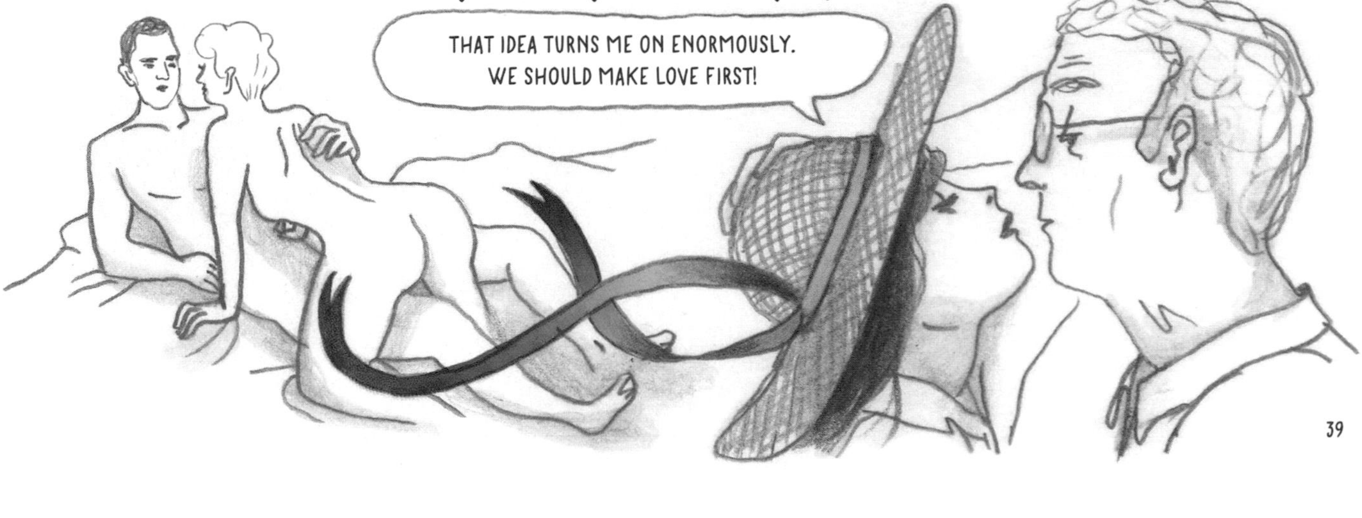

THAT IDEA TURNS ME ON ENORMOUSLY. WE SHOULD MAKE LOVE FIRST!

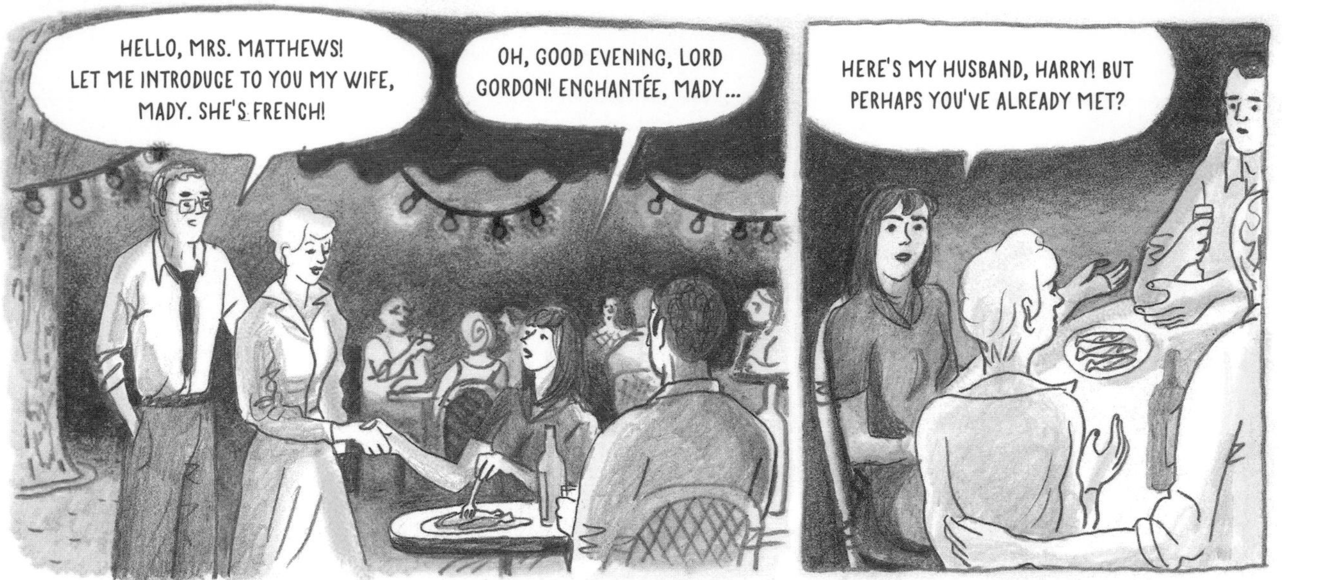
HELLO, MRS. MATTHEWS!
LET ME INTRODUCE TO YOU MY WIFE, MADY. SHE'S FRENCH!
OH, GOOD EVENING, LORD GORDON! ENCHANTÉE, MADY...
HERE'S MY HUSBAND, HARRY! BUT PERHAPS YOU'VE ALREADY MET?

I had an enormous mousetrap stuck in my chest. I couldn't sleep anymore...
my nights and days withered away, like the slimy foam torn from dying waves.

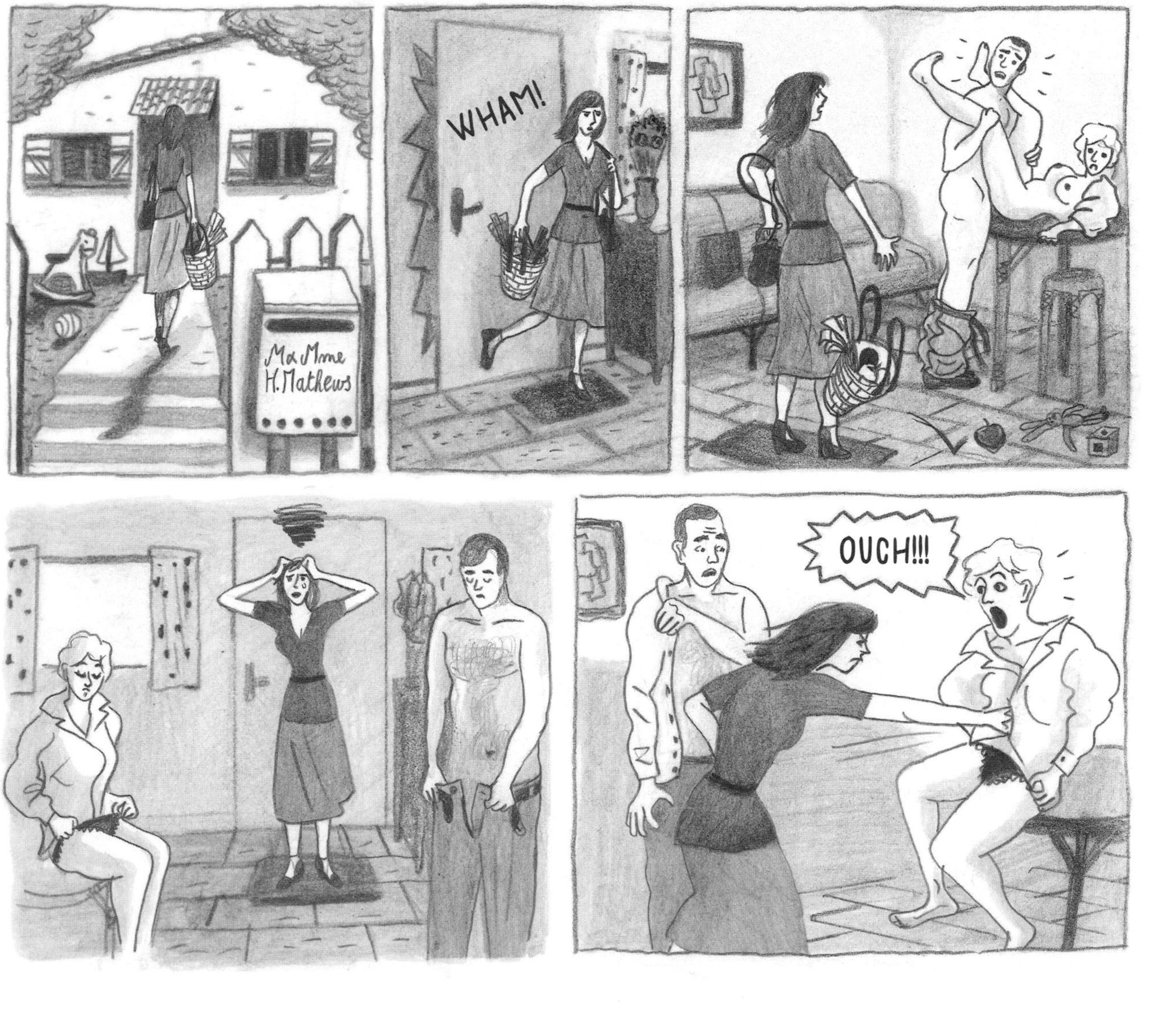
M & Mme
H. Mathews
WHAM!
OUCH!!!

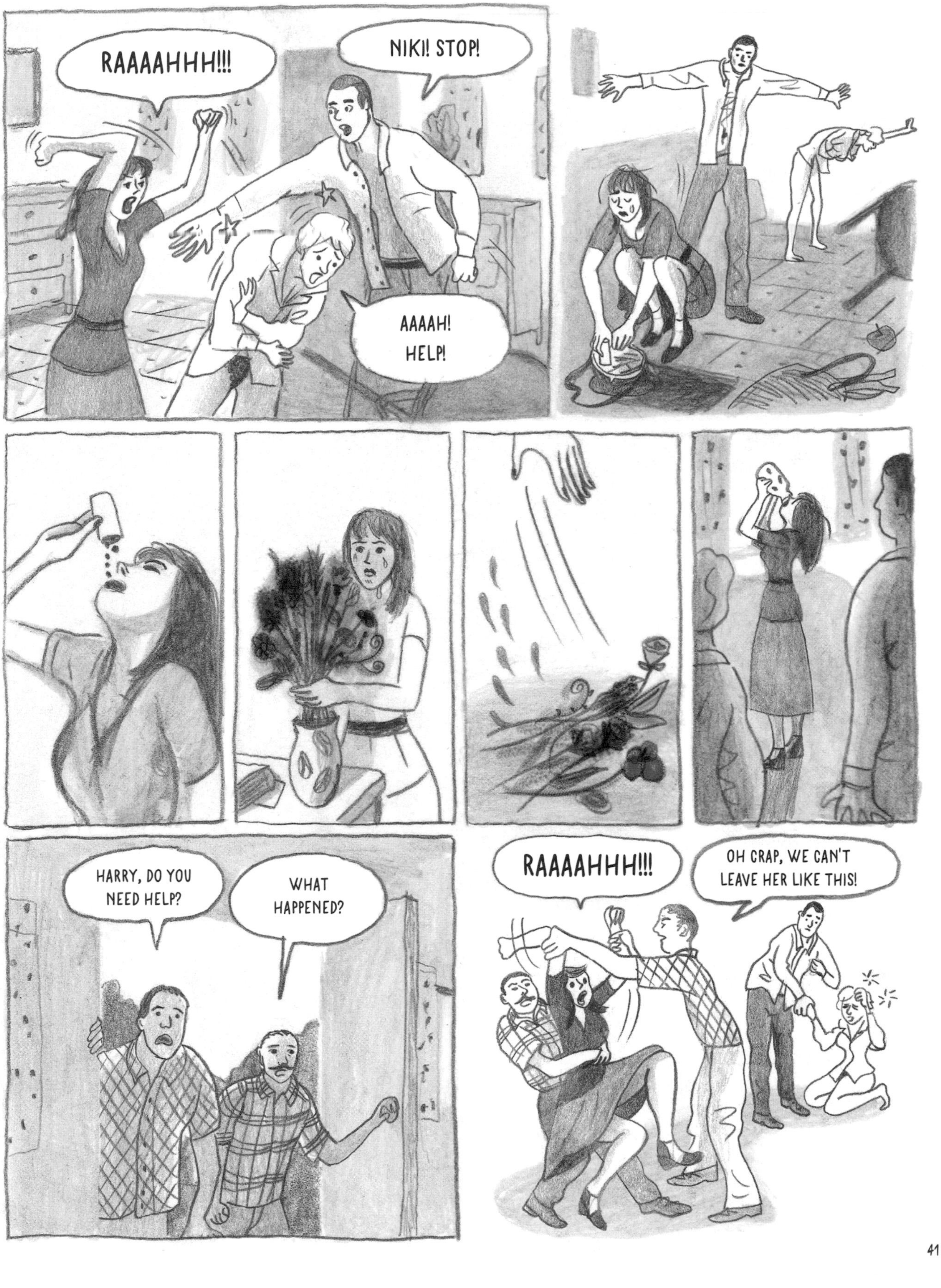
RAAAAHHH!!!
NIKI! STOP!
AAAAH! HELP!
HARRY, DO YOU NEED HELP?
WHAT HAPPENED?
RAAAAHHH!!!
OH CRAP, WE CAN'T LEAVE HER LIKE THIS!

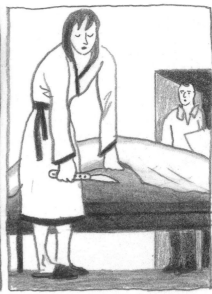

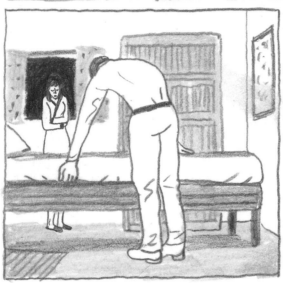

NICE, FRANCE, PSYCHIATRIC WARD, THAT SAME NIGHT.

THANK YOU VERY MUCH, MADAME. YOU DID WELL TO COME.

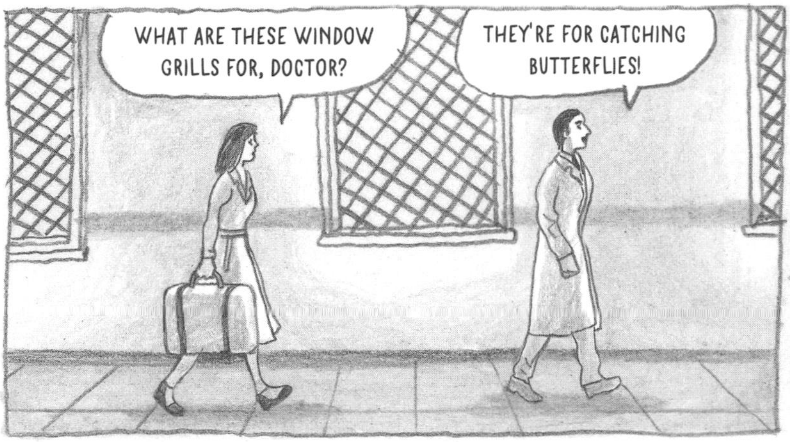
WHAT ARE THESE WINDOW GRILLS FOR, DOCTOR?
THEY'RE FOR CATCHING BUTTERFLIES!

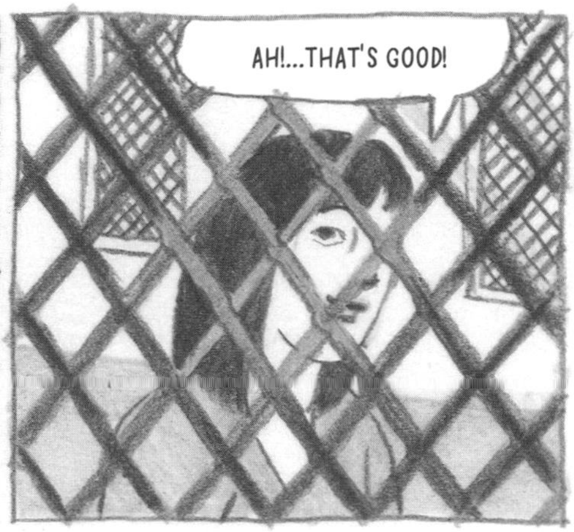
AH!...THAT'S GOOD!

The insulin treatment was very painful because it removes all of your body's sugar, and it was necessary to replace it afterwards. Then came the shock therapy

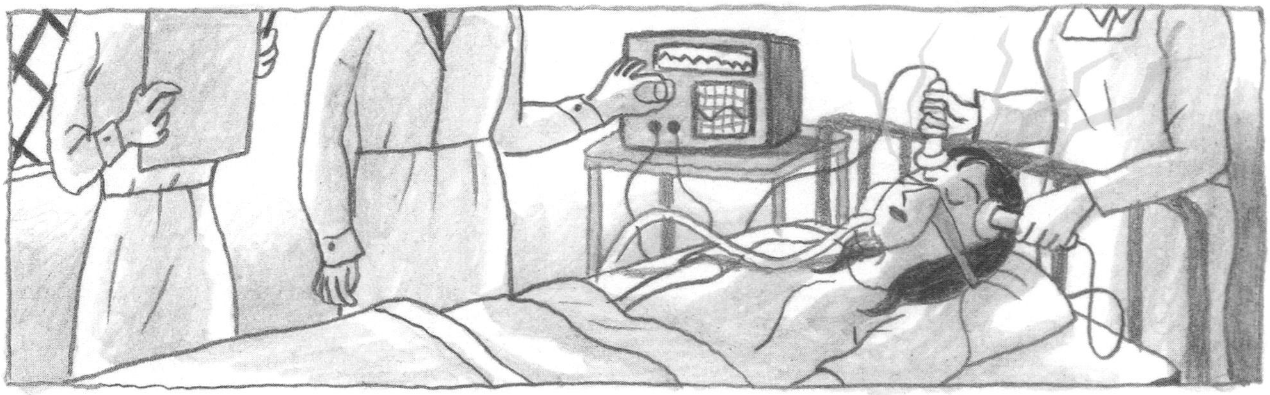

The doctor had sedated me, so I don't remember anything. But I awoke to a fog of no memory that caused me terrible anguish...Are the rats inside me?

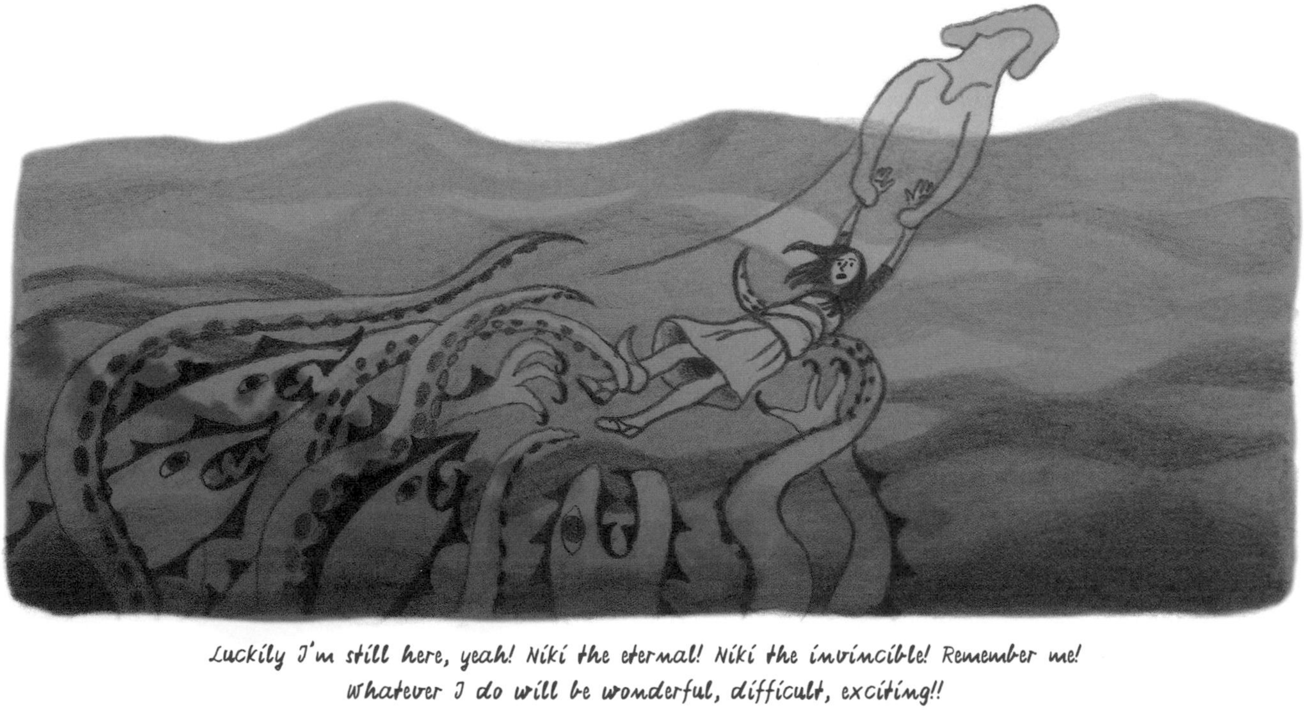

Luckily I'm still here, yeah! Niki the eternal! Niki the invincible! Remember me! Whatever I do will be wonderful, difficult, exciting!!

TEN ELECTROSHOCKS AND SIX WEEKS LATER.

*I came in crazy, I'll come out painting...*

NIKI! YOU'RE GOING HOME! AND TO SAY DR. COSSA THOUGHT HE MIGHT HAVE TO KEEP YOU FOR FIVE YEARS!

ONE FRIDAY...

"MY DEAR DAUGHTER, I'M SURE YOU REMEMBER THAT, WHEN YOU WERE ELEVEN YEARS OLD, I TRIED TO MAKE YOU MY MISTRESS..."

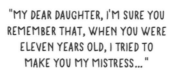

*For years, a violent migraine would take hold of me every Friday whenever the mailman came by.*

NOW, NOW, MRS. MATTHEWS... YOUR FATHER CANNOT HAVE COMMITTED SUCH AN ACT!

I'LL ANSWER HIM. LET ME SEE TO IT!

# CHAPTER 5

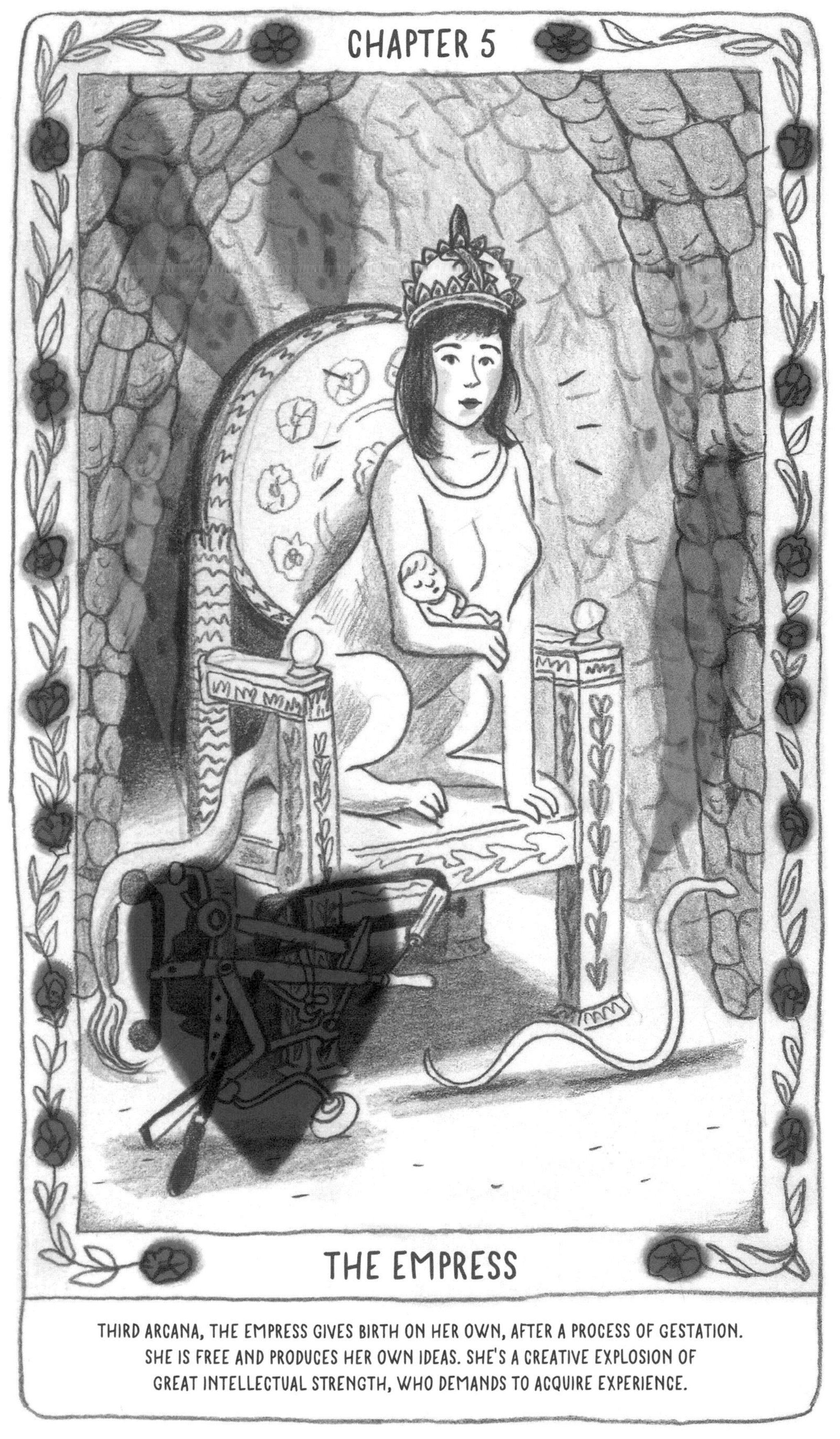

## THE EMPRESS

THIRD ARCANA, THE EMPRESS GIVES BIRTH ON HER OWN, AFTER A PROCESS OF GESTATION. SHE IS FREE AND PRODUCES HER OWN IDEAS. SHE'S A CREATIVE EXPLOSION OF GREAT INTELLECTUAL STRENGTH, WHO DEMANDS TO ACQUIRE EXPERIENCE.

SUMMER 1954: BACK TO PARIS.

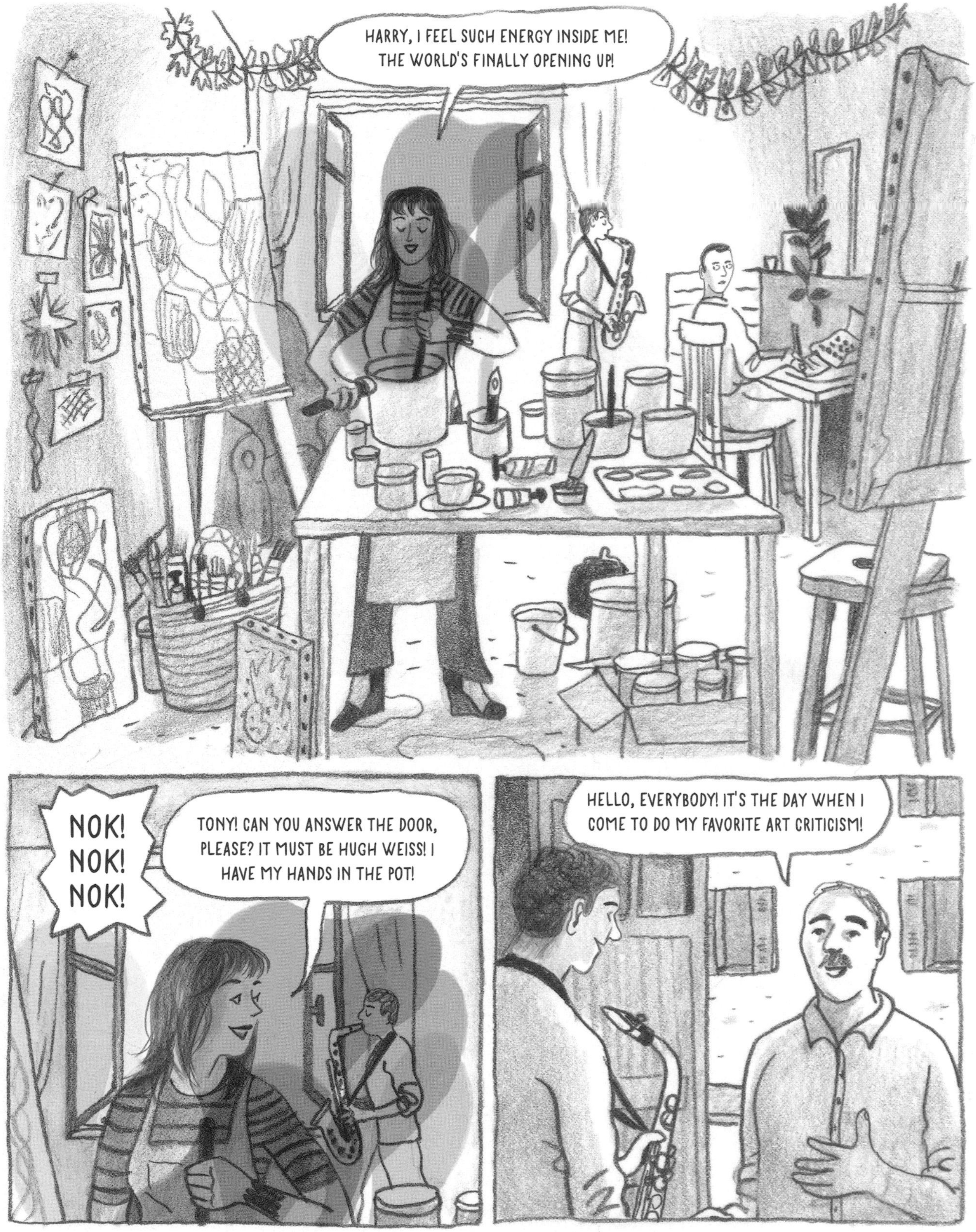
HARRY, I FEEL SUCH ENERGY INSIDE ME! THE WORLD'S FINALLY OPENING UP!
NOK! NOK! NOK!
TONY! CAN YOU ANSWER THE DOOR, PLEASE? IT MUST BE HUGH WEISS! I HAVE MY HANDS IN THE POT!
HELLO, EVERYBODY! IT'S THE DAY WHEN I COME TO DO MY FAVORITE ART CRITICISM!

*Our friend Tony the jazzman introduced Hugh to me as the best mentor I could have...*

For years, Hugh enlightened me with his advice, dissuading me from taking classroom classes.
He said I ought to keep my freshness as a self-taught artist.

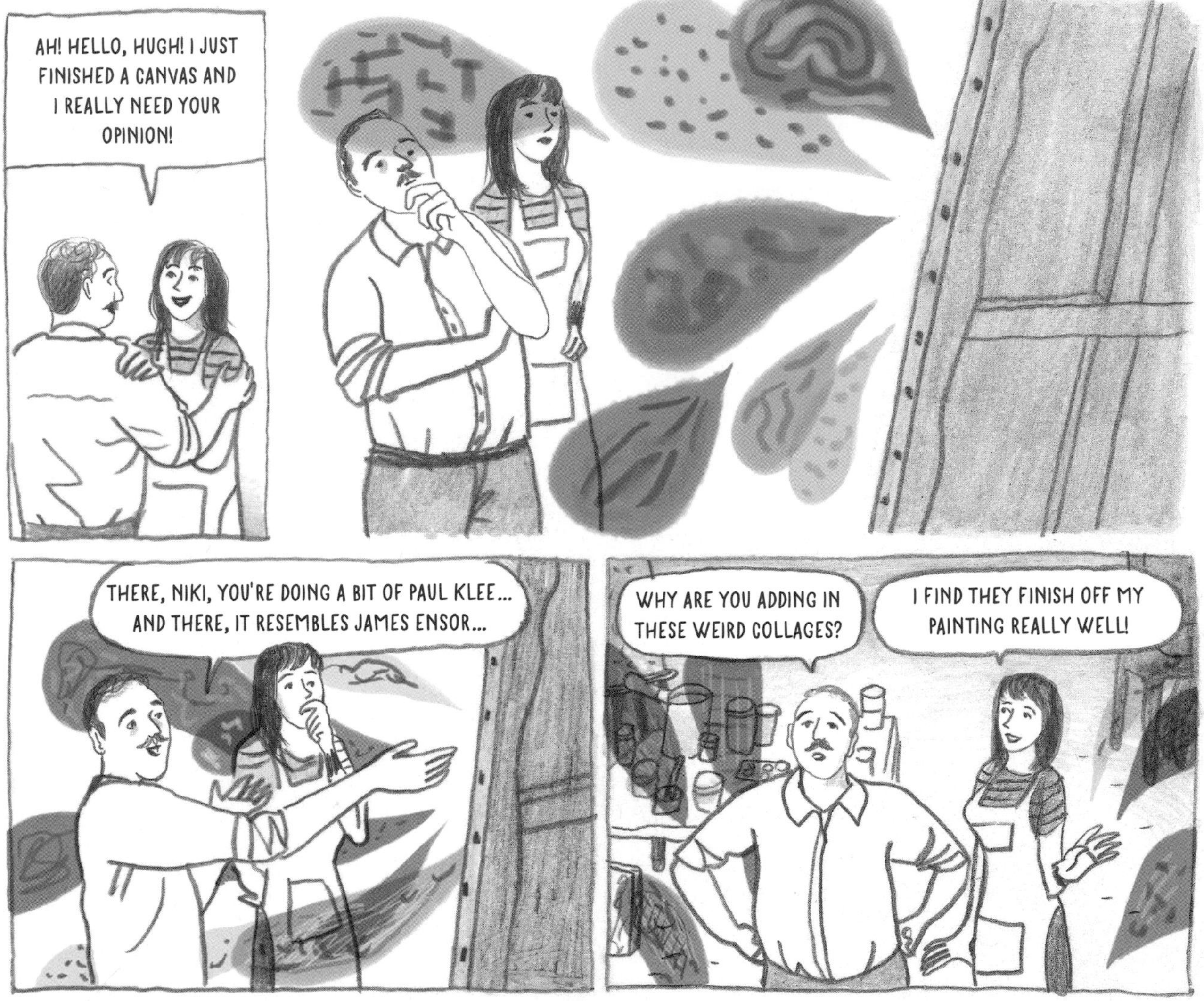
AH! HELLO, HUGH! I JUST FINISHED A CANVAS AND I REALLY NEED YOUR OPINION!
THERE, NIKI, YOU'RE DOING A BIT OF PAUL KLEE... AND THERE, IT RESEMBLES JAMES ENSOR...
WHY ARE YOU ADDING IN THESE WEIRD COLLAGES?
I FIND THEY FINISH OFF MY PAINTING REALLY WELL!

For Hugh, painting needed to remain... painting!

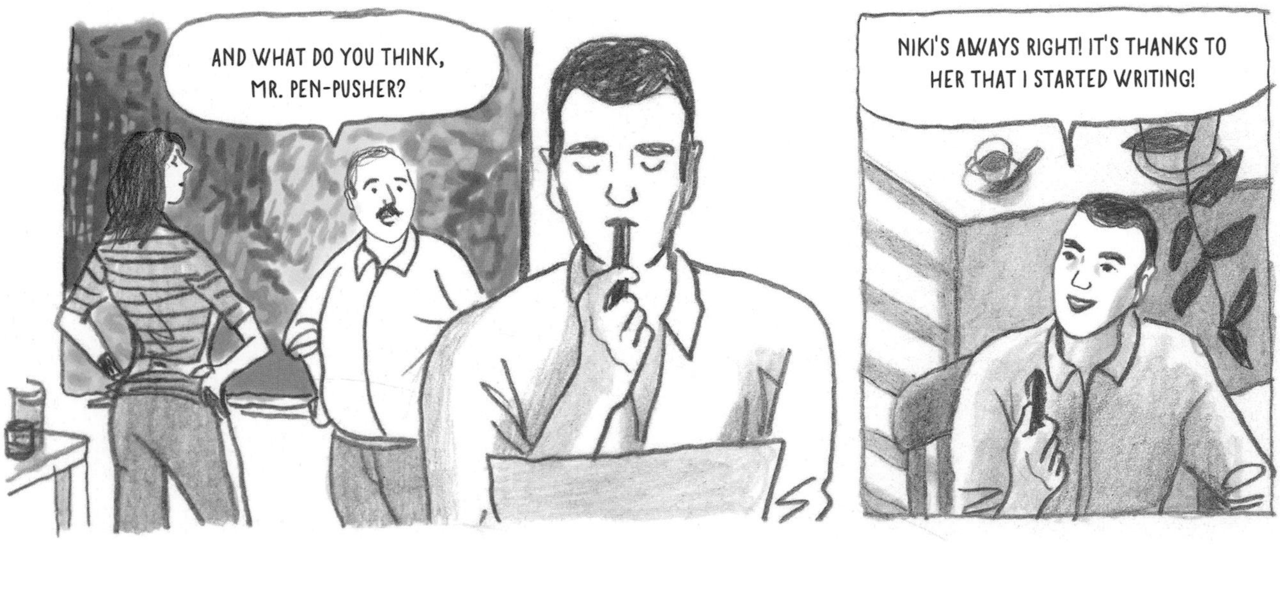
AND WHAT DO YOU THINK, MR. PEN-PUSHER?
NIKI'S ALWAYS RIGHT! IT'S THANKS TO HER THAT I STARTED WRITING!

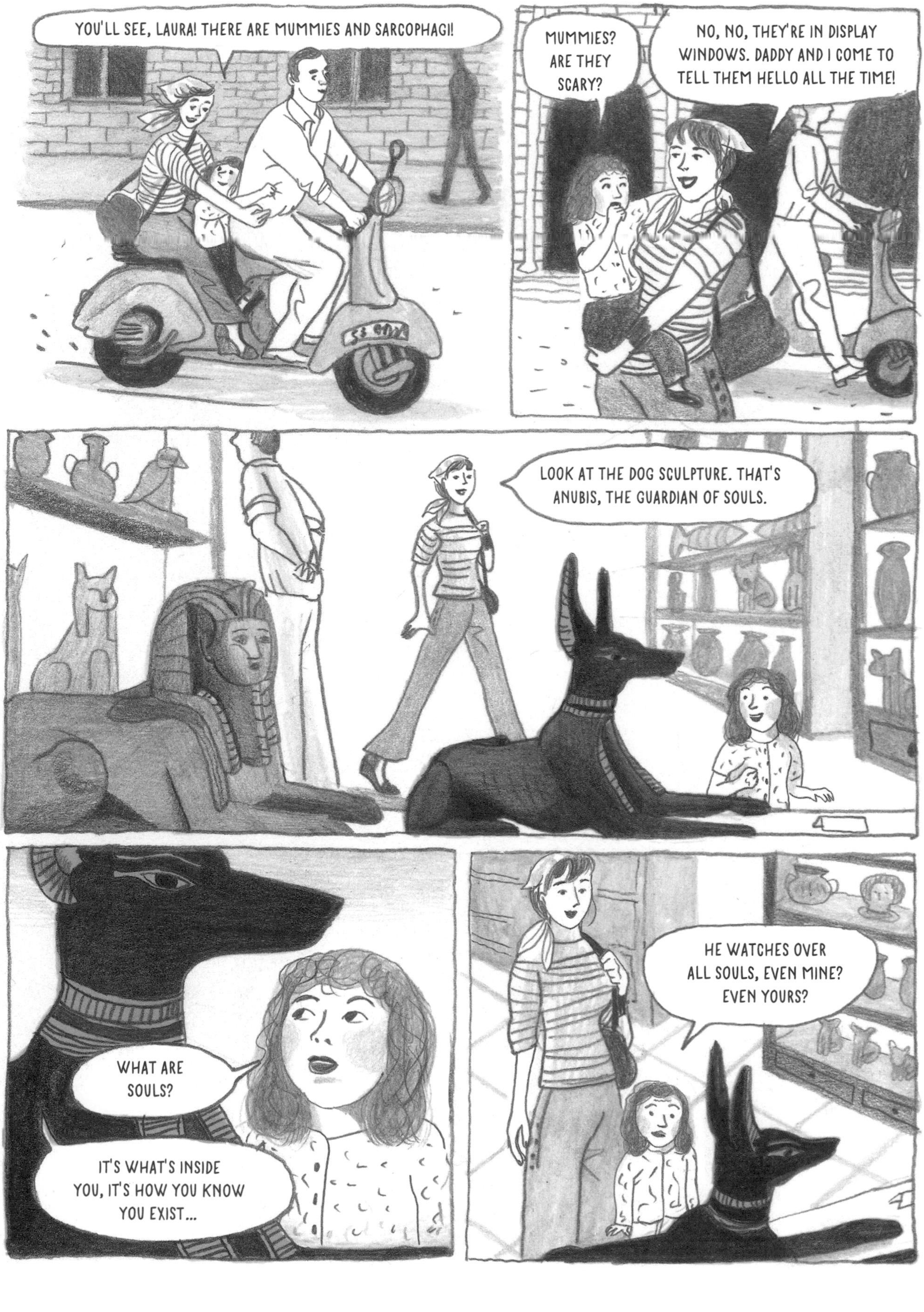
YOU'LL SEE, LAURA! THERE ARE MUMMIES AND SARCOPHAGI!
MUMMIES? ARE THEY SCARY?
NO, NO, THEY'RE IN DISPLAY WINDOWS. DADDY AND I COME TO TELL THEM HELLO ALL THE TIME!
LOOK AT THE DOG SCULPTURE. THAT'S ANUBIS, THE GUARDIAN OF SOULS.
WHAT ARE SOULS?
IT'S WHAT'S INSIDE YOU, IT'S HOW YOU KNOW YOU EXIST...
HE WATCHES OVER ALL SOULS, EVEN MINE? EVEN YOURS?

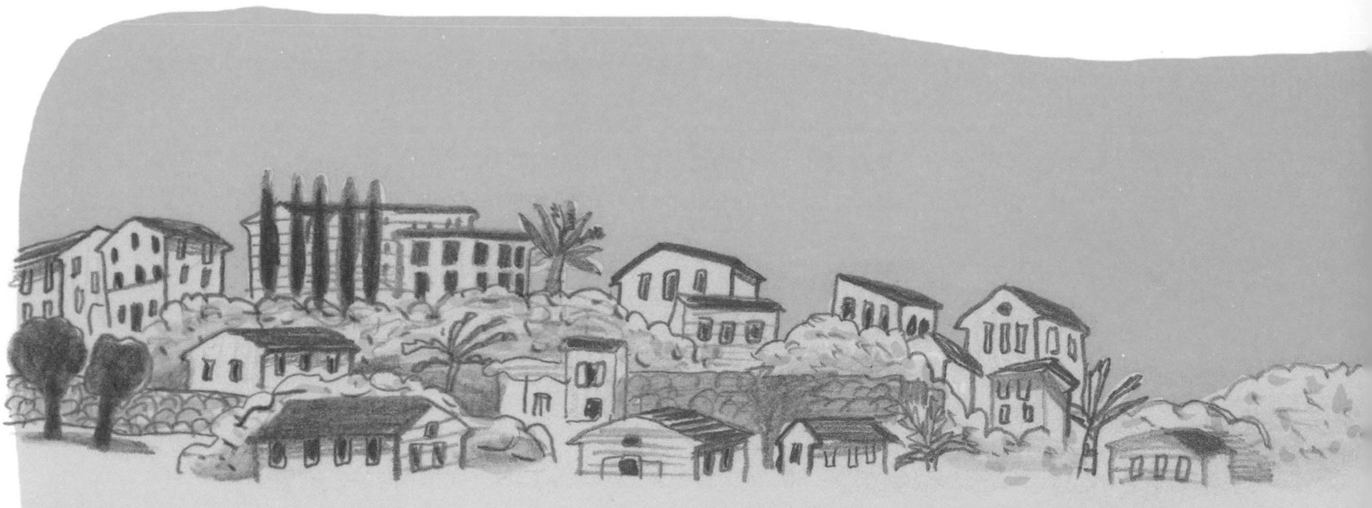

Our constant need for change brought us to a corner of paradise: Deià in Majorca...Harry, who was an only child, wanted a second child so much, and I was pregnant again! After prescribed bedrest of three months to protect the baby, once again I was allowed to resume "a normal life." Spain, here we come!

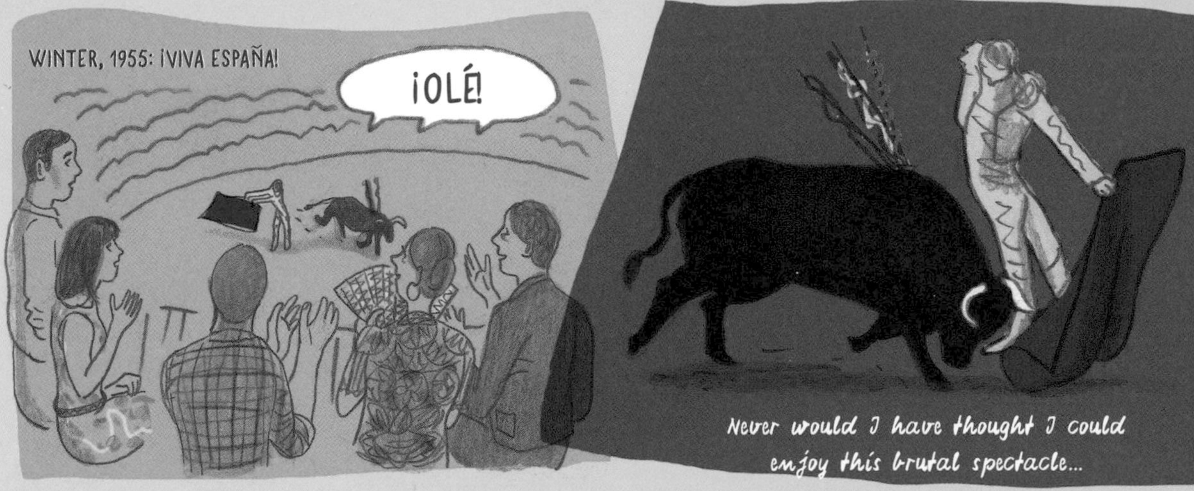
WINTER, 1955: ¡VIVA ESPAÑA!
¡OLÉ!
Never would I have thought I could enjoy this brutal spectacle...

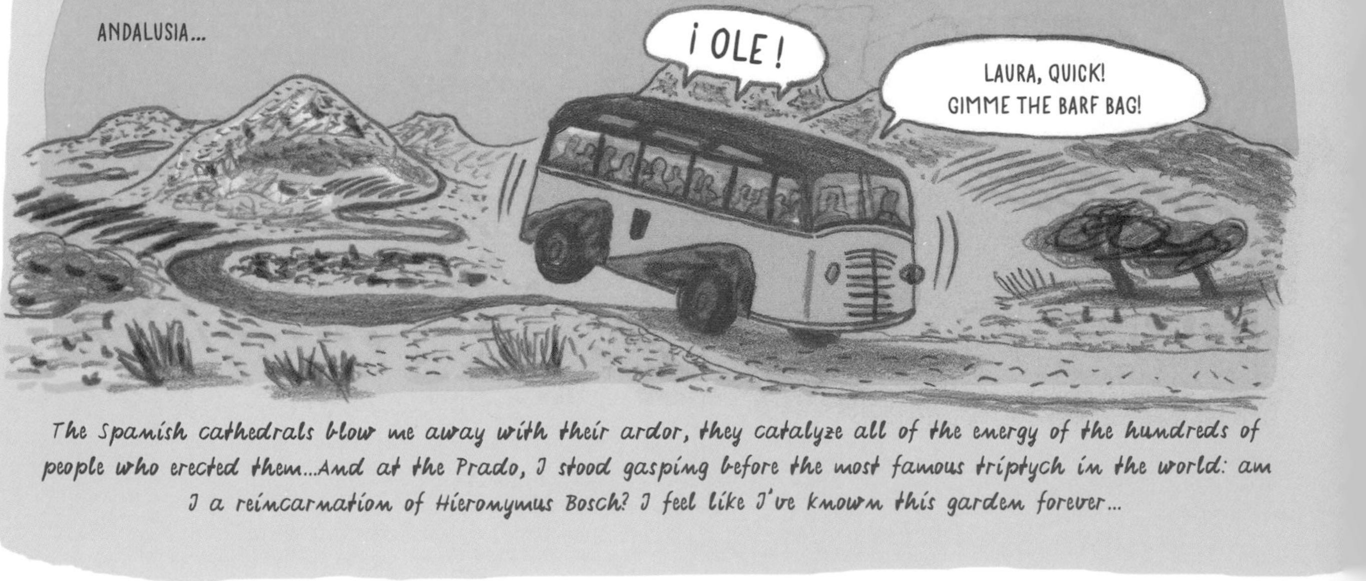
ANDALUSIA...
¡ OLE !
LAURA, QUICK! GIMME THE BARF BAG!

The Spanish cathedrals blow me away with their ardor, they catalyze all of the energy of the hundreds of people who erected them...And at the Prado, I stood gasping before the most famous triptych in the world: am I a reincarnation of Hieronymus Bosch? I feel like I've known this garden forever...

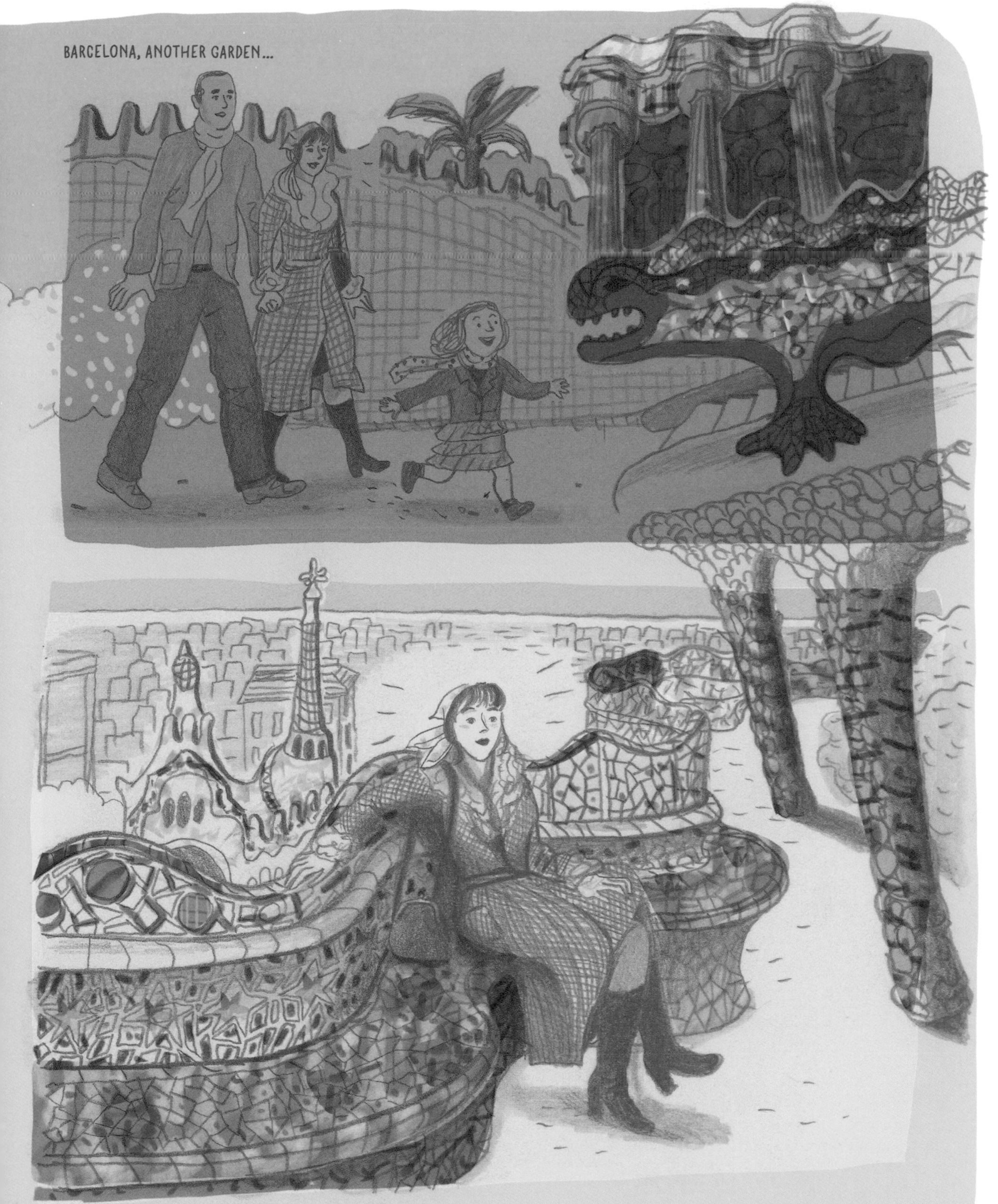
BARCELONA, ANOTHER GARDEN...
It's a cosmic ray crossing through me: I MUST create a garden like this one, that'll be the source of people's joy! It's my DESTINY!

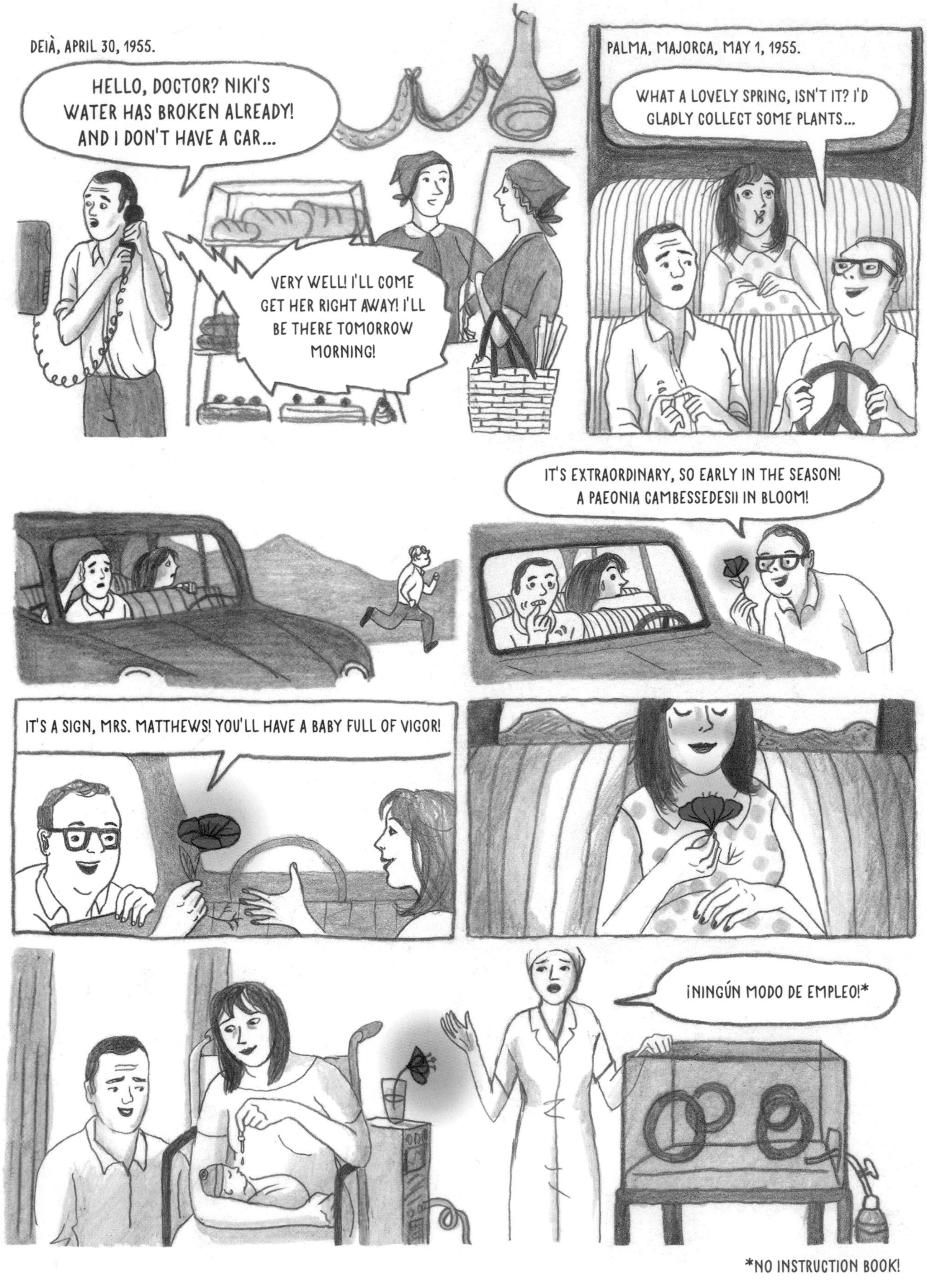
DEIÀ, APRIL 30, 1955.
HELLO, DOCTOR? NIKI'S WATER HAS BROKEN ALREADY! AND I DON'T HAVE A CAR...
VERY WELL! I'LL COME GET HER RIGHT AWAY! I'LL BE THERE TOMORROW MORNING!
PALMA, MAJORCA, MAY 1, 1955.
WHAT A LOVELY SPRING, ISN'T IT? I'D GLADLY COLLECT SOME PLANTS...
IT'S EXTRAORDINARY, SO EARLY IN THE SEASON! A PAEONIA CAMBESSEDESII IN BLOOM!
IT'S A SIGN, MRS. MATTHEWS! YOU'LL HAVE A BABY FULL OF VIGOR!
¡NINGÚN MODO DE EMPLEO!*



*NO INSTRUCTION BOOK!

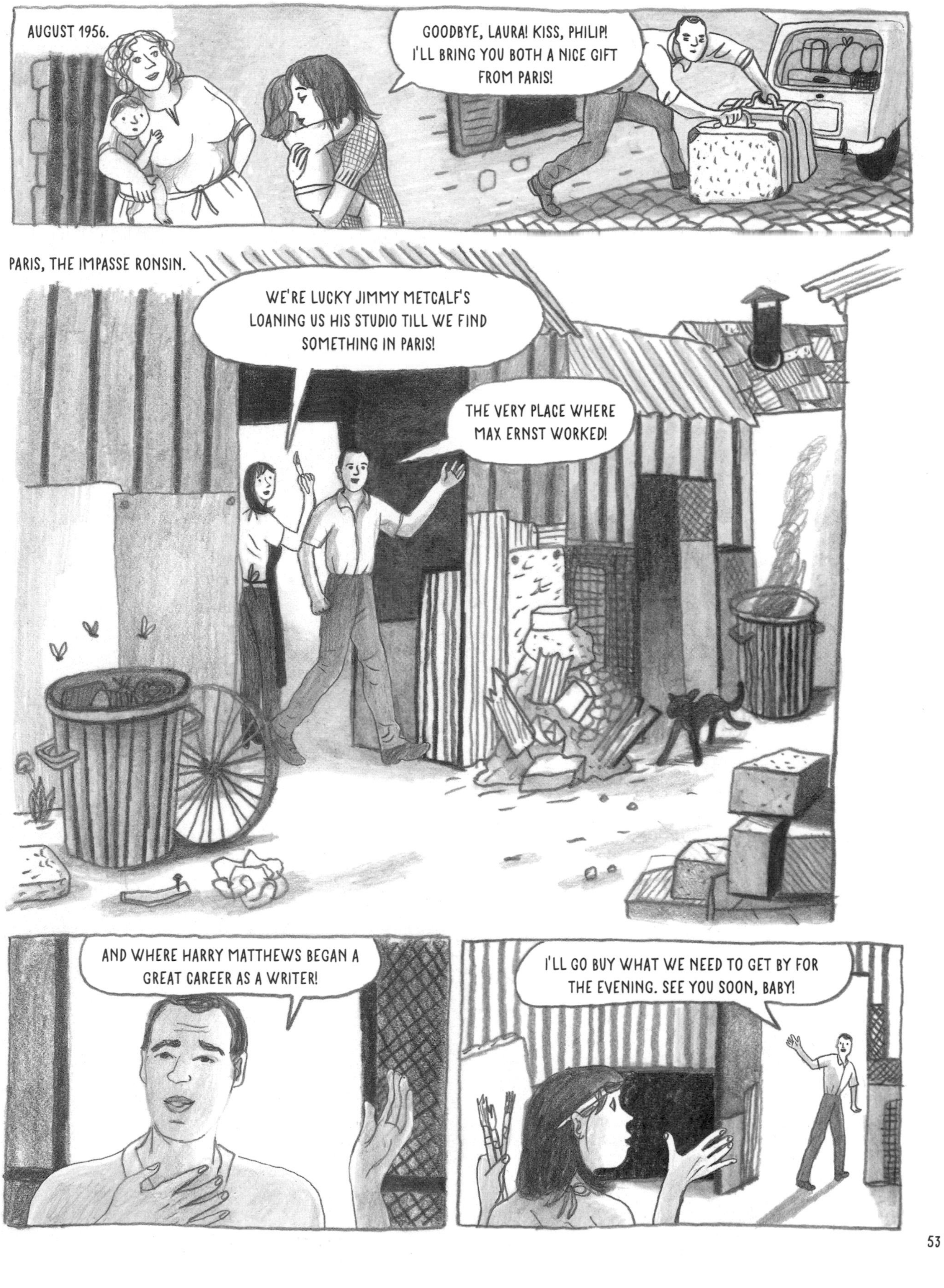
AUGUST 1956.
GOODBYE, LAURA! KISS, PHILIP! I'LL BRING YOU BOTH A NICE GIFT FROM PARIS!
PARIS, THE IMPASSE RONSIN.
WE'RE LUCKY JIMMY METCALF'S LOANING US HIS STUDIO TILL WE FIND SOMETHING IN PARIS!
THE VERY PLACE WHERE MAX ERNST WORKED!
AND WHERE HARRY MATTHEWS BEGAN A GREAT CAREER AS A WRITER!
I'LL GO BUY WHAT WE NEED TO GET BY FOR THE EVENING. SEE YOU SOON, BABY!

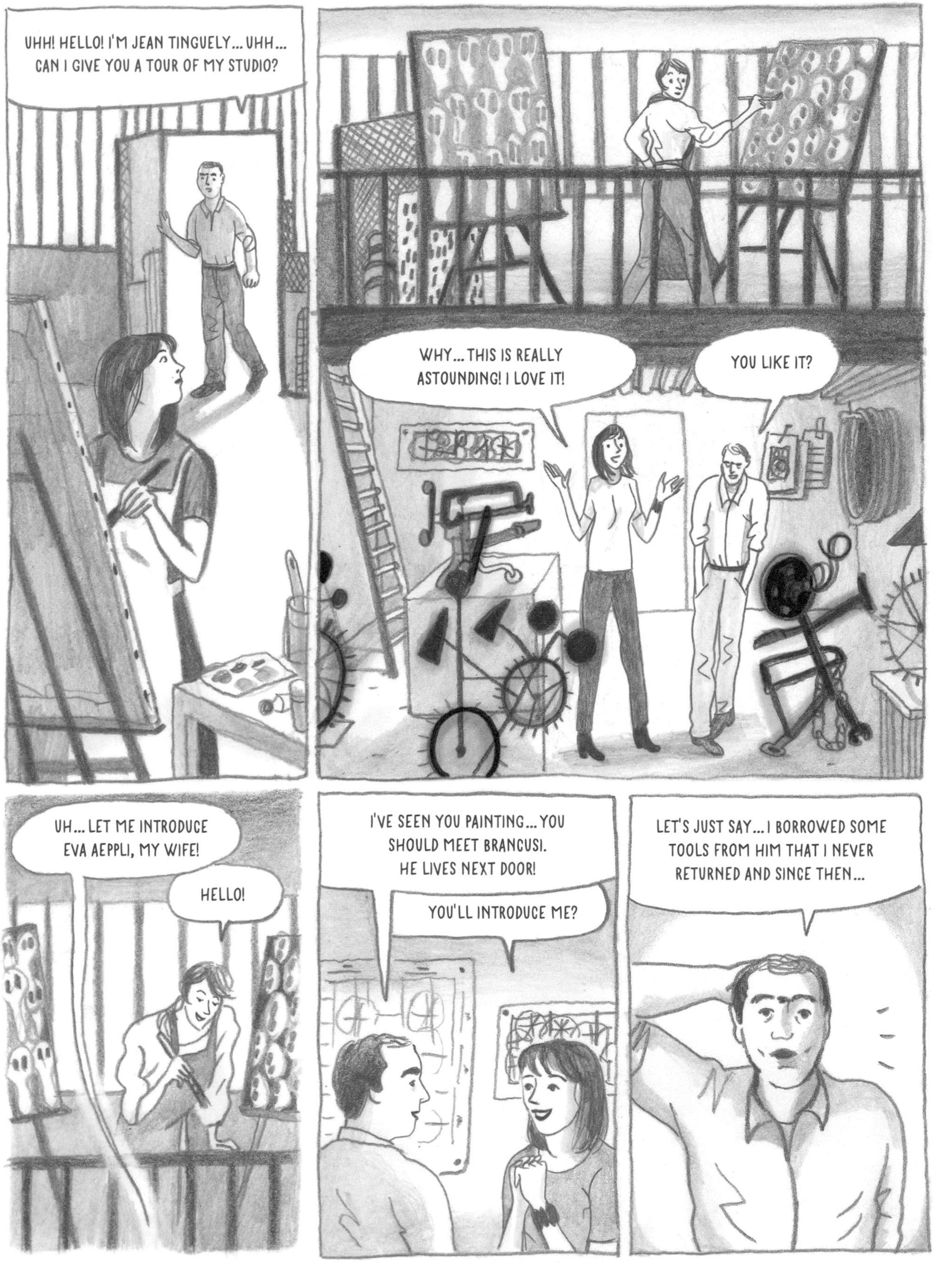
UHH! HELLO! I'M JEAN TINGUELY... UHH... CAN I GIVE YOU A TOUR OF MY STUDIO?
WHY... THIS IS REALLY ASTOUNDING! I LOVE IT!
YOU LIKE IT?
UH... LET ME INTRODUCE EVA AEPPLI, MY WIFE!
HELLO!
I'VE SEEN YOU PAINTING... YOU SHOULD MEET BRANCUSI. HE LIVES NEXT DOOR!
YOU'LL INTRODUCE ME?
LET'S JUST SAY... I BORROWED SOME TOOLS FROM HIM THAT I NEVER RETURNED AND SINCE THEN...

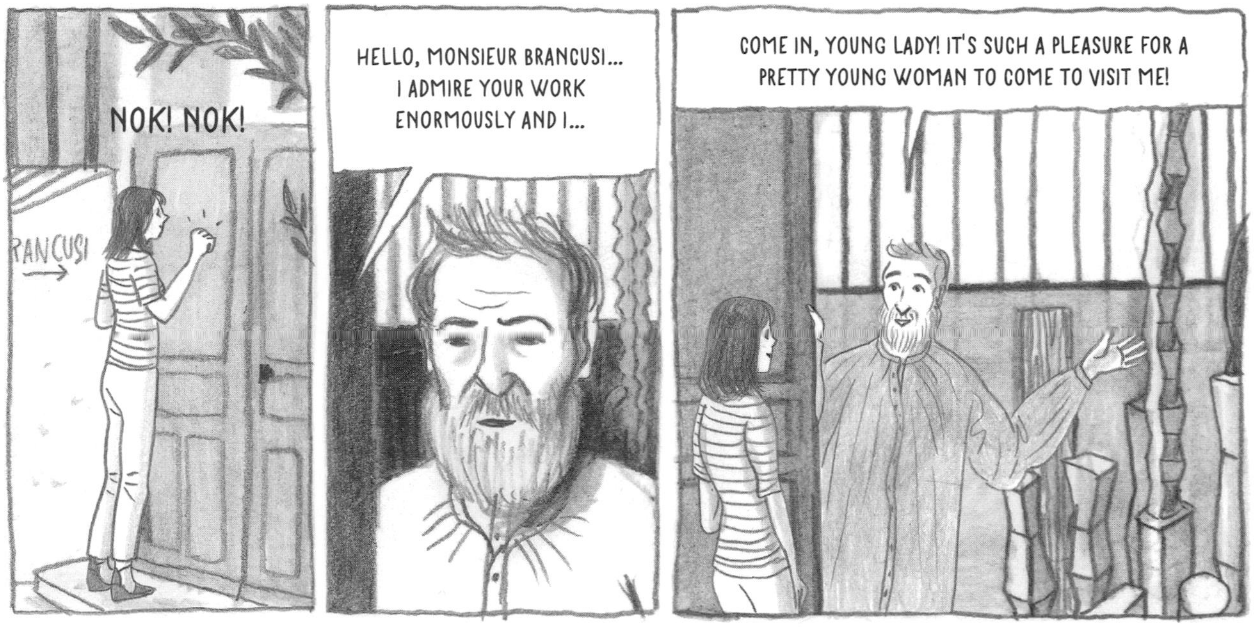
NOK! NOK!
RANCUSI
HELLO, MONSIEUR BRANCUSI... I ADMIRE YOUR WORK ENORMOUSLY AND I...
COME IN, YOUNG LADY! IT'S SUCH A PLEASURE FOR A PRETTY YOUNG WOMAN TO COME TO VISIT ME!

*These magnetic encounters, that faith in Art, that selflessness of material contingencies...*
*I felt at home in this wretched impasse that exuded total freedom and the thirst for the absolute!*

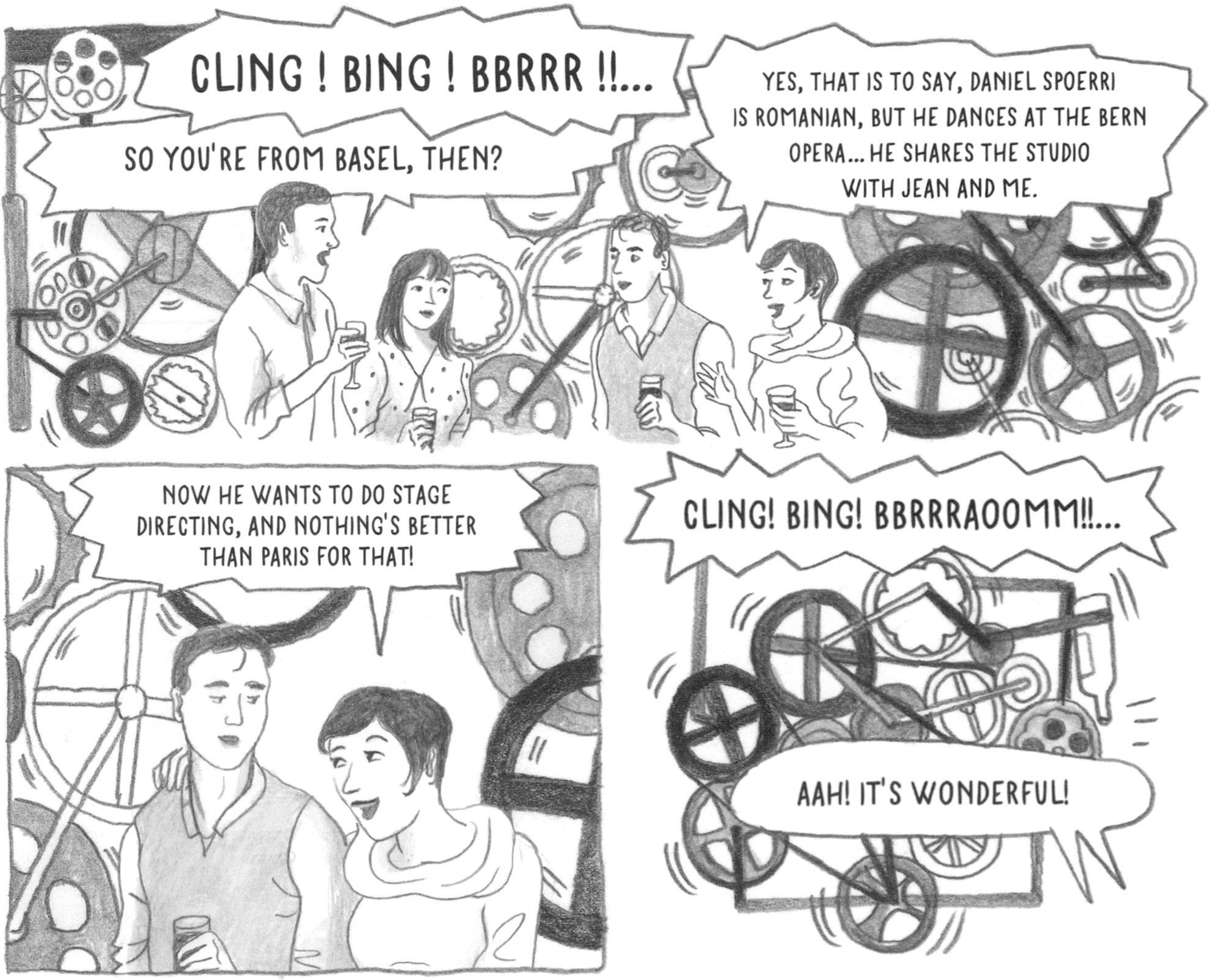
CLING ! BING ! BBRRR !!...
SO YOU'RE FROM BASEL, THEN?
YES, THAT IS TO SAY, DANIEL SPOERRI IS ROMANIAN, BUT HE DANCES AT THE BERN OPERA... HE SHARES THE STUDIO WITH JEAN AND ME.
NOW HE WANTS TO DO STAGE DIRECTING, AND NOTHING'S BETTER THAN PARIS FOR THAT!
CLING! BING! BBRRRAOOMM!!...
AAH! IT'S WONDERFUL!

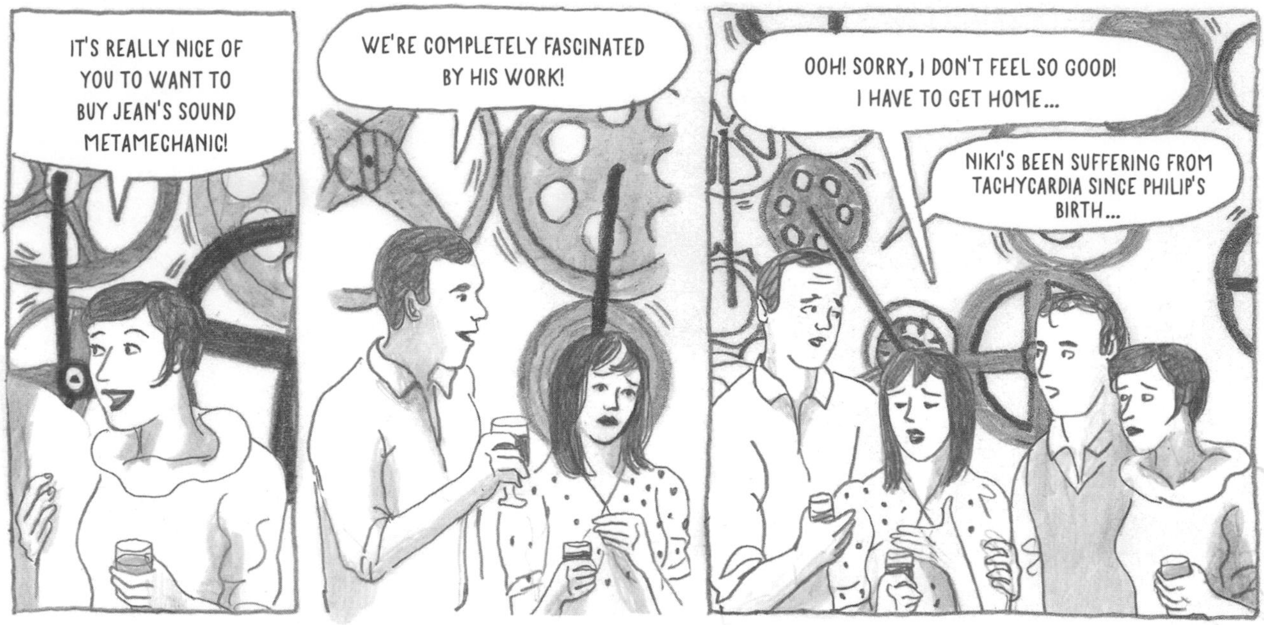
IT'S REALLY NICE OF YOU TO WANT TO BUY JEAN'S SOUND METAMECHANIC!
WE'RE COMPLETELY FASCINATED BY HIS WORK!
OOH! SORRY, I DON'T FEEL SO GOOD! I HAVE TO GET HOME...
NIKI'S BEEN SUFFERING FROM TACHYCARDIA SINCE PHILIP'S BIRTH...

*Philip suffered from an unknown form of hypoglycemia, which inflicted frightening convulsions on his hurt, little body and plunged him at various times into a woeful comatose state. As for me, my thyroid gland started skittering around like a gigantic garden spider at the center of its trap.*

BEGINNING OF 1958, THE AMERICAN HOSPITAL IN PARIS.

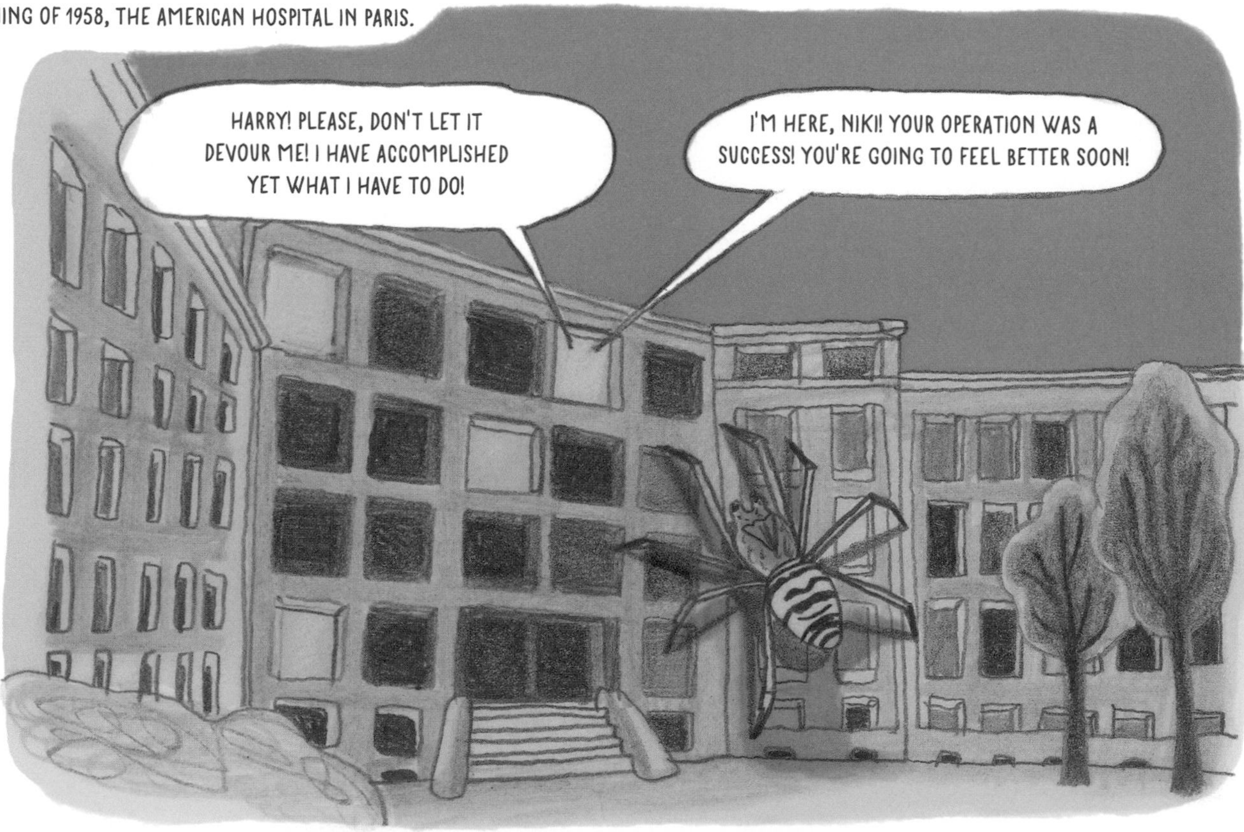
HARRY! PLEASE, DON'T LET IT DEVOUR ME! I HAVE ACCOMPLISHED YET WHAT I HAVE TO DO!
I'M HERE, NIKI! YOUR OPERATION WAS A SUCCESS! YOU'RE GOING TO FEEL BETTER SOON!

*Those two years tortured both Philip's body and my own so much...They unleashed an ill wind that soon caused our magnificent house of cards to come crumbling down. It was as though happiness had abandoned us...*

# CHAPTER 6

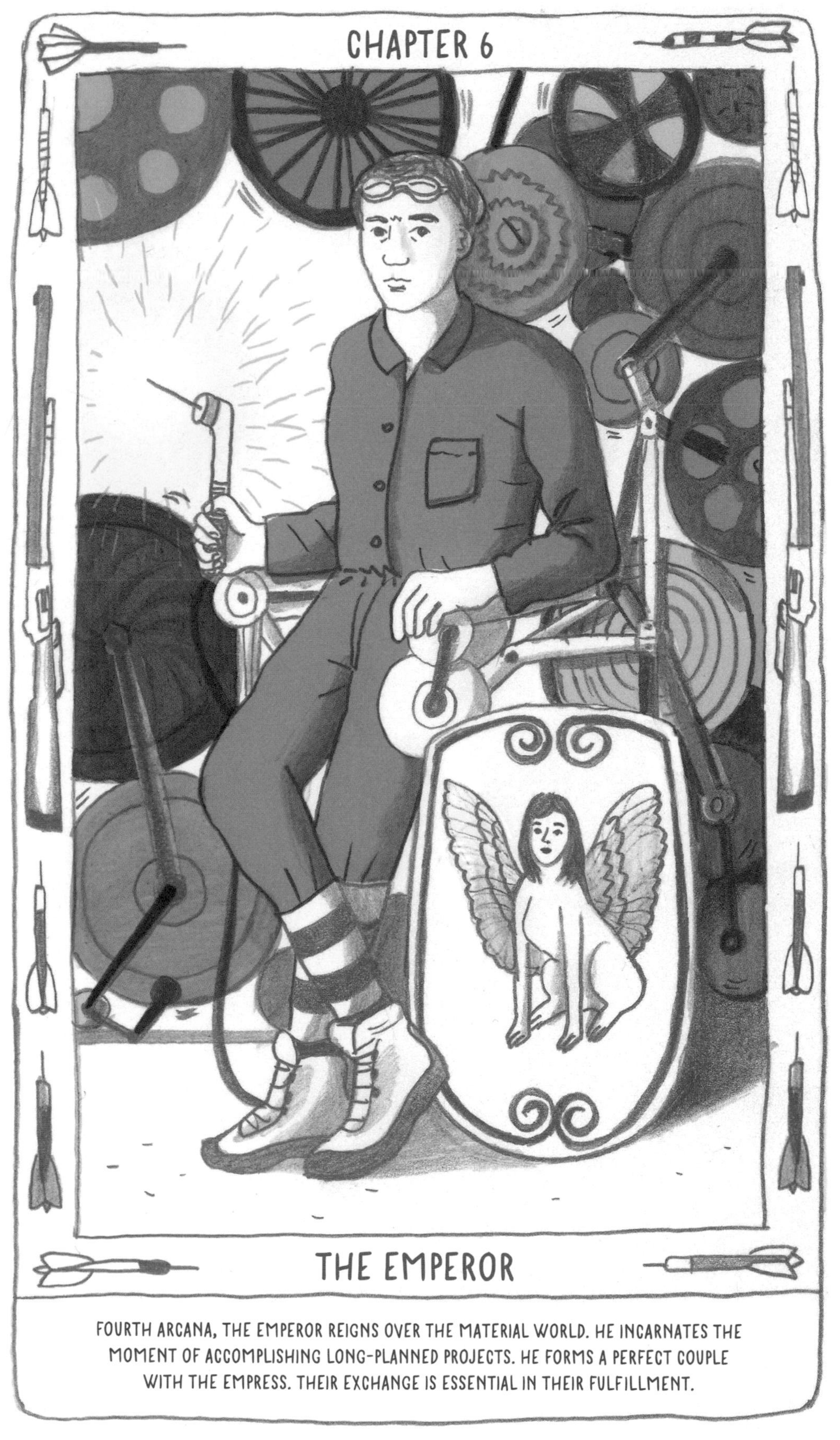

## THE EMPEROR

FOURTH ARCANA, THE EMPEROR REIGNS OVER THE MATERIAL WORLD. HE INCARNATES THE MOMENT OF ACCOMPLISHING LONG-PLANNED PROJECTS. HE FORMS A PERFECT COUPLE WITH THE EMPRESS. THEIR EXCHANGE IS ESSENTIAL IN THEIR FULFILLMENT.

1958, CONVALESCENCE IN LANS, FRANCE. *Little by little, the composition grew, like something organic, miraculous... I take refuge in painting, but chaos is never very far away.*

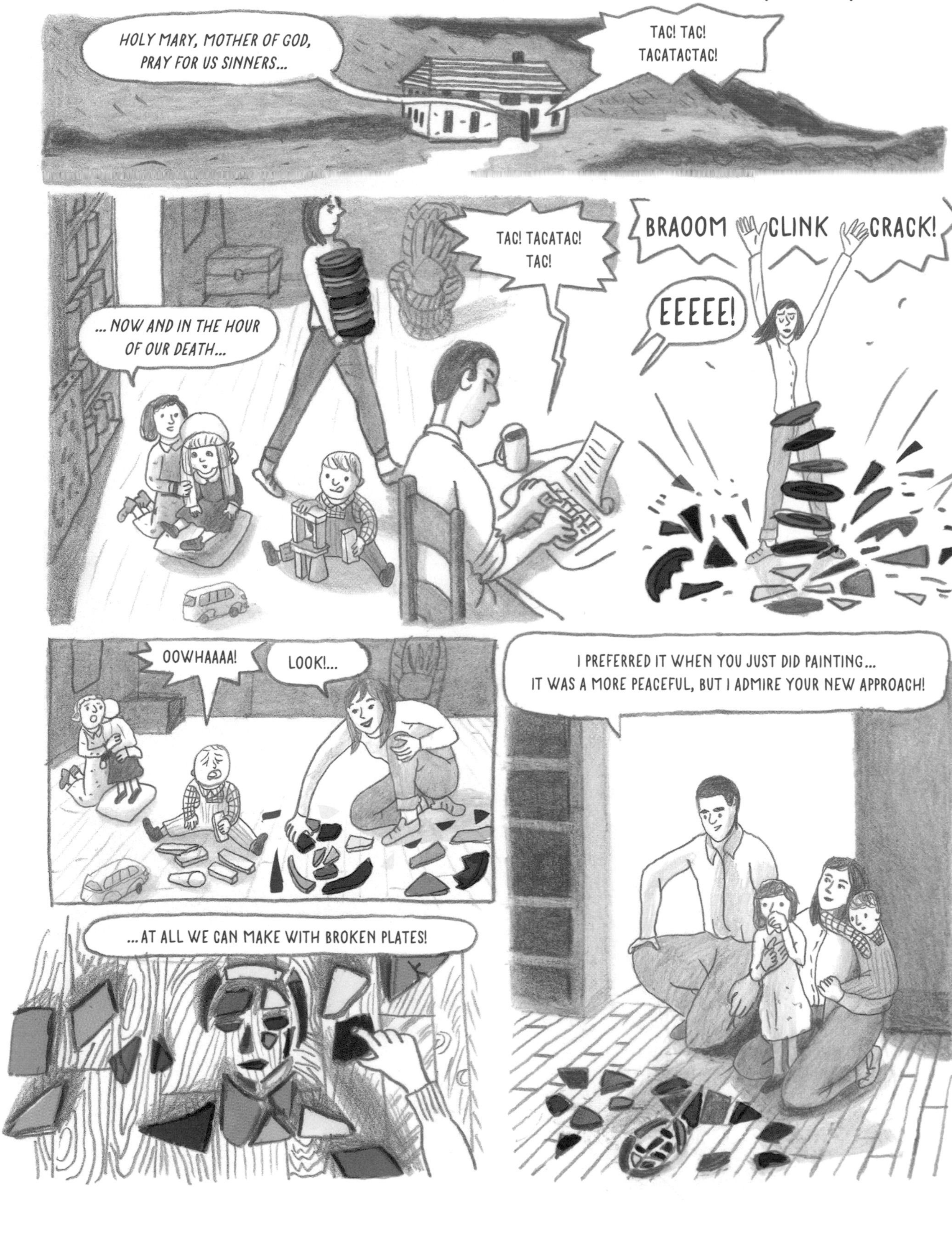
HOLY MARY, MOTHER OF GOD, PRAY FOR US SINNERS...
TAC! TAC! TACATACTAC!
TAC! TACATAC! TAC!
... NOW AND IN THE HOUR OF OUR DEATH...
BRAOOM
CLINK
CRACK!
EEEEE!
OOWHAAAA!
LOOK!...
I PREFERRED IT WHEN YOU JUST DID PAINTING... IT WAS A MORE PEACEFUL, BUT I ADMIRE YOUR NEW APPROACH!
...AT ALL WE CAN MAKE WITH BROKEN PLATES!

1959, PARIS. In our new apartment on Rue Alfred-Durand-Claye, I wanted to transform the children's bedroom into a real "Land of Dreams," to make us forget the awful mouth of the closed fireplace looming over the center of the room. I got the idea of a fantastically voluminous tree, but I didn't know how to pull it off...I asked Jean, my new partner in crime, to help me out...

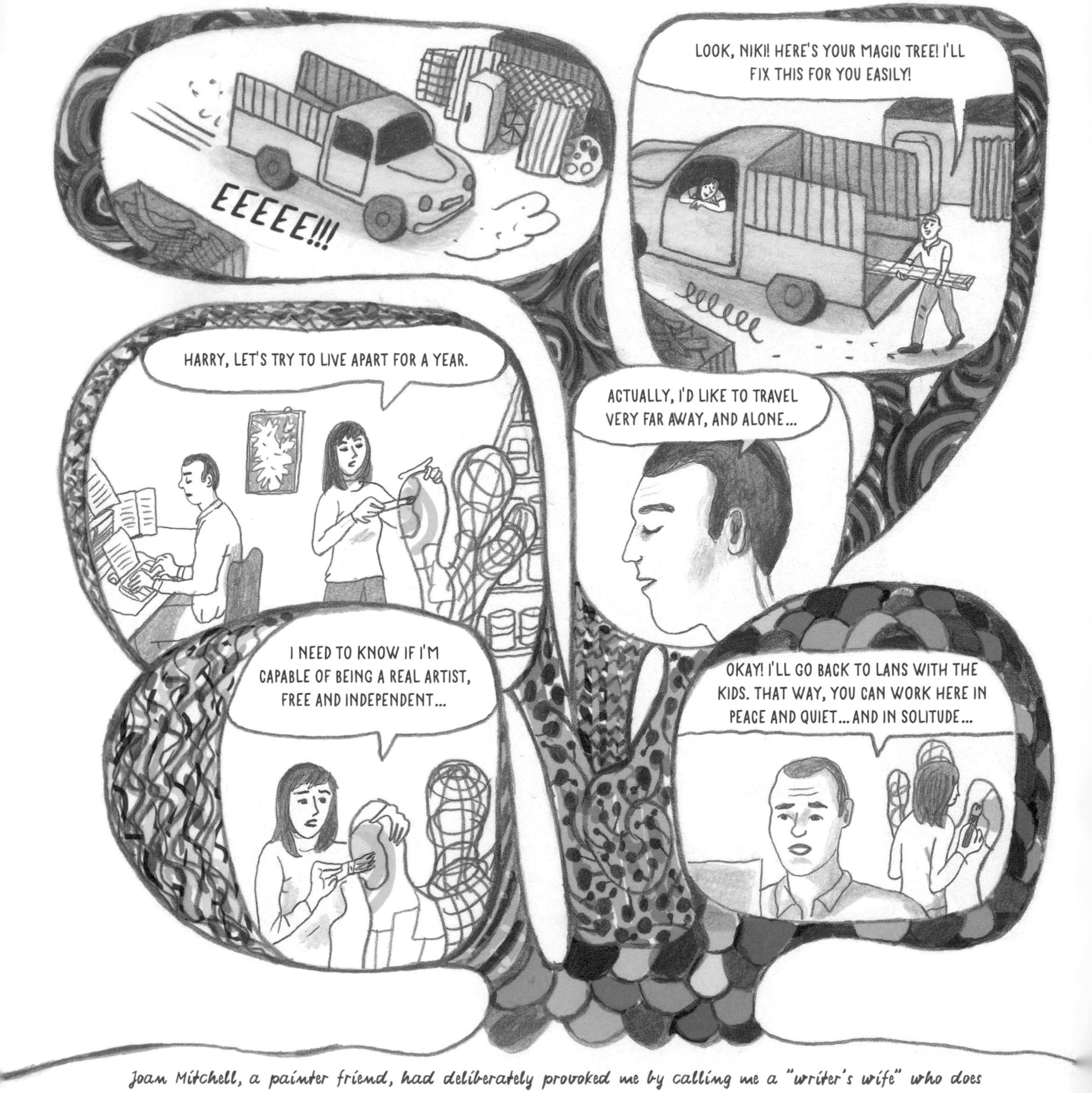
EEEEE!!!
LOOK, NIKI! HERE'S YOUR MAGIC TREE! I'LL FIX THIS FOR YOU EASILY!
HARRY, LET'S TRY TO LIVE APART FOR A YEAR.
ACTUALLY, I'D LIKE TO TRAVEL VERY FAR AWAY, AND ALONE...
I NEED TO KNOW IF I'M CAPABLE OF BEING A REAL ARTIST, FREE AND INDEPENDENT...
OKAY! I'LL GO BACK TO LANS WITH THE KIDS. THAT WAY, YOU CAN WORK HERE IN PEACE AND QUIET... AND IN SOLITUDE...

Joan Mitchell, a painter friend, had deliberately provoked me by calling me a "writer's wife" who does painting on the side. Her sarcastic comments had deeply wounded me. I couldn't wash away the sticky froth of those thoughts that were clumping together in the depths of my brain.

END OF 1960: A MOTIONLESS CATACLYSM.

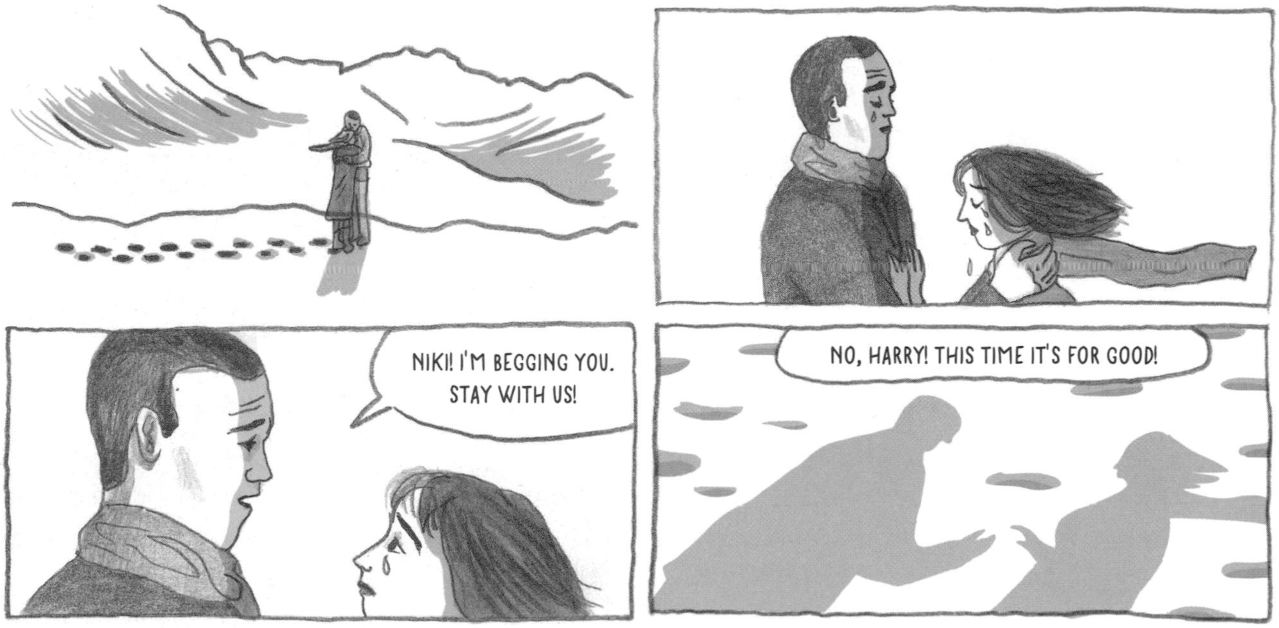
NIKI! I'M BEGGING YOU. STAY WITH US!
NO, HARRY! THIS TIME IT'S FOR GOOD!

*My mother devoured her family. I didn't want to repeat the same pattern. I wanted to pursue my way in Art, even if that would be extremely painful for all of us...All four of us would return to Paris, but our addresses would be different from now on.*

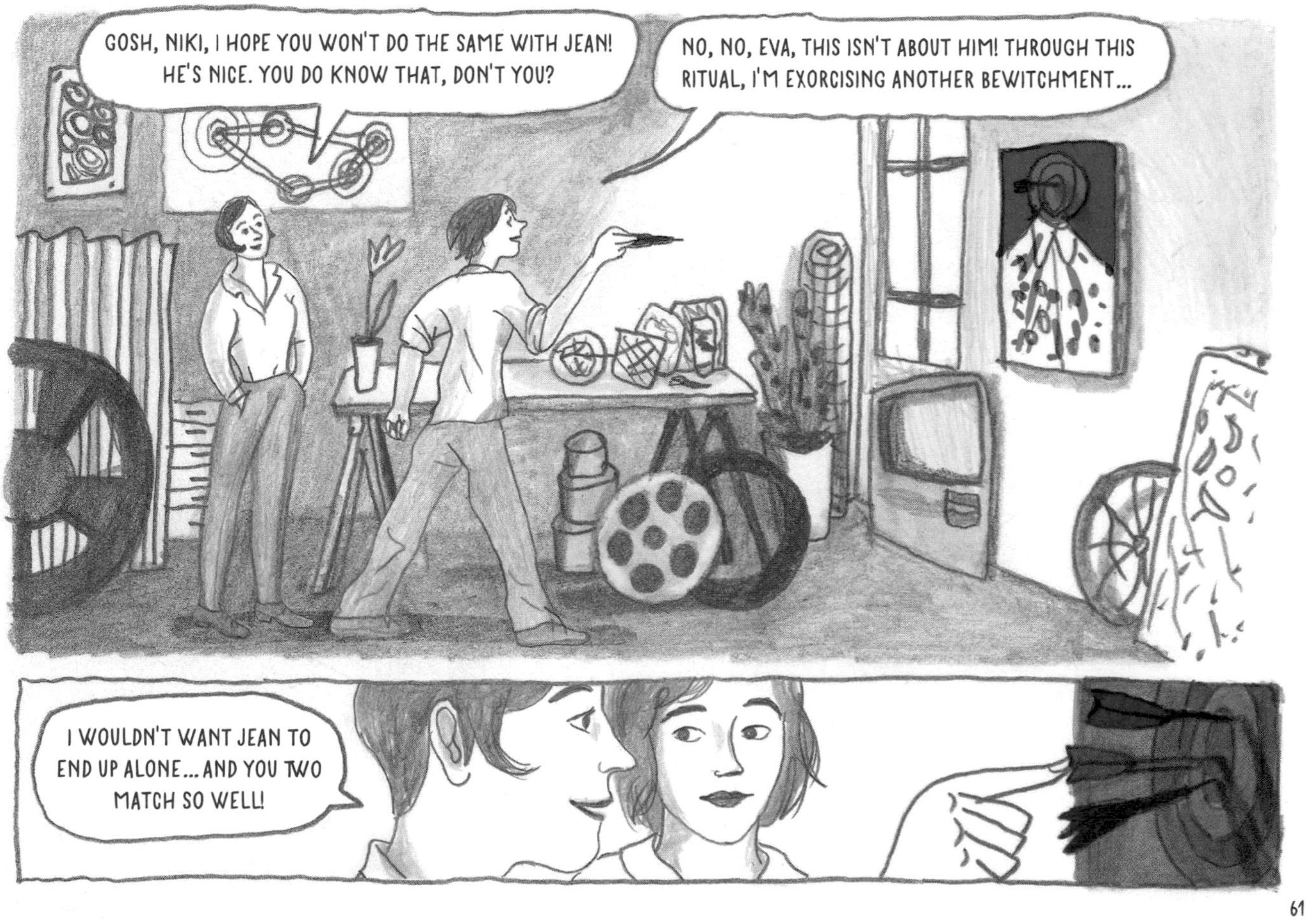
GOSH, NIKI, I HOPE YOU WON'T DO THE SAME WITH JEAN! HE'S NICE. YOU DO KNOW THAT, DON'T YOU?
NO, NO, EVA, THIS ISN'T ABOUT HIM! THROUGH THIS RITUAL, I'M EXORCISING ANOTHER BEWITCHMENT...
I WOULDN'T WANT JEAN TO END UP ALONE... AND YOU TWO MATCH SO WELL!

1961: SHOOTINGS!

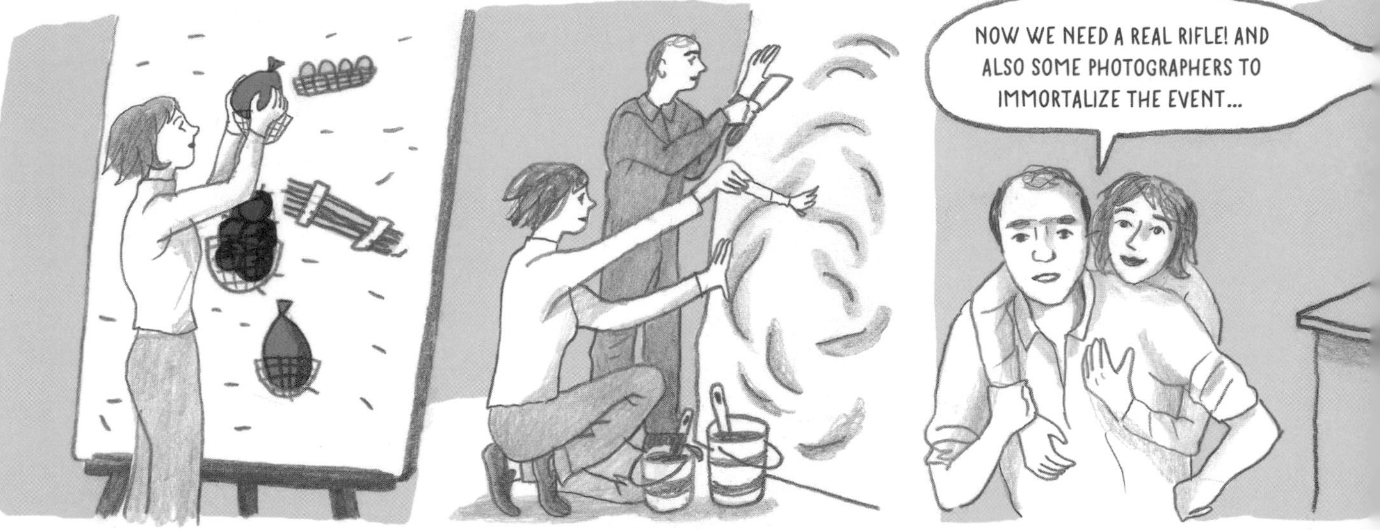
NOW WE NEED A REAL RIFLE! AND ALSO SOME PHOTOGRAPHERS TO IMMORTALIZE THE EVENT...

*I'm wounded and I want everything around me to bleed! The painting must bleed, to expiate in the place of beings! No more darts, I found a more expeditious means! Anger! Fascination, war, vengeance, immense pleasure, black, white, red, blue magic! A pure instant of "scorpionic" grace!*

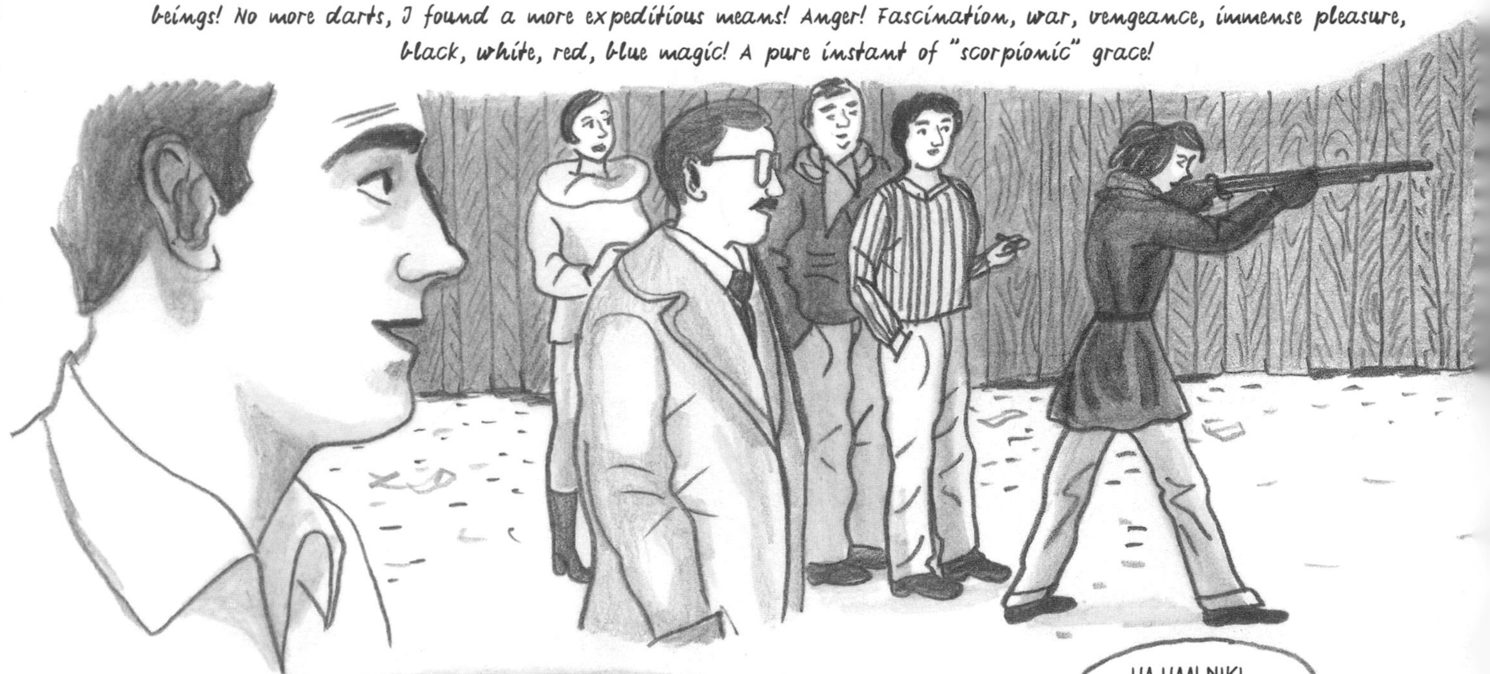

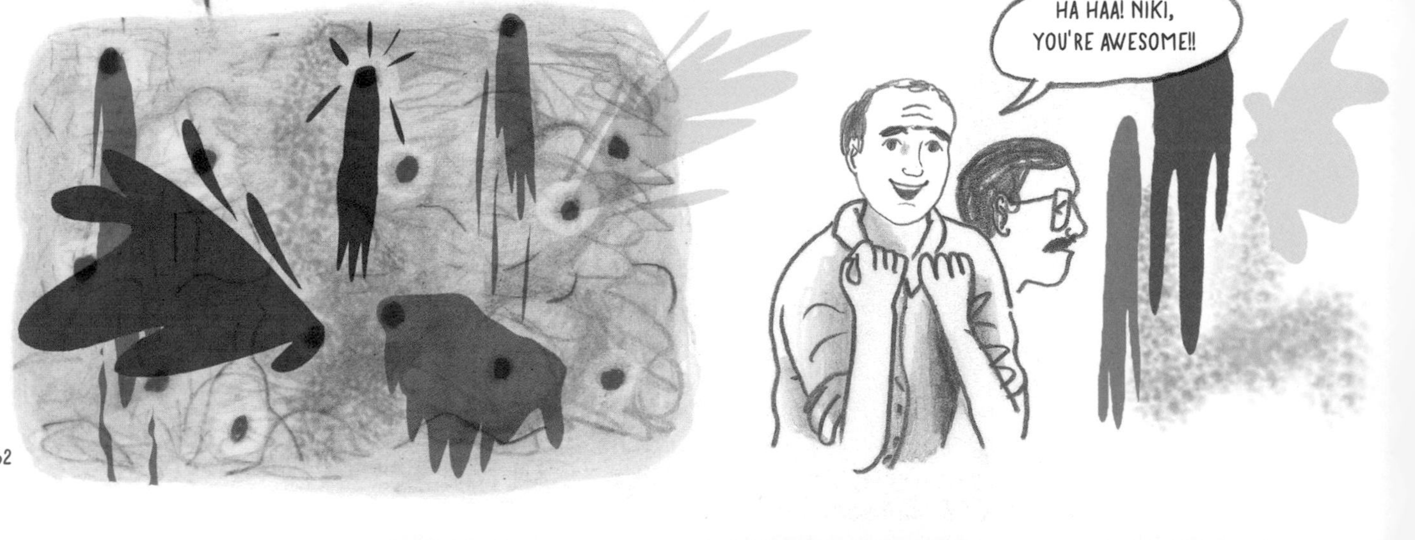
HA HAA! NIKI, YOU'RE AWESOME!!

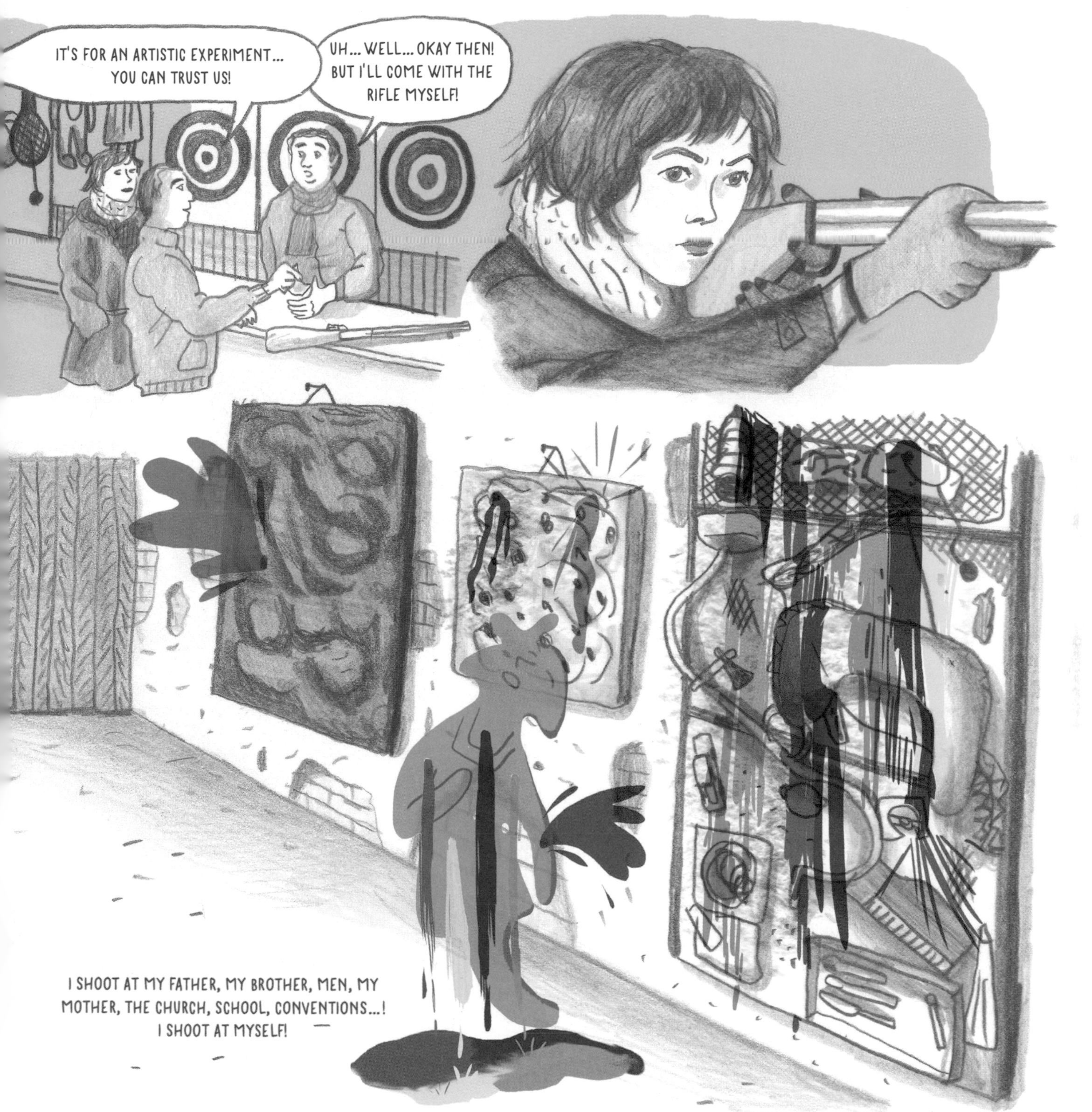
IT'S FOR AN ARTISTIC EXPERIMENT... YOU CAN TRUST US!
UH... WELL... OKAY THEN! BUT I'LL COME WITH THE RIFLE MYSELF!
I SHOOT AT MY FATHER, MY BROTHER, MEN, MY MOTHER, THE CHURCH, SCHOOL, CONVENTIONS...! I SHOOT AT MYSELF!

*I've abandoned my children! I've become the monster that pursued me for so long! Now, and until my death, I have to prove to the whole world that it was worthwhile. I must create a powerful and immortal body of work.*

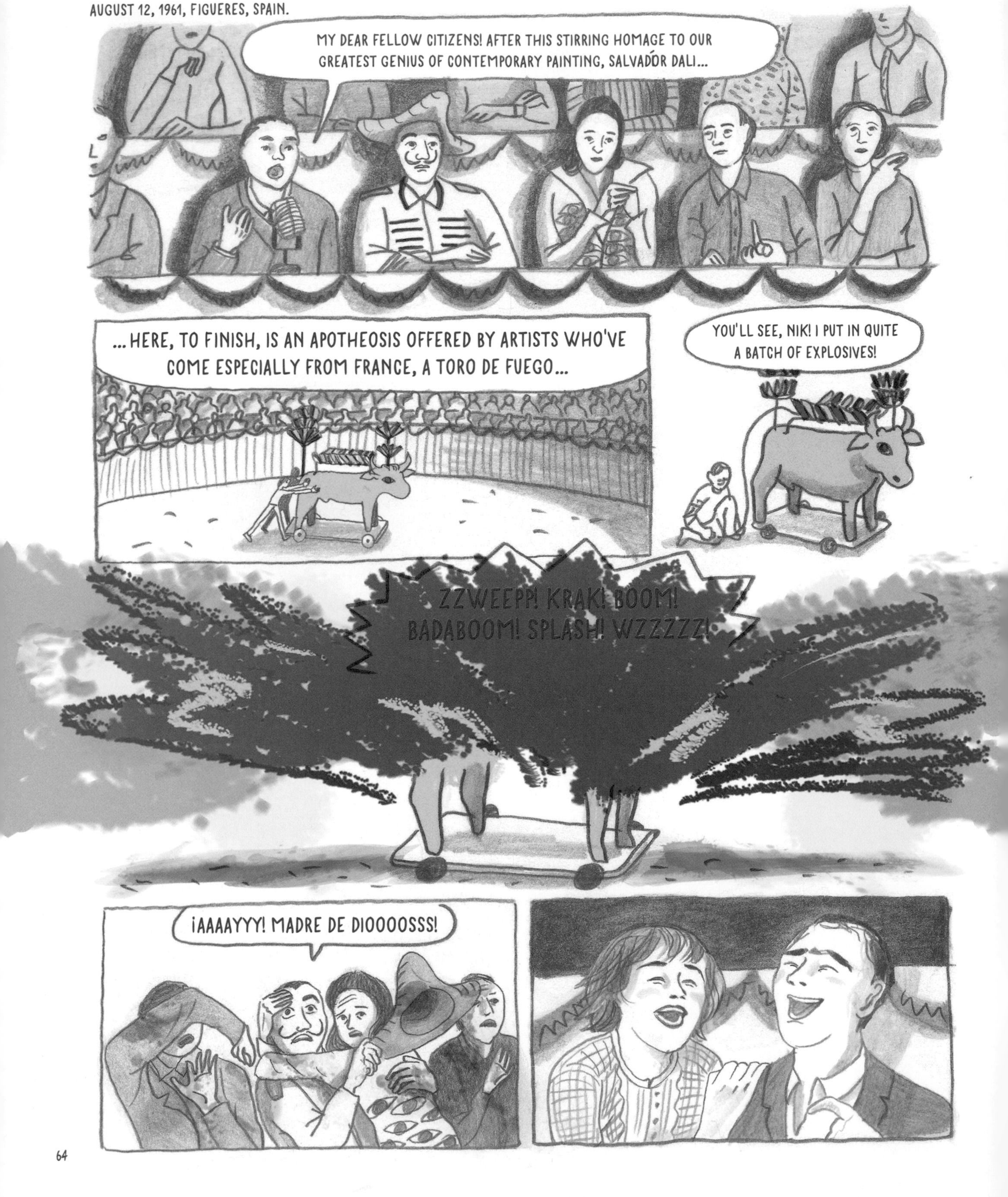
AUGUST 12, 1961, FIGUERES, SPAIN.
MY DEAR FELLOW CITIZENS! AFTER THIS STIRRING HOMAGE TO OUR GREATEST GENIUS OF CONTEMPORARY PAINTING, SALVADÓR DALI...
... HERE, TO FINISH, IS AN APOTHEOSIS OFFERED BY ARTISTS WHO'VE COME ESPECIALLY FROM FRANCE, A TORO DE FUEGO...
YOU'LL SEE, NIK! I PUT IN QUITE A BATCH OF EXPLOSIVES!
ZZWEEPP! KRAK! BOOM! BADABOOM! SPLASH! WZZZZZ!
¡AAAAYYY! MADRE DE DIOOOOSSS!

# CHAPTER 7

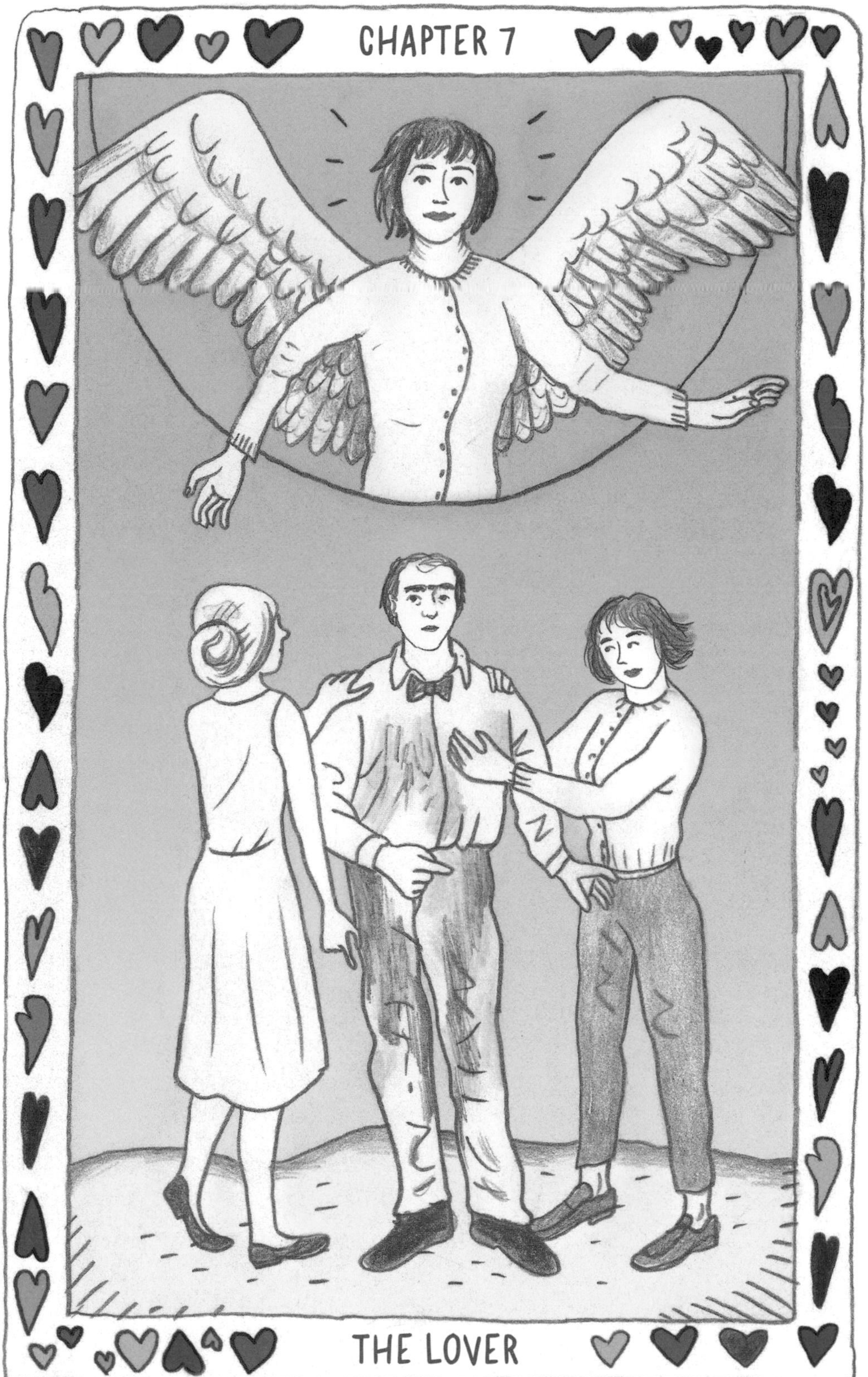

## THE LOVER

SIXTH ARCANA, THE LOVER EXPRESSES THE HEART'S CHOICE. IT'S THE MOMENT TO START DOING WHAT YOU LOVE. IT'S ALSO THE TIME FOR SOCIAL AND EMOTIONAL CHOICES, THE CHOICE OF UNION OR DISUNION...

OCTOBER 1962, NYC. *Mother had refused to welcome Jean the previous year. In order to examine him up close, she'd finally organized a family dinner by inviting us along with my favorite uncle and Luisa, his fascinating wife.*

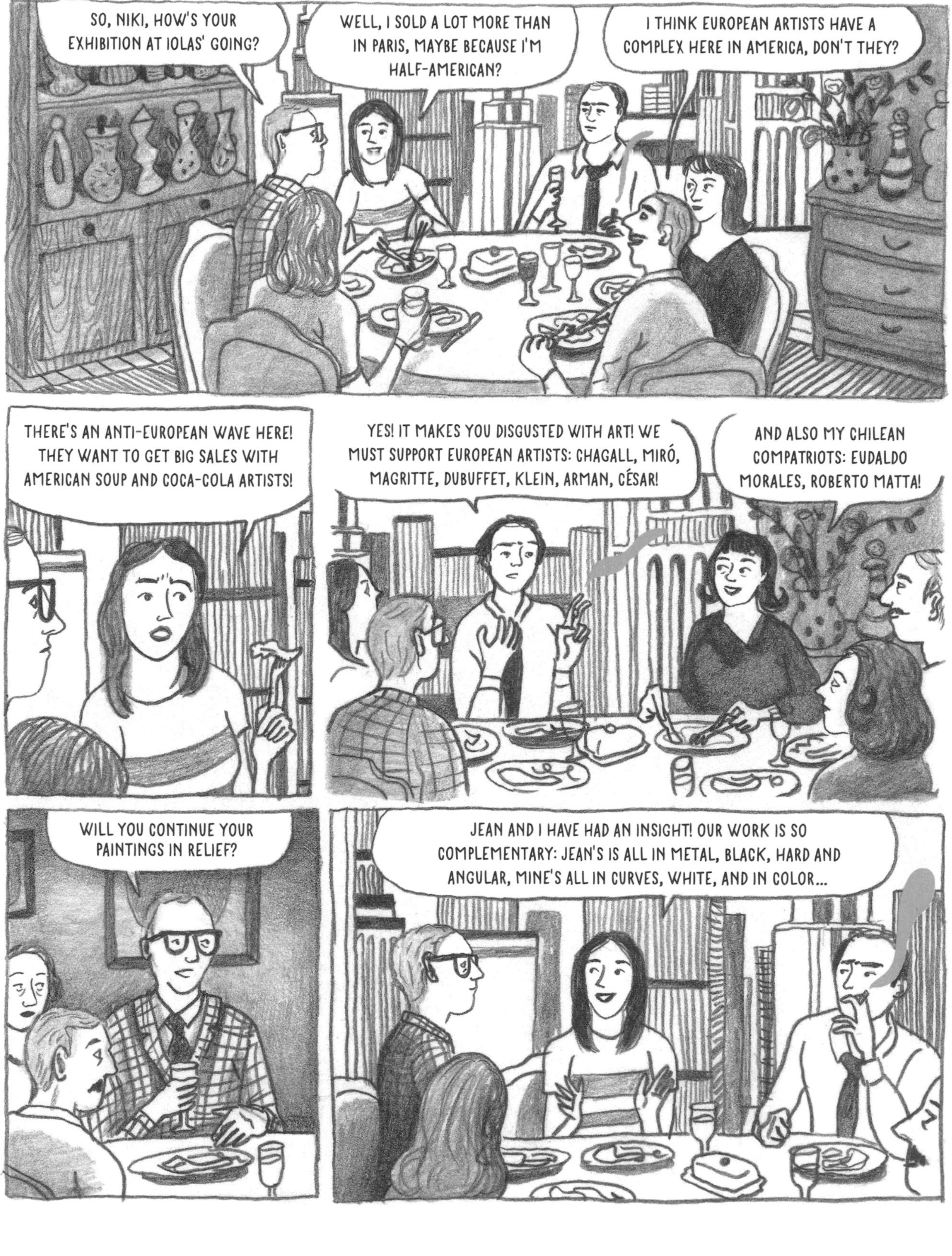
SO, NIKI, HOW'S YOUR EXHIBITION AT IOLAS' GOING?
WELL, I SOLD A LOT MORE THAN IN PARIS, MAYBE BECAUSE I'M HALF-AMERICAN?
I THINK EUROPEAN ARTISTS HAVE A COMPLEX HERE IN AMERICA, DON'T THEY?
THERE'S AN ANTI-EUROPEAN WAVE HERE! THEY WANT TO GET BIG SALES WITH AMERICAN SOUP AND COCA-COLA ARTISTS!
YES! IT MAKES YOU DISGUSTED WITH ART! WE MUST SUPPORT EUROPEAN ARTISTS: CHAGALL, MIRÓ, MAGRITTE, DUBUFFET, KLEIN, ARMAN, CÉSAR!
AND ALSO MY CHILEAN COMPATRIOTS: EUDALDO MORALES, ROBERTO MATTA!
WILL YOU CONTINUE YOUR PAINTINGS IN RELIEF?
JEAN AND I HAVE HAD AN INSIGHT! OUR WORK IS SO COMPLEMENTARY: JEAN'S IS ALL IN METAL, BLACK, HARD AND ANGULAR, MINE'S ALL IN CURVES, WHITE, AND IN COLOR...

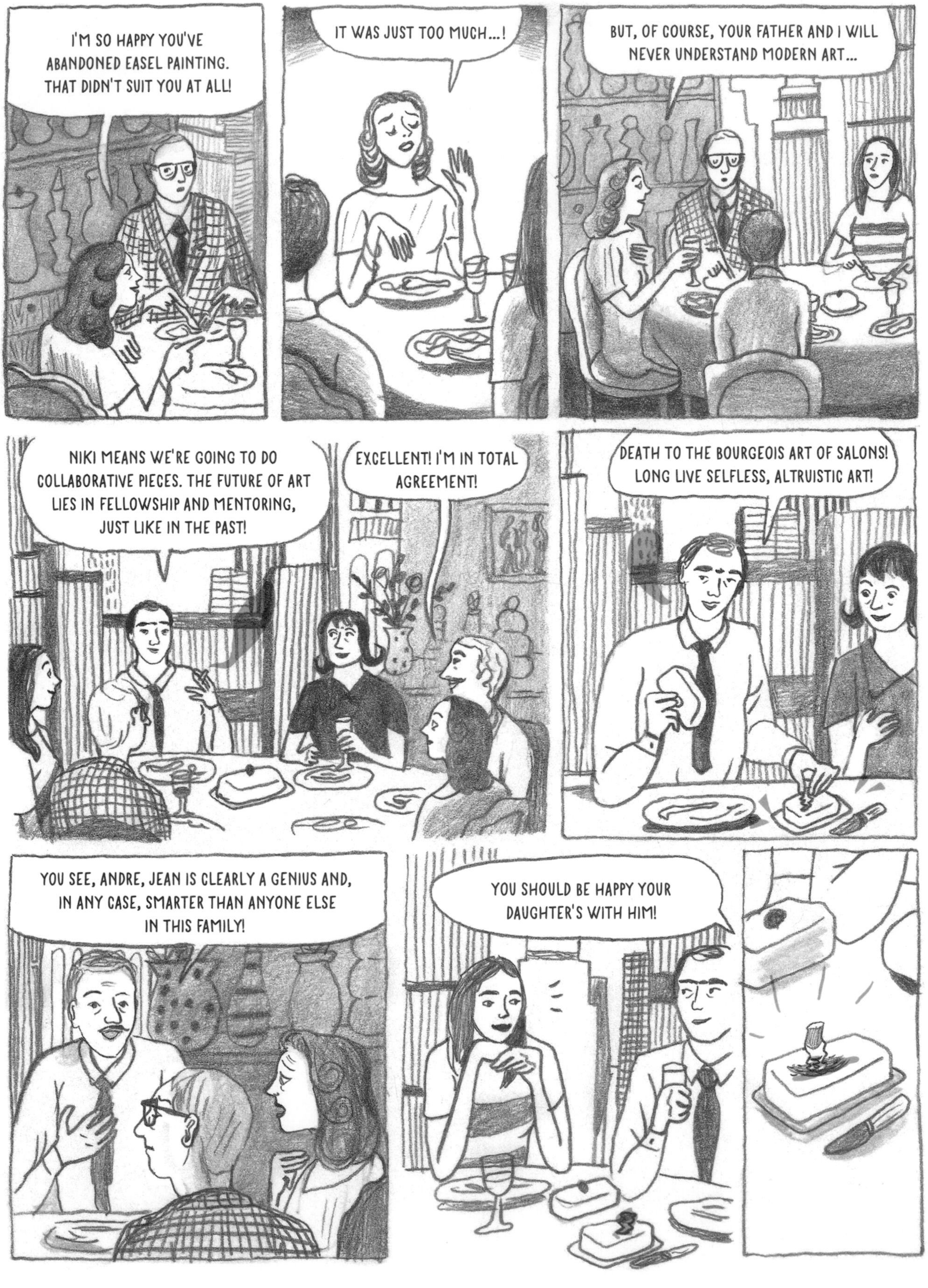
I'M SO HAPPY YOU'VE ABANDONED EASEL PAINTING. THAT DIDN'T SUIT YOU AT ALL!
IT WAS JUST TOO MUCH...!
BUT, OF COURSE, YOUR FATHER AND I WILL NEVER UNDERSTAND MODERN ART...
NIKI MEANS WE'RE GOING TO DO COLLABORATIVE PIECES. THE FUTURE OF ART LIES IN FELLOWSHIP AND MENTORING, JUST LIKE IN THE PAST!
EXCELLENT! I'M IN TOTAL AGREEMENT!
DEATH TO THE BOURGEOIS ART OF SALONS! LONG LIVE SELFLESS, ALTRUISTIC ART!
YOU SEE, ANDRE, JEAN IS CLEARLY A GENIUS AND, IN ANY CASE, SMARTER THAN ANYONE ELSE IN THIS FAMILY!
YOU SHOULD BE HAPPY YOUR DAUGHTER'S WITH HIM!

WINTER 1964, SOISY-SUR-ÉCOLE, FRANCE.. *I'm totally obsessed with creation. Men have power, women have creation! Men have fire, and I'll steal the fire from them!"*

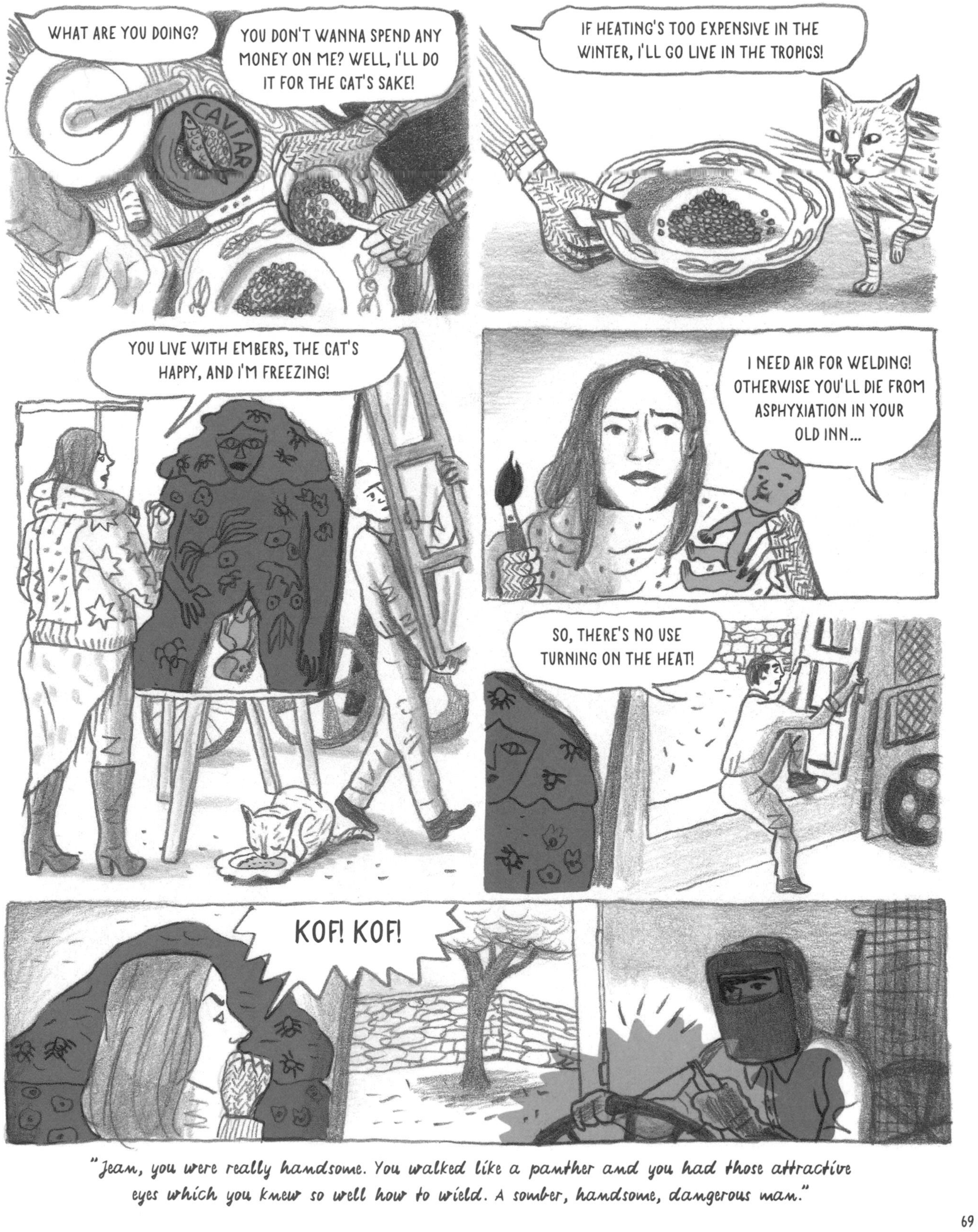

WHAT ARE YOU DOING?
YOU DON'T WANNA SPEND ANY MONEY ON ME? WELL, I'LL DO IT FOR THE CAT'S SAKE!
CAVIAR
IF HEATING'S TOO EXPENSIVE IN THE WINTER, I'LL GO LIVE IN THE TROPICS!
YOU LIVE WITH EMBERS, THE CAT'S HAPPY, AND I'M FREEZING!
I NEED AIR FOR WELDING! OTHERWISE YOU'LL DIE FROM ASPHYXIATION IN YOUR OLD INN...
SO, THERE'S NO USE TURNING ON THE HEAT!
KOF! KOF!


*"Jean, you were really handsome. You walked like a panther and you had those attractive eyes which you knew so well how to wield. A somber, handsome, dangerous man."*

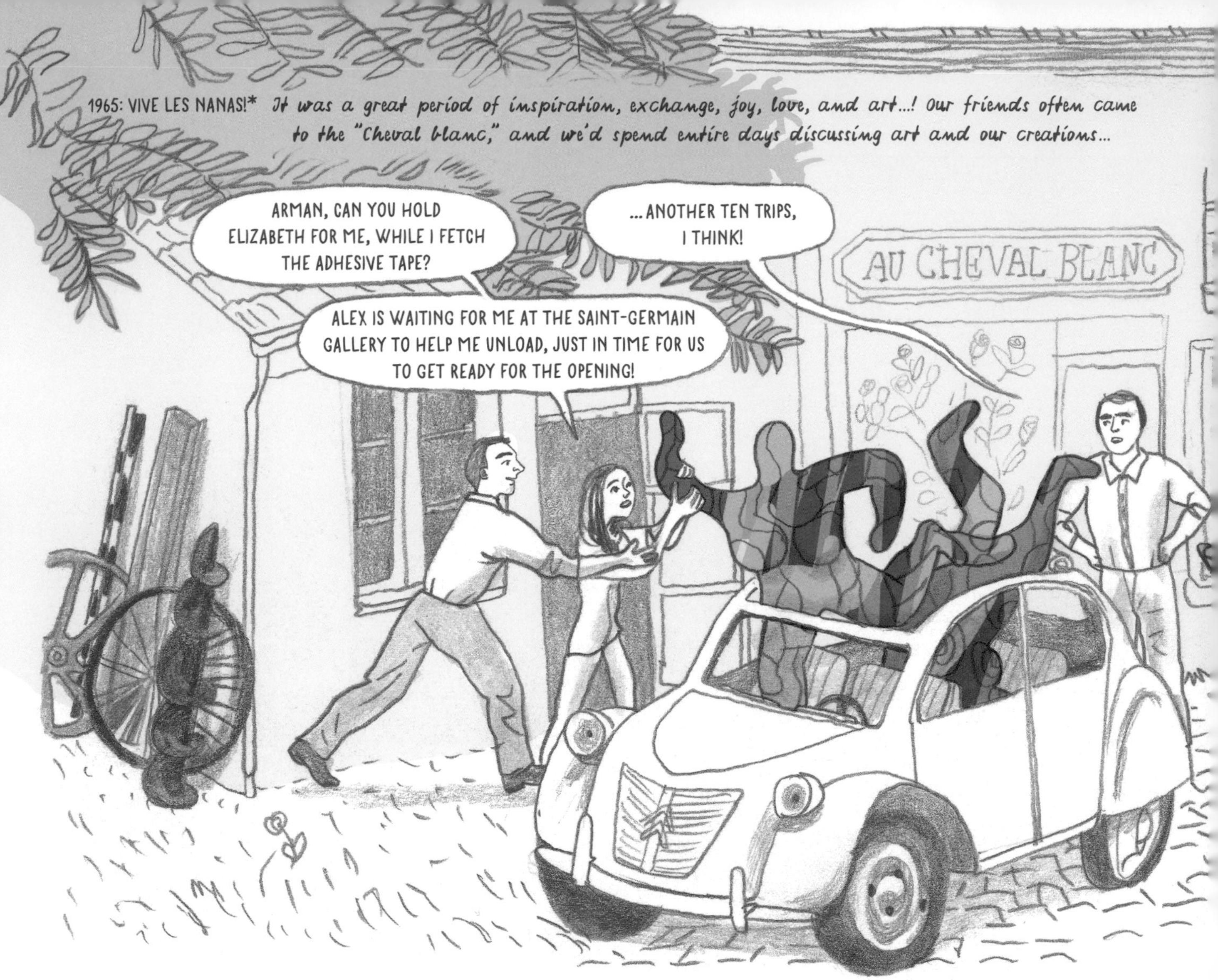
1965: VIVE LES NANAS!* It was a great period of inspiration, exchange, joy, love, and art...! Our friends often came to the "Cheval blanc," and we'd spend entire days discussing art and our creations...
ARMAN, CAN YOU HOLD ELIZABETH FOR ME, WHILE I FETCH THE ADHESIVE TAPE?
...ANOTHER TEN TRIPS, I THINK!
ALEX IS WAITING FOR ME AT THE SAINT-GERMAIN GALLERY TO HELP ME UNLOAD, JUST IN TIME FOR US TO GET READY FOR THE OPENING!
AU CHEVAL BLANC

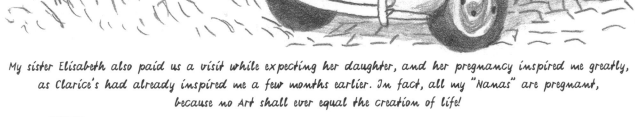

*My sister Elisabeth also paid us a visit while expecting her daughter, and her pregnancy inspired me greatly, as Clarice's had already inspired me a few months earlier. In fact, all my "Nanas" are pregnant, because no Art shall ever equal the creation of life!*

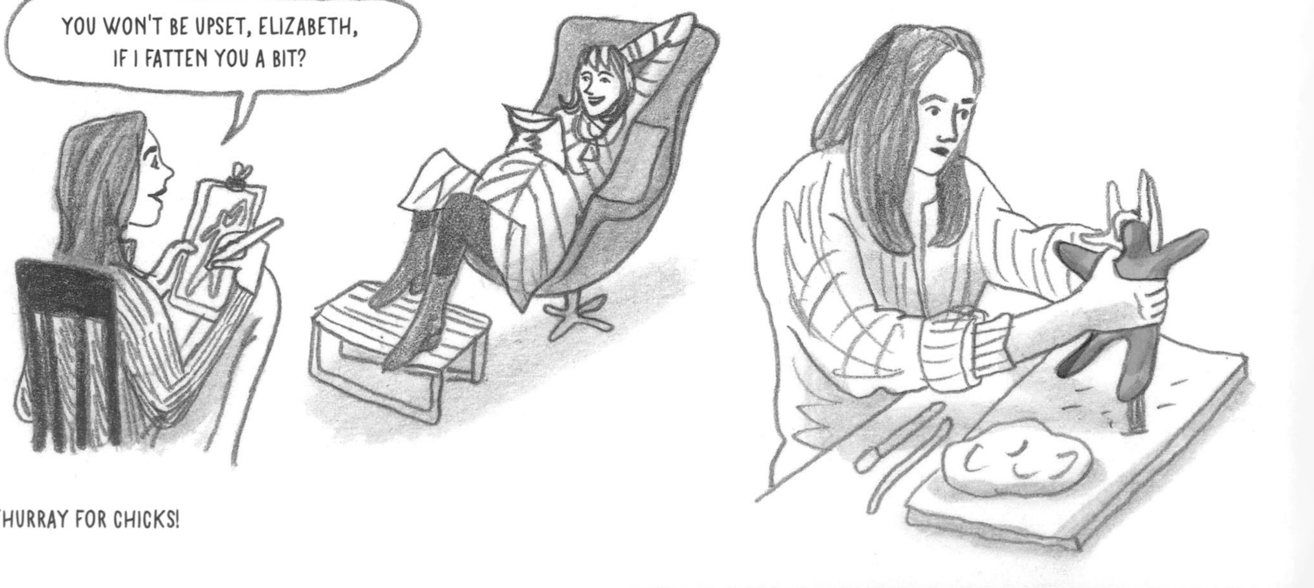
YOU WON'T BE UPSET, ELIZABETH, IF I FATTEN YOU A BIT?

*HURRAY FOR CHICKS!

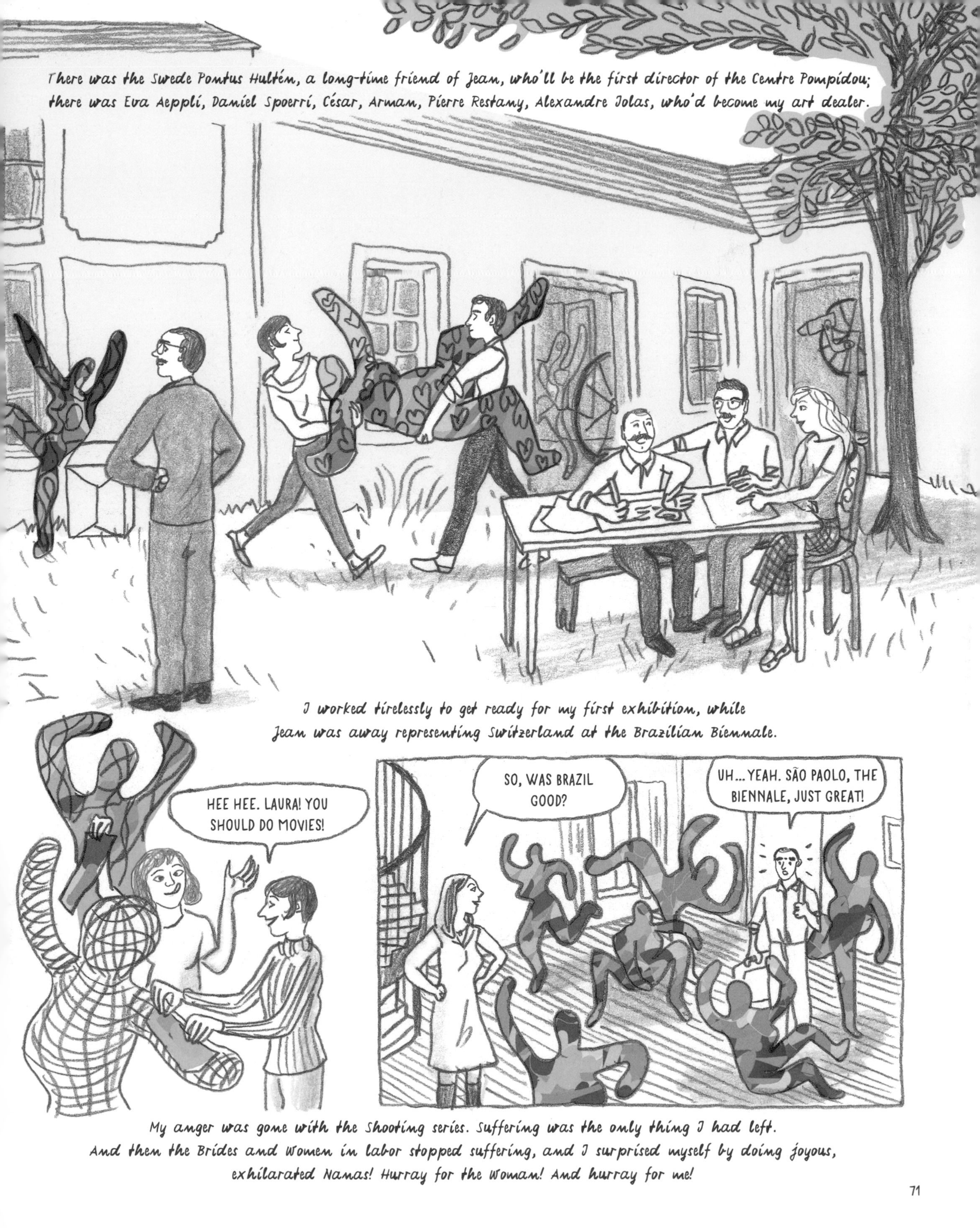
There was the Swede Pontus Hultén, a long-time friend of Jean, who'll be the first director of the Centre Pompidou;
there was Eva Aepplí, Daníel Spoerrí, César, Arman, Píerre Restany, Alexandre Jolas, who'd become my art dealer.
I worked tirelessly to get ready for my first exhibition, while
Jean was away representing Switzerland at the Brazilian Biennale.
HEE HEE. LAURA! YOU SHOULD DO MOVIES!
SO, WAS BRAZIL GOOD?
UH... YEAH. SÃO PAOLO, THE BIENNALE, JUST GREAT!
My anger was gone with the Shooting series. Suffering was the only thing I had left.
And then the Brides and Women in labor stopped suffering, and I surprised myself by doing joyous,
exhilarated Nanas! Hurray for the Woman! And hurray for me!

SPRING 1966, MODERNA MUSEET, STOCKHOLM.

Pontus Hultén had invited us to organize a big, mainstream exhibition. He wanted to bring Art to the largest number possible, in his Stockholm museum, and to create a real event, thanks to the collaborative work of three artists...Only five weeks from the opening, and we still don't have a plan...

WHAT IF YOU IMAGINE A HUGE "NANA" BY NIKI, LYING ON HER BACK, WHICH VISITORS CAN GO INTO TO DISCOVER ALL SORTS OF FUN?

OH, OF COURSE! PEOPLE WOULD COME AND EXIT THROUGH THE VAGINA. SHE'D BE THE GREATEST PROSTITUTE OF ALL TIME!

THERE'D BE A CINEMA THEATER, A MILK BAR INSIDE A BREAST...

A PLANETARIUM INSIDE HER HEAD, A TOBOGGAN IN A LEG... MADDENING MACHINES PLAYING BACH!

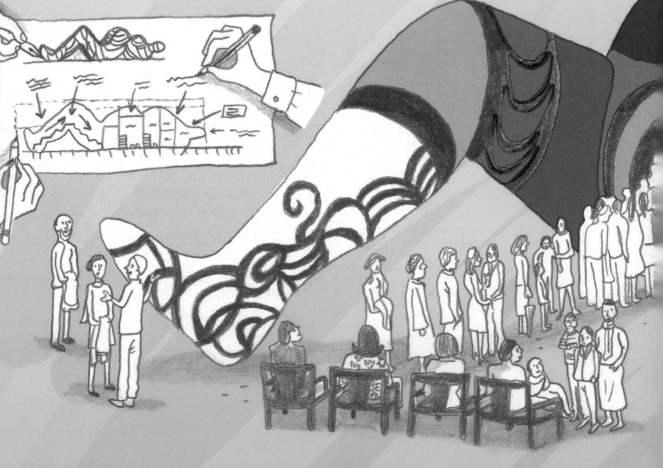

Jean, Per Olof Ultvedt and I worked like crazy! Putting together the plans, building, dressing the giant, painting her skin, filling her body with attractive organs We called her "Hon," or "She" in Swedish.....

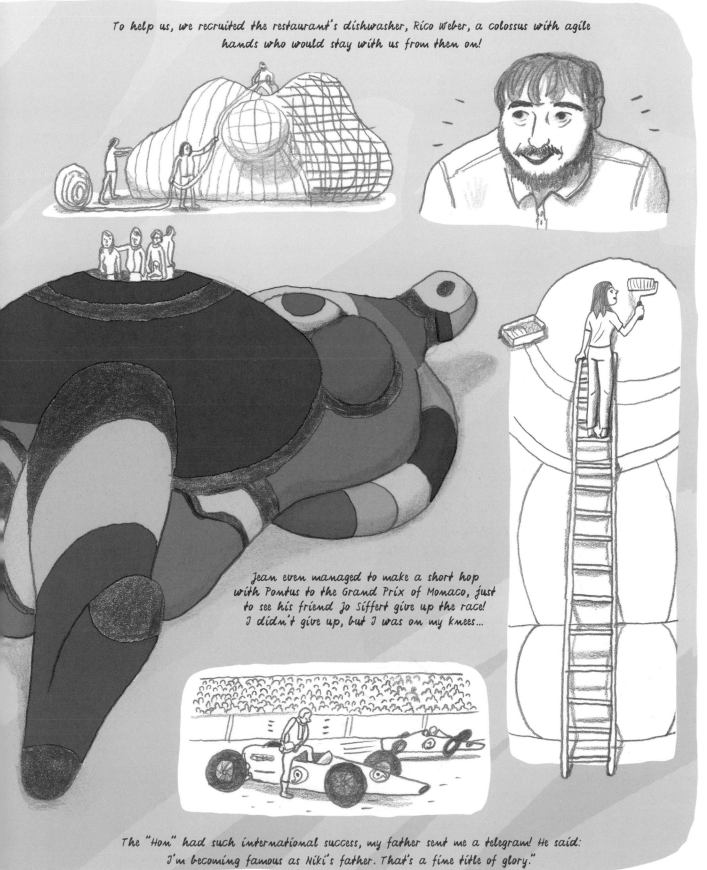

To help us, we recruited the restaurant's dishwasher, Rico Weber, a colossus with agile hands who would stay with us from then on!

Jean even managed to make a short hop with Pontus to the Grand Prix of Monaco, just to see his friend Jo Siffert give up the race! I didn't give up, but I was on my knees...

The "Hon" had such international success, my father sent me a telegram! He said: "I'm becoming famous as Niki's father. That's a fine title of glory."

OCTOBER 1966, PARIS, DIRECTOR GENERAL OF ARTS AND HUMANITIES.

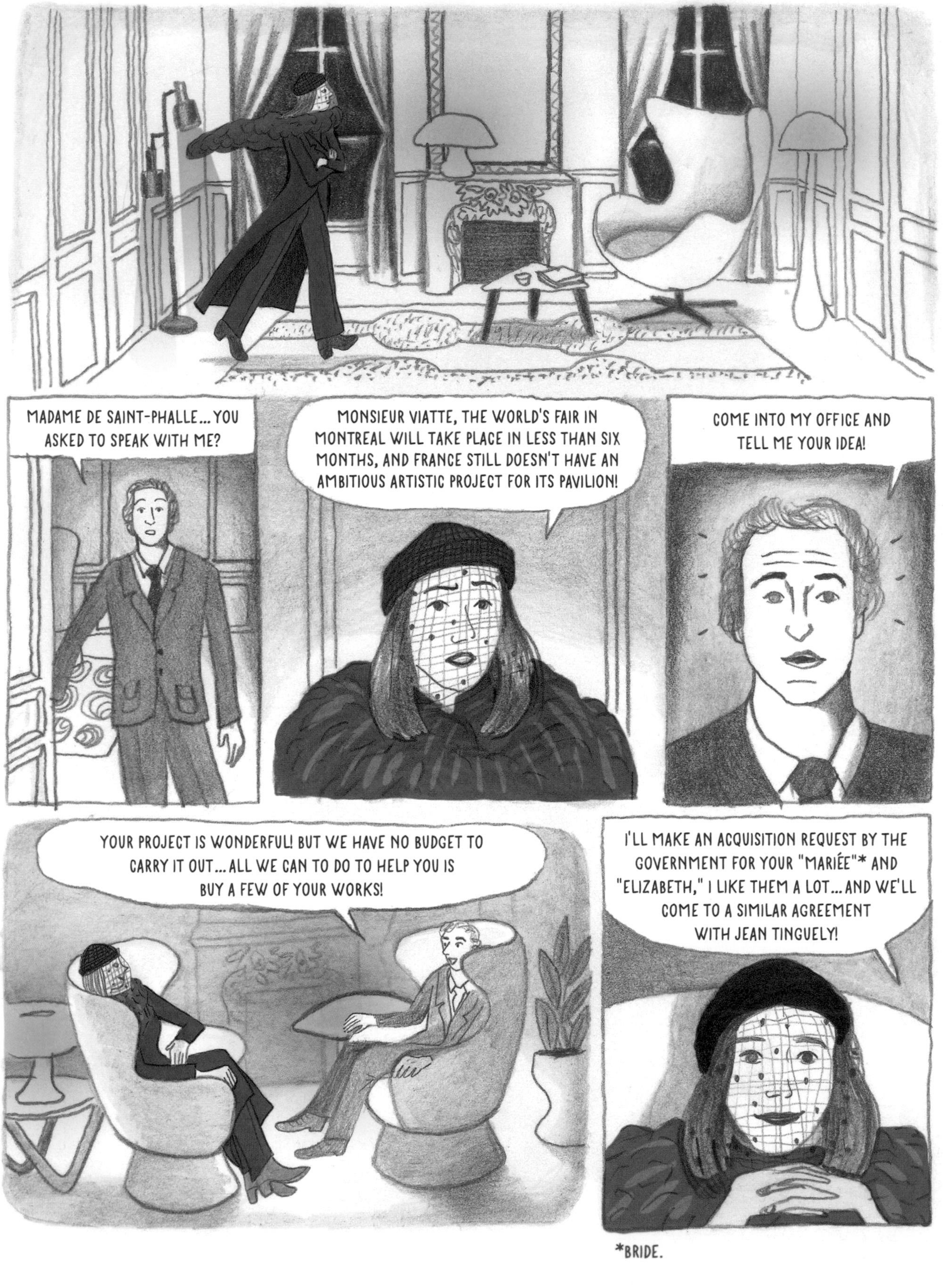
MADAME DE SAINT-PHALLE... YOU ASKED TO SPEAK WITH ME?
MONSIEUR VIATTE, THE WORLD'S FAIR IN MONTREAL WILL TAKE PLACE IN LESS THAN SIX MONTHS, AND FRANCE STILL DOESN'T HAVE AN AMBITIOUS ARTISTIC PROJECT FOR ITS PAVILION!
COME INTO MY OFFICE AND TELL ME YOUR IDEA!
YOUR PROJECT IS WONDERFUL! BUT WE HAVE NO BUDGET TO CARRY IT OUT... ALL WE CAN TO DO TO HELP YOU IS BUY A FEW OF YOUR WORKS!
I'LL MAKE AN ACQUISITION REQUEST BY THE GOVERNMENT FOR YOUR "MARIÉE"* AND "ELIZABETH," I LIKE THEM A LOT... AND WE'LL COME TO A SIMILAR AGREEMENT WITH JEAN TINGUELY!



*BRIDE.

APRIL 1967, MONTREAL, THE FRENCH PAVILION AT EXPO 67.

*Our "Fantastic Paradise" arrived in Montreal via a French army cargo plane! Nanas resisting the assaults of Jean's aggressive machines...Creating them exhausted me: I lost almost 16 lbs in the process and caught a new bout of pneumonia. But the "battle of the sexes" with Jean was worth the sacrifice.*

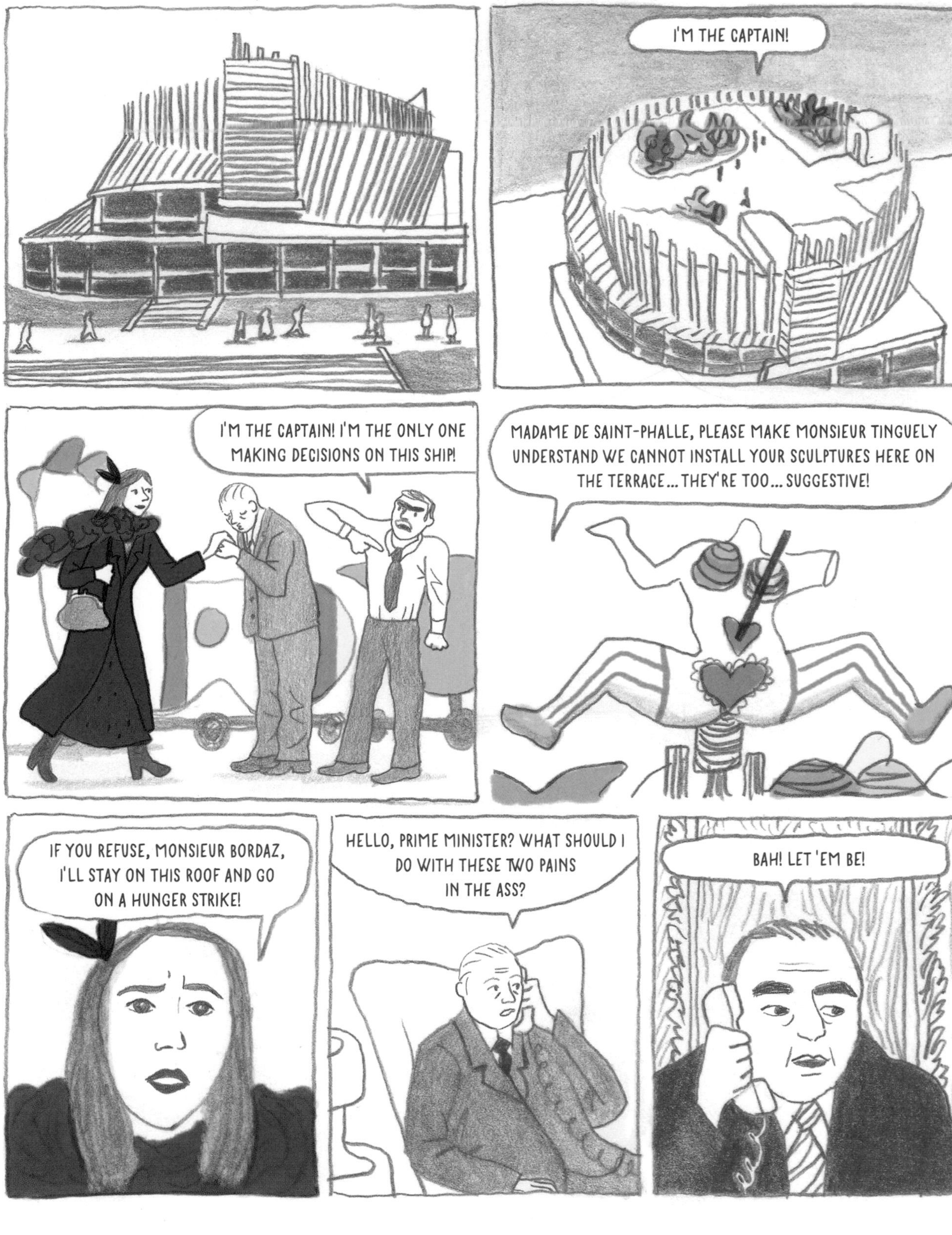

I'M THE CAPTAIN!
I'M THE CAPTAIN! I'M THE ONLY ONE MAKING DECISIONS ON THIS SHIP!
MADAME DE SAINT-PHALLE, PLEASE MAKE MONSIEUR TINGUELY UNDERSTAND WE CANNOT INSTALL YOUR SCULPTURES HERE ON THE TERRACE... THEY'RE TOO... SUGGESTIVE!
IF YOU REFUSE, MONSIEUR BORDAZ, I'LL STAY ON THIS ROOF AND GO ON A HUNGER STRIKE!
HELLO, PRIME MINISTER? WHAT SHOULD I DO WITH THESE TWO PAINS IN THE ASS?
BAH! LET 'EM BE!

AUGUST 17, 1967, CHOCORUA LAKE, NEW HAMPSHIRE.

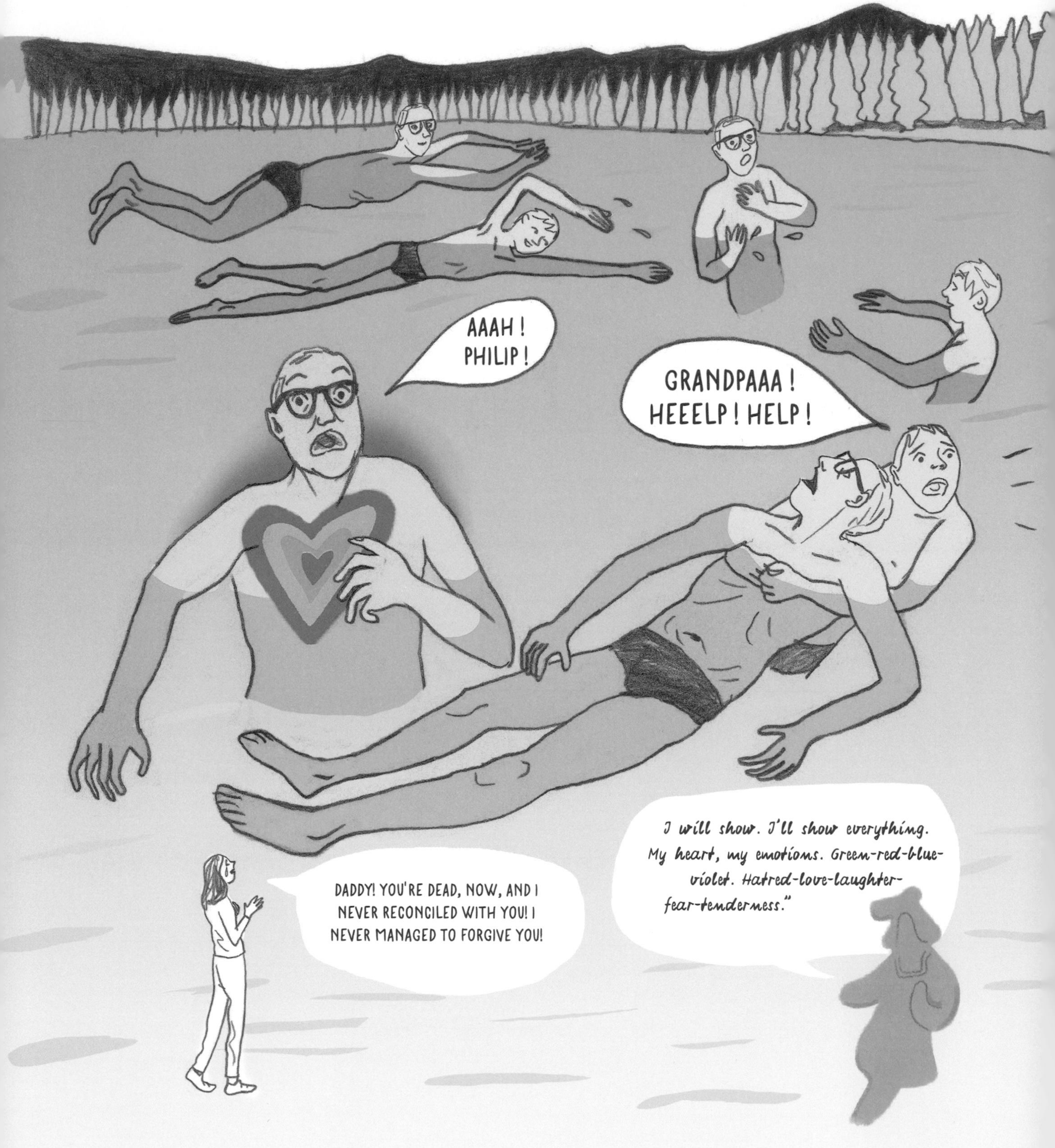
AAAH ! PHILIP !
GRANDPAAA ! HEEELP ! HELP !
I will show. I'll show everything. My heart, my emotions. Green-red-blue-violet. Hatred-love-laughter-fear-tenderness."
DADDY! YOU'RE DEAD, NOW, AND I NEVER RECONCILED WITH YOU! I NEVER MANAGED TO FORGIVE YOU!

# CHAPTER 8

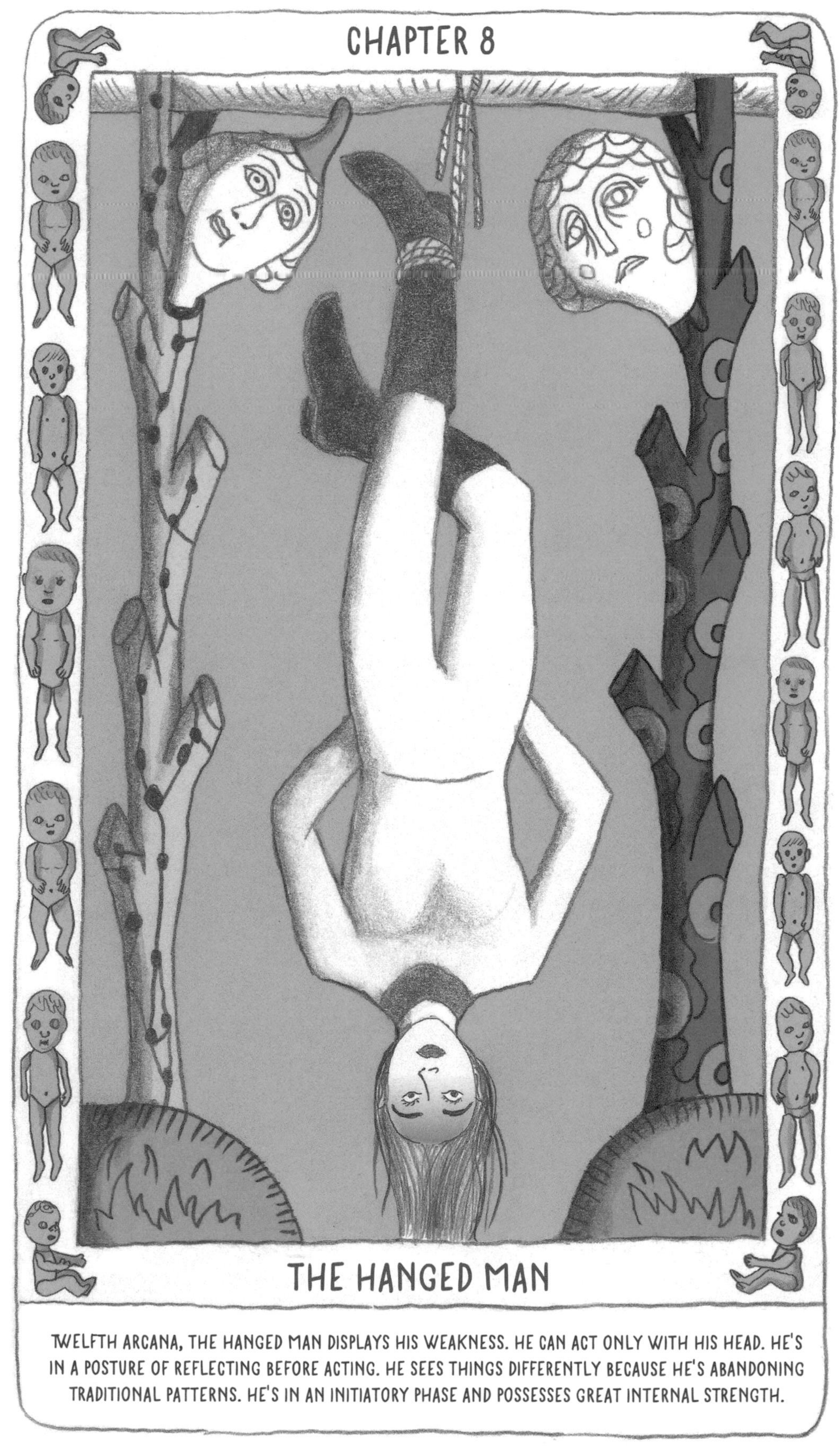

## THE HANGED MAN

TWELFTH ARCANA, THE HANGED MAN DISPLAYS HIS WEAKNESS. HE CAN ACT ONLY WITH HIS HEAD. HE'S IN A POSTURE OF REFLECTING BEFORE ACTING. HE SEES THINGS DIFFERENTLY BECAUSE HE'S ABANDONING TRADITIONAL PATTERNS. HE'S IN AN INITIATORY PHASE AND POSSESSES GREAT INTERNAL STRENGTH.

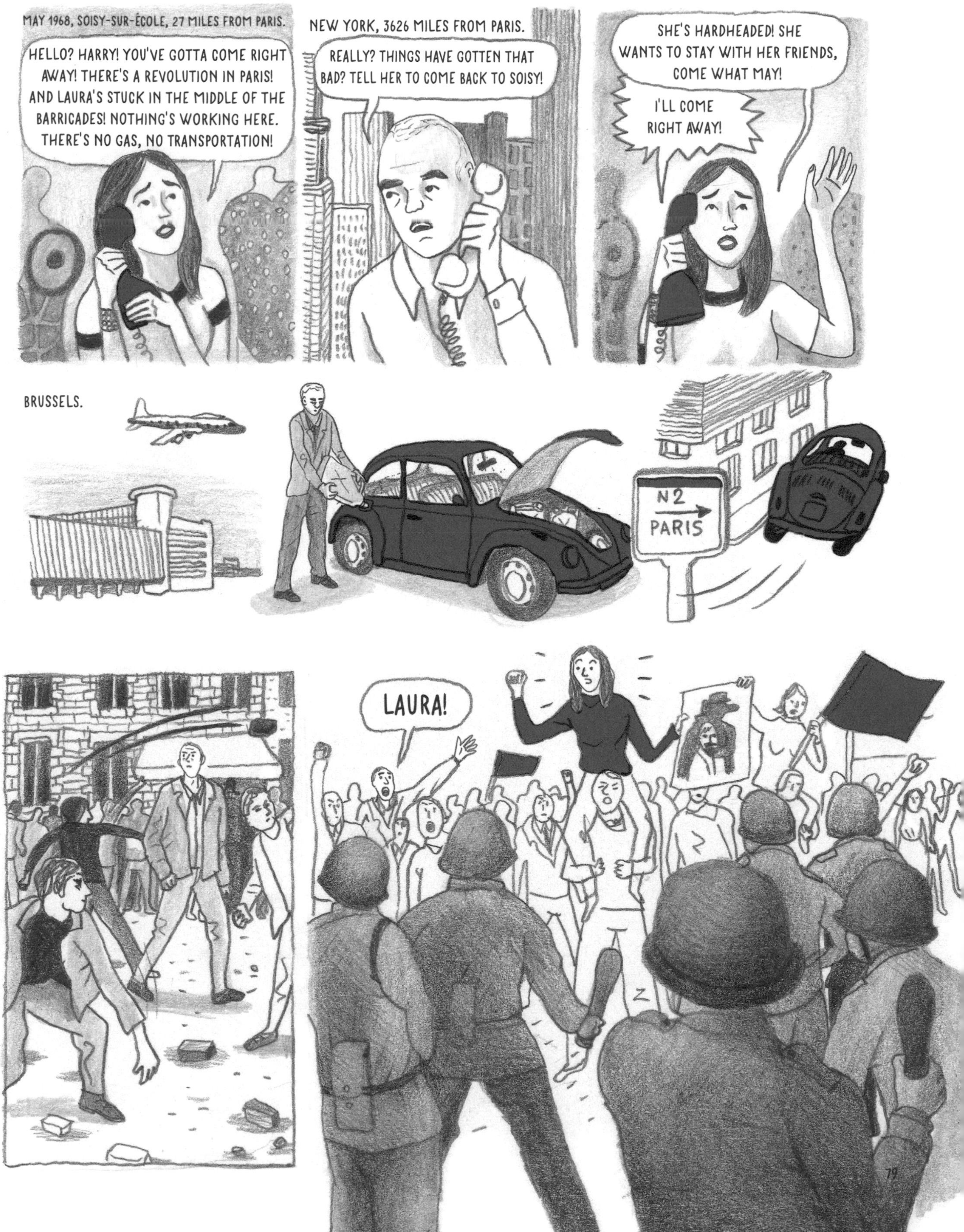
MAY 1968, SOISY-SUR-ÉCOLE, 27 MILES FROM PARIS.
HELLO? HARRY! YOU'VE GOTTA COME RIGHT AWAY! THERE'S A REVOLUTION IN PARIS! AND LAURA'S STUCK IN THE MIDDLE OF THE BARRICADES! NOTHING'S WORKING HERE. THERE'S NO GAS, NO TRANSPORTATION!
NEW YORK, 3626 MILES FROM PARIS.
REALLY? THINGS HAVE GOTTEN THAT BAD? TELL HER TO COME BACK TO SOISY!
SHE'S HARDHEADED! SHE WANTS TO STAY WITH HER FRIENDS, COME WHAT MAY!
I'LL COME RIGHT AWAY!
BRUSSELS.
N2
PARIS
LAURA!

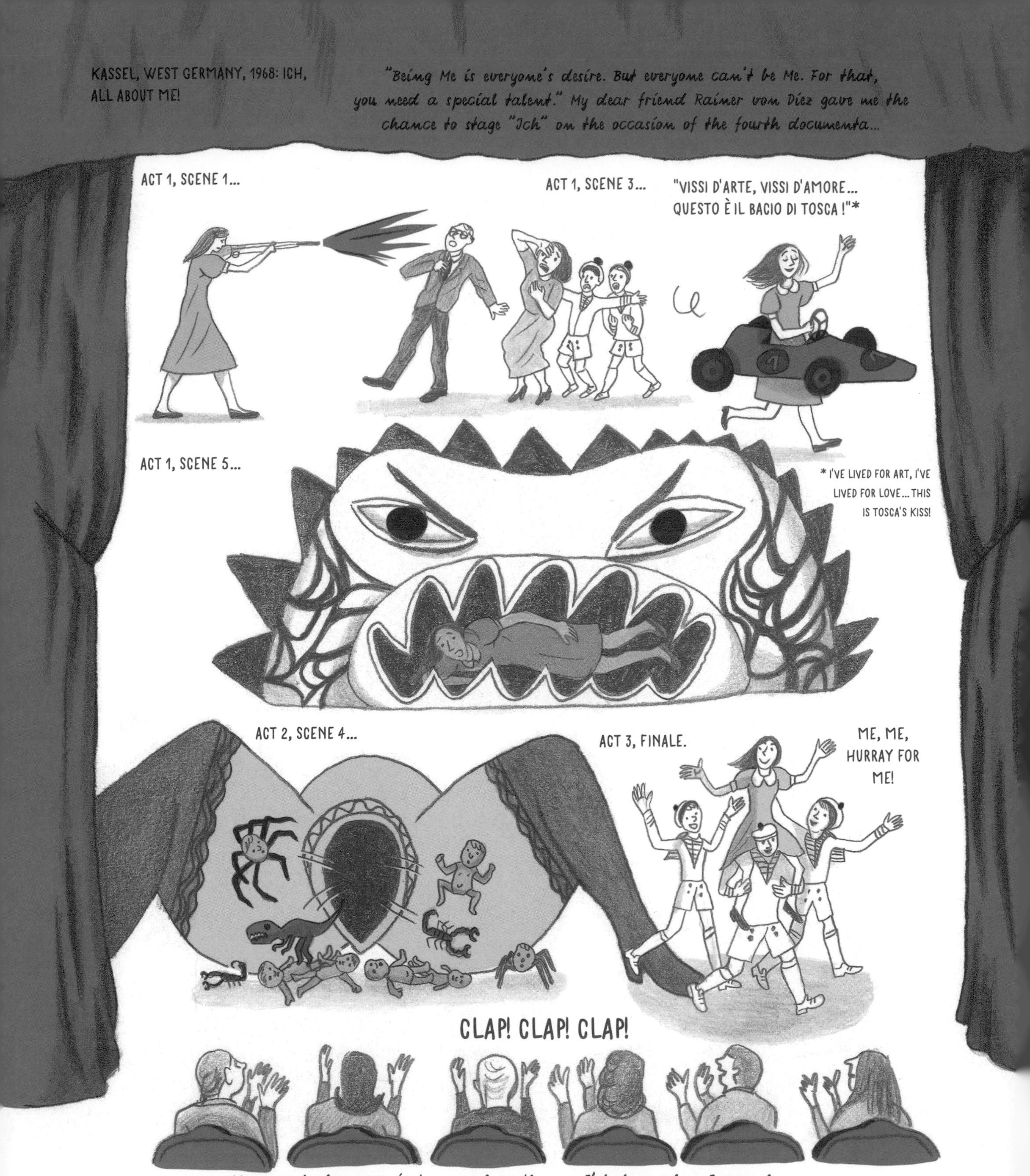
KASSEL, WEST GERMANY, 1968: ICH, ALL ABOUT ME!
"Being Me is everyone's desire. But everyone can't be Me. For that, you need a special talent." My dear friend Rainer von Díez gave me the chance to stage "Ich" on the occasion of the fourth documenta...
ACT 1, SCENE 1...
ACT 1, SCENE 3...
"VISSI D'ARTE, VISSI D'AMORE... QUESTO È IL BACIO DI TOSCA !"*
ACT 1, SCENE 5...
* I'VE LIVED FOR ART, I'VE LIVED FOR LOVE... THIS IS TOSCA'S KISS!
ACT 2, SCENE 4...
ACT 3, FINALE.
ME, ME, HURRAY FOR ME!
CLAP! CLAP! CLAP!

My second play was just as cruel as the one I'd done when I was eleven... With its subject "Me," I completely assumed my megalomania! The little Ich was as detestable as the immense Hon was loveable. But quite curiously, it won the public's approval!

NEYRUZ, SWITZERLAND: BETRAYAL.

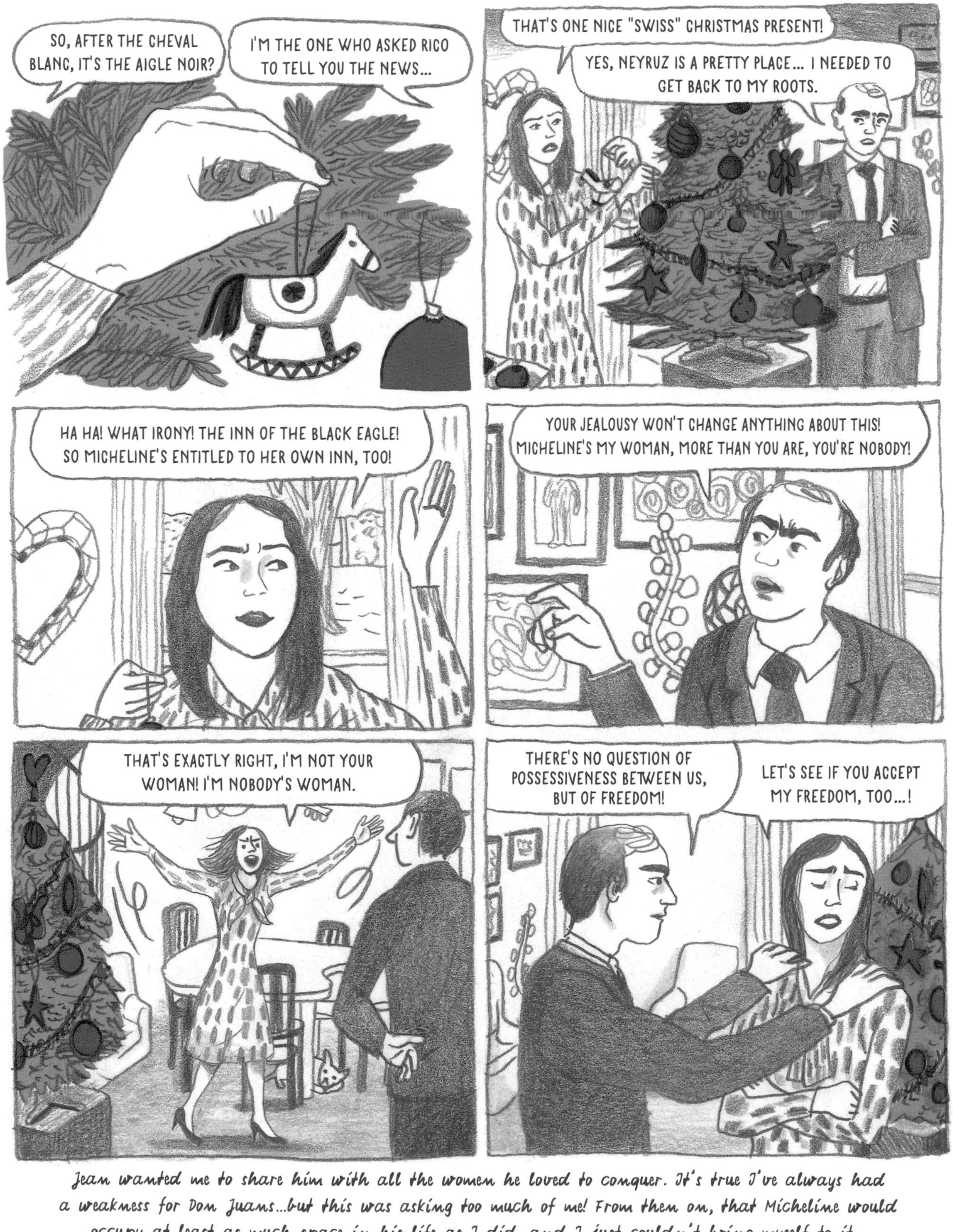
SO, AFTER THE CHEVAL BLANC, IT'S THE AIGLE NOIR?
I'M THE ONE WHO ASKED RICO TO TELL YOU THE NEWS...
THAT'S ONE NICE "SWISS" CHRISTMAS PRESENT!
YES, NEYRUZ IS A PRETTY PLACE... I NEEDED TO GET BACK TO MY ROOTS.
HA HA! WHAT IRONY! THE INN OF THE BLACK EAGLE! SO MICHELINE'S ENTITLED TO HER OWN INN, TOO!
YOUR JEALOUSY WON'T CHANGE ANYTHING ABOUT THIS! MICHELINE'S MY WOMAN, MORE THAN YOU ARE, YOU'RE NOBODY!
THAT'S EXACTLY RIGHT, I'M NOT YOUR WOMAN! I'M NOBODY'S WOMAN.
THERE'S NO QUESTION OF POSSESSIVENESS BETWEEN US, BUT OF FREEDOM!
LET'S SEE IF YOU ACCEPT MY FREEDOM, TOO...!

*Jean wanted me to share him with all the women he loved to conquer. It's true I've always had a weakness for Don Juans...but this was asking too much of me! From then on, that Micheline would occupy at least as much space in his life as I did, and I just couldn't bring myself to it...*

1969, MILLY-LA-FORÊT, FRANCE: THE CYCLOPS. *Despite the fracture in our relationship, we continued our collaborative projects. Jean wanted to construct his own "Sagrada Familia" by involving all of his artist friends in it. Slowly, the project took the shape of an immense head whose body would forever remain buried in the depths of the forest soil.*

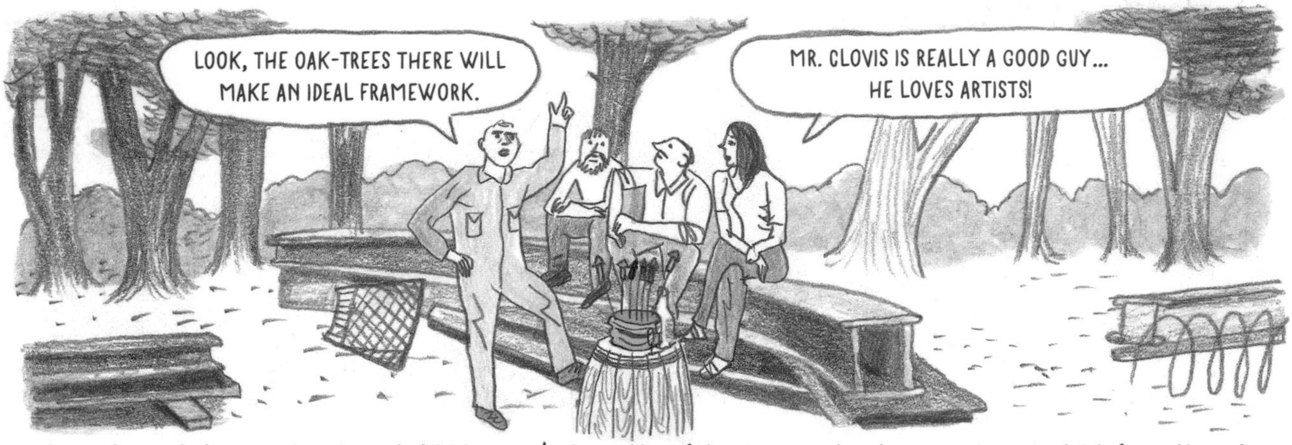

LOOK, THE OAK-TREES THERE WILL MAKE AN IDEAL FRAMEWORK.
MR. CLOVIS IS REALLY A GOOD GUY... HE LOVES ARTISTS!


*The Swiss sculptor Bernhard Luginbühl, Jean's long-time friend, came to give us a hand right from the get-go.*

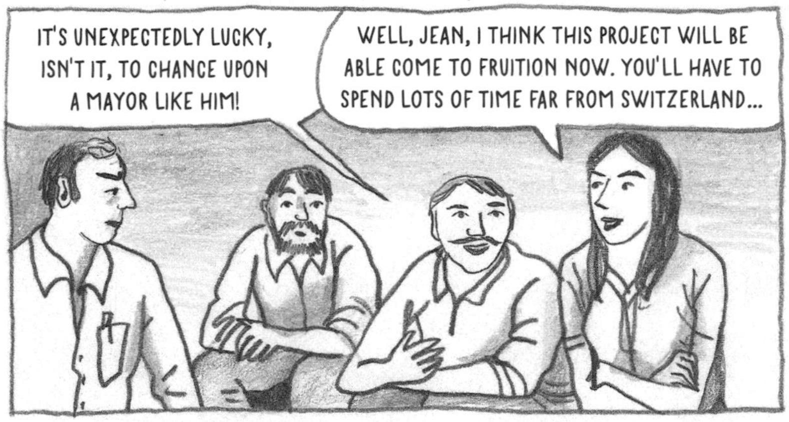

IT'S UNEXPECTEDLY LUCKY, ISN'T IT, TO CHANCE UPON A MAYOR LIKE HIM!
WELL, JEAN, I THINK THIS PROJECT WILL BE ABLE COME TO FRUITION NOW. YOU'LL HAVE TO SPEND LOTS OF TIME FAR FROM SWITZERLAND...


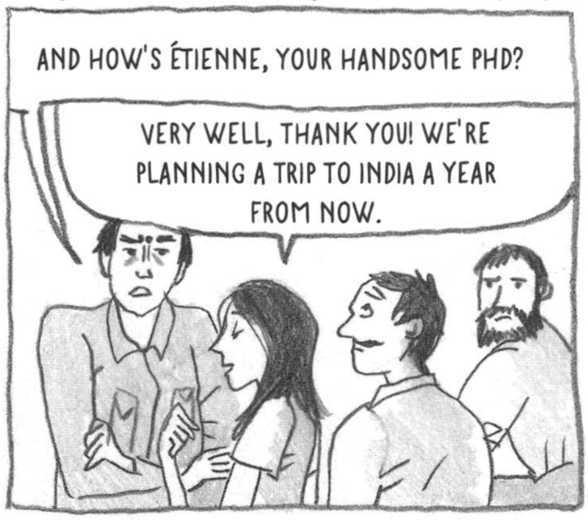

AND HOW'S ÉTIENNE, YOUR HANDSOME PHD?
VERY WELL, THANK YOU! WE'RE PLANNING A TRIP TO INDIA A YEAR FROM NOW.


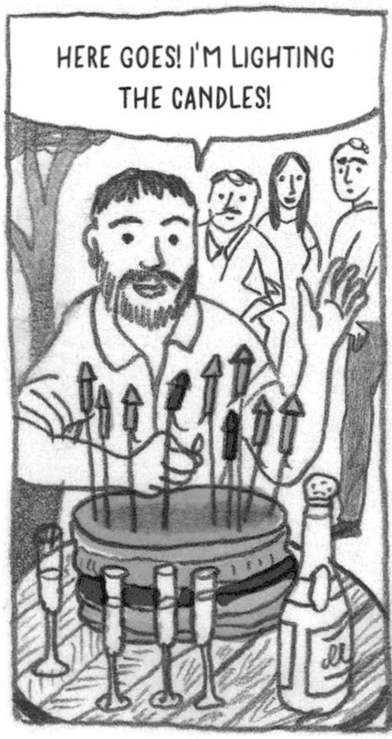

HERE GOES! I'M LIGHTING THE CANDLES!


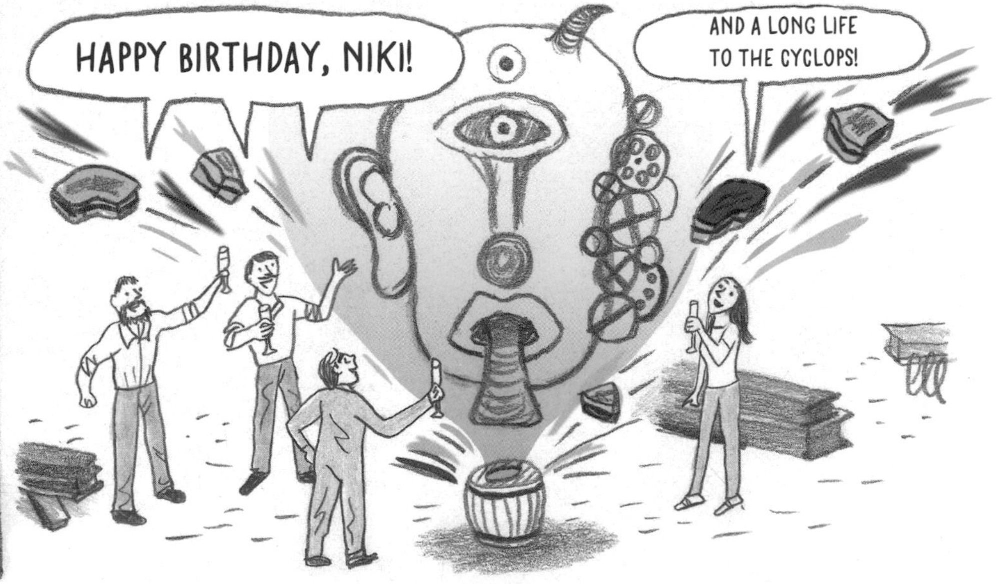

HAPPY BIRTHDAY, NIKI!
AND A LONG LIFE TO THE CYCLOPS!


*That head would take thirty years to sprout and fill out... In order to be closer to the worksite, Jean bought La Commanderie, an old building of the Templars in a neighboring village. Between the insatiable "Cyclops" and his stays in Neyruz, we didn't see each other very much anymore.*

1970, DEVOURING MOTHERS.

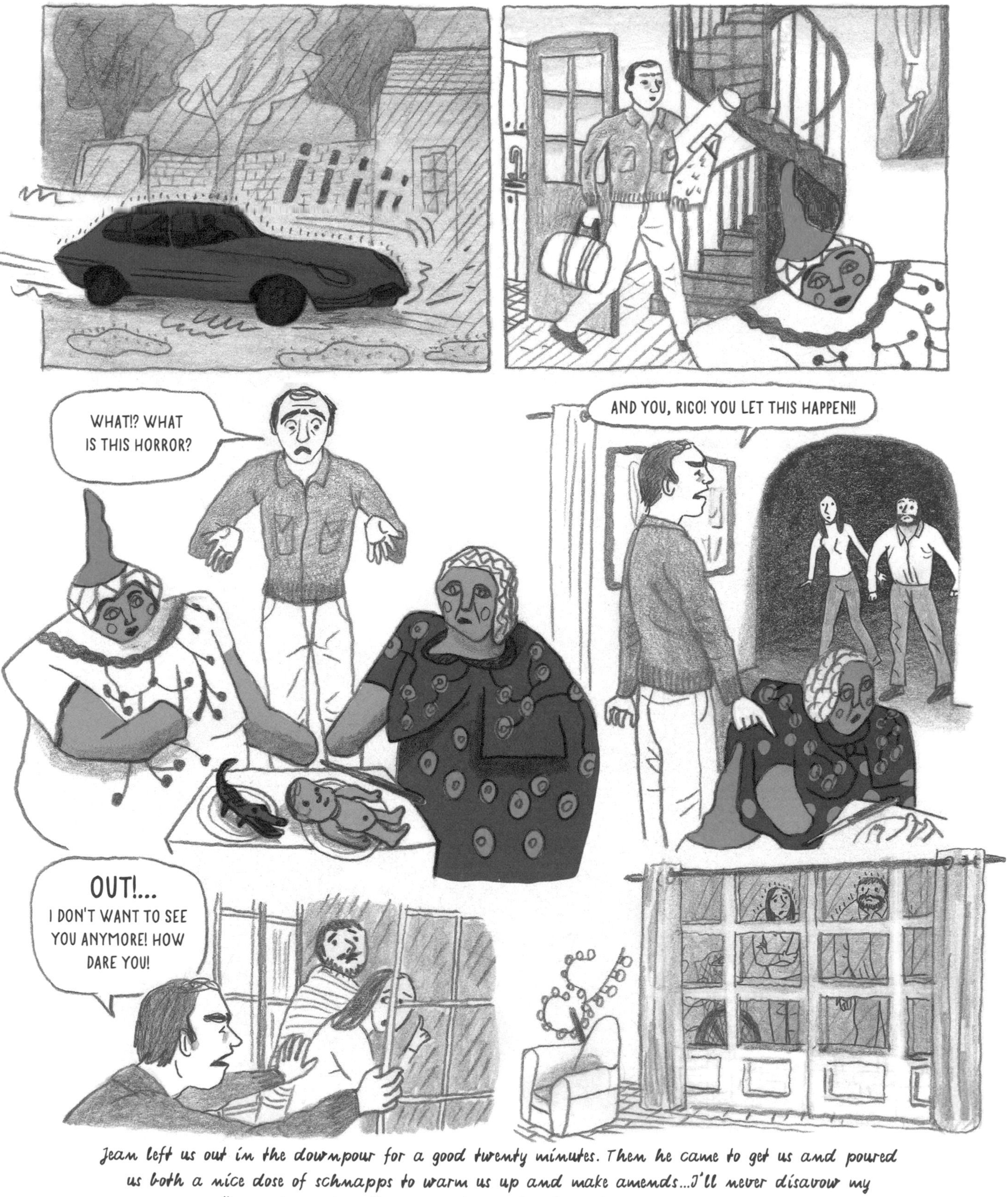
WHAT!? WHAT IS THIS HORROR?
AND YOU, RICO! YOU LET THIS HAPPEN!!
OUT!... I DON'T WANT TO SEE YOU ANYMORE! HOW DARE YOU!

*Jean left us out in the downpour for a good twenty minutes. Then he came to get us and poured us both a nice dose of schnapps to warm us up and make amends...I'll never disavow my "Devouring Mothers." They are the somber face of my luminous Nanas.*

1971, BLACK EAGLES... *I pushed Jean away again and again, not wanting to live the pain of this sharing. But each time, he managed to win me back again! I ended up giving in and even came to an understanding with Micheline.*

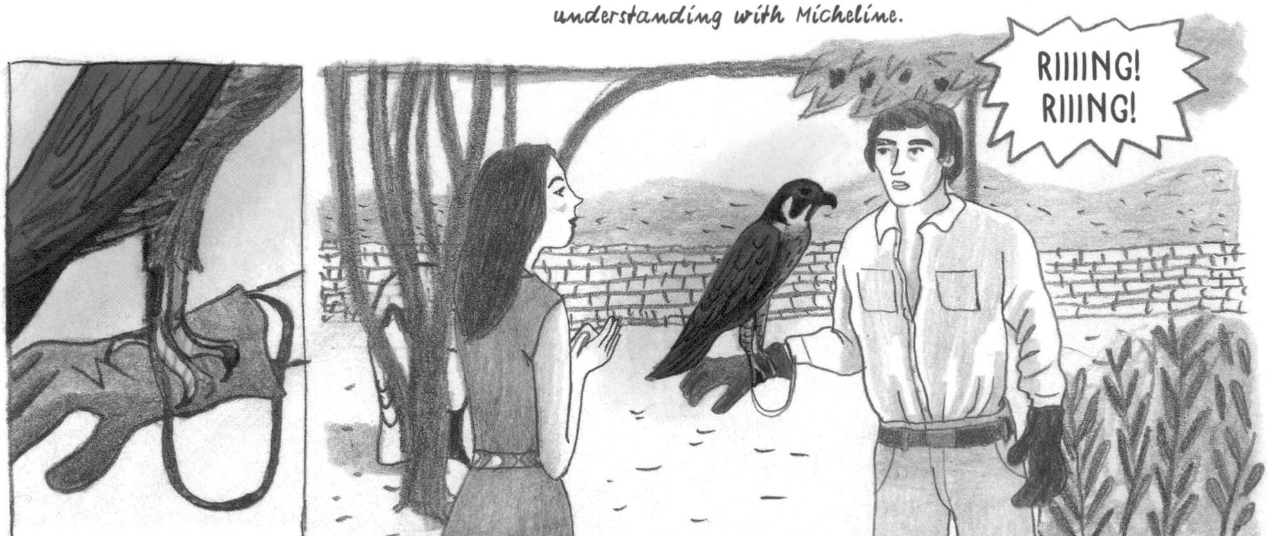
RIIIING!
RIIING!

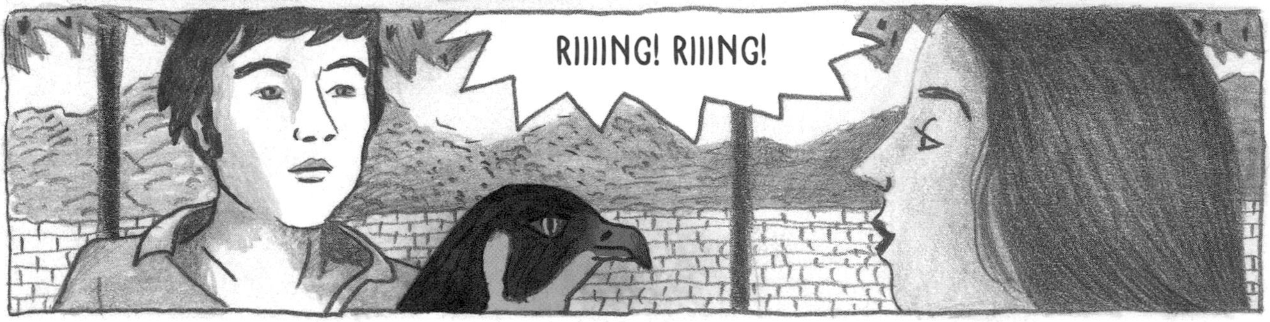
RIIIING! RIIING!

*Jean wanted a kid. I refused. From now on, I'd create only my artwork. My time for childbearing had passed. What's more, I was going to be a grandmother soon and was awaiting that birth with great impatience and great joy.*

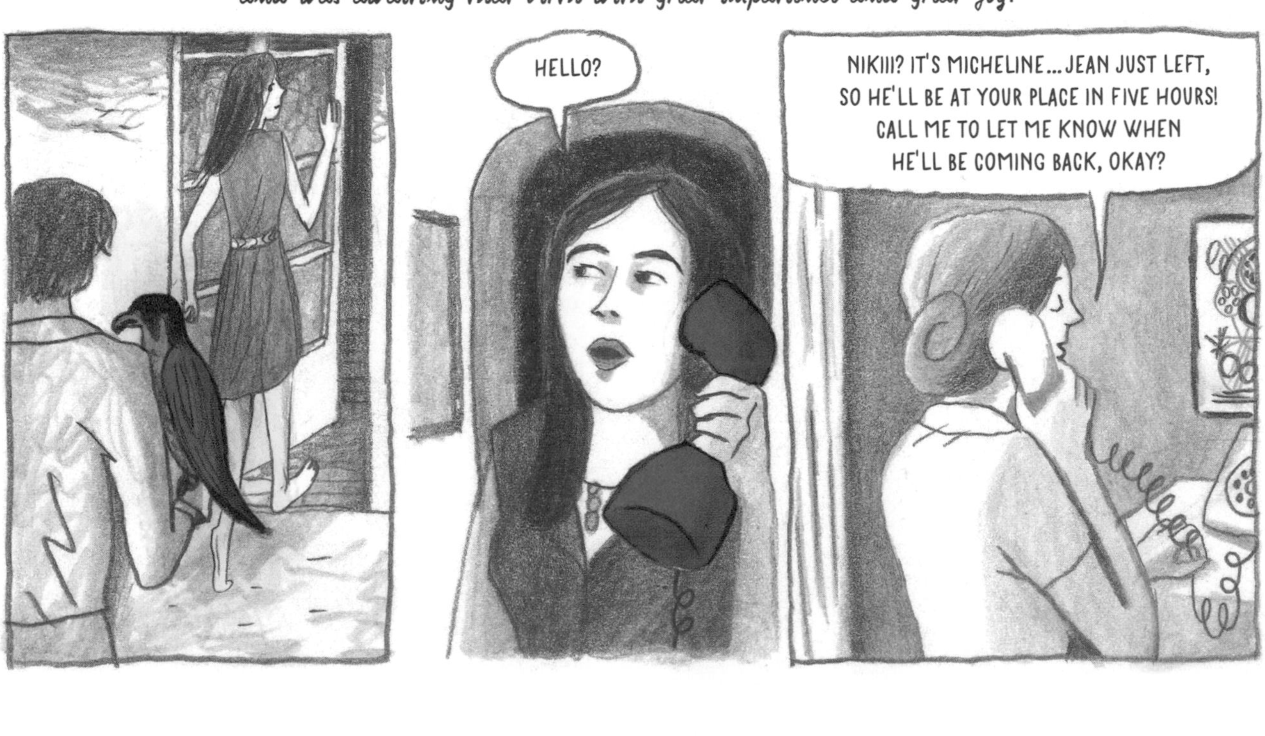
HELLO?
NIKIII? IT'S MICHELINE... JEAN JUST LEFT, SO HE'LL BE AT YOUR PLACE IN FIVE HOURS! CALL ME TO LET ME KNOW WHEN HE'LL BE COMING BACK, OKAY?

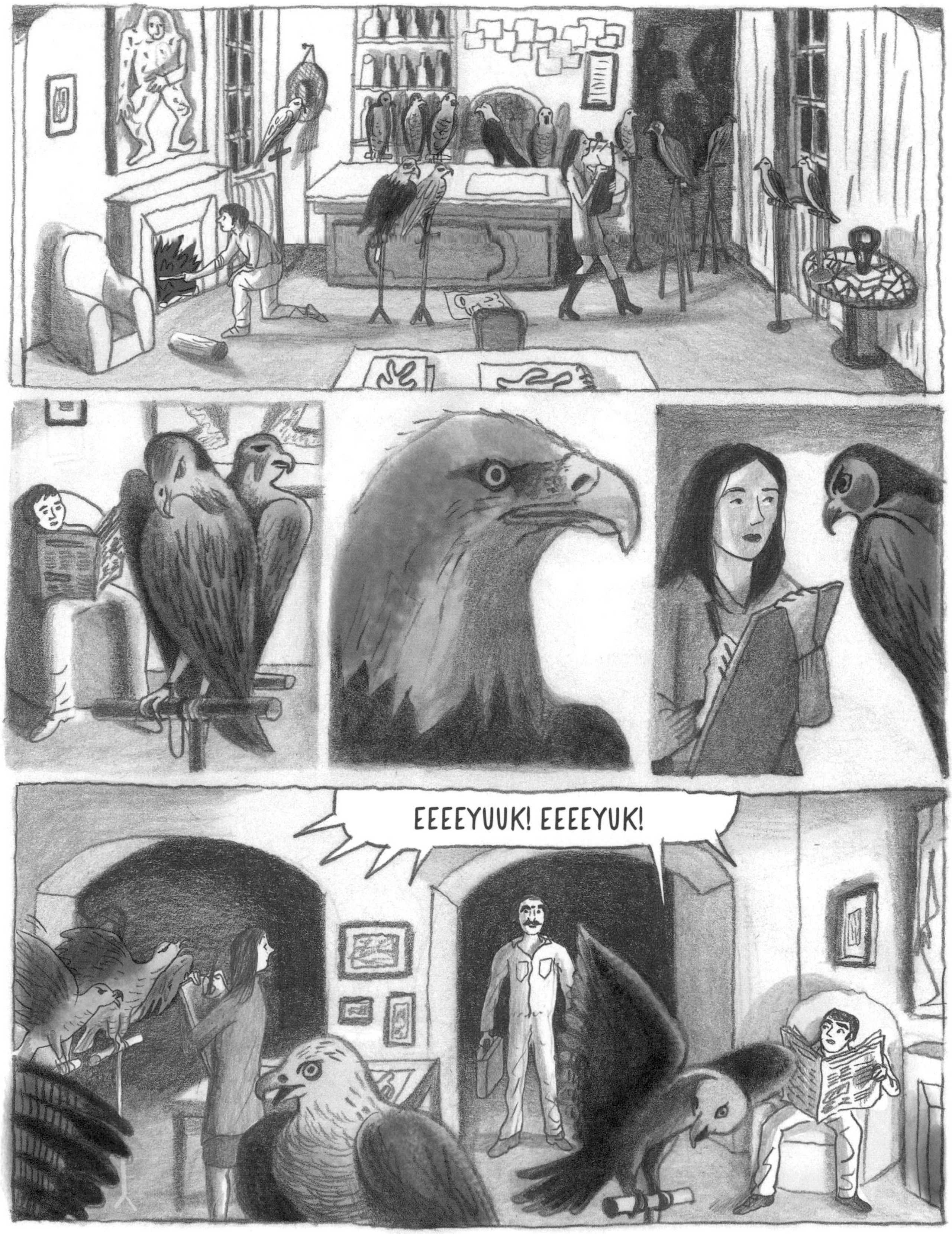
EEEEYUUK! EEEEYUK!

*How I loved you with your piercing gaze, man and bird, you frightful sphinx...*
*Your sublime enigma subjugated me for so long.*

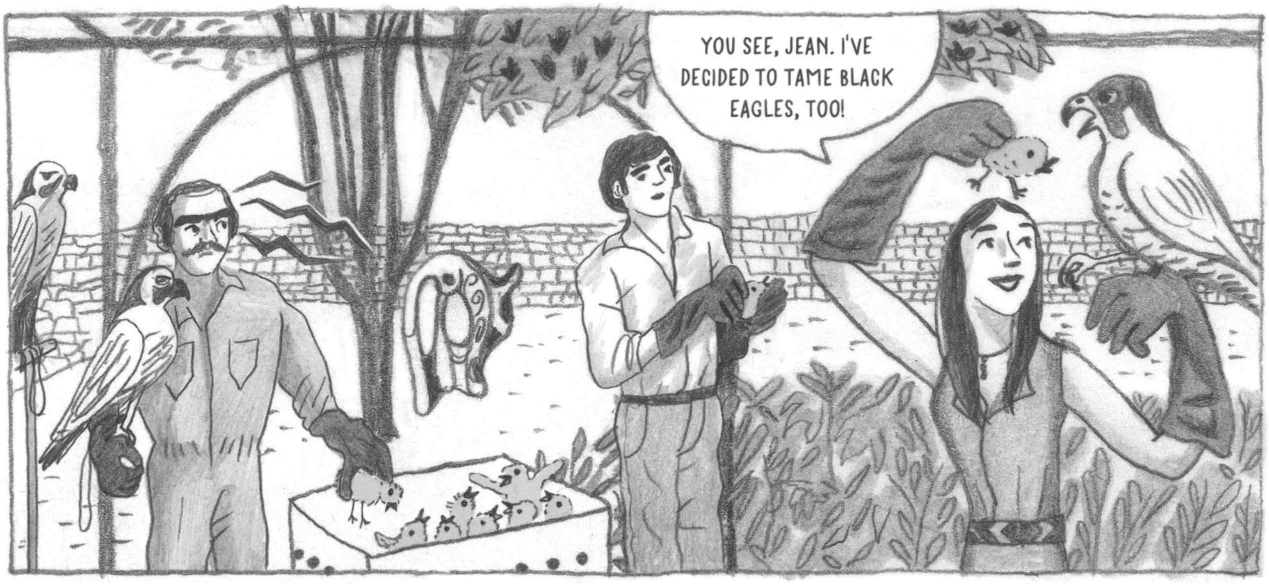
YOU SEE, JEAN. I'VE DECIDED TO TAME BLACK EAGLES, TOO!

A CYCLOPEAN WORK... After the "Cyclops" went trough a few collapses due to Jean and Bernhard's lack of expertise as welders and, thanks to the judicious choice of Micheline, we soon recruited an excellent Swiss welder via want ads. His name is Seppi Imhof. He's unafraid of heights and also possesses the marvelous virtue of knowing how to play jass...*

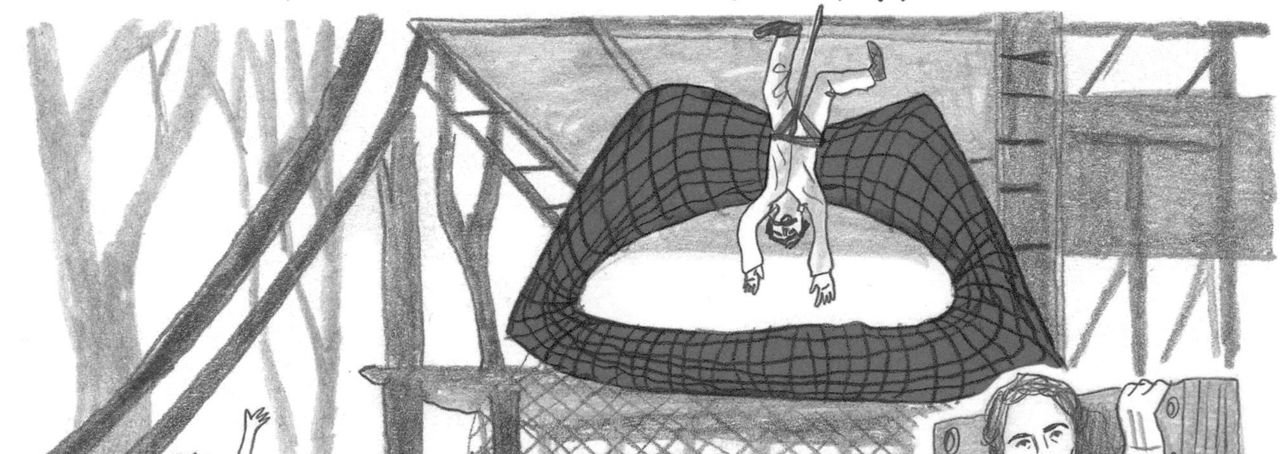

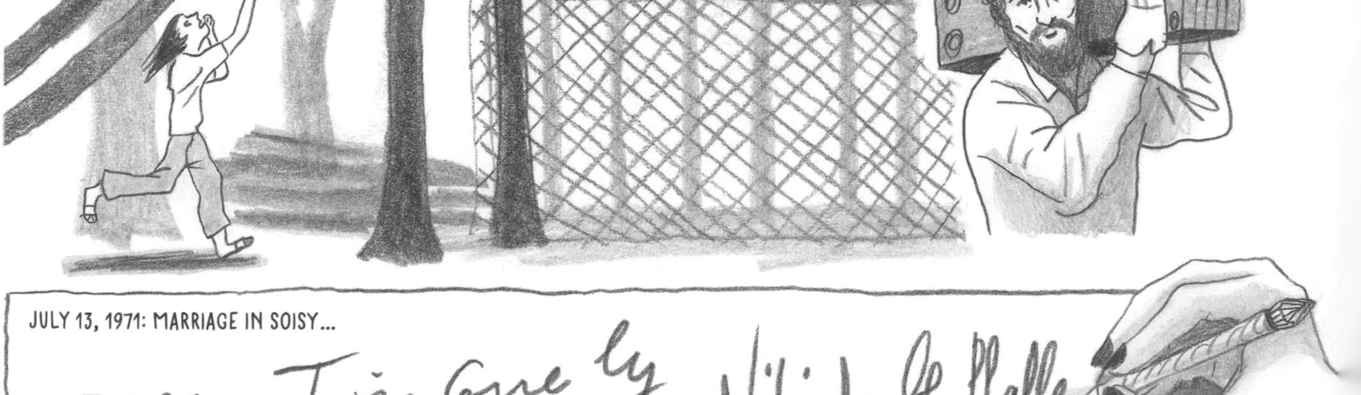
JULY 13, 1971: MARRIAGE IN SOISY...
Jean Tinguely
Niki de St Phalle

Jean refused to marry Micheline, although she wanted to have his child. Our marriage remained secret for a long time.... The month following our marriage, Laura gave birth to my little Bloum.



*a card game played in Switzerland.

# CHAPTER 9

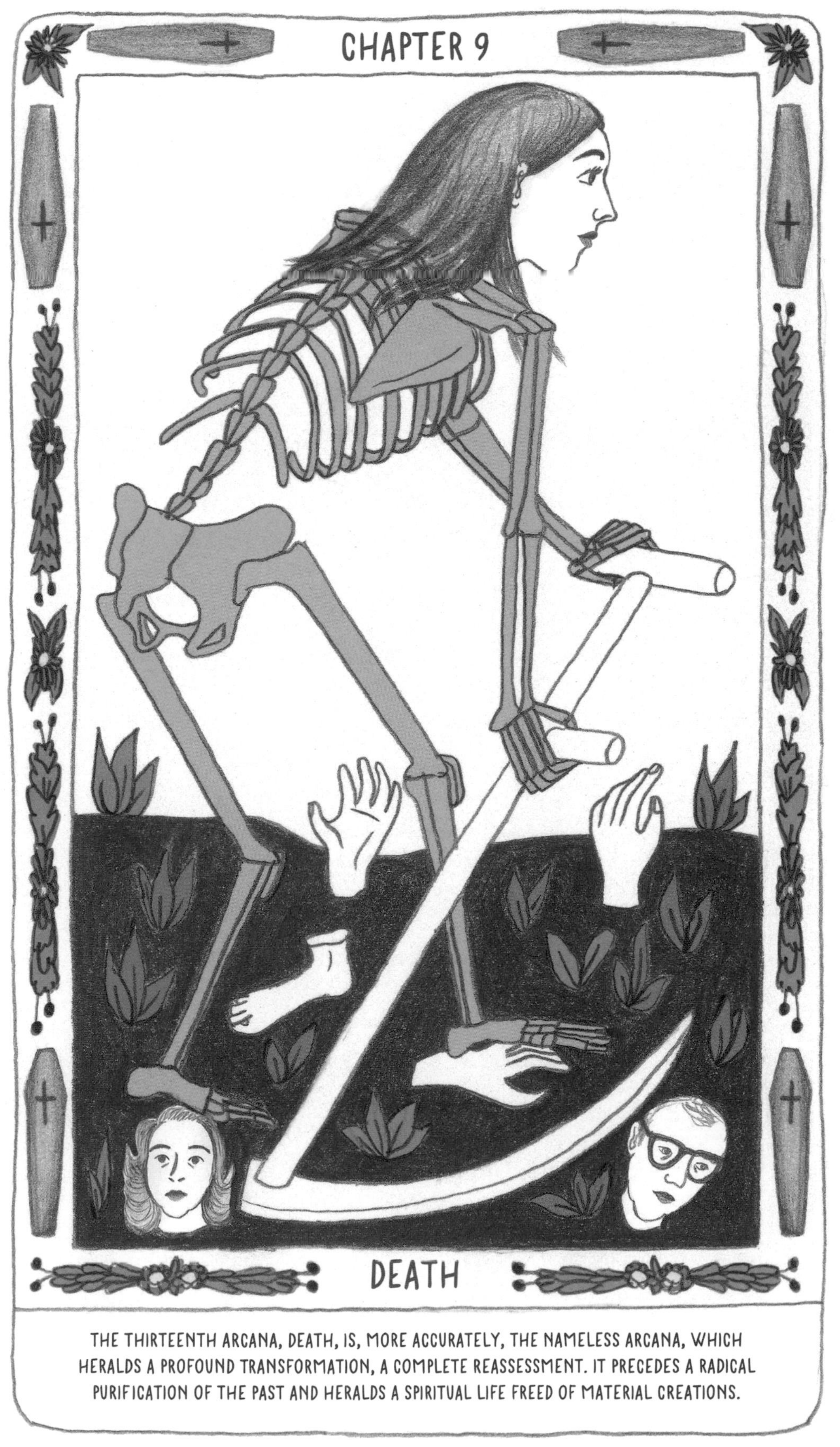

## DEATH

THE THIRTEENTH ARCANA, DEATH, IS, MORE ACCURATELY, THE NAMELESS ARCANA, WHICH HERALDS A PROFOUND TRANSFORMATION, A COMPLETE REASSESSMENT. IT PRECEDES A RADICAL PURIFICATION OF THE PAST AND HERALDS A SPIRITUAL LIFE FREED OF MATERIAL CREATIONS.

1972: FROM ONE GIANT TO ANOTHER. *Thanks to the patronage of Prince Michael of Greece and Marina, friends for the past few years, the "Cyclops" was making giant strides, even though it didn't have any legs, like those Olmec heads that had inspired Jean and me!*

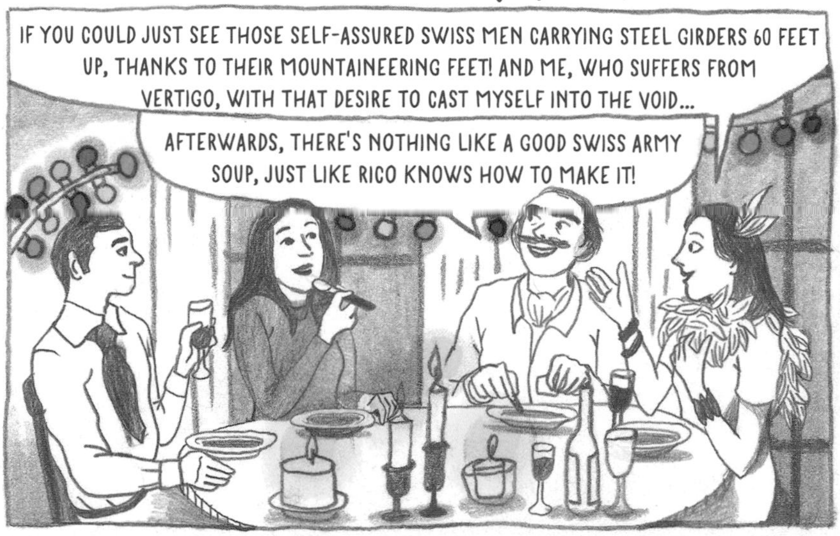
IF YOU COULD JUST SEE THOSE SELF-ASSURED SWISS MEN CARRYING STEEL GIRDERS 60 FEET UP, THANKS TO THEIR MOUNTAINEERING FEET! AND ME, WHO SUFFERS FROM VERTIGO, WITH THAT DESIRE TO CAST MYSELF INTO THE VOID...
AFTERWARDS, THERE'S NOTHING LIKE A GOOD SWISS ARMY SOUP, JUST LIKE RICO KNOWS HOW TO MAKE IT!

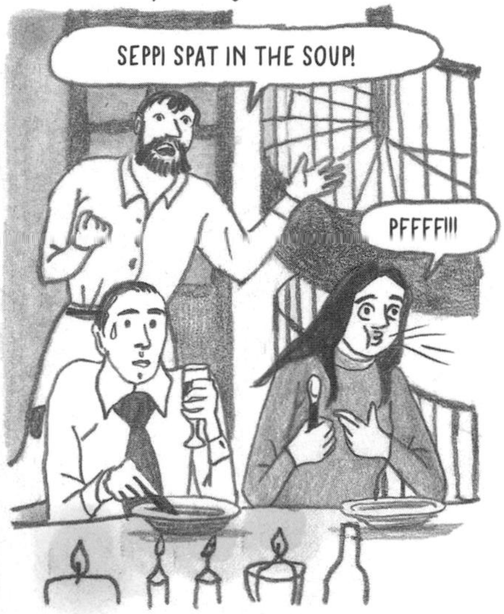
SEPPI SPAT IN THE SOUP!
PFFFF!!!

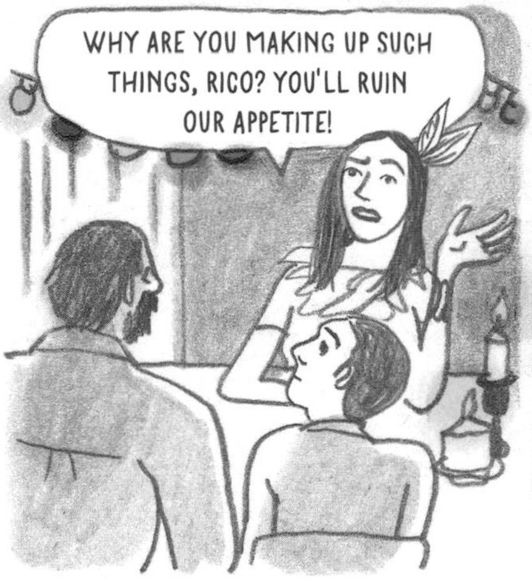
WHY ARE YOU MAKING UP SUCH THINGS, RICO? YOU'LL RUIN OUR APPETITE!

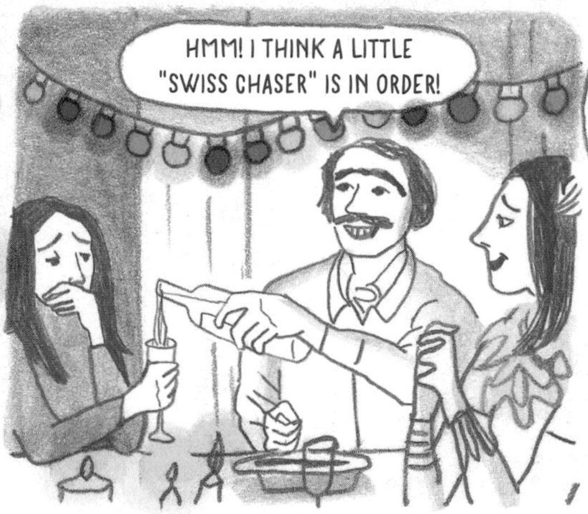
HMM! I THINK A LITTLE "SWISS CHASER" IS IN ORDER!

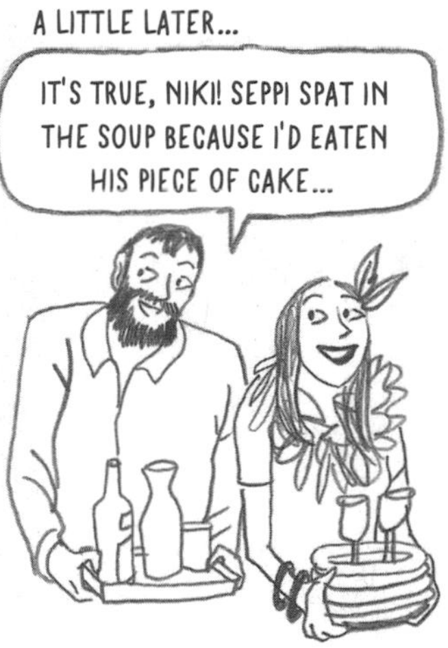
A LITTLE LATER...
IT'S TRUE, NIKI! SEPPI SPAT IN THE SOUP BECAUSE I'D EATEN HIS PIECE OF CAKE...

*About that same time, my own giant head project was coming to fruition in Israel: a Golem, a gentle monster with tongue slides that would spit out the spellbound children of Jerusalem, be they Arabs or Jews!*

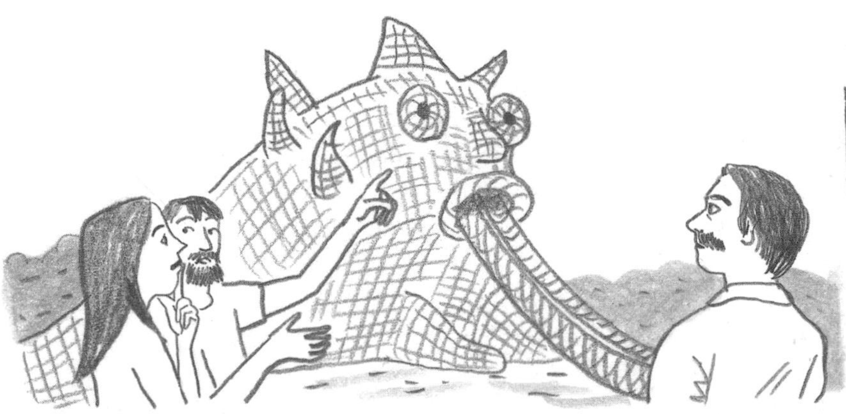

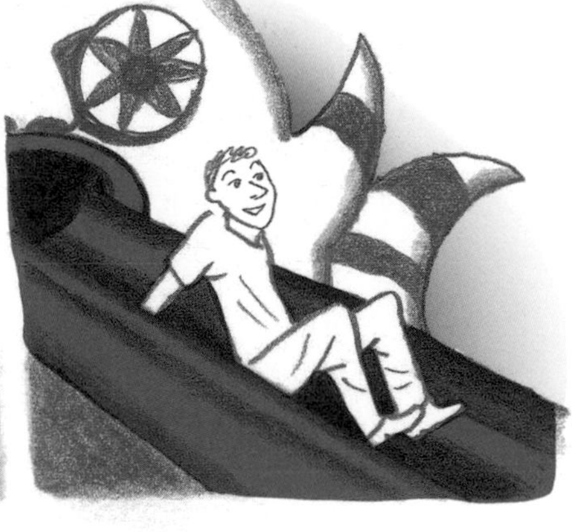

*"The monster has come back. It changes colors endlessly... I'd like to be a bird as big as a plane and fly away... Why must birds die? Why does love die? Everything my eyes sees will die. Even you and I."*

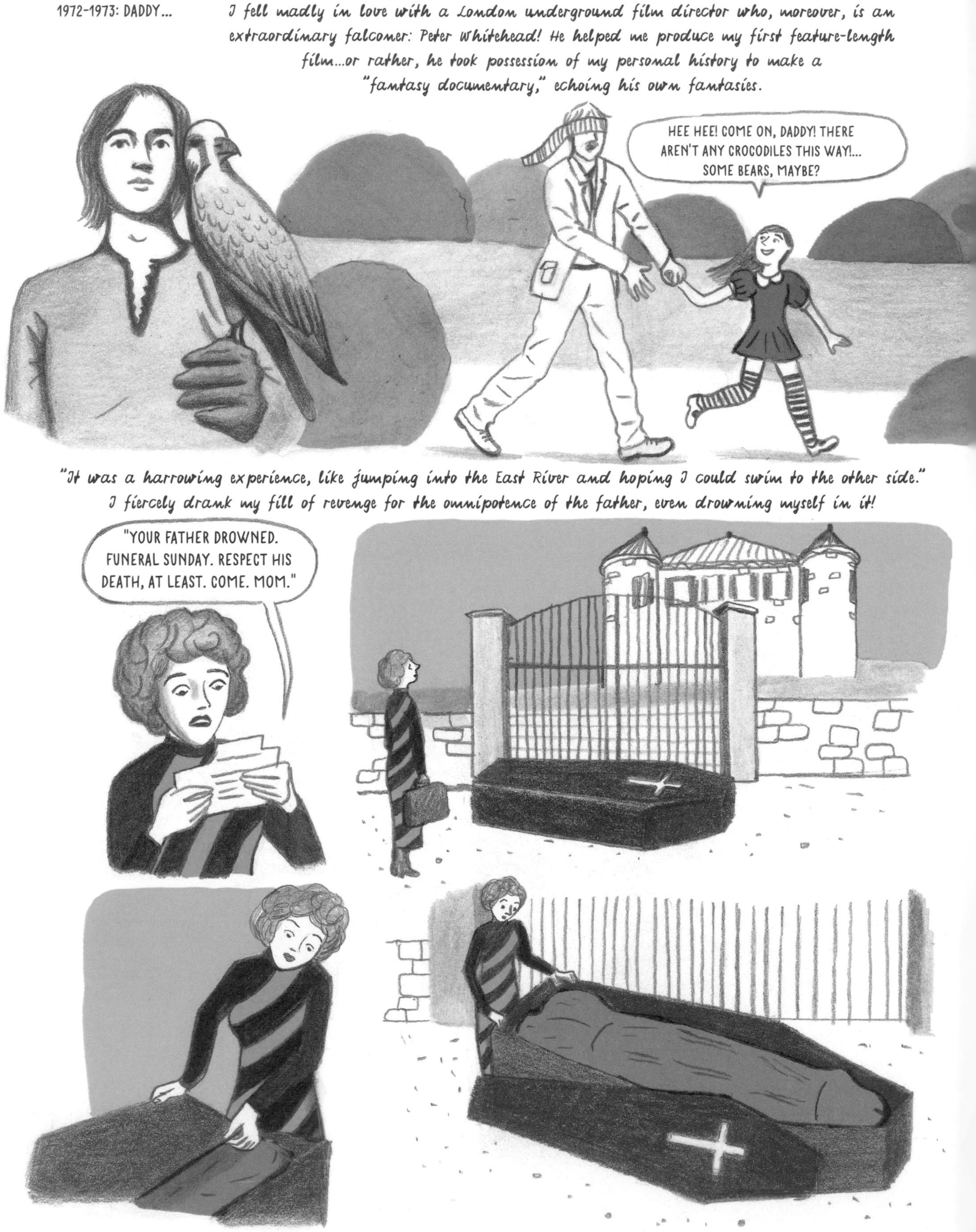
1972–1973: DADDY...
I fell madly in love with a London underground film director who, moreover, is an extraordinary falconer: Peter Whitehead! He helped me produce my first feature-length film...or rather, he took possession of my personal history to make a "fantasy documentary," echoing his own fantasies.
HEE HEE! COME ON, DADDY! THERE AREN'T ANY CROCODILES THIS WAY!... SOME BEARS, MAYBE?
"It was a harrowing experience, like jumping into the East River and hoping I could swim to the other side." I fiercely drank my fill of revenge for the omnipotence of the father, even drowning myself in it!
"YOUR FATHER DROWNED. FUNERAL SUNDAY. RESPECT HIS DEATH, AT LEAST. COME. MOM."

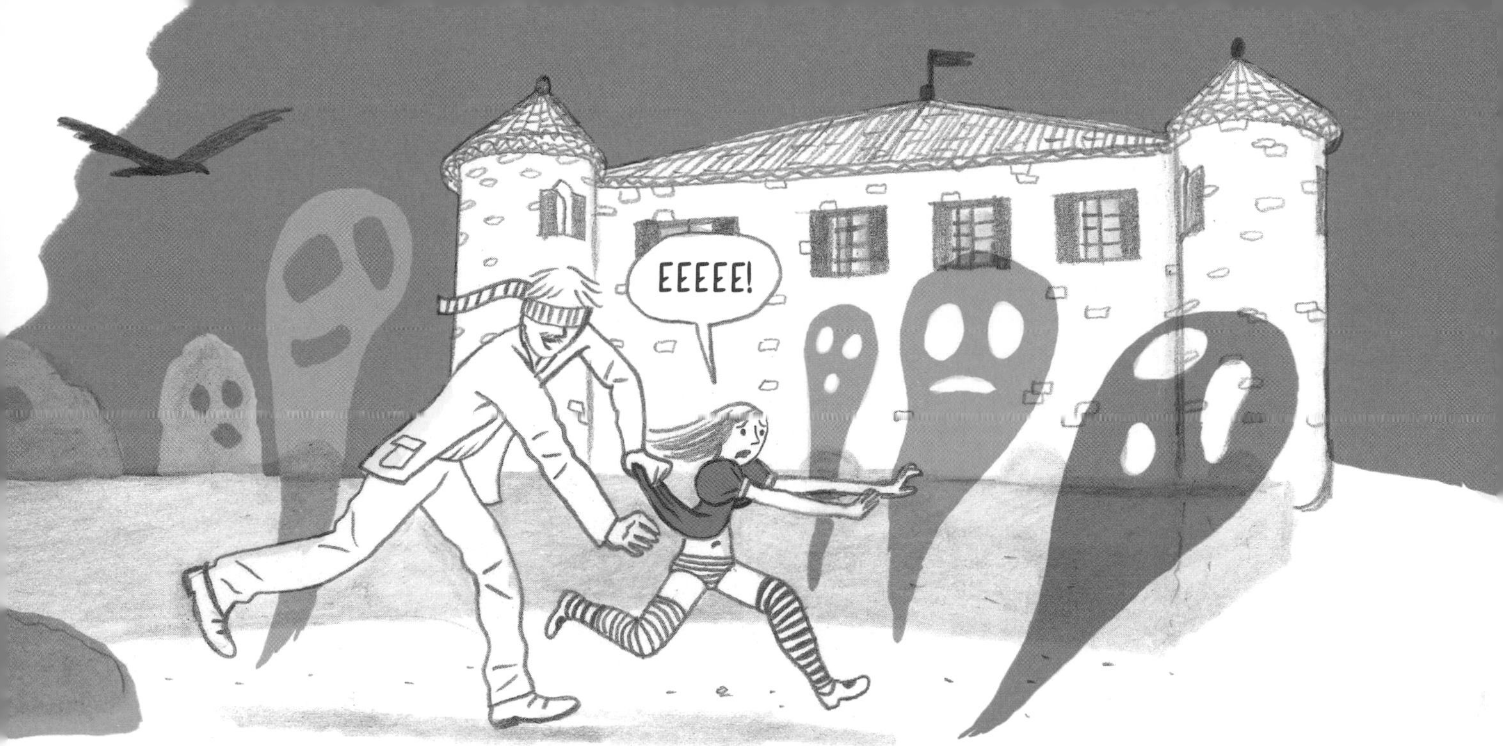
EEEEE!

We exploded all the taboos, and I finally admitted that children are sexual beings, too.
"In the end, who violated whom? It's an event of my life I've not managed to reconstitute... I was a very sexy little girl, and I still am"

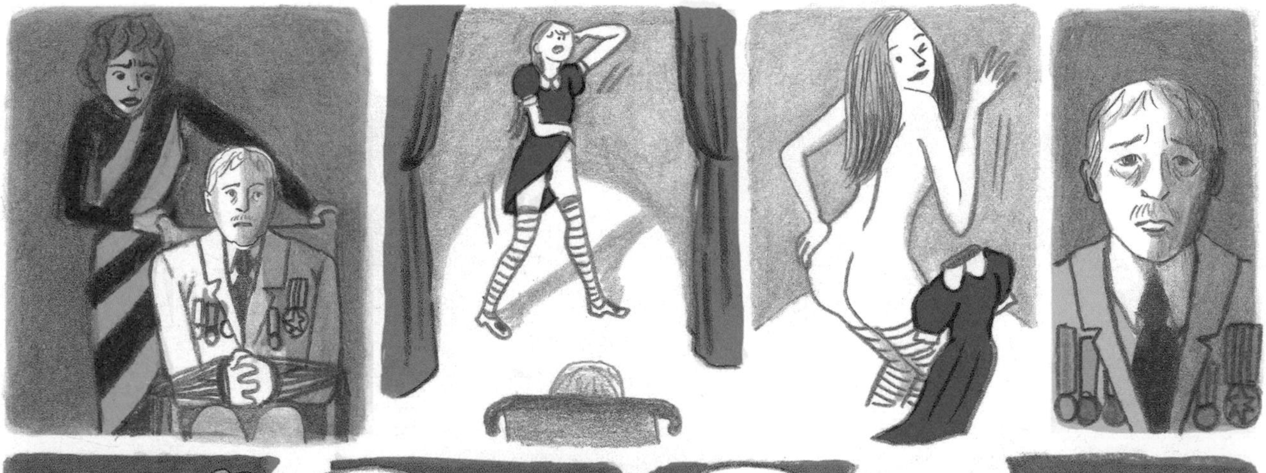

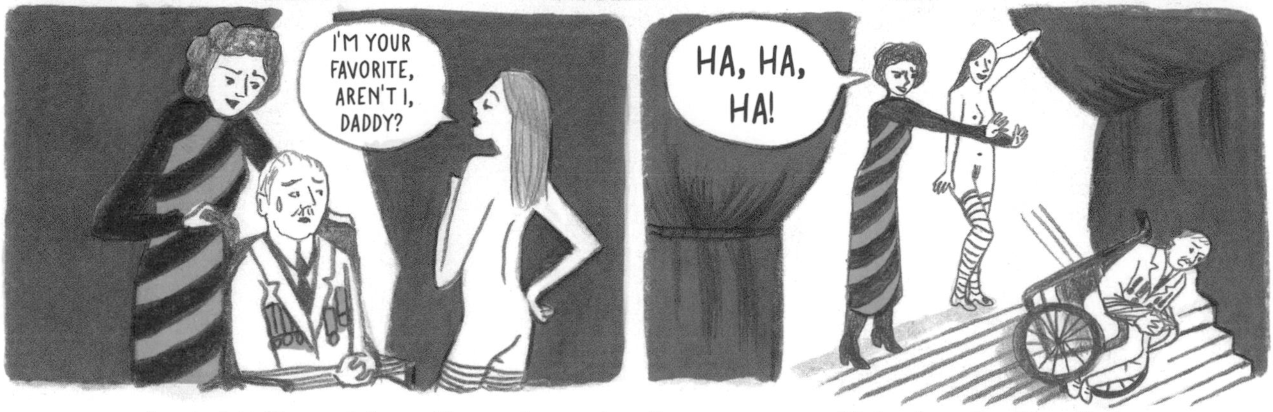
I'M YOUR FAVORITE, AREN'T I, DADDY?
HA, HA, HA!

I asked Mother not to see the movie, arguing it was a paranoid fantasy. Purely artistic. The film shocked even Jean...

*Mother followed my advice. She's never seen the film. But she supported me.*

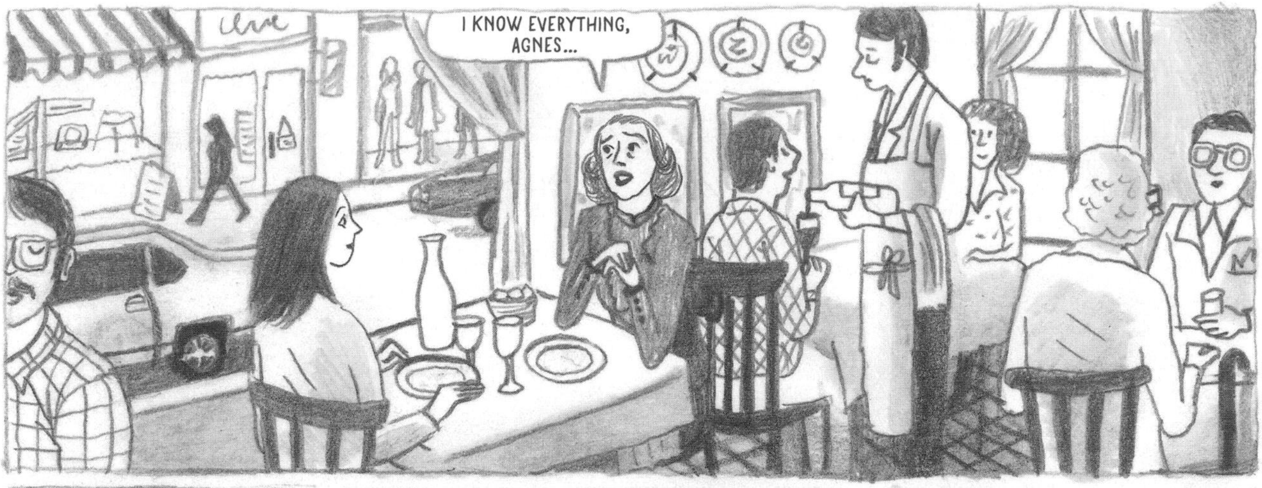
I KNOW EVERYTHING, AGNES...

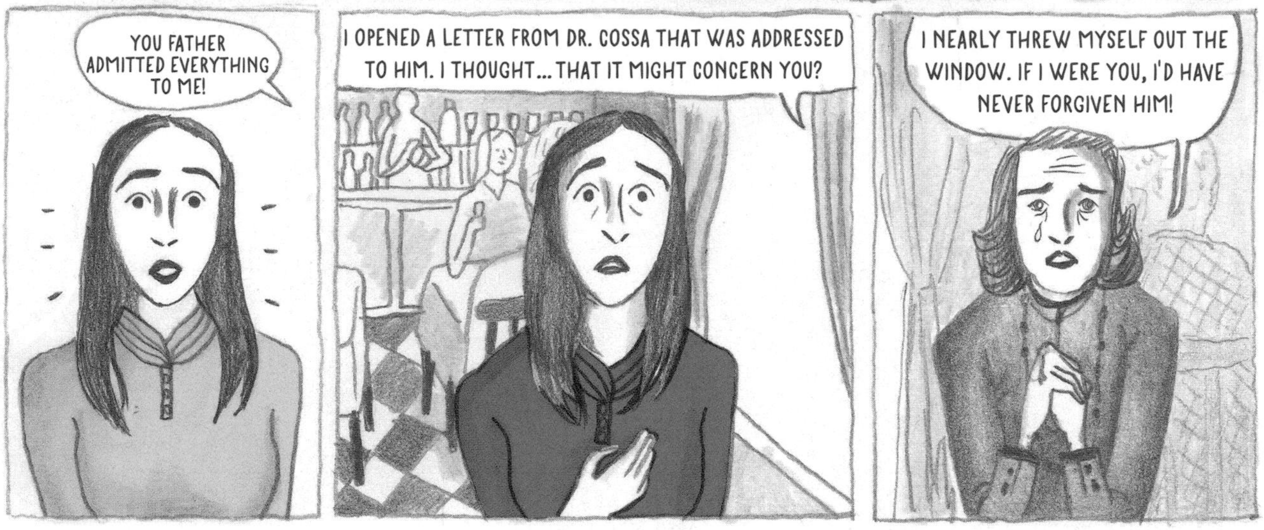
YOU FATHER ADMITTED EVERYTHING TO ME!
I OPENED A LETTER FROM DR. COSSA THAT WAS ADDRESSED TO HIM. I THOUGHT... THAT IT MIGHT CONCERN YOU?
I NEARLY THREW MYSELF OUT THE WINDOW. IF I WERE YOU, I'D HAVE NEVER FORGIVEN HIM!

*That day, for the first time since my early childhood, I felt the desire to throw myself into her arms...*

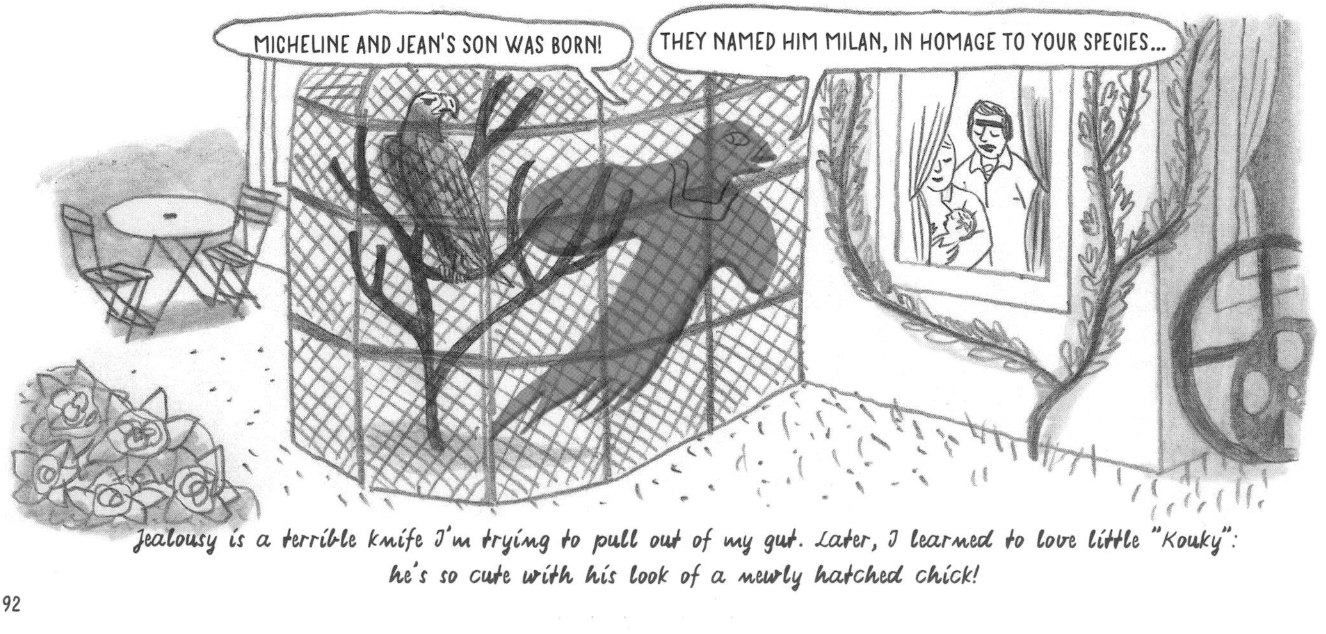
MICHELINE AND JEAN'S SON WAS BORN!
THEY NAMED HIM MILAN, IN HOMAGE TO YOUR SPECIES...

*Jealousy is a terrible knife I'm trying to pull out of my gut. Later, I learned to love little "Kouky": he's so cute with his look of a newly hatched chick!*

THE COMMANDERIE... *An acute pulmonary inflammation nearly did me in at the beginning of 1974... I thought I was over it, but my immune defenses are in a poor condition. Fortunately, Étienne Beaulieu comes all the way to Dannemois to give me shots! Who would of thought of such a thing! Here I am being supported by two of the loves of my life!*

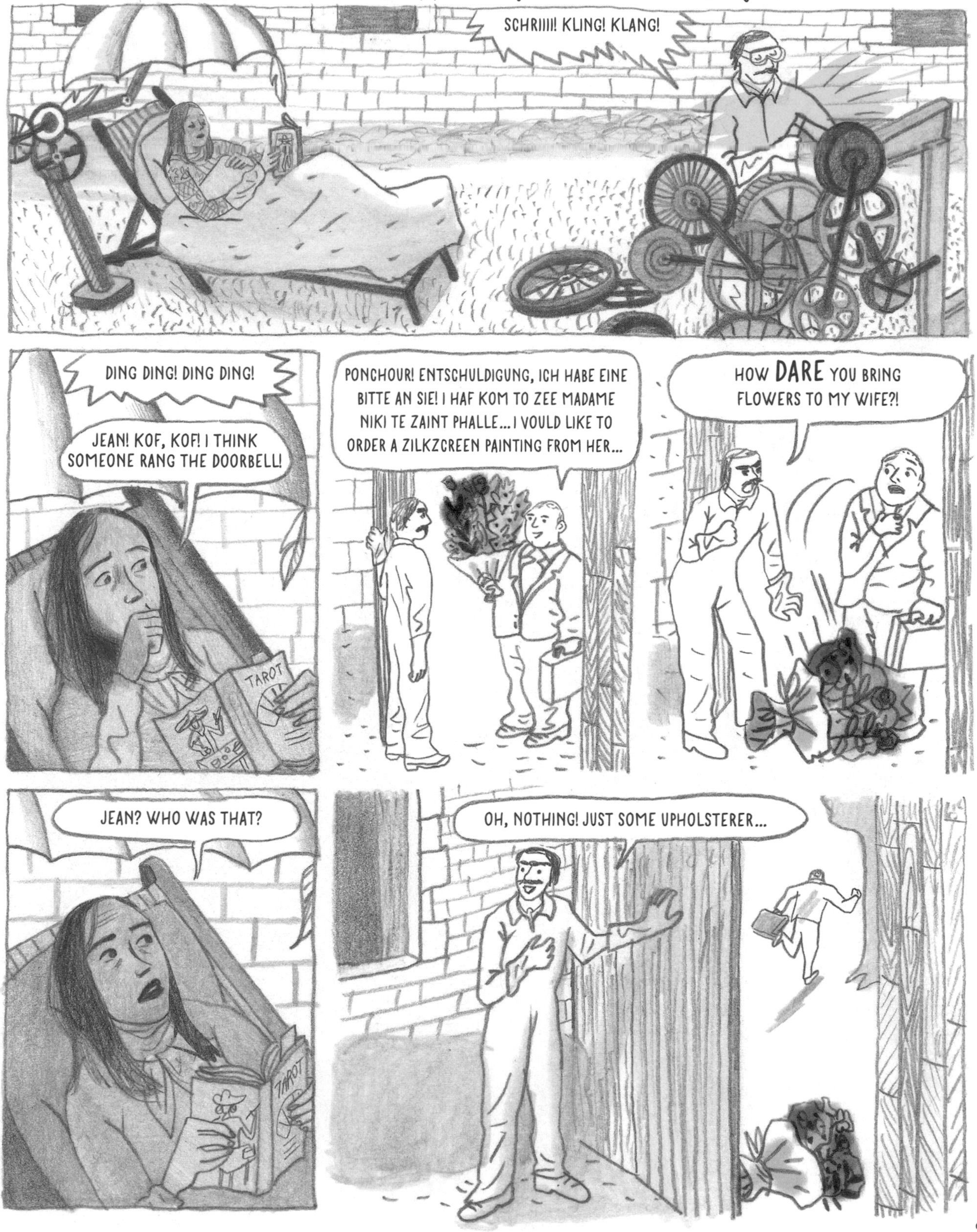
SCHRIIII! KLING! KLANG!
DING DING! DING DING!
JEAN! KOF, KOF! I THINK SOMEONE RANG THE DOORBELL!
TAROT
PONCHOUR! ENTSCHULDIGUNG, ICH HABE EINE BITTE AN SIE! I HAF KOM TO ZEE MADAME NIKI TE ZAINT PHALLE... I VOULD LIKE TO ORDER A ZILKZCREEN PAINTING FROM HER...
HOW DARE YOU BRING FLOWERS TO MY WIFE?!
JEAN? WHO WAS THAT?
TAROT
OH, NOTHING! JUST SOME UPHOLSTERER...

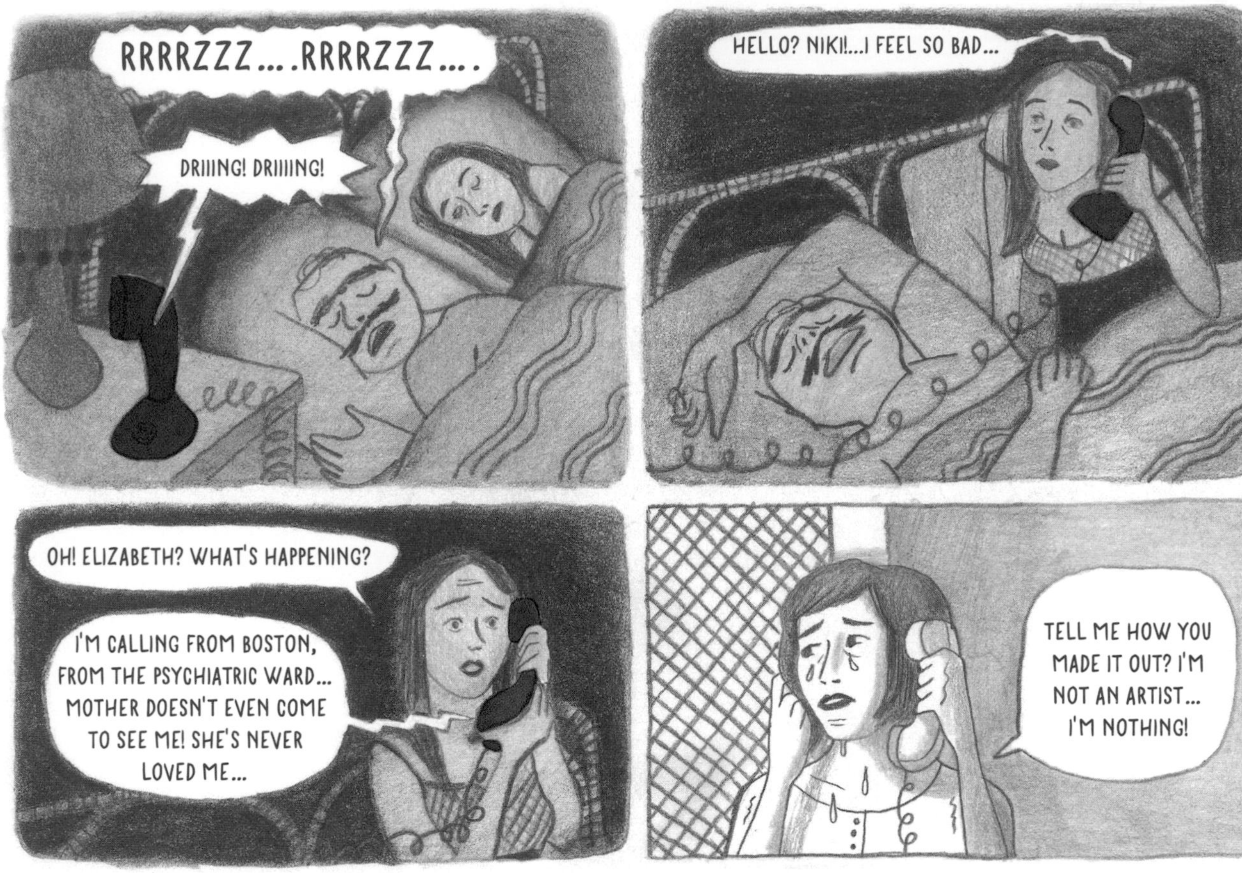
RRRRZZZ.....RRRRZZZ....
DRIIING! DRIIING!
HELLO? NIKI!...I FEEL SO BAD...
OH! ELIZABETH? WHAT'S HAPPENING?
I'M CALLING FROM BOSTON, FROM THE PSYCHIATRIC WARD... MOTHER DOESN'T EVEN COME TO SEE ME! SHE'S NEVER LOVED ME...
TELL ME HOW YOU MADE IT OUT? I'M NOT AN ARTIST... I'M NOTHING!

*A few weeks later, another phone call informed me of Elizabeth's "car accident"...*

THE HALIGON STATUE REPRODUCTION ATELIER, PÉRIGNY, FRANCE.

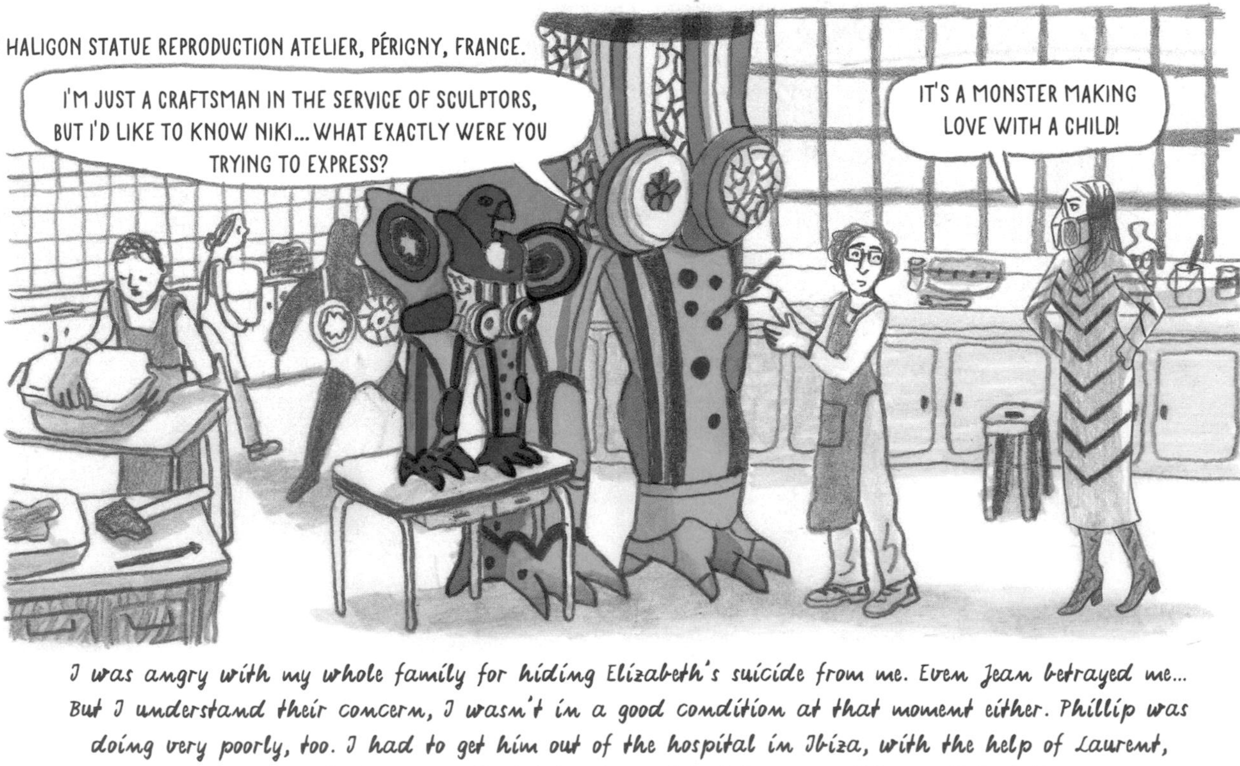
I'M JUST A CRAFTSMAN IN THE SERVICE OF SCULPTORS, BUT I'D LIKE TO KNOW NIKI... WHAT EXACTLY WERE YOU TRYING TO EXPRESS?
IT'S A MONSTER MAKING LOVE WITH A CHILD!

*I was angry with my whole family for hiding Elizabeth's suicide from me. Even Jean betrayed me... But I understand their concern, I wasn't in a good condition at that moment either. Phillip was doing very poorly, too. I had to get him out of the hospital in Ibiza, with the help of Laurent, my dear son-in-law. Now that he's at my side, I hope everything will be better...*

# CHAPTER 10

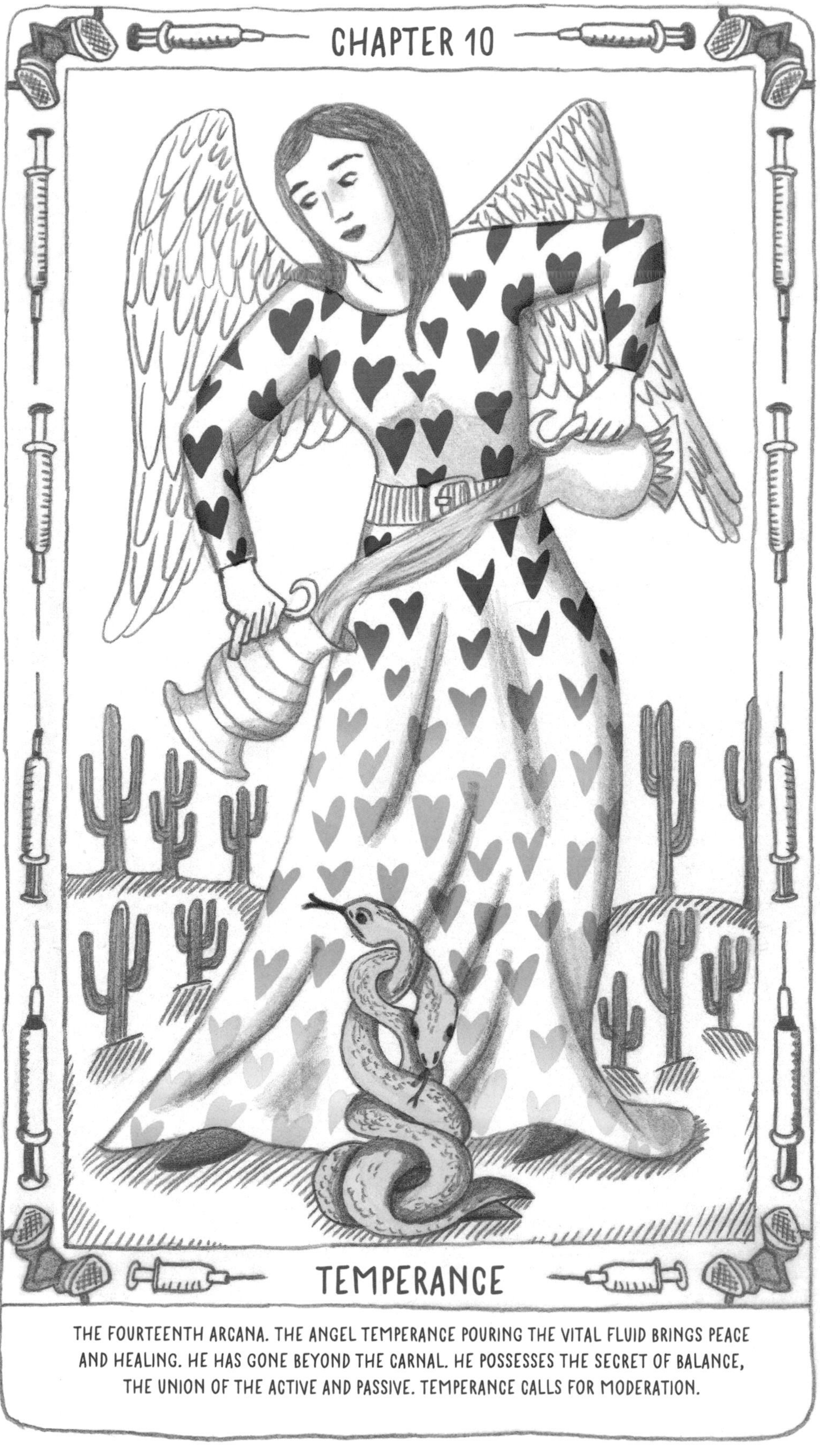

## TEMPERANCE

THE FOURTEENTH ARCANA. THE ANGEL TEMPERANCE POURING THE VITAL FLUID BRINGS PEACE AND HEALING. HE HAS GONE BEYOND THE CARNAL. HE POSSESSES THE SECRET OF BALANCE, THE UNION OF THE ACTIVE AND PASSIVE. TEMPERANCE CALLS FOR MODERATION.

END OF 1974: OUT OF BREATH.

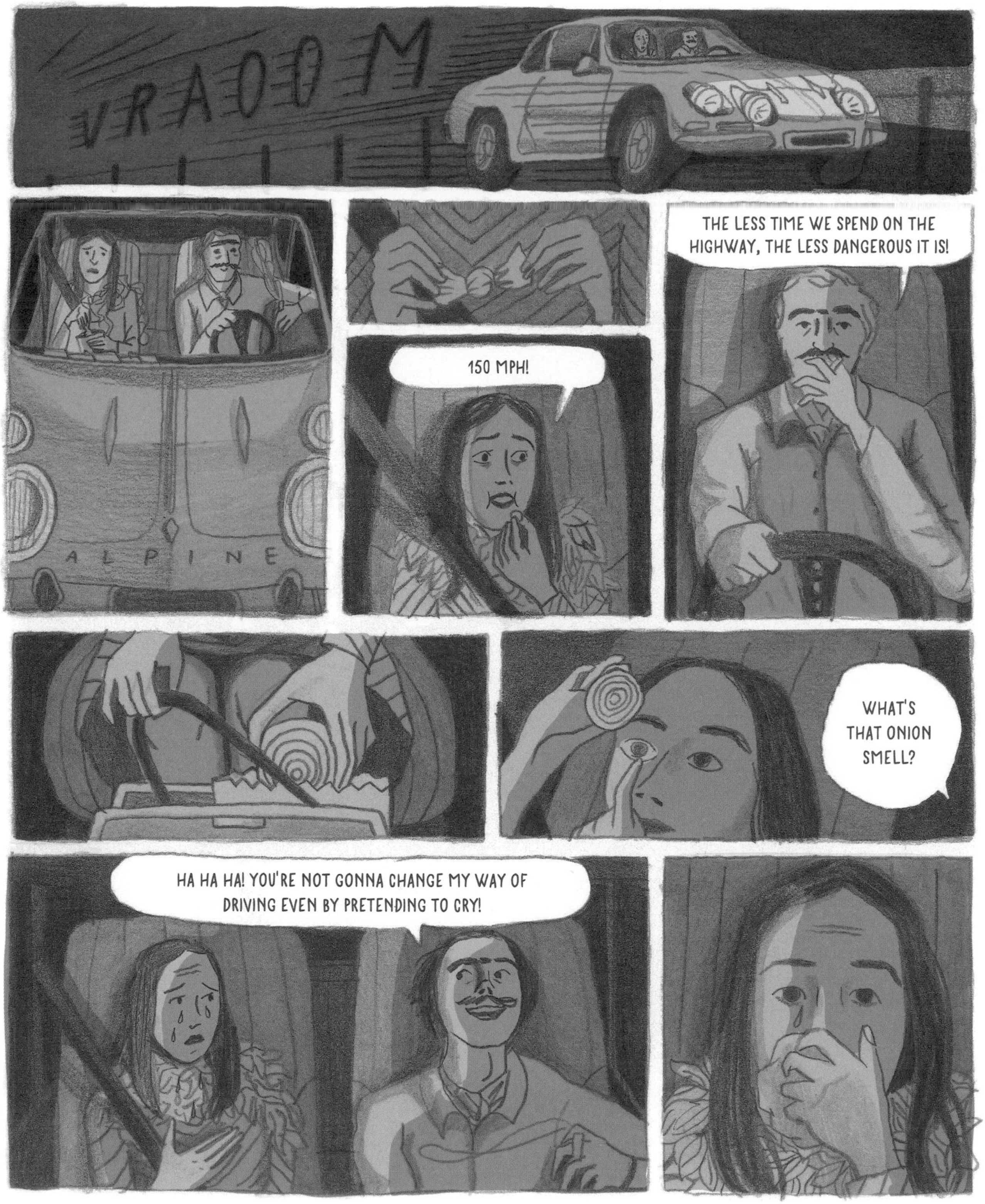
VRAOOM
ALPINE
THE LESS TIME WE SPEND ON THE HIGHWAY, THE LESS DANGEROUS IT IS!
150 MPH!
WHAT'S THAT ONION SMELL?
HA HA HA! YOU'RE NOT GONNA CHANGE MY WAY OF DRIVING EVEN BY PRETENDING TO CRY!

*Because my respiratory problems aren't giving me any respite, I went to take up residence in Switzerland for a while, to be closer to the "Tiefenauspital" in Bern, where Professor Silvio Barandun, an immunologist, had been treating me for a few years.*

In the end, I was transported there by ambulance because of a pulmonary abscess.
Micheline cried a lot. Jean and Marina spent nights at my bedside.

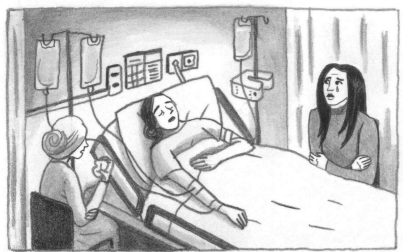

UNFORTUNATELY, HER CONDITION IS CRITICAL...

YOU'RE NOT LEAVING ME! DO YOU HEAR?! I FORBID YOU TO DIE!

...JEAN...! PROMISE ME YOU'LL BURN ME IN MY PRETTIEST DRESS, ON A BIG PYRE LIKE IN INDIA, AT THE FOOT OF THE "CYCLOPS"... AND TO HAVE A HUGE PARTY WITH ALL MY FRIENDS AND LOTS OF WINE!

AGNES IS AN ANGEL... OH! THERE'S TOO MUCH ELECTRICITY IN SPACE! ALL THE BEINGS OF THE COSMOS ARE CONNECTED BY ELECTRICITY AND THEY'RE TANGLED TOGETHER, TANGLED!

ALL THOSE CROSSED WIRES HAVE MADE A FINE MESS IN THE UNIVERSE! WE MUST EXCHANGE FLUIDS!... WHY HASN'T NIKI COME TO SEE ME?

ARIZONA DREAM. I ended up with pulmonary emphysema. I could barely walk a few yards without getting winded. The hospital radiologist told me I wouldn't make it past my fiftieth birthday. I left for two months in Arizona to rebuild my health. My whole family came to see me: Jean, Laura and Laurent Condominas, and little Bloum!

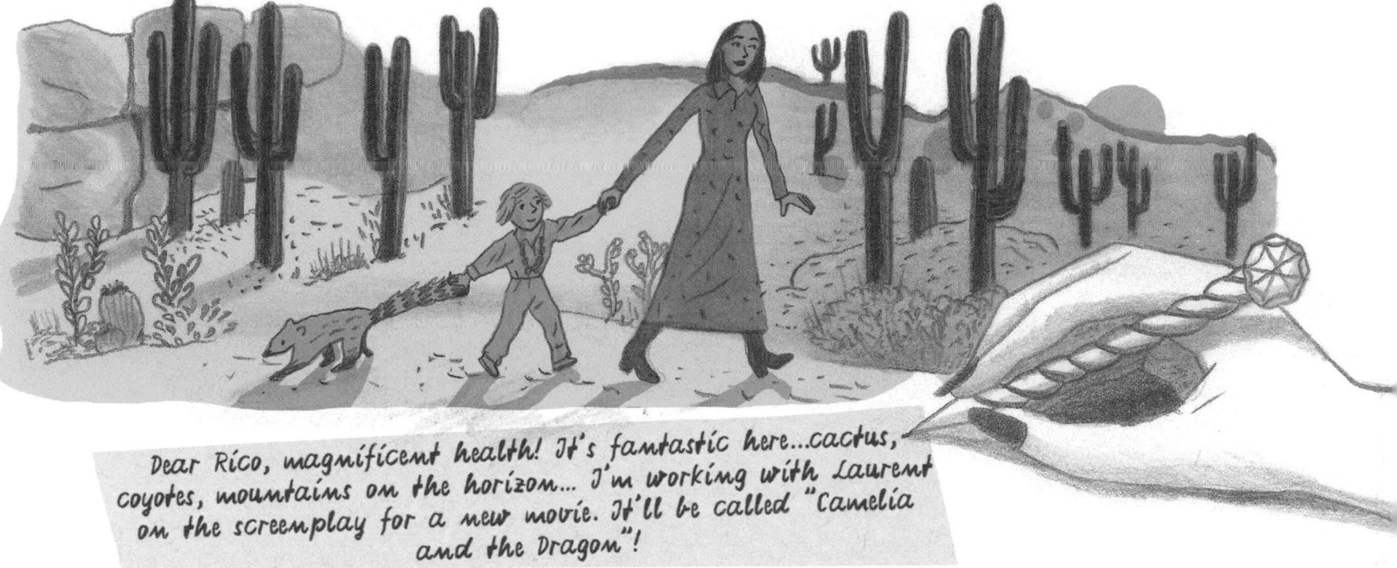
Dear Rico, magnificent health! It's fantastic here...cactus, coyotes, mountains on the horizon... I'm working with Laurent on the screenplay for a new movie. It'll be called "Camelia and the Dragon"!

1975, LA PUNT, SWITZERLAND, ALBERTINI HOUSE. Back in Europe, I had a prolonged stay in the Swiss Alps: still in search of pure air... To occupy my convalescence, I began animation work on "Camelia."

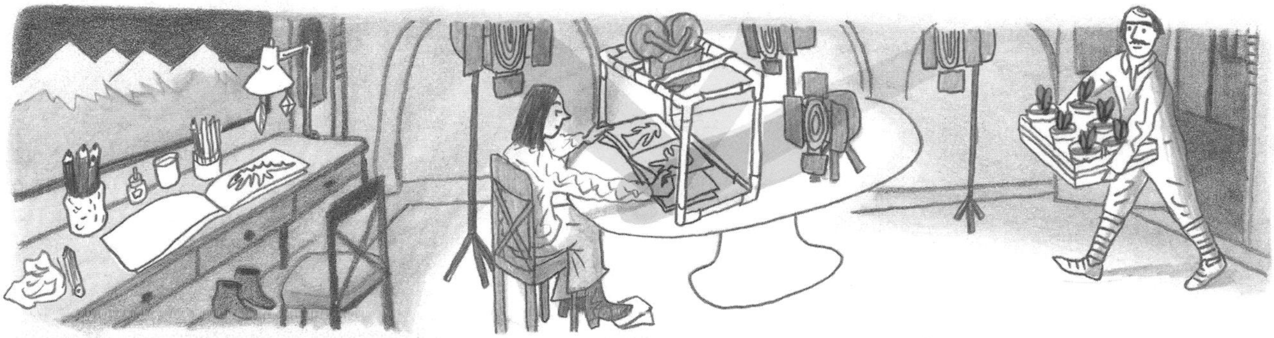

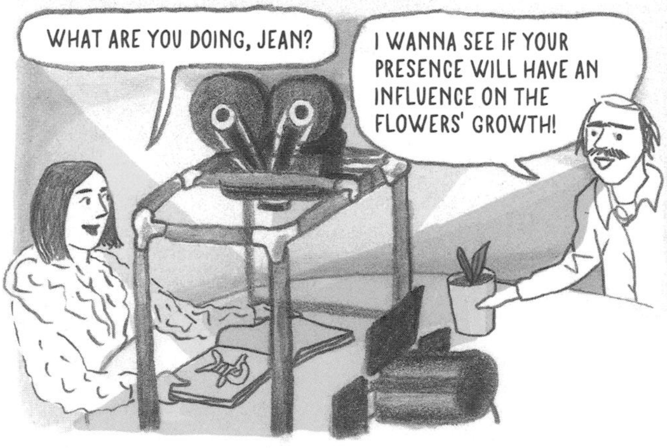
WHAT ARE YOU DOING, JEAN?
I WANNA SEE IF YOUR PRESENCE WILL HAVE AN INFLUENCE ON THE FLOWERS' GROWTH!

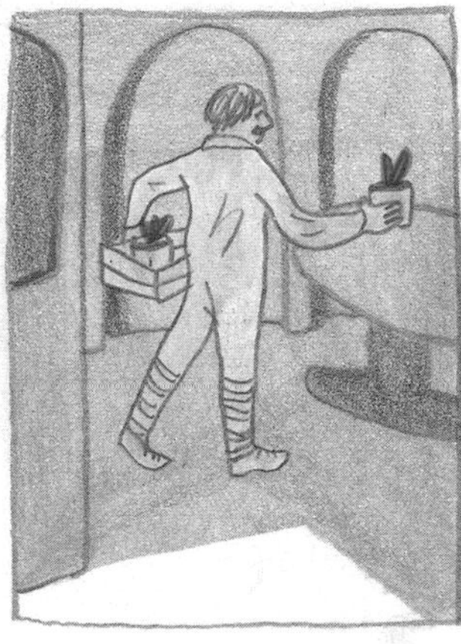

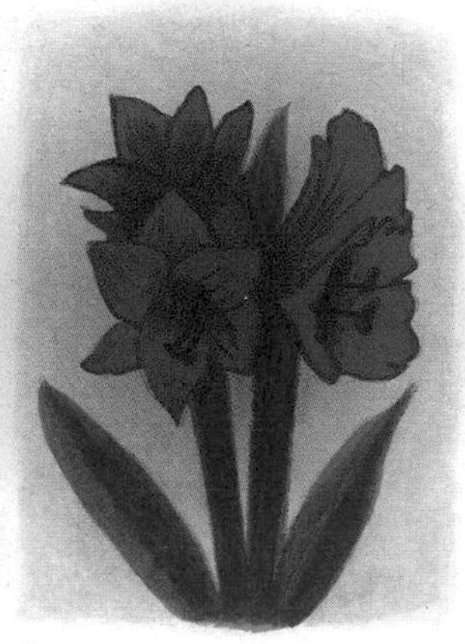

I felt myself gently coming back to life, like those bulb flowers that resume germination at winter's end...I was like Jean's amaryllises. I needed to be surrounded with love, music, and future projects! I listened to Bach, Mozart, and the Beatles. And the flowers that were close to me bloomed twice as fast as the ones isolated in an empty room!

ST. MORITZ, SWITZERLAND. *Jean was coming to see me less often. He was spending time with his son Milan.*

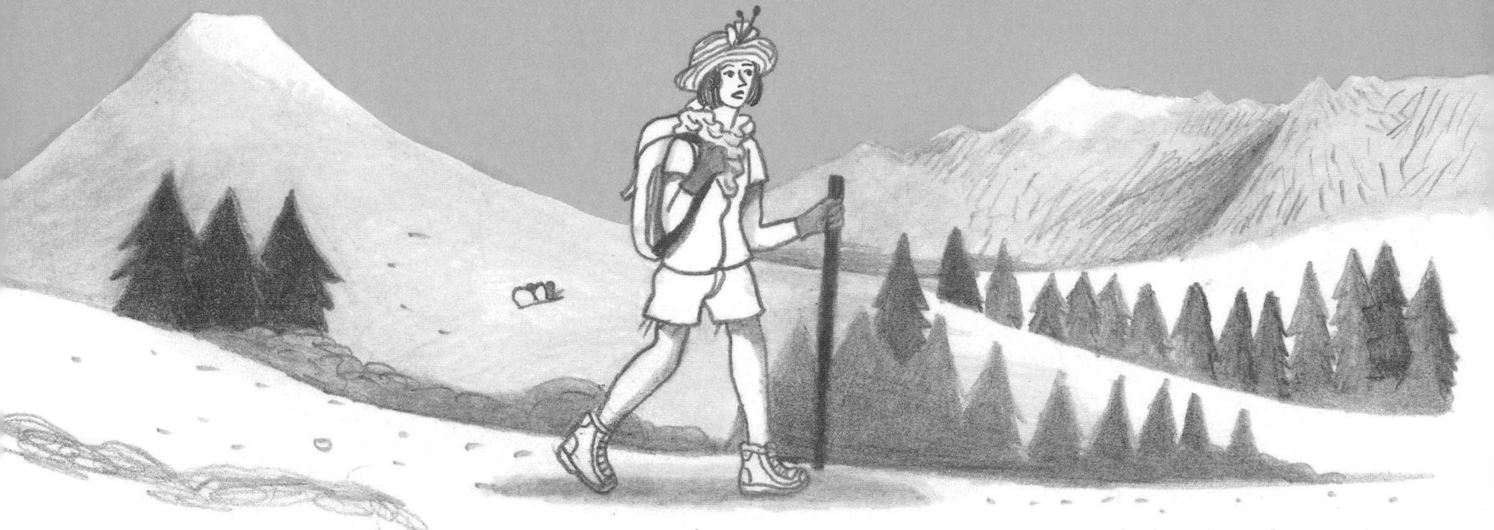

*He asked his friend Niki Lauda (another Niki!) to loan me her trainer, Günter Traub, the champion speed skater. That's how I spent a whole year gently regaining my wind, thanks to his advice.*

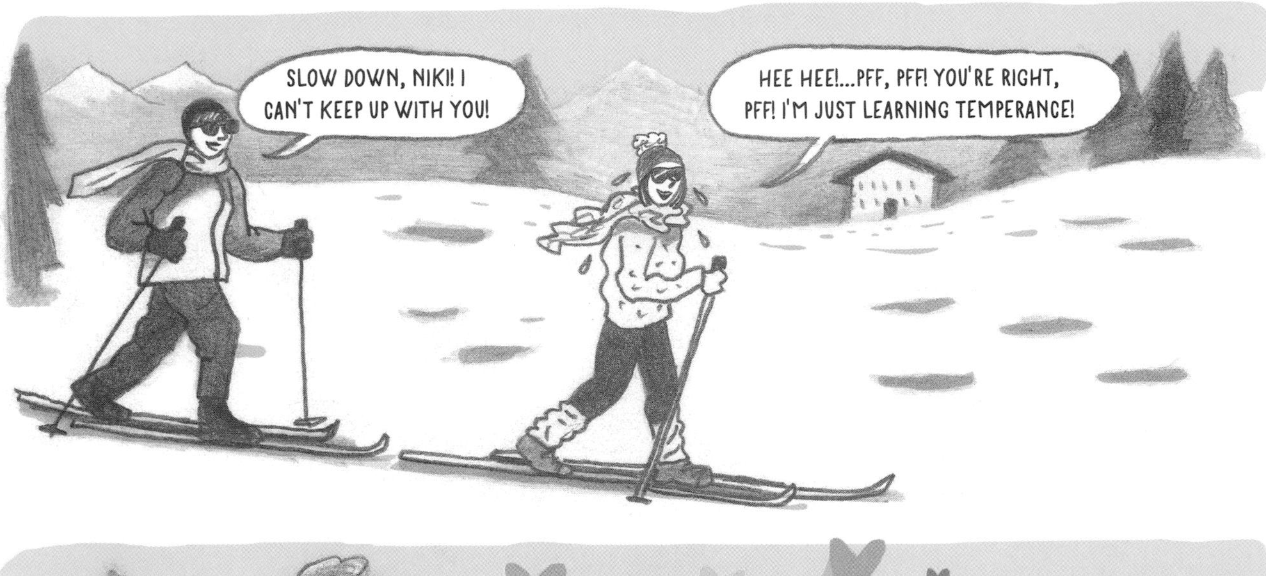
SLOW DOWN, NIKI! I CAN'T KEEP UP WITH YOU!
HEE HEE!...PFF, PFF! YOU'RE RIGHT, PFF! I'M JUST LEARNING TEMPERANCE!

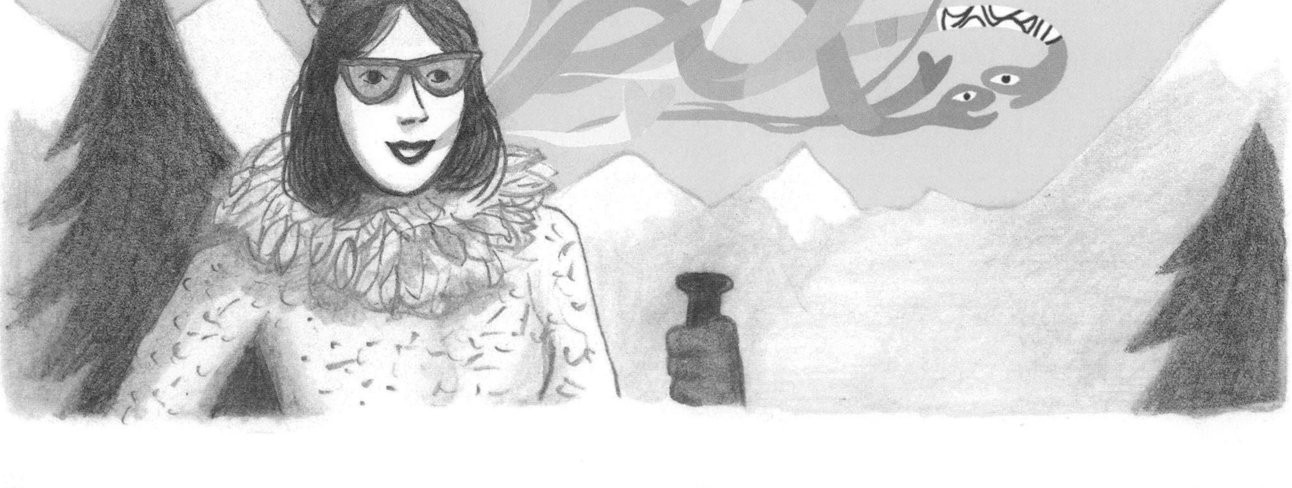

## CHAPTER 11

## THE STAR

THE SEVENTEENTH ARCANA, THE STAR SYMBOLIZES THE PERFECTION OF GIVING. IT'S A BEING ENTIRELY
CONNECTED TO THE WORLD, THE UNIVERSAL FORCE PASSES THROUGH IT. PURIFYING ITS PAST,
THE STAR ALSO PURIFIES ITS ENTOURAGE AND ITS FUTURE.

SUMMER 1975: AN EFFERVESCENT REMISSION!

*Despite the physicians' pessimistic predictions, I felt myself coming to life again with a new appetite for creation. My animated film project evolved into a real film shoot! No more settling of scores...This time, I was going to create a pure initiation story!*

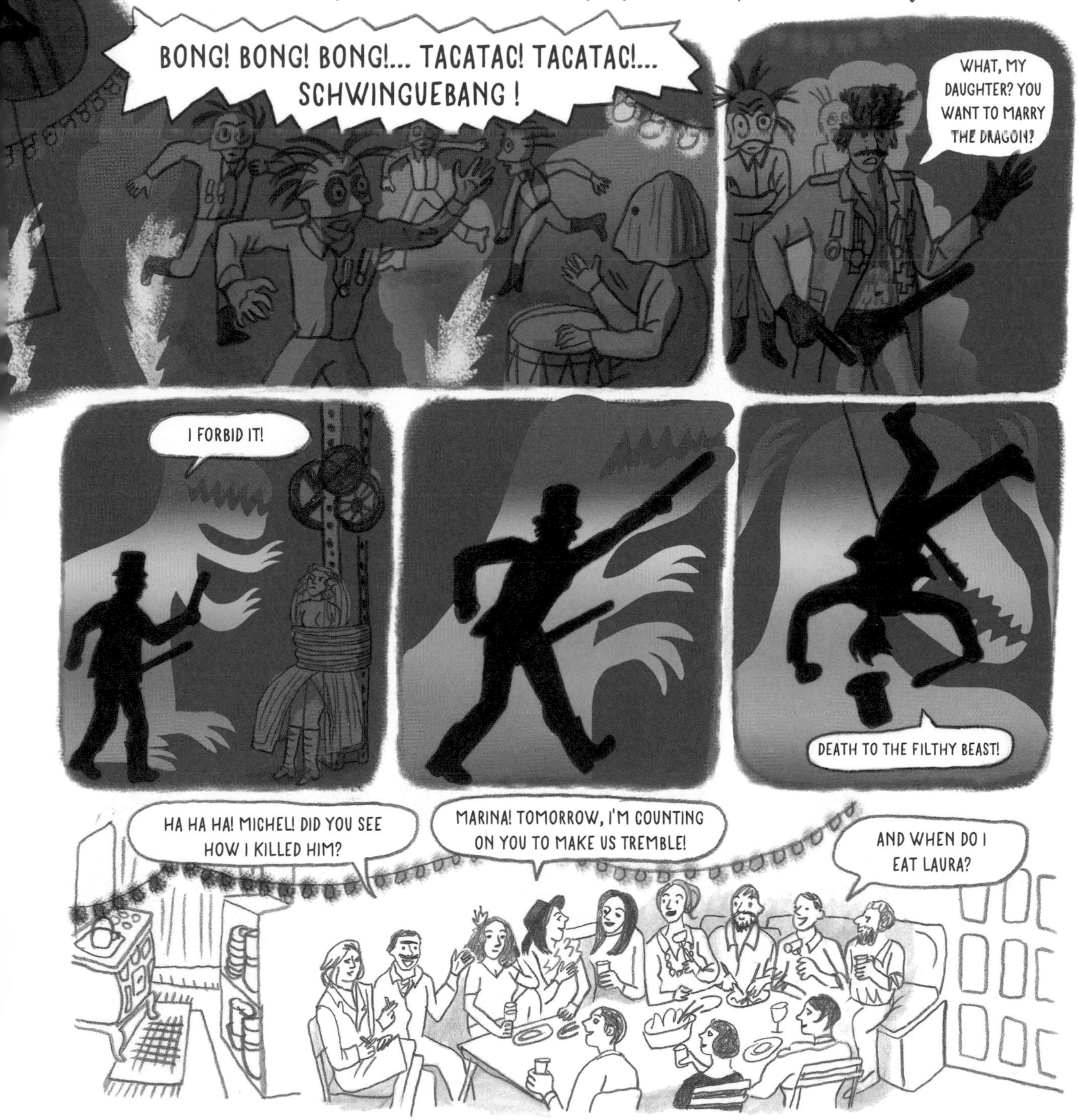
BONG! BONG! BONG!... TACATAC! TACATAC!... SCHWINGUEBANG !
WHAT, MY DAUGHTER? YOU WANT TO MARRY THE DRAGON?
I FORBID IT!
DEATH TO THE FILTHY BEAST!
HA HA HA! MICHEL! DID YOU SEE HOW I KILLED HIM?
MARINA! TOMORROW, I'M COUNTING ON YOU TO MAKE US TREMBLE!
AND WHEN DO I EAT LAURA?

*"Camelia and the Dragon" becomes "A Dream Longer than the Night," thanks to Frédéric Rossif, who helped me with the film editing. I assembled all of my friends and family around this film shoot: Laura in the title role, Jean playing her father as a crazy general, Laurent as Death, Marina Karella, the witch. I also had Silvio Barandun, Régine Deforges, Andrée Putman participating as actors.*

*Laura had made her acting debut in the role of Guinevere for "Lancelot of the Lake," a film by Robert Bresson, who'd received the Foreign Press award at Cannes... To say I'd refused that same role twenty years before!*

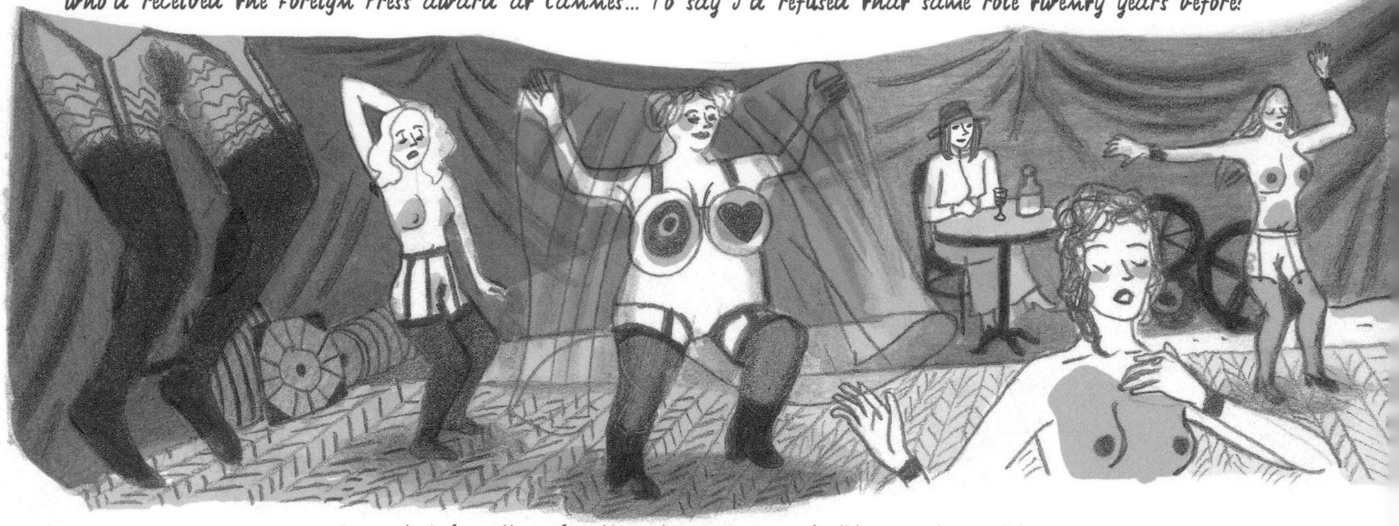

*I created furniture for the set, and Jean built several machines. Eva also positioned her disturbing fabric mannequins.*

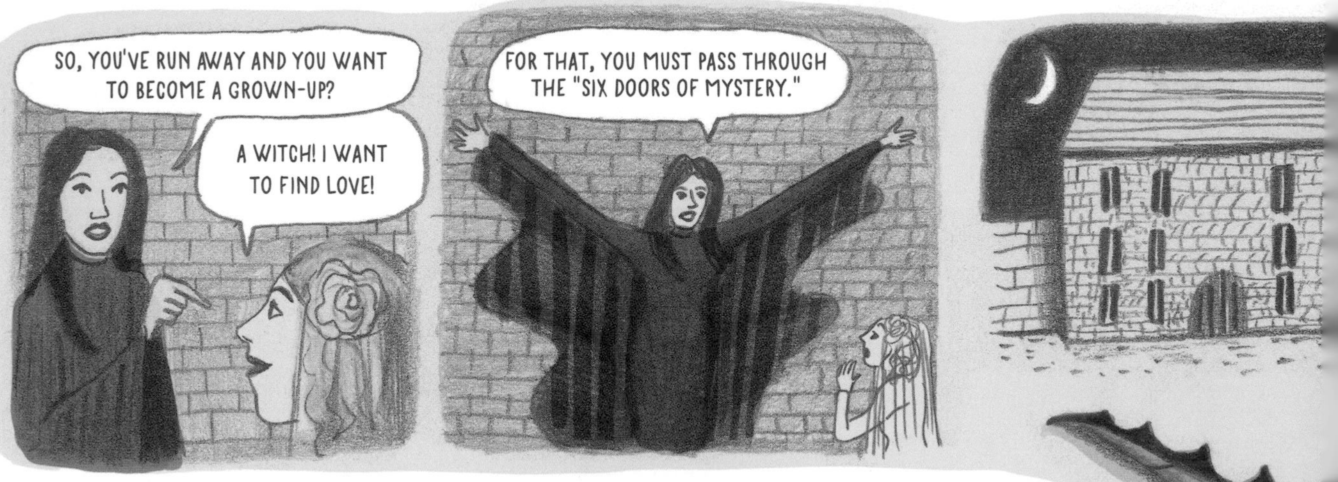
SO, YOU'VE RUN AWAY AND YOU WANT TO BECOME A GROWN-UP?
A WITCH! I WANT TO FIND LOVE!
FOR THAT, YOU MUST PASS THROUGH THE "SIX DOORS OF MYSTERY."

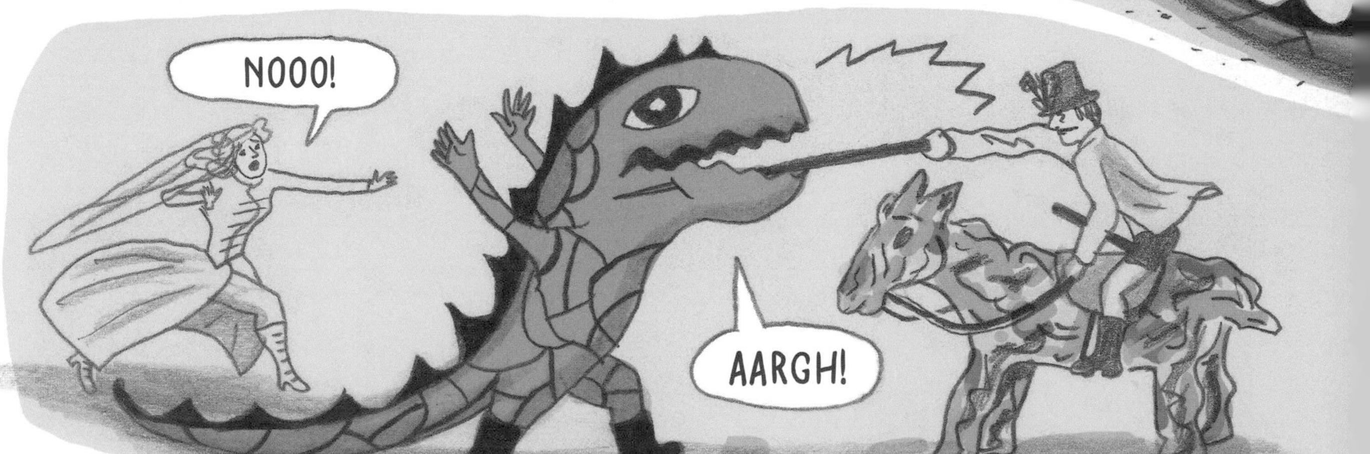
NOOO!
AARGH!

*Rico played the role of the dragon. The poor fellow sweated so much beneath his heavy costume, he lost a few pounds during the film shoot!*

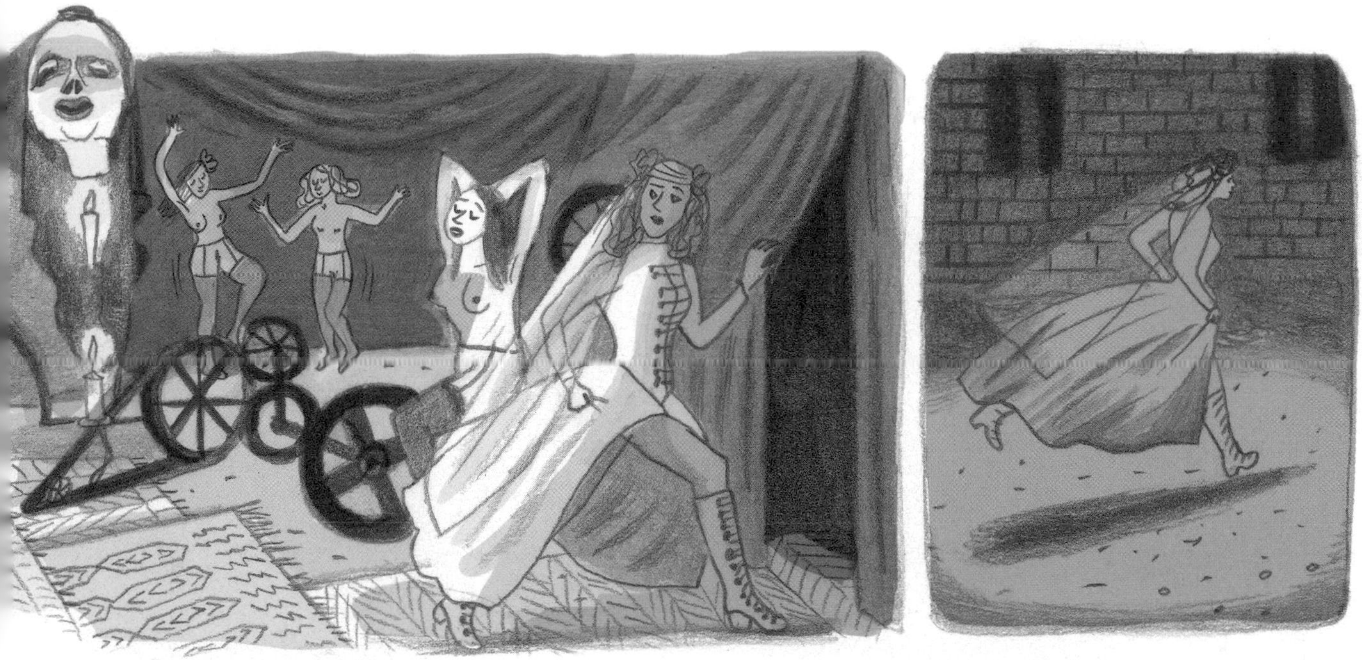

Everyone totally threw themselves into this astonishing adventure, into a whirlwind of collective creativity!

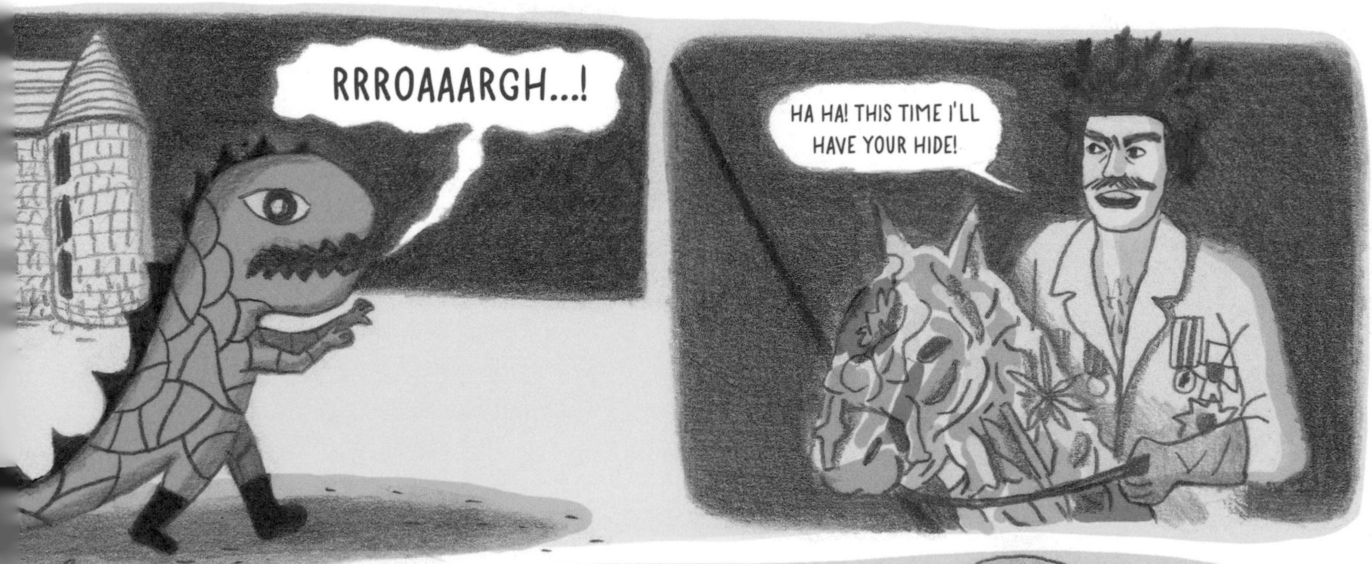
RRROAAARGH...!
HA HA! THIS TIME I'LL HAVE YOUR HIDE!

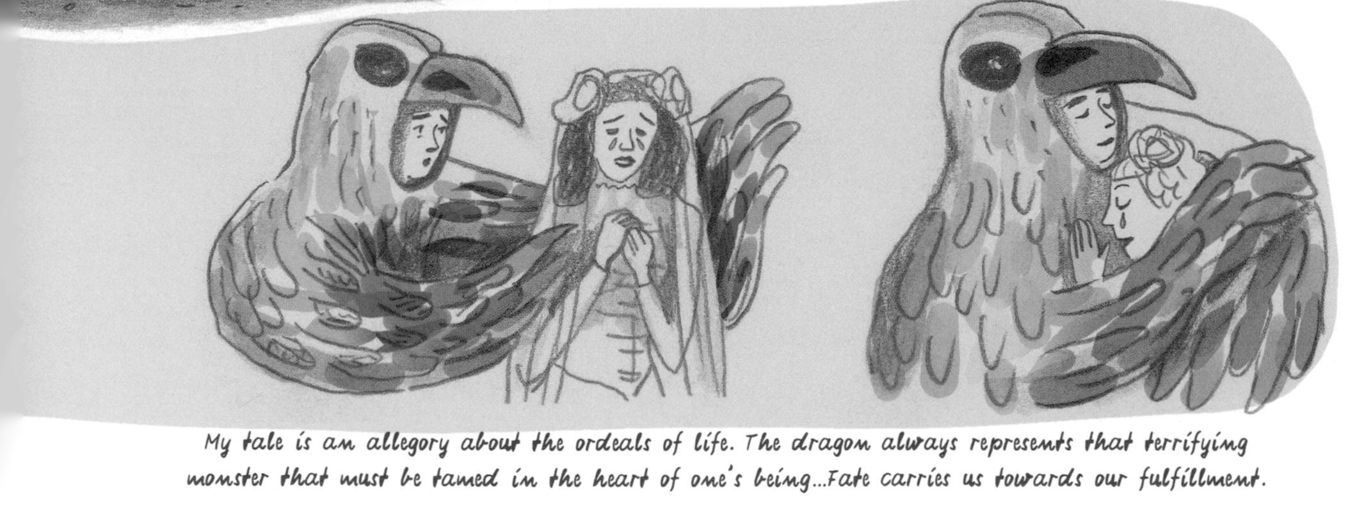

My tale is an allegory about the ordeals of life. The dragon always represents that terrifying monster that must be tamed in the heart of one's being...Fate carries us towards our fulfillment.

A CYCLOPS THAT DOESN'T LACK FOR AIR!

A CYCLOPS THAT DOESN'T LACK FOR AIR!

Jean was very absorbed by the construction of his "Cylops." He scoured the area's scrapyards, ever in search of material to salvage...one night, I accompanied him to the Beaubourg construction site; the adventure seemed very exciting to me!

LOOK AT THAT, NIKI! ISN'T IT FABULOUS?

BRRMMM...

THEY'RE LIKE THE MOUTHS OF HELL...

ARE YOU SURE IT'S NOT FOR USE IN CONSTRUCTION?

NIKIE, ACTIVATE THE LEVER FOR THE HYDRAULIC DUMP!

GO AHEAD NOW! LOWER THE BOX-BED!

"BONNIE AND CLYDE, BONNIE AND CLY...YDE"

# CHAPTER 12

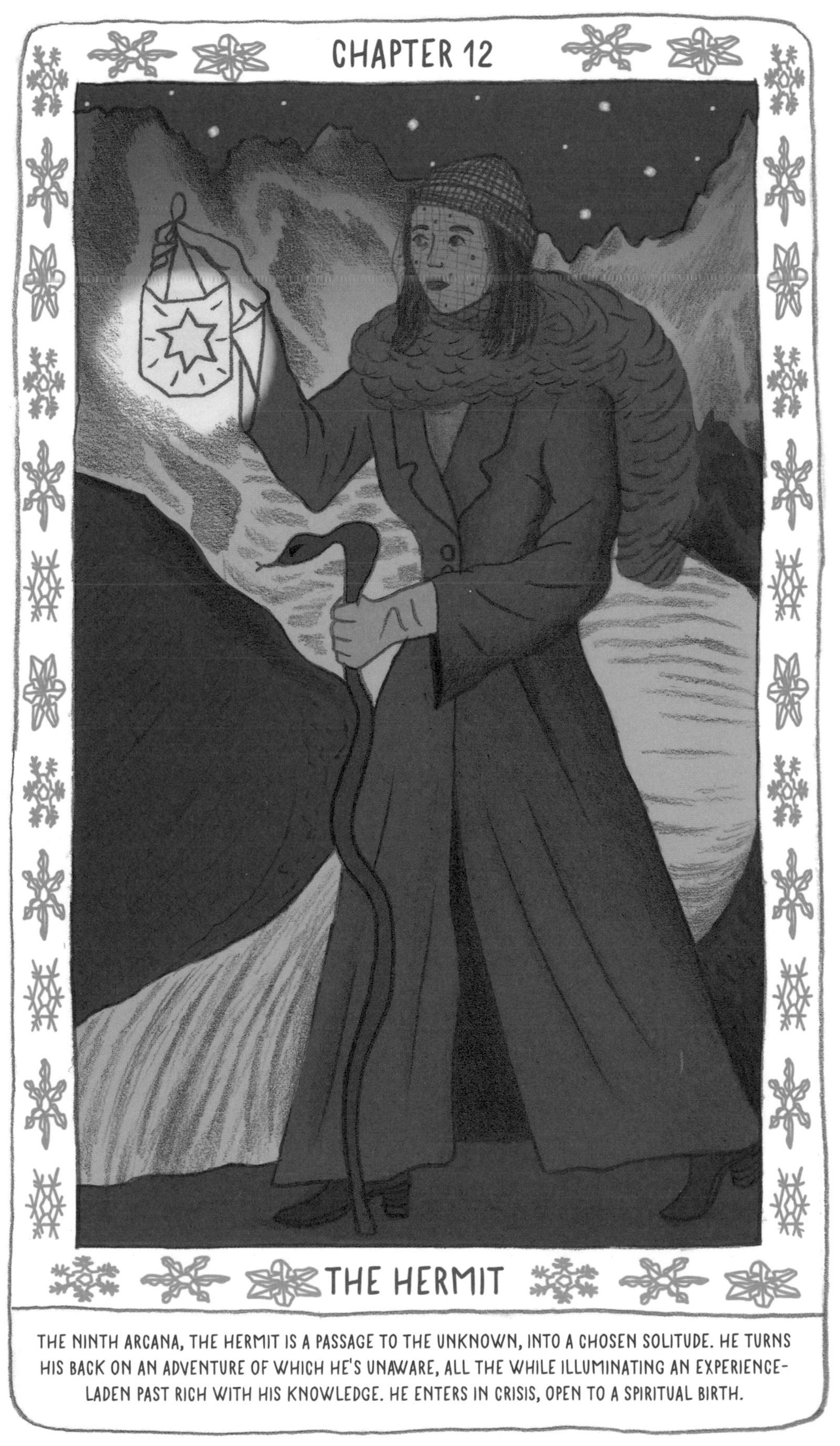

# THE HERMIT

THE NINTH ARCANA, THE HERMIT IS A PASSAGE TO THE UNKNOWN, INTO A CHOSEN SOLITUDE. HE TURNS HIS BACK ON AN ADVENTURE OF WHICH HE'S UNAWARE, ALL THE WHILE ILLUMINATING AN EXPERIENCE-LADEN PAST RICH WITH HIS KNOWLEDGE. HE ENTERS IN CRISIS, OPEN TO A SPIRITUAL BIRTH.

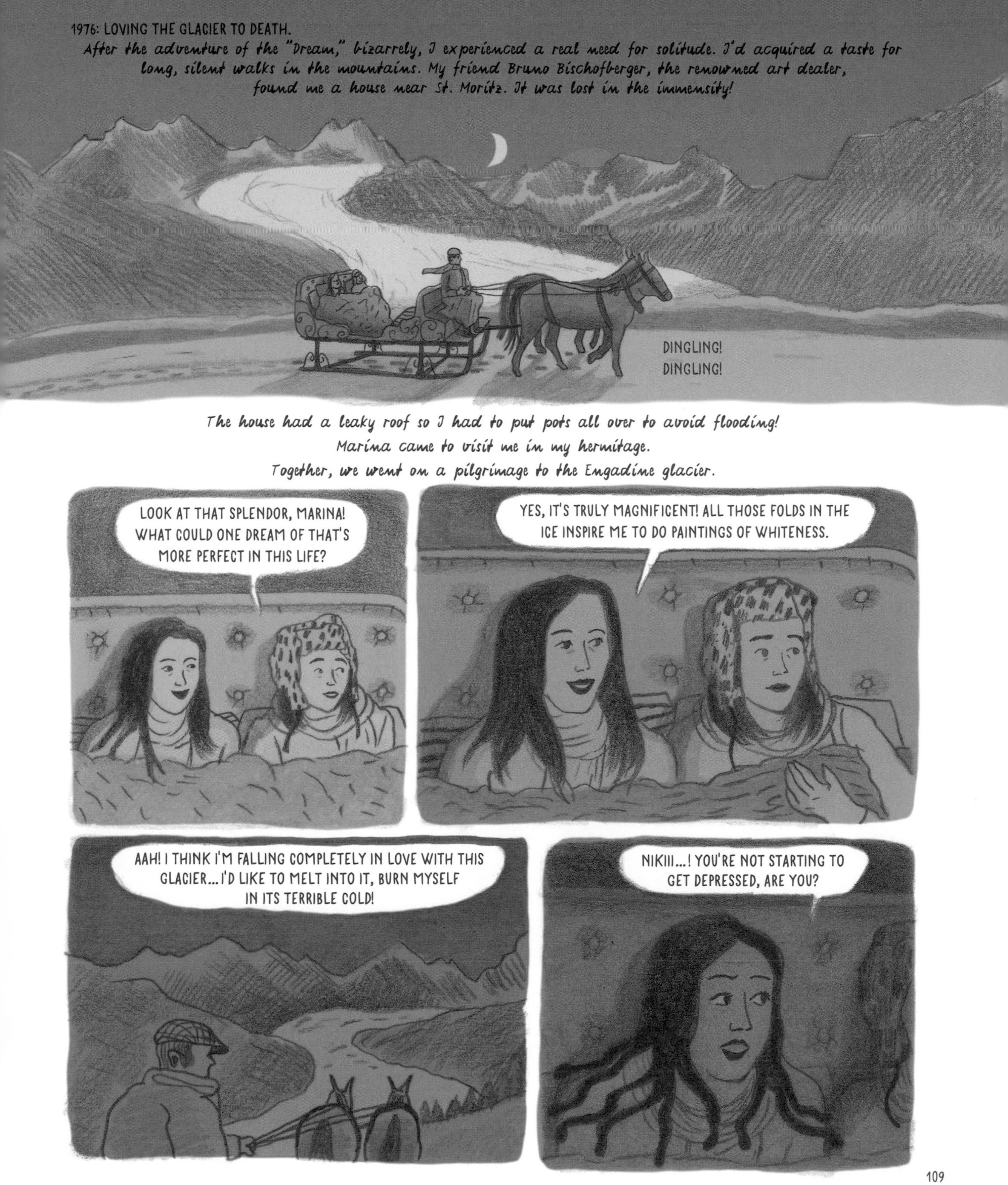
1976: LOVING THE GLACIER TO DEATH.
After the adventure of the "Dream," bizarrely, I experienced a real need for solitude. I'd acquired a taste for long, silent walks in the mountains. My friend Bruno Bischofberger, the renowned art dealer, found me a house near St. Moritz. It was lost in the immensity!
DINGLING! DINGLING!
The house had a leaky roof so I had to put pots all over to avoid flooding! Marina came to visit me in my hermitage. Together, we went on a pilgrimage to the Engadine glacier.
LOOK AT THAT SPLENDOR, MARINA! WHAT COULD ONE DREAM OF THAT'S MORE PERFECT IN THIS LIFE?
YES, IT'S TRULY MAGNIFICENT! ALL THOSE FOLDS IN THE ICE INSPIRE ME TO DO PAINTINGS OF WHITENESS.
AAH! I THINK I'M FALLING COMPLETELY IN LOVE WITH THIS GLACIER... I'D LIKE TO MELT INTO IT, BURN MYSELF IN ITS TERRIBLE COLD!
NIKIII...! YOU'RE NOT STARTING TO GET DEPRESSED, ARE YOU?

*I'd believed that the creation of Daddy would free me...be a therapy. And I was sinking again.*

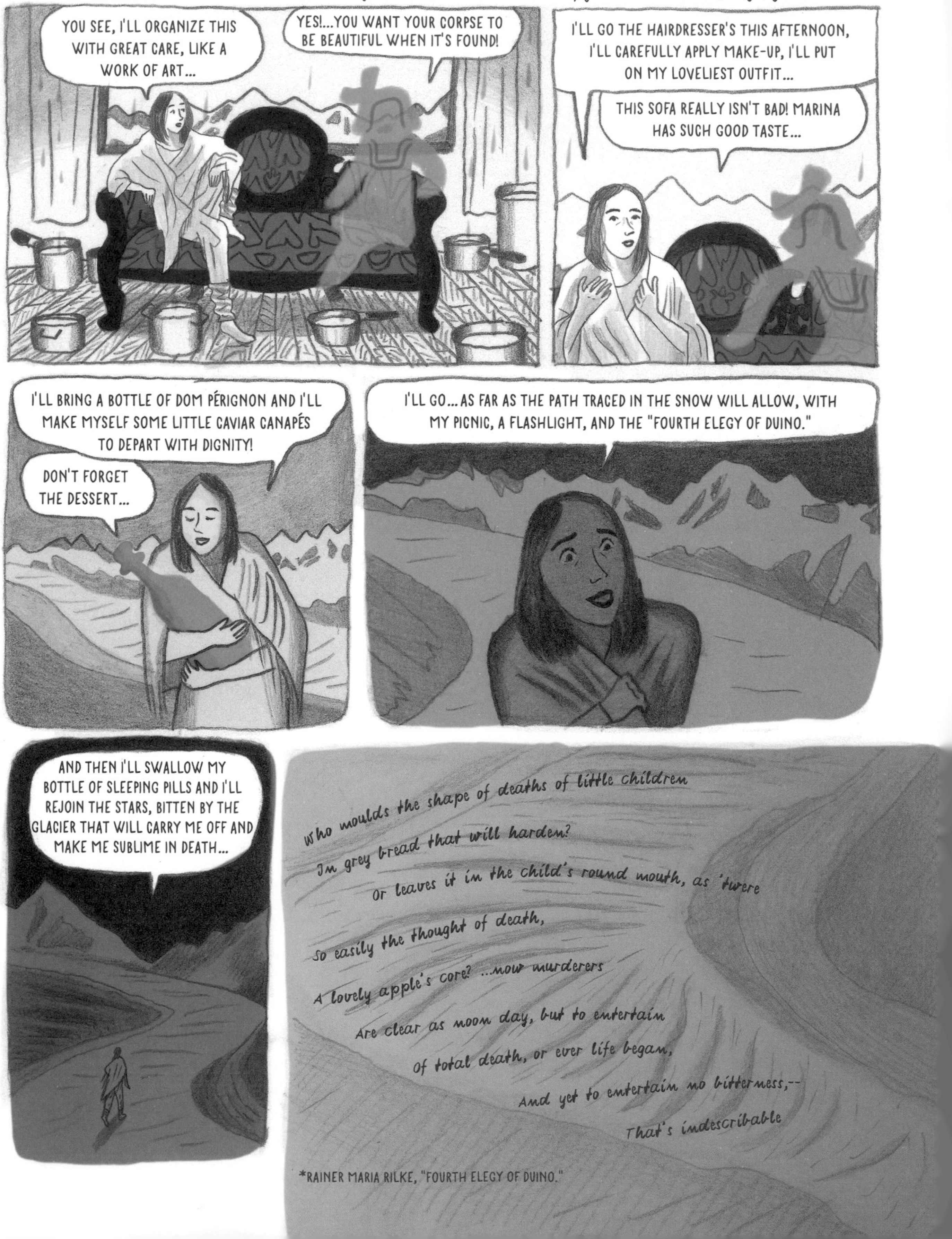

YOU SEE, I'LL ORGANIZE THIS WITH GREAT CARE, LIKE A WORK OF ART...
YES!...YOU WANT YOUR CORPSE TO BE BEAUTIFUL WHEN IT'S FOUND!
I'LL GO THE HAIRDRESSER'S THIS AFTERNOON, I'LL CAREFULLY APPLY MAKE-UP, I'LL PUT ON MY LOVELIEST OUTFIT...
THIS SOFA REALLY ISN'T BAD! MARINA HAS SUCH GOOD TASTE...
I'LL BRING A BOTTLE OF DOM PÉRIGNON AND I'LL MAKE MYSELF SOME LITTLE CAVIAR CANAPÉS TO DEPART WITH DIGNITY!
DON'T FORGET THE DESSERT...
I'LL GO... AS FAR AS THE PATH TRACED IN THE SNOW WILL ALLOW, WITH MY PICNIC, A FLASHLIGHT, AND THE "FOURTH ELEGY OF DUINO."
AND THEN I'LL SWALLOW MY BOTTLE OF SLEEPING PILLS AND I'LL REJOIN THE STARS, BITTEN BY THE GLACIER THAT WILL CARRY ME OFF AND MAKE ME SUBLIME IN DEATH...
Who moulds the shape of deaths of little children
In grey bread that will harden?
Or leaves it in the child's round mouth, as 'twere
So easily the thought of death,
A lovely apple's core? ...now murderers
Are clear as noon day, but to entertain
Of total death, or ever life began,
And yet to entertain no bitterness,--
That's indescribable
*RAINER MARIA RILKE, "FOURTH ELEGY OF DUINO."

*Forty-eight hours before the date I'd chosen for my suicide, I unwillingly found myself in an ambulance en route to the Bern hospital with pneumonia! I was so disappointed about that missed appointment I couldn't speak for three days...*

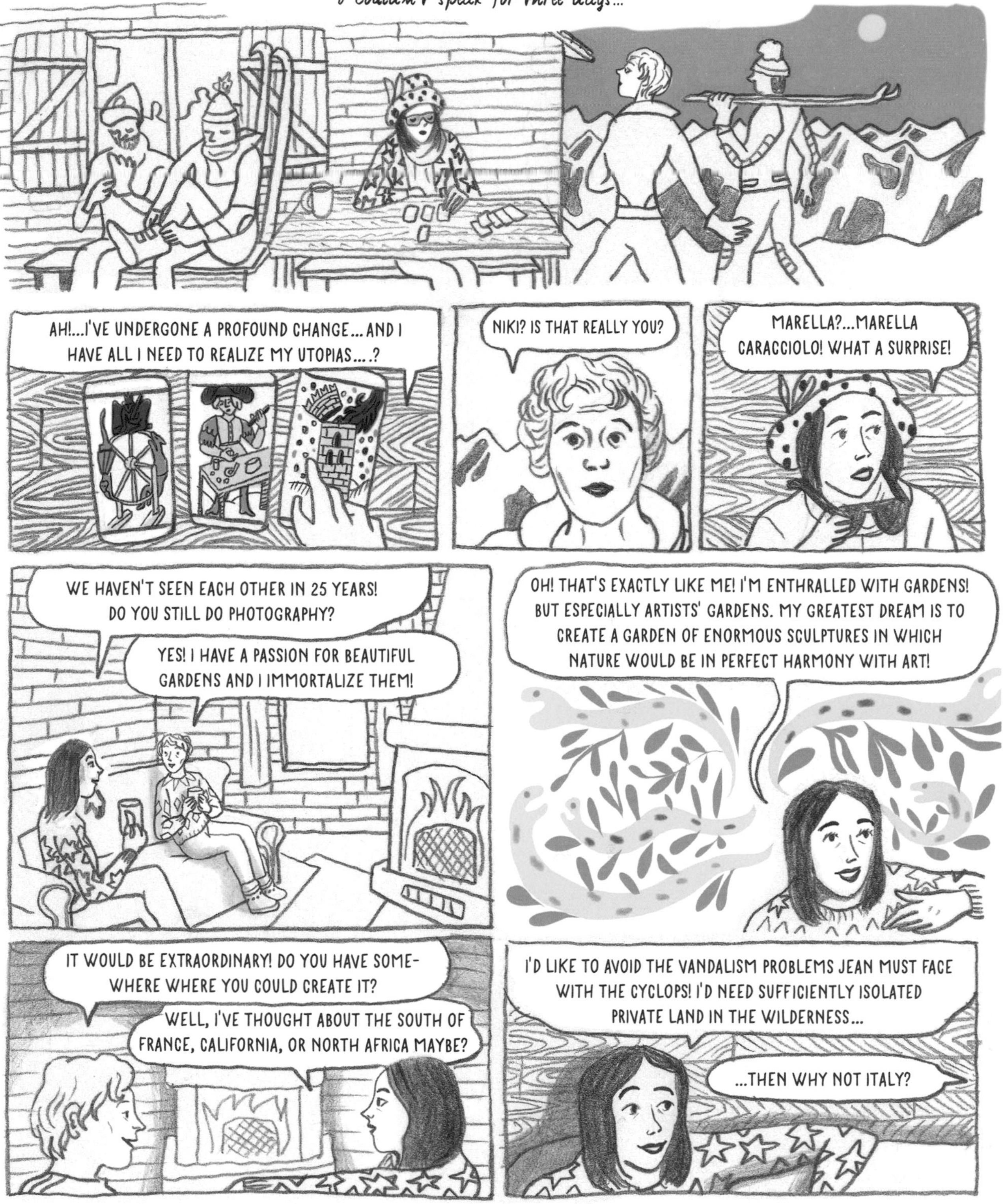
AH!...I'VE UNDERGONE A PROFOUND CHANGE... AND I HAVE ALL I NEED TO REALIZE MY UTOPIAS... .?
NIKI? IS THAT REALLY YOU?
MARELLA?...MARELLA CARACCIOLO! WHAT A SURPRISE!
WE HAVEN'T SEEN EACH OTHER IN 25 YEARS! DO YOU STILL DO PHOTOGRAPHY?
YES! I HAVE A PASSION FOR BEAUTIFUL GARDENS AND I IMMORTALIZE THEM!
OH! THAT'S EXACTLY LIKE ME! I'M ENTHRALLED WITH GARDENS! BUT ESPECIALLY ARTISTS' GARDENS. MY GREATEST DREAM IS TO CREATE A GARDEN OF ENORMOUS SCULPTURES IN WHICH NATURE WOULD BE IN PERFECT HARMONY WITH ART!
IT WOULD BE EXTRAORDINARY! DO YOU HAVE SOMEWHERE WHERE YOU COULD CREATE IT?
WELL, I'VE THOUGHT ABOUT THE SOUTH OF FRANCE, CALIFORNIA, OR NORTH AFRICA MAYBE?
I'D LIKE TO AVOID THE VANDALISM PROBLEMS JEAN MUST FACE WITH THE CYCLOPS! I'D NEED SUFFICIENTLY ISOLATED PRIVATE LAND IN THE WILDERNESS...
...THEN WHY NOT ITALY?

*The patron and wife of Giovanni Agnelli, heir of the Fiat group, Marella is also a princess! She told me about her brothers Carlo and Nicolai, who owned a huge, unused plot of land in Tuscany...*

THE MARQUIS POET...

*The new prospect of creating this garden, which had obsessed me for so many years, acted like a resurrection on me! I began to consult a phenomenal quantity of books and documents on the different religions of the world. I wanted to create a "Garden of the Gods" that would offer a universal synthesis of mysticisms...*

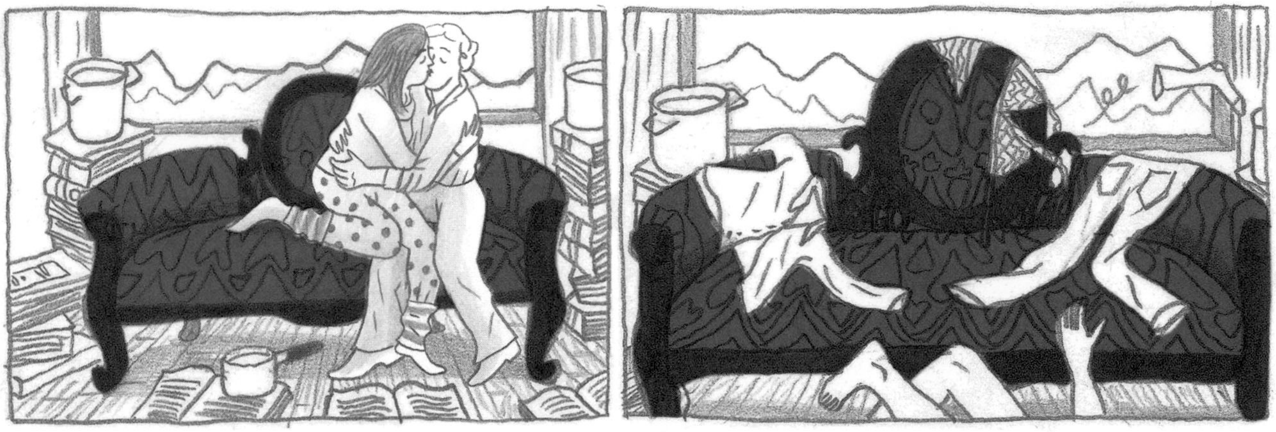

*Marina sent me a young poet friend, Constantin Mulgrave, to help me in my research, and also to keep me company. We fell madly in love with one another...I'm really not made for living alone!*

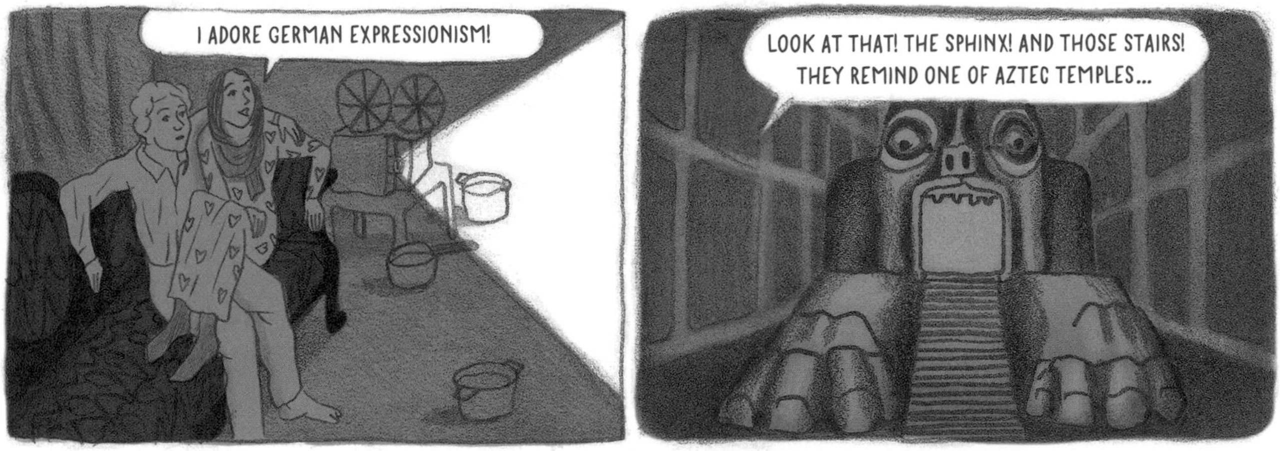
I ADORE GERMAN EXPRESSIONISM!
LOOK AT THAT! THE SPHINX! AND THOSE STAIRS! THEY REMIND ONE OF AZTEC TEMPLES...

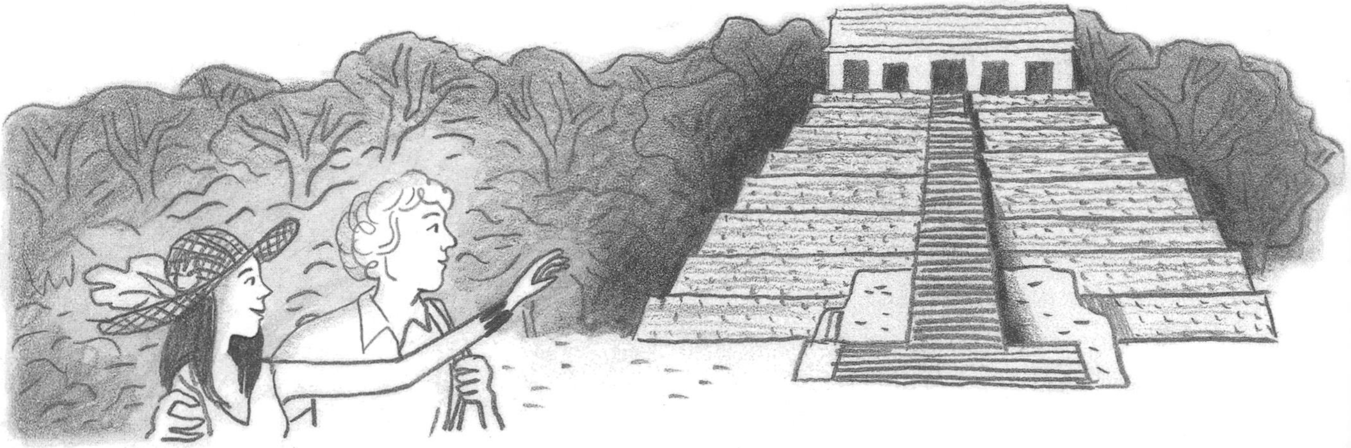

*At the end of 1977, after the opening of my exhibition in New York at the Gimpel Weitzenhoffer Gallery, we took off for a trip into pre-Columbian times...Palenque impressed me greatly. I'd draw inspiration from it for my garden!*

# CHAPTER 13

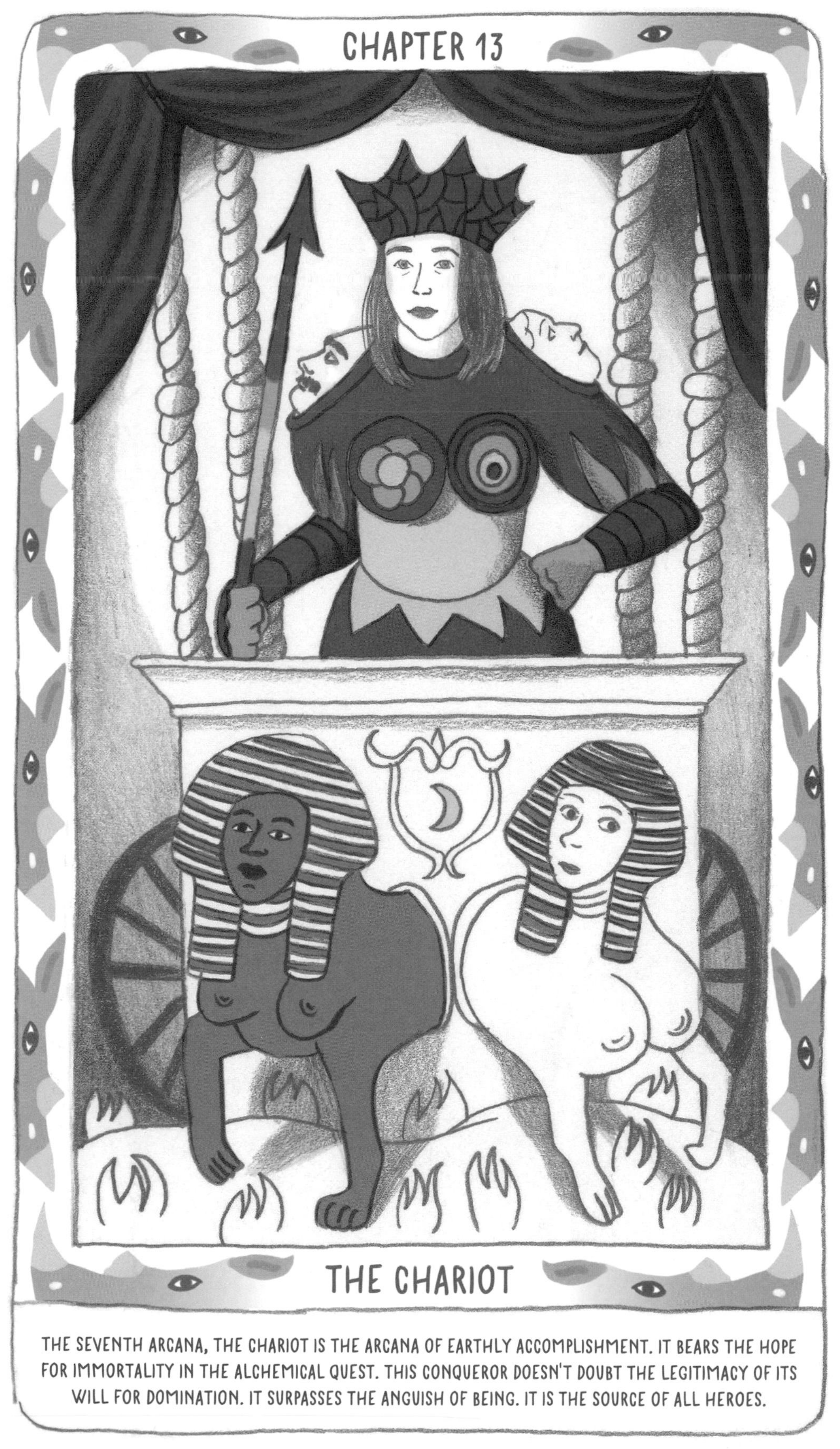

## THE CHARIOT

THE SEVENTH ARCANA, THE CHARIOT IS THE ARCANA OF EARTHLY ACCOMPLISHMENT. IT BEARS THE HOPE FOR IMMORTALITY IN THE ALCHEMICAL QUEST. THIS CONQUEROR DOESN'T DOUBT THE LEGITIMACY OF ITS WILL FOR DOMINATION. IT SURPASSES THE ANGUISH OF BEING. IT IS THE SOURCE OF ALL HEROES.

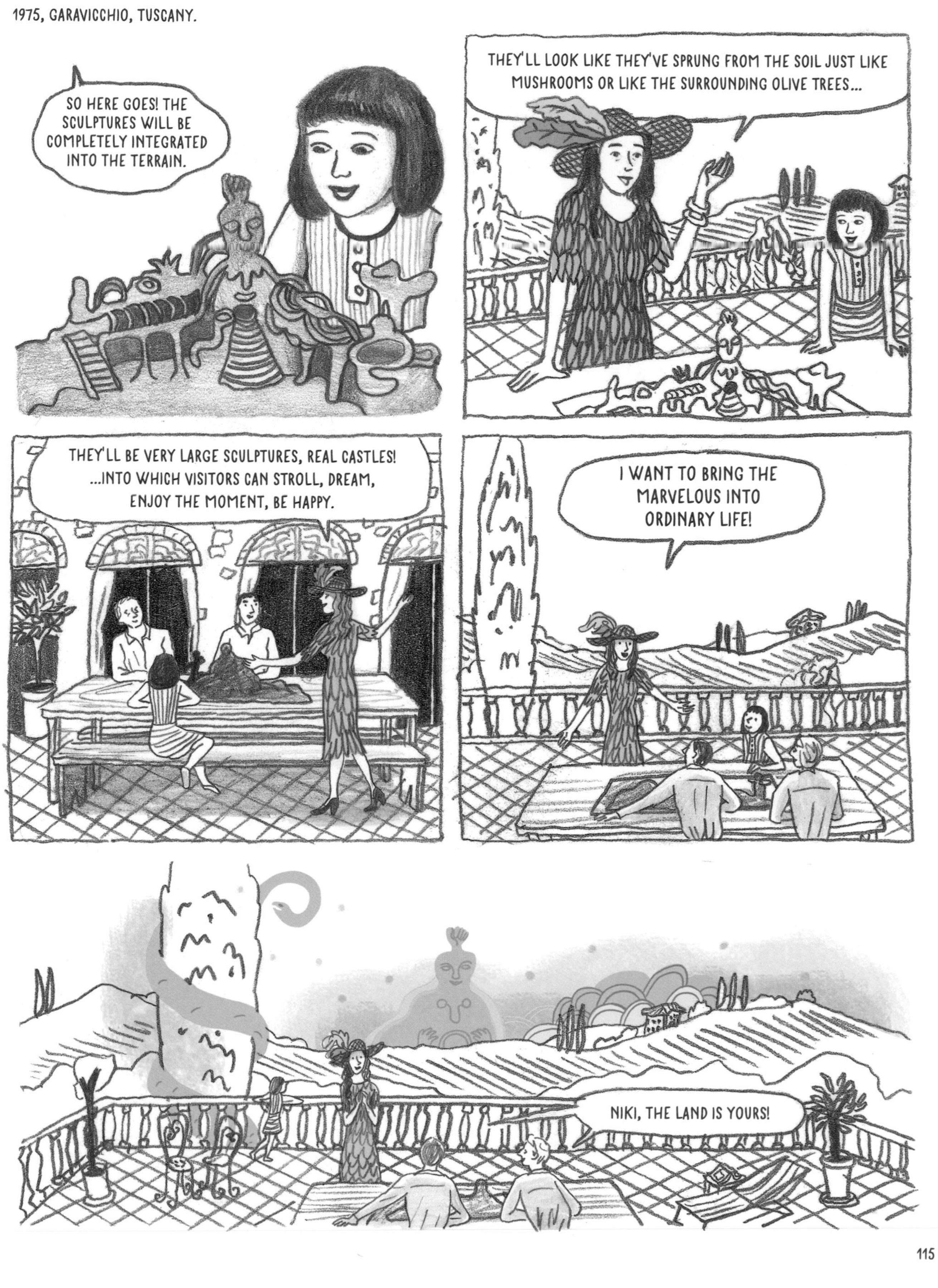
1975, GARAVICCHIO, TUSCANY.
SO HERE GOES! THE SCULPTURES WILL BE COMPLETELY INTEGRATED INTO THE TERRAIN.
THEY'LL LOOK LIKE THEY'VE SPRUNG FROM THE SOIL JUST LIKE MUSHROOMS OR LIKE THE SURROUNDING OLIVE TREES...
THEY'LL BE VERY LARGE SCULPTURES, REAL CASTLES! ...INTO WHICH VISITORS CAN STROLL, DREAM, ENJOY THE MOMENT, BE HAPPY.
I WANT TO BRING THE MARVELOUS INTO ORDINARY LIFE!
NIKI, THE LAND IS YOURS!

MAY 1978: MOTHER, I DEVOURED YOU.

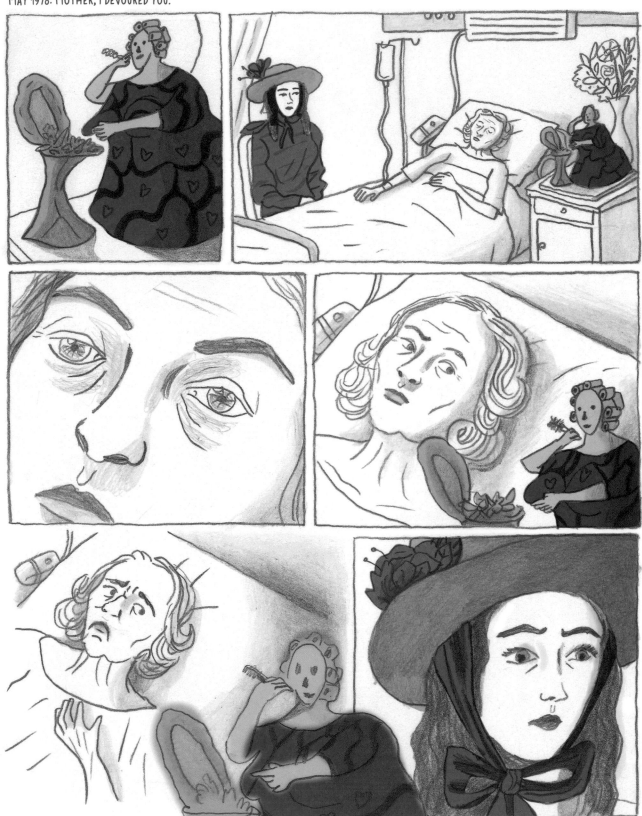

*Mother has died. Jean likes to say I finished her off because she didn't appreciate my farewell gift!*

*Here we are back in Soisy, France. I'd moved Constantin into my home, and we continued to work a lot. Jean was living in Switzerland most of the time.*

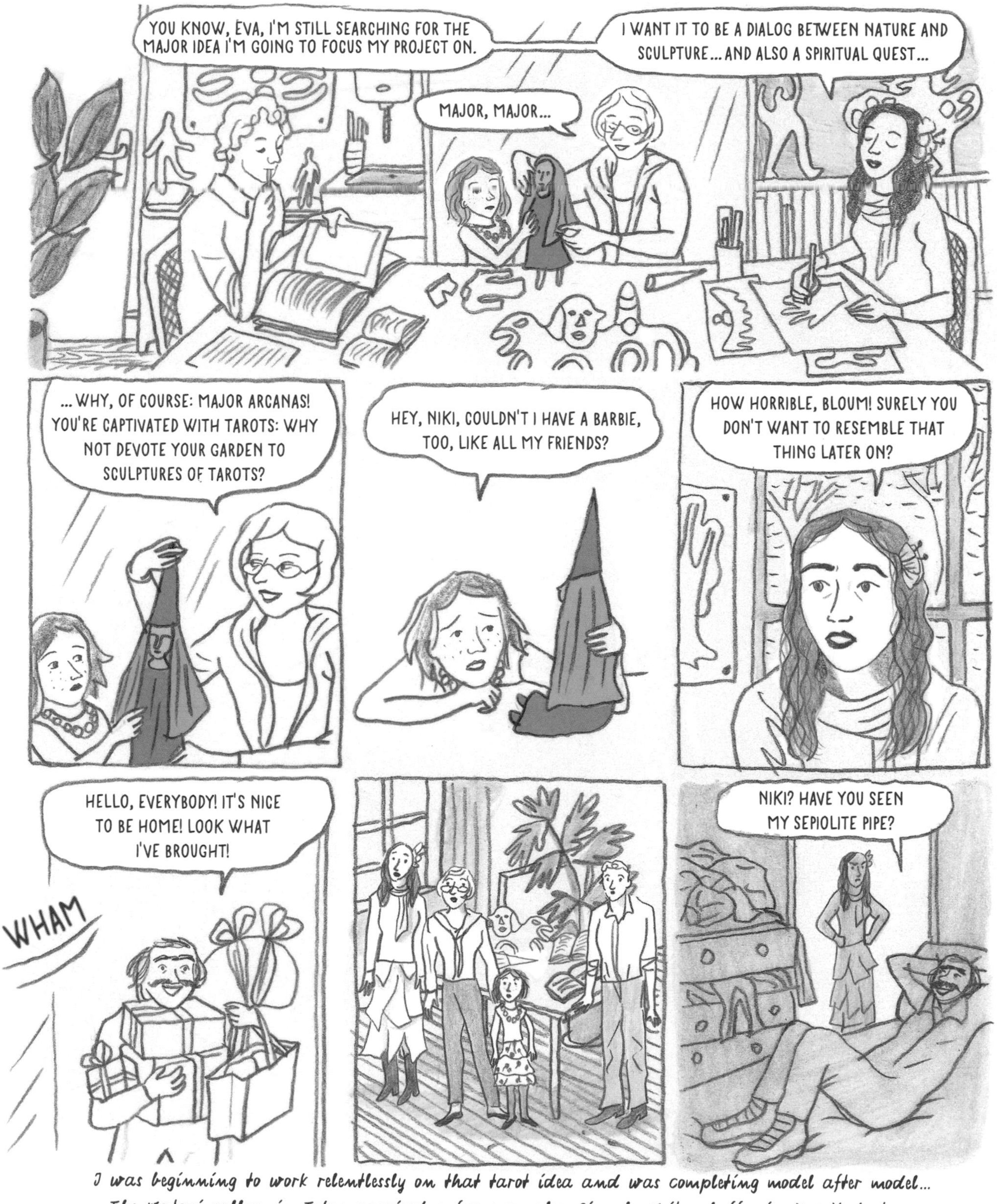

YOU KNOW, EVA, I'M STILL SEARCHING FOR THE MAJOR IDEA I'M GOING TO FOCUS MY PROJECT ON.
I WANT IT TO BE A DIALOG BETWEEN NATURE AND SCULPTURE... AND ALSO A SPIRITUAL QUEST...
MAJOR, MAJOR...
...WHY, OF COURSE: MAJOR ARCANAS! YOU'RE CAPTIVATED WITH TAROTS: WHY NOT DEVOTE YOUR GARDEN TO SCULPTURES OF TAROTS?
HEY, NIKI, COULDN'T I HAVE A BARBIE, TOO, LIKE ALL MY FRIENDS?
HOW HORRIBLE, BLOUM! SURELY YOU DON'T WANT TO RESEMBLE THAT THING LATER ON?
HELLO, EVERYBODY! IT'S NICE TO BE HOME! LOOK WHAT I'VE BROUGHT!
WHAM
NIKI? HAVE YOU SEEN MY SEPIOLITE PIPE?


*I was beginning to work relentlessly on that tarot idea and was completing model after model... The Watari gallery in Tokyo acquired a few examples, Gimpel Weitzenhoffer in New York, too. I felt close to something that resembled signs of completion!*

1979: THE EPIC BEGINS!

*What euphoria carried me away when, FINALLY, the trucks loaded with material arrived at the site of the future garden! I began by having the soil leveled, then had water and electricity brought in.*

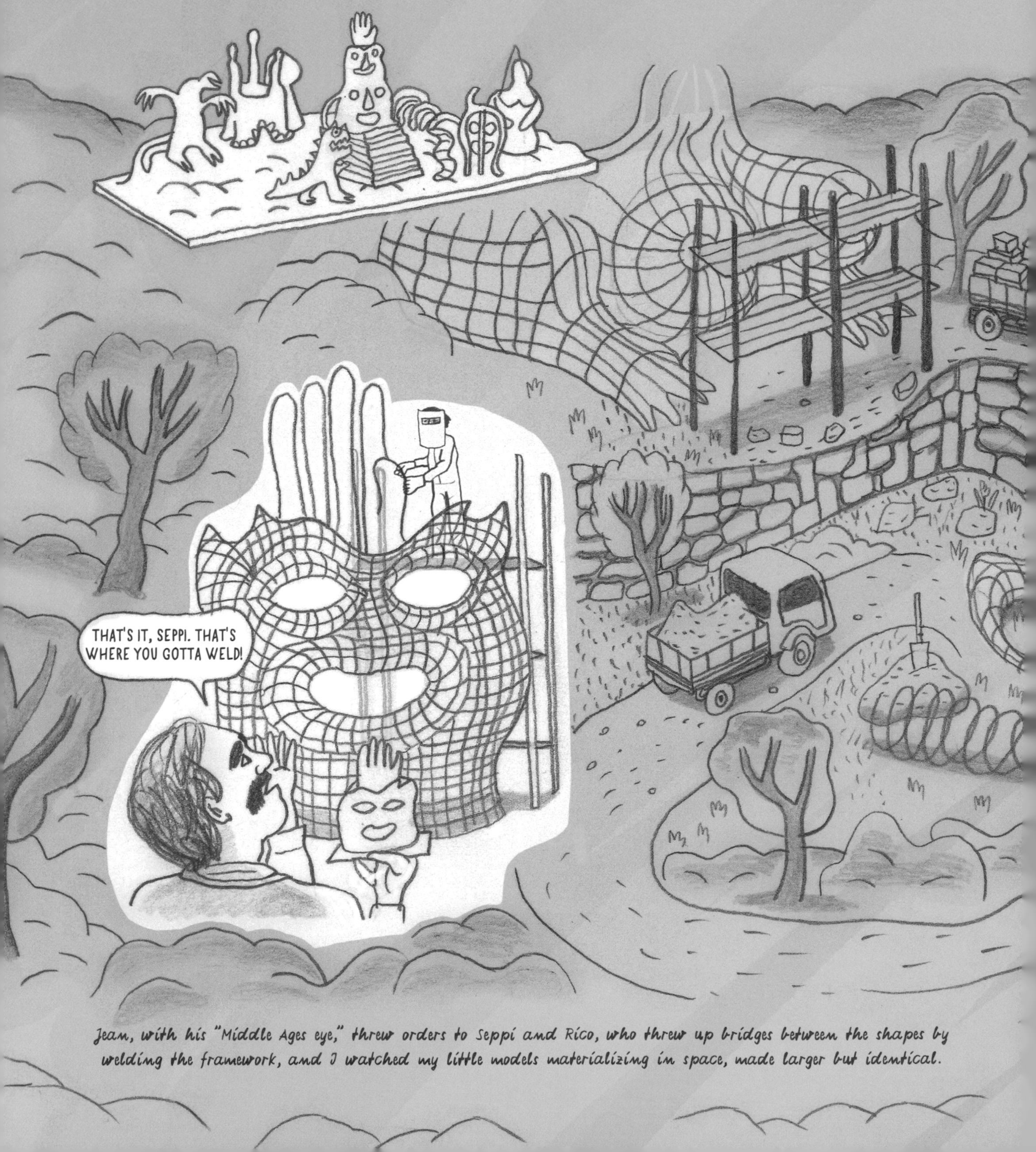
THAT'S IT, SEPPI. THAT'S WHERE YOU GOTTA WELD!

*Jean, with his "Middle Ages eye," threw orders to Seppi and Rico, who threw up bridges between the shapes by welding the framework, and I watched my little models materializing in space, made larger but identical.*

A new friend came into my life: Ricardo Menon, an Argentine. He'd become my right-hand man, ever attentive to my needs and in service to my great could. I could no longer do without him over the next ten years! He was simultaneously a gardener, handyman, party organizer, nurse, and gay...

NIKI, IS THAT GIANT HAND WAVING AT THE NUCLEAR POWER PLANT ACROSS THE WAY OR TELLING IT "STOP"?

HEE HA! MY MAGICIAN SCOFFS AT ATOMIC REACTORS! HE'S DIRECTLY CONNECTED TO COSMIC RAYS!

DERNA! TUOI GNOCCHI ALLA ROMANA SONO SUBLIMISSIMES!

two Etruscan tombs were discovered in the area. I took this coincidence as a sign. My garden was truly at the place where it should be! At the heart of the great European civilization of the Quattrocento, and ready to welcome into it the best artisan heirs to that tradition.

JULY 1980: RETROSPECTIVE AT THE CENTRE GEORGES POMPIDOU.

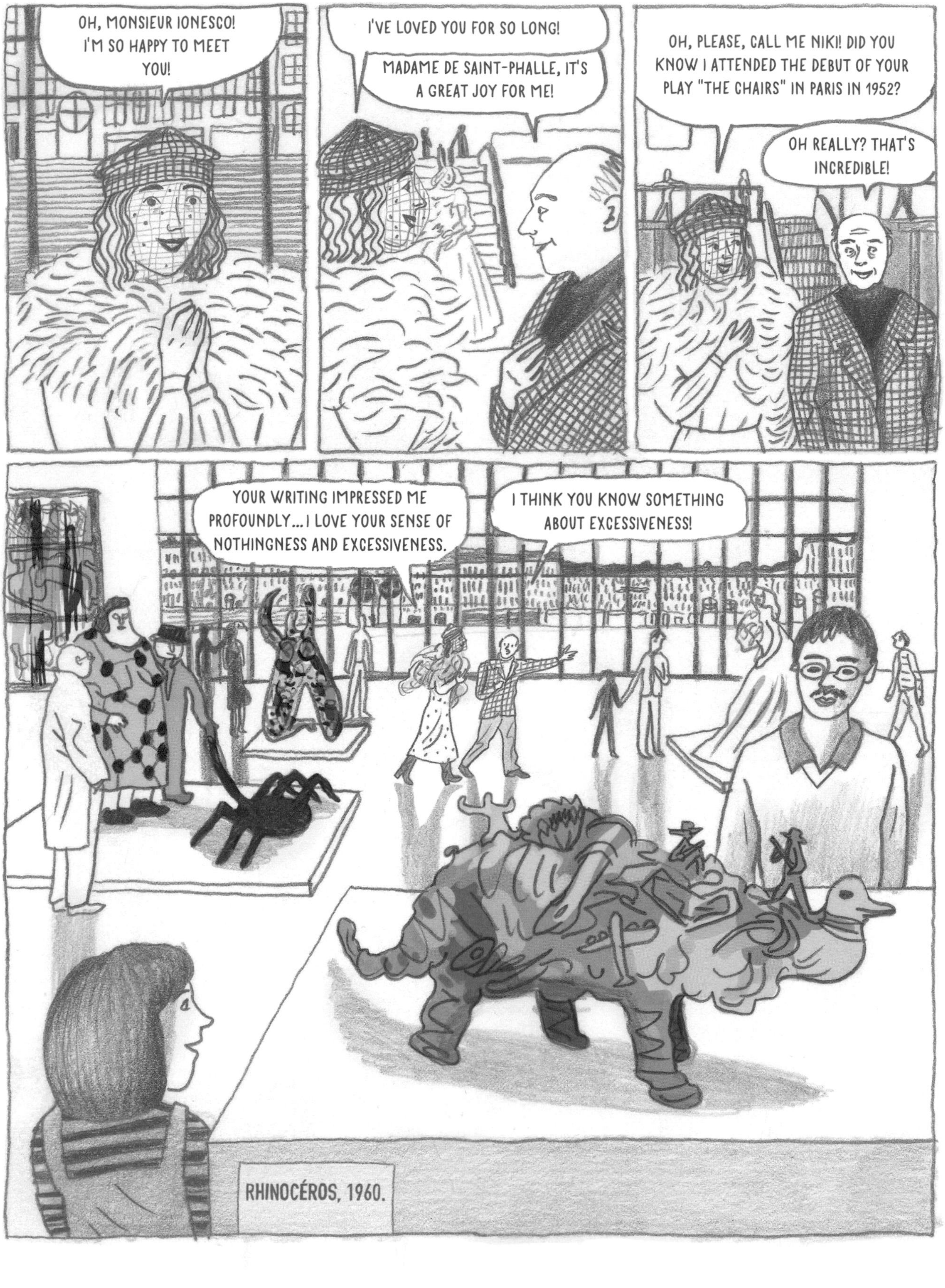
OH, MONSIEUR IONESCO! I'M SO HAPPY TO MEET YOU!
I'VE LOVED YOU FOR SO LONG!
MADAME DE SAINT-PHALLE, IT'S A GREAT JOY FOR ME!
OH, PLEASE, CALL ME NIKI! DID YOU KNOW I ATTENDED THE DEBUT OF YOUR PLAY "THE CHAIRS" IN PARIS IN 1952?
OH REALLY? THAT'S INCREDIBLE!
YOUR WRITING IMPRESSED ME PROFOUNDLY... I LOVE YOUR SENSE OF NOTHINGNESS AND EXCESSIVENESS.
I THINK YOU KNOW SOMETHING ABOUT EXCESSIVENESS!
RHINOCÉROS, 1960.

# CHAPTER 14

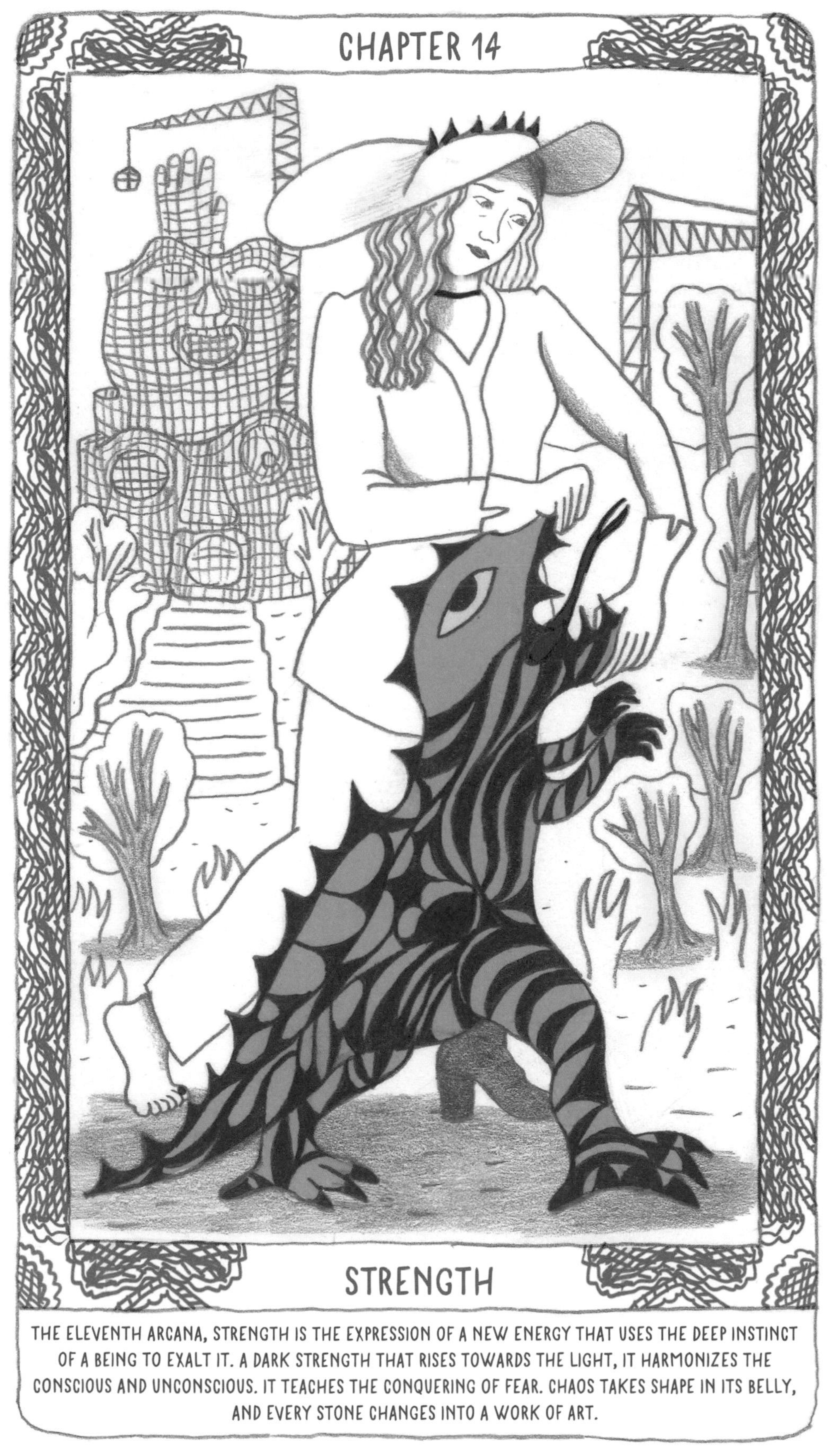

## STRENGTH

THE ELEVENTH ARCANA, STRENGTH IS THE EXPRESSION OF A NEW ENERGY THAT USES THE DEEP INSTINCT OF A BEING TO EXALT IT. A DARK STRENGTH THAT RISES TOWARDS THE LIGHT, IT HARMONIZES THE CONSCIOUS AND UNCONSCIOUS. IT TEACHES THE CONQUERING OF FEAR. CHAOS TAKES SHAPE IN ITS BELLY, AND EVERY STONE CHANGES INTO A WORK OF ART.

JUNE 6, 1981, LE BOURGET AIRPORT, PARIS.

*A transatlantic air race was organized for the fiftieth anniversary of Costes and Bellonte's crossing. A cigarette foundation, the sponsor of Team 43, proposed that I paint the Piper Aerostar that was to participate in it... I made a model that was then executed on the plane in England. It was very funny to see my painting flying!*

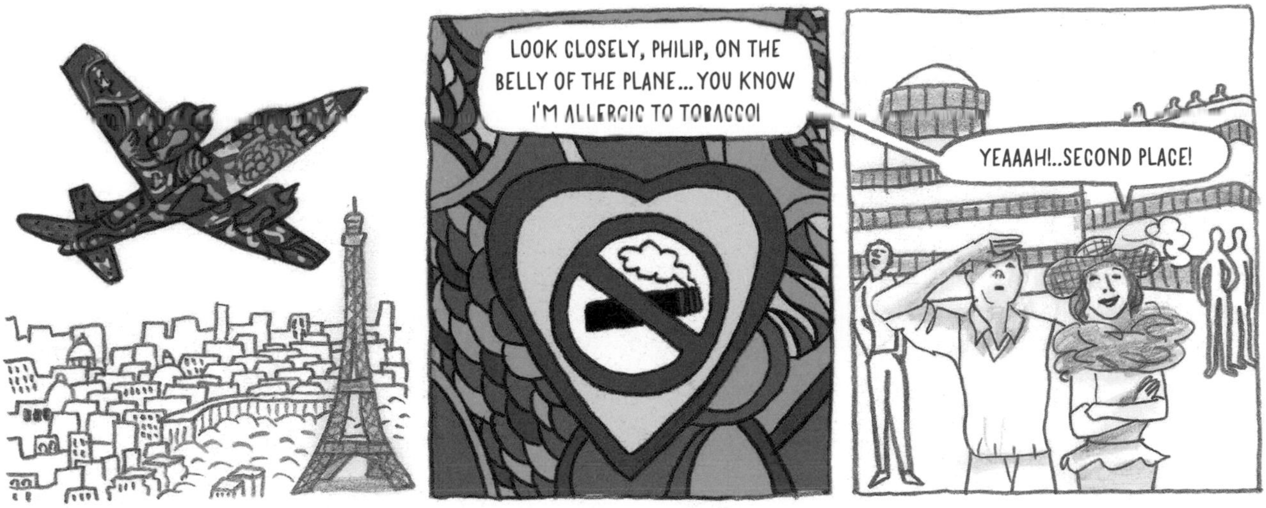
LOOK CLOSELY, PHILIP, ON THE BELLY OF THE PLANE... YOU KNOW I'M ALLERGIC TO TOBACCO!
YEAAAH!..SECOND PLACE!

*The day after the inauguration of my retrospective at Beaubourg, I'd been struck by an acute bout of rheumatoid arthritis. My right wrist swelled like a balloon and caused me much suffering. These flare ups would multiply over the course of the following years... With fewer and fewer remissions.*

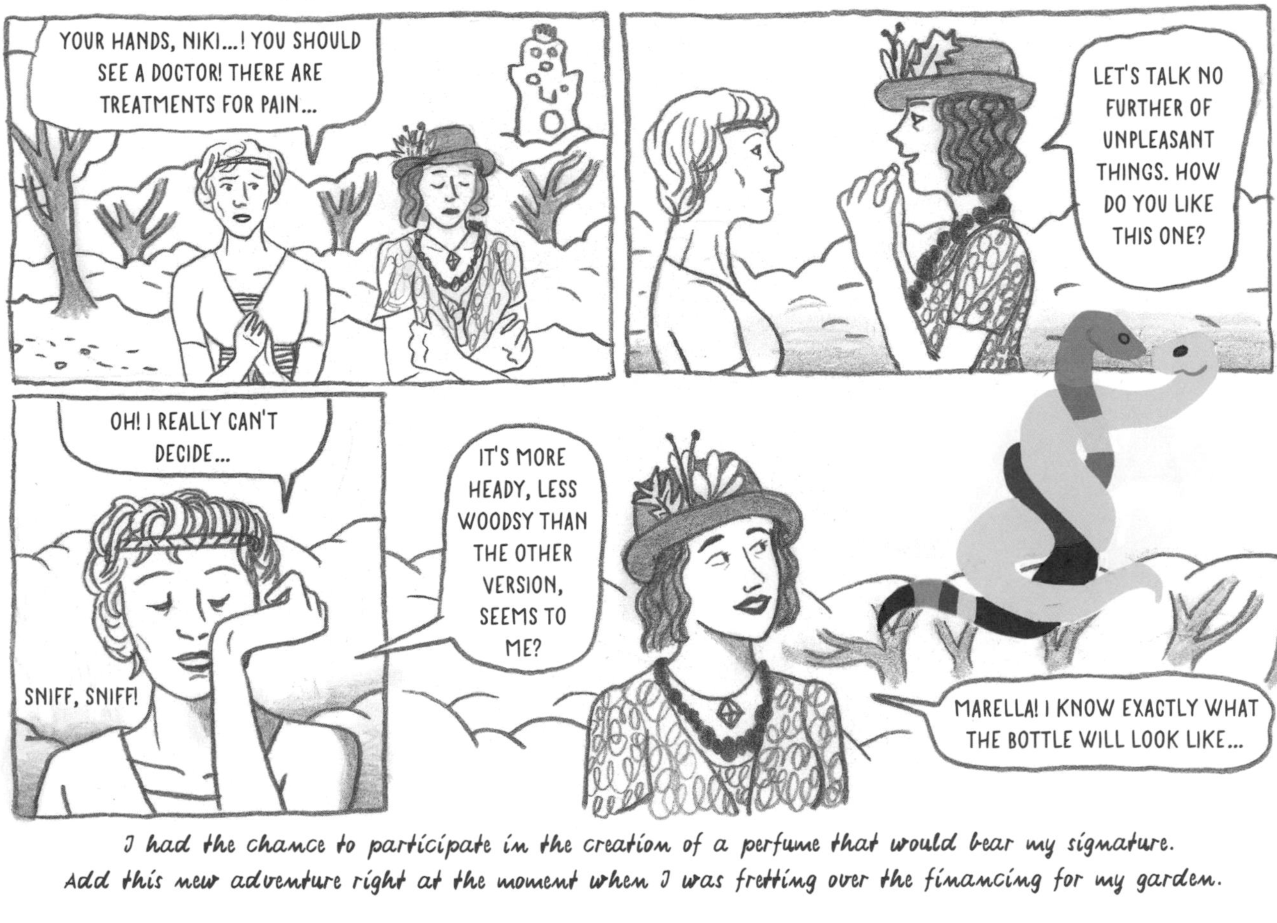
YOUR HANDS, NIKI...! YOU SHOULD SEE A DOCTOR! THERE ARE TREATMENTS FOR PAIN...
LET'S TALK NO FURTHER OF UNPLEASANT THINGS. HOW DO YOU LIKE THIS ONE?
OH! I REALLY CAN'T DECIDE...
SNIFF, SNIFF!
IT'S MORE HEADY, LESS WOODSY THAN THE OTHER VERSION, SEEMS TO ME?
MARELLA! I KNOW EXACTLY WHAT THE BOTTLE WILL LOOK LIKE...

*I had the chance to participate in the creation of a perfume that would bear my signature. Add this new adventure right at the moment when I was fretting over the financing for my garden.*

AUGUST 30, 1982, NYC.

*My hopes would be fulfilled: it hadn't been unusual for me to be two months from insolvency with all the people working for me at Garavicchio. The perfume would pay for a third of the garden!*

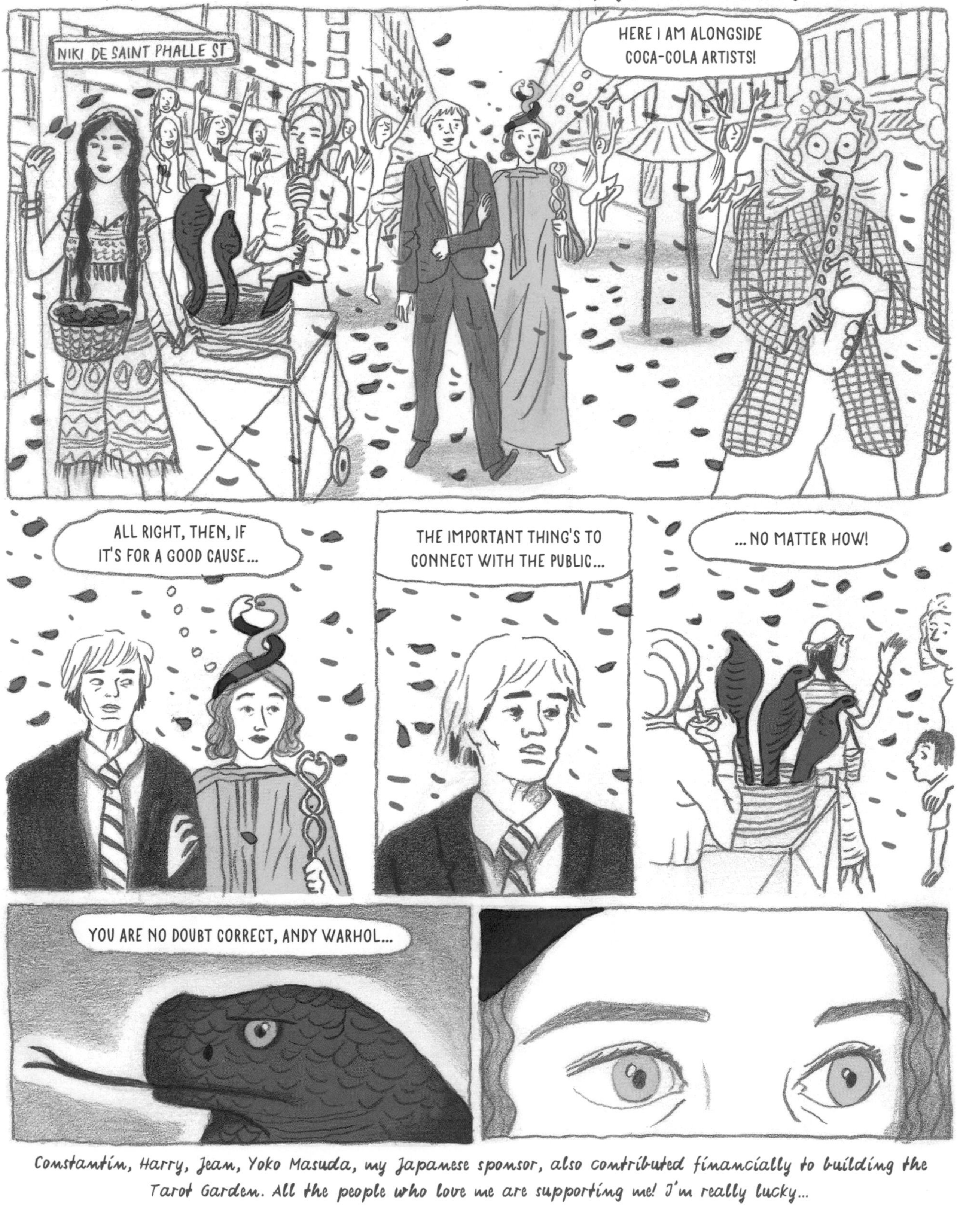
NIKI DE SAINT PHALLE ST
HERE I AM ALONGSIDE COCA-COLA ARTISTS!
ALL RIGHT, THEN, IF IT'S FOR A GOOD CAUSE...
THE IMPORTANT THING'S TO CONNECT WITH THE PUBLIC...
...NO MATTER HOW!
YOU ARE NO DOUBT CORRECT, ANDY WARHOL...

*Constantin, Harry, Jean, Yoko Masuda, my Japanese sponsor, also contributed financially to building the Tarot Garden. All the people who love me are supporting me! I'm really lucky...*

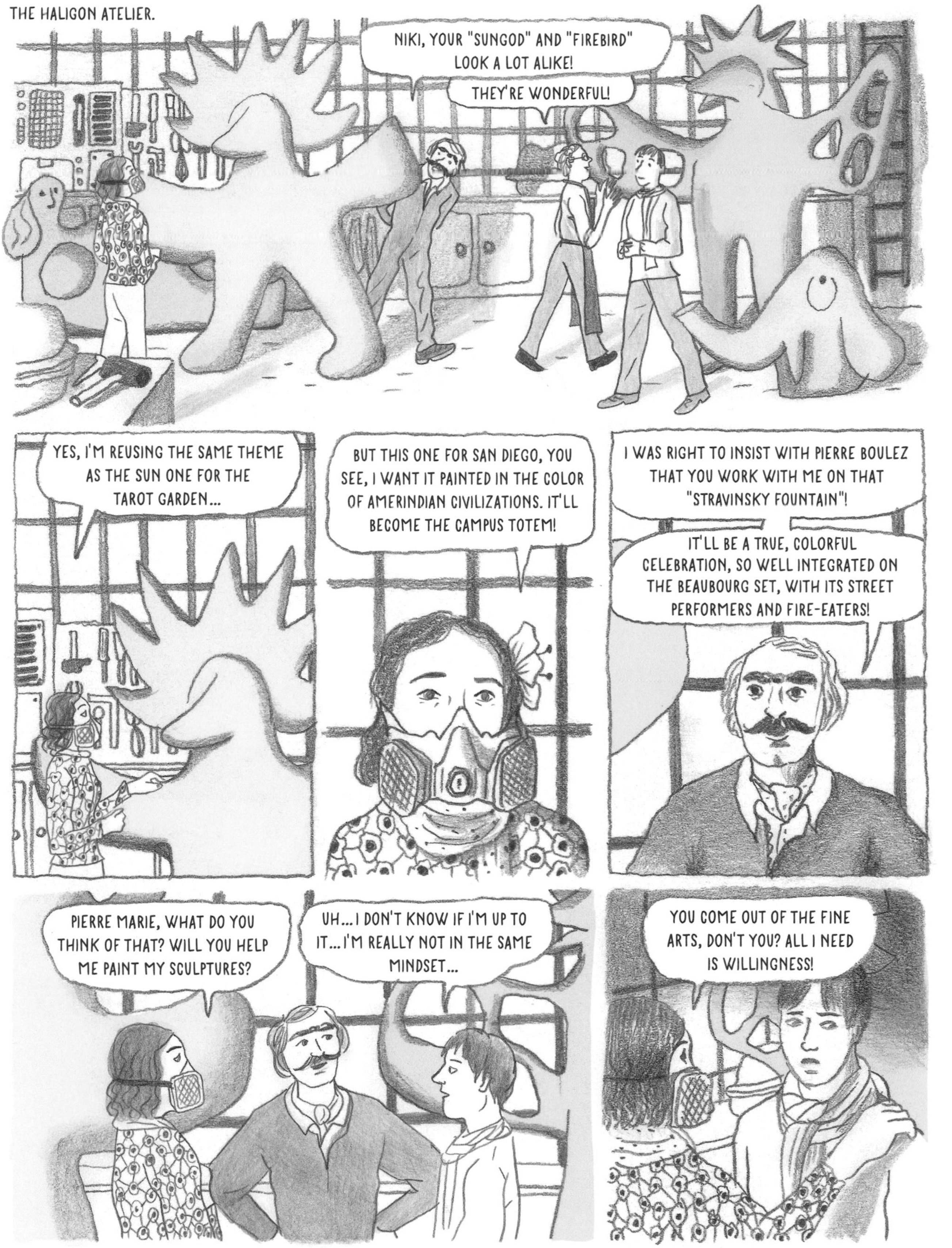
THE HALIGON ATELIER.
NIKI, YOUR "SUNGOD" AND "FIREBIRD" LOOK A LOT ALIKE!
THEY'RE WONDERFUL!
YES, I'M REUSING THE SAME THEME AS THE SUN ONE FOR THE TAROT GARDEN...
BUT THIS ONE FOR SAN DIEGO, YOU SEE, I WANT IT PAINTED IN THE COLOR OF AMERINDIAN CIVILIZATIONS. IT'LL BECOME THE CAMPUS TOTEM!
I WAS RIGHT TO INSIST WITH PIERRE BOULEZ THAT YOU WORK WITH ME ON THAT "STRAVINSKY FOUNTAIN"!
IT'LL BE A TRUE, COLORFUL CELEBRATION, SO WELL INTEGRATED ON THE BEAUBOURG SET, WITH ITS STREET PERFORMERS AND FIRE-EATERS!
PIERRE MARIE, WHAT DO YOU THINK OF THAT? WILL YOU HELP ME PAINT MY SCULPTURES?
UH... I DON'T KNOW IF I'M UP TO IT... I'M REALLY NOT IN THE SAME MINDSET...
YOU COME OUT OF THE FINE ARTS, DON'T YOU? ALL I NEED IS WILLINGNESS!

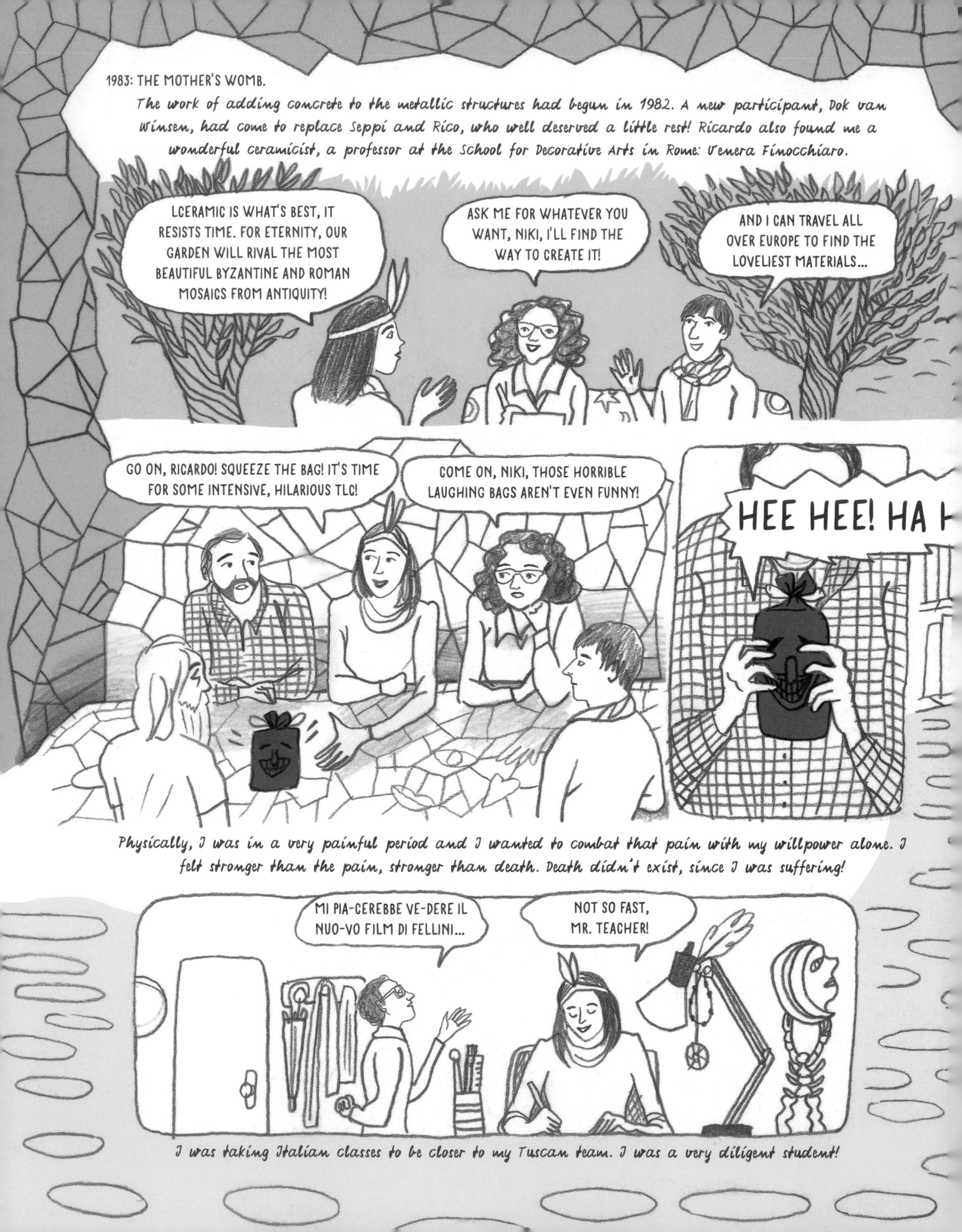
1983: THE MOTHER'S WOMB.
The work of adding concrete to the metallic structures had begun in 1982. A new participant, Dok van Winsen, had come to replace Seppi and Rico, who well deserved a little rest! Ricardo also found me a wonderful ceramicist, a professor at the School for Decorative Arts in Rome: Venera Finocchiaro.
LCERAMIC IS WHAT'S BEST, IT RESISTS TIME. FOR ETERNITY, OUR GARDEN WILL RIVAL THE MOST BEAUTIFUL BYZANTINE AND ROMAN MOSAICS FROM ANTIQUITY!
ASK ME FOR WHATEVER YOU WANT, NIKI, I'LL FIND THE WAY TO CREATE IT!
AND I CAN TRAVEL ALL OVER EUROPE TO FIND THE LOVELIEST MATERIALS...
GO ON, RICARDO! SQUEEZE THE BAG! IT'S TIME FOR SOME INTENSIVE, HILARIOUS TLC!
COME ON, NIKI, THOSE HORRIBLE LAUGHING BAGS AREN'T EVEN FUNNY!
HEE HEE! HA H
Physically, I was in a very painful period and I wanted to combat that pain with my willpower alone. I felt stronger than the pain, stronger than death. Death didn't exist, since I was suffering!
MI PIA-CEREBBE VE-DERE IL NUO-VO FILM DI FELLINI...
NOT SO FAST, MR. TEACHER!
I was taking Italian classes to be closer to my Tuscan team. I was a very diligent student!

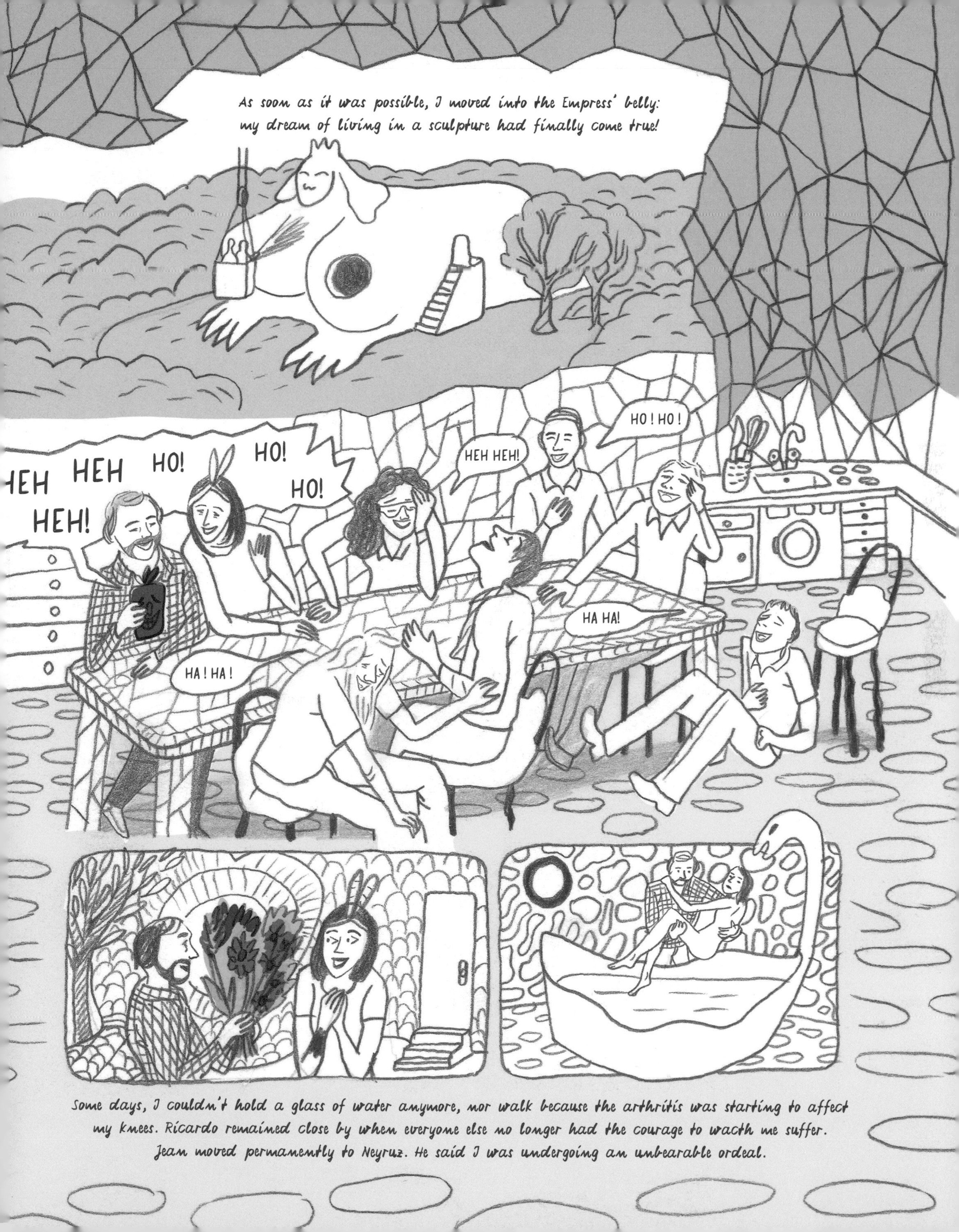
As soon as it was possible, I moved into the Empress' belly: my dream of living in a sculpture had finally come true!
HEH HEH HEH!
HO! HO! HO!
HEH HEH!
HO! HO!
HA HA!
HA! HA!
Some days, I couldn't hold a glass of water anymore, nor walk because the arthritis was starting to affect my knees. Ricardo remained close by when everyone else no longer had the courage to wacth me suffer. Jean moved permanently to Neyruz. He said I was undergoing an unbearable ordeal.

1984: CORTISONE AND OLD LACE.

*Finally, after two years of intense suffering and insufficient alternative medicine treatments, I resolved to undergo a cortisone treatment. I felt myself come to life again, but my mood had changed, I'd become irascible!*

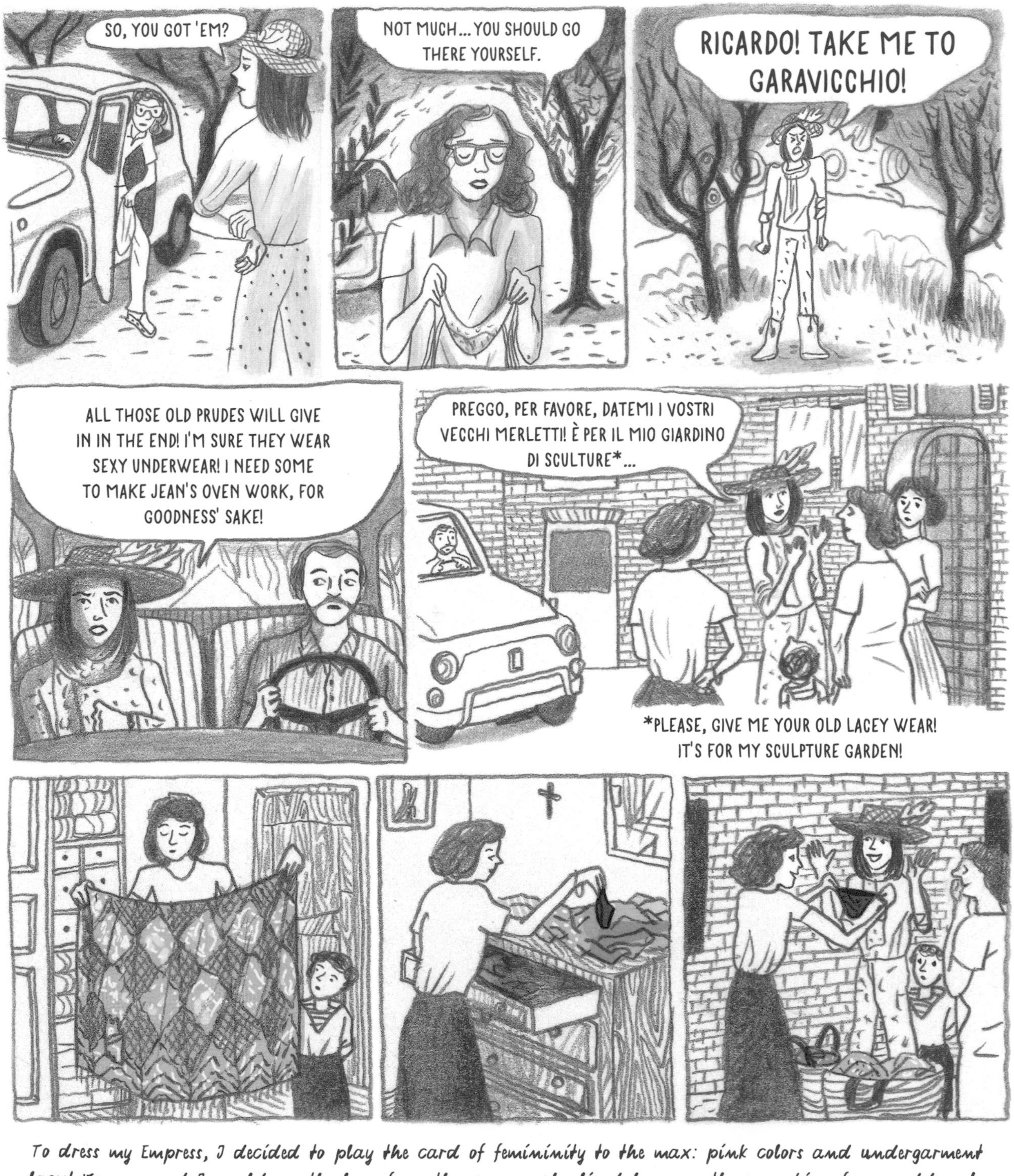

SO, YOU GOT 'EM?
NOT MUCH... YOU SHOULD GO THERE YOURSELF.
RICARDO! TAKE ME TO GARAVICCHIO!
ALL THOSE OLD PRUDES WILL GIVE IN IN THE END! I'M SURE THEY WEAR SEXY UNDERWEAR! I NEED SOME TO MAKE JEAN'S OVEN WORK, FOR GOODNESS' SAKE!
PREGGO, PER FAVORE, DATEMI I VOSTRI VECCHI MERLETTI! È PER IL MIO GIARDINO DI SCULTURE*...
*PLEASE, GIVE ME YOUR OLD LACEY WEAR! IT'S FOR MY SCULPTURE GARDEN!


*To dress my Empress, I decided to play the card of femininity to the max: pink colors and undergarment laces! Venera and I would use the lace from the women who lived here, on the very skin of our goddess, by immortalizing their fingerprints in the clay of the tesserae! But I think the women of Garavicchio didn't entirely understand my approach...*

# CHAPTER 15

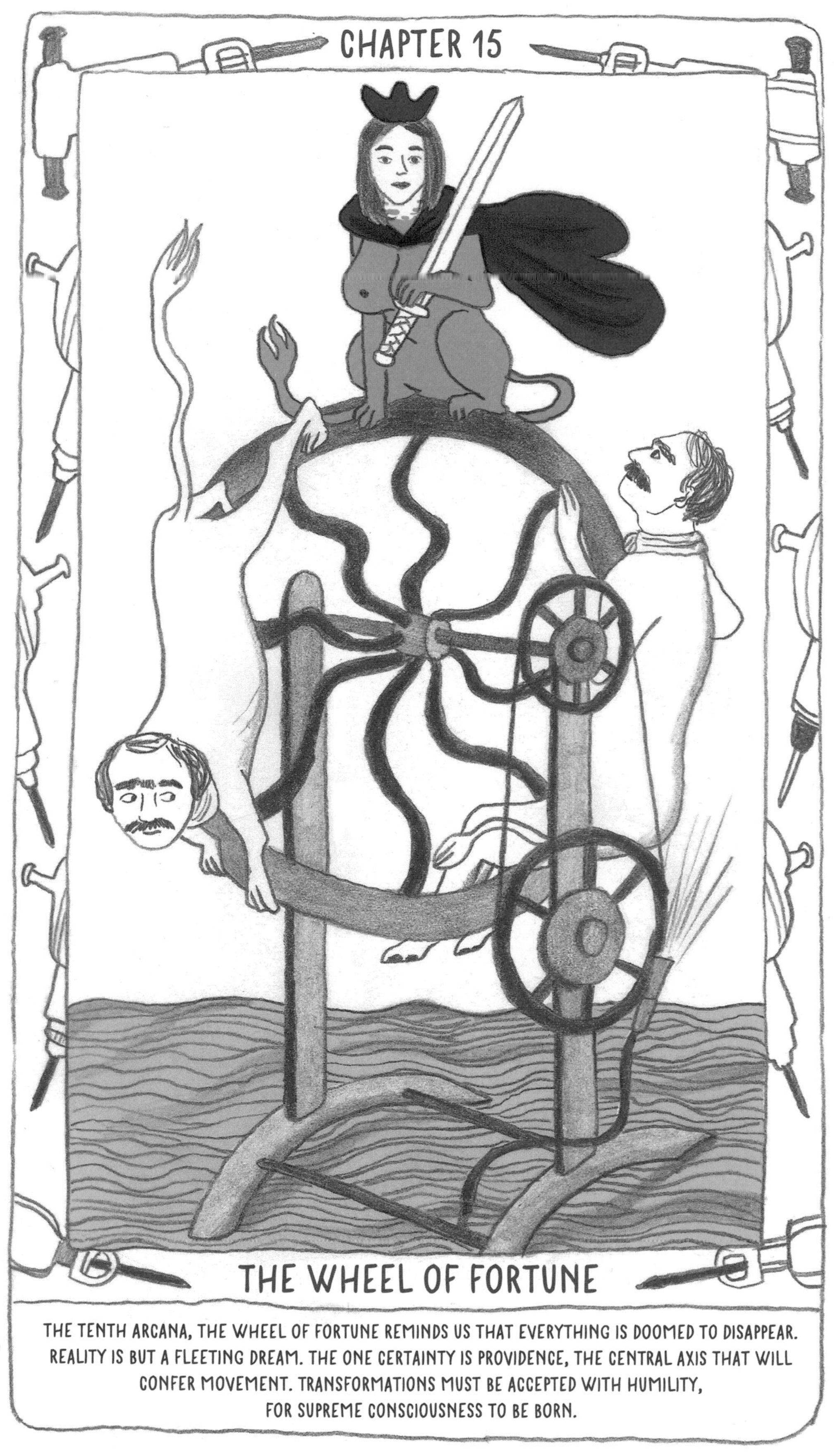

## THE WHEEL OF FORTUNE

THE TENTH ARCANA, THE WHEEL OF FORTUNE REMINDS US THAT EVERYTHING IS DOOMED TO DISAPPEAR. REALITY IS BUT A FLEETING DREAM. THE ONE CERTAINTY IS PROVIDENCE, THE CENTRAL AXIS THAT WILL CONFER MOVEMENT. TRANSFORMATIONS MUST BE ACCEPTED WITH HUMILITY, FOR SUPREME CONSCIOUSNESS TO BE BORN.

THE INFERNAL TOWER.

*I didn't know how to successfully complete the Emperor's Tower. It was too high and was eating the space over the other sculptures. I called Jean to the rescue...*

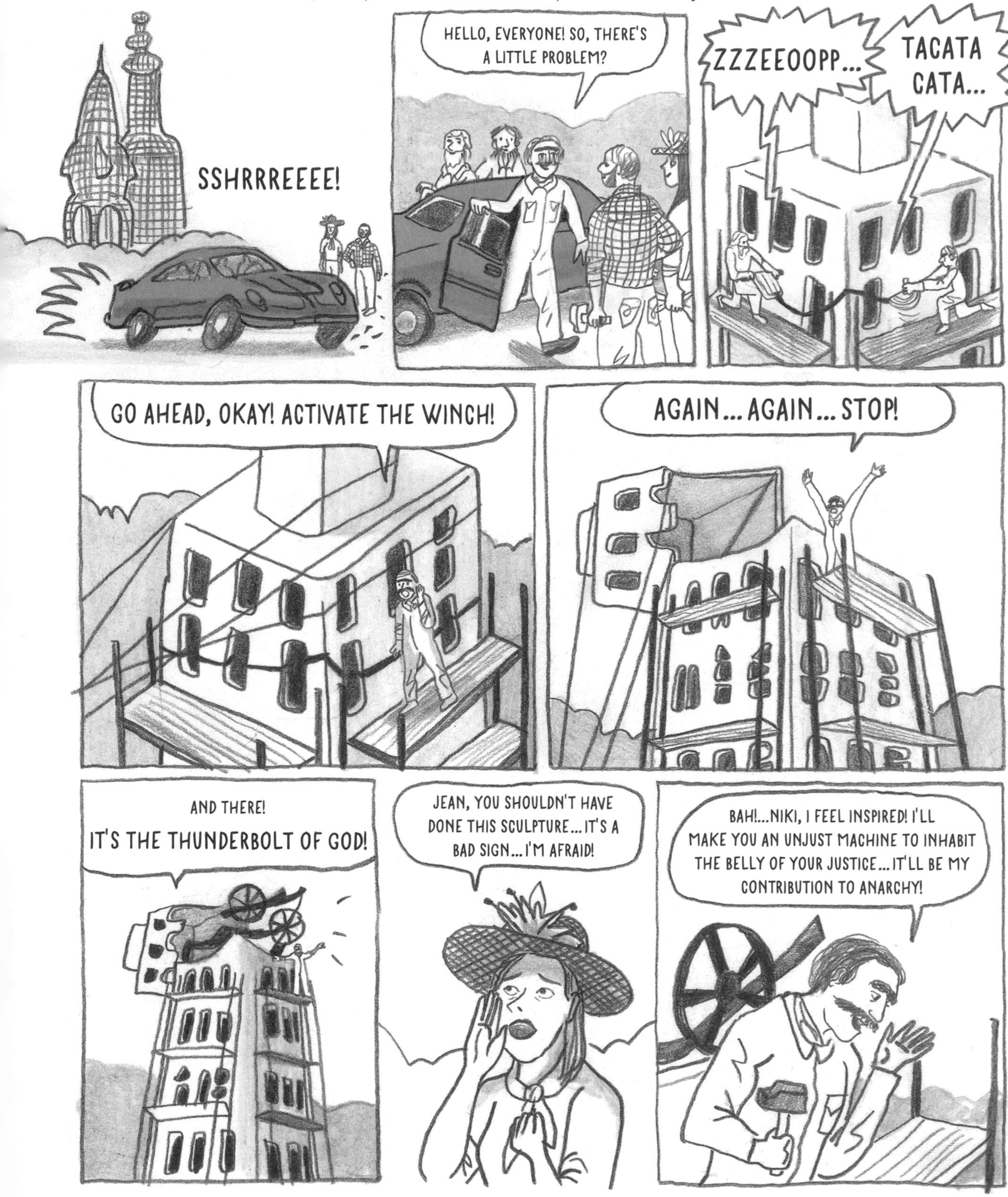
SSHRRREEEE!
HELLO, EVERYONE! SO, THERE'S A LITTLE PROBLEM?
ZZZEEOOPP...
TACATA CATA...
GO AHEAD, OKAY! ACTIVATE THE WINCH!
AGAIN... AGAIN... STOP!
AND THERE! IT'S THE THUNDERBOLT OF GOD!
JEAN, YOU SHOULDN'T HAVE DONE THIS SCULPTURE... IT'S A BAD SIGN... I'M AFRAID!
BAH!...NIKI, I FEEL INSPIRED! I'LL MAKE YOU AN UNJUST MACHINE TO INHABIT THE BELLY OF YOUR JUSTICE... IT'LL BE MY CONTRIBUTION TO ANARCHY!

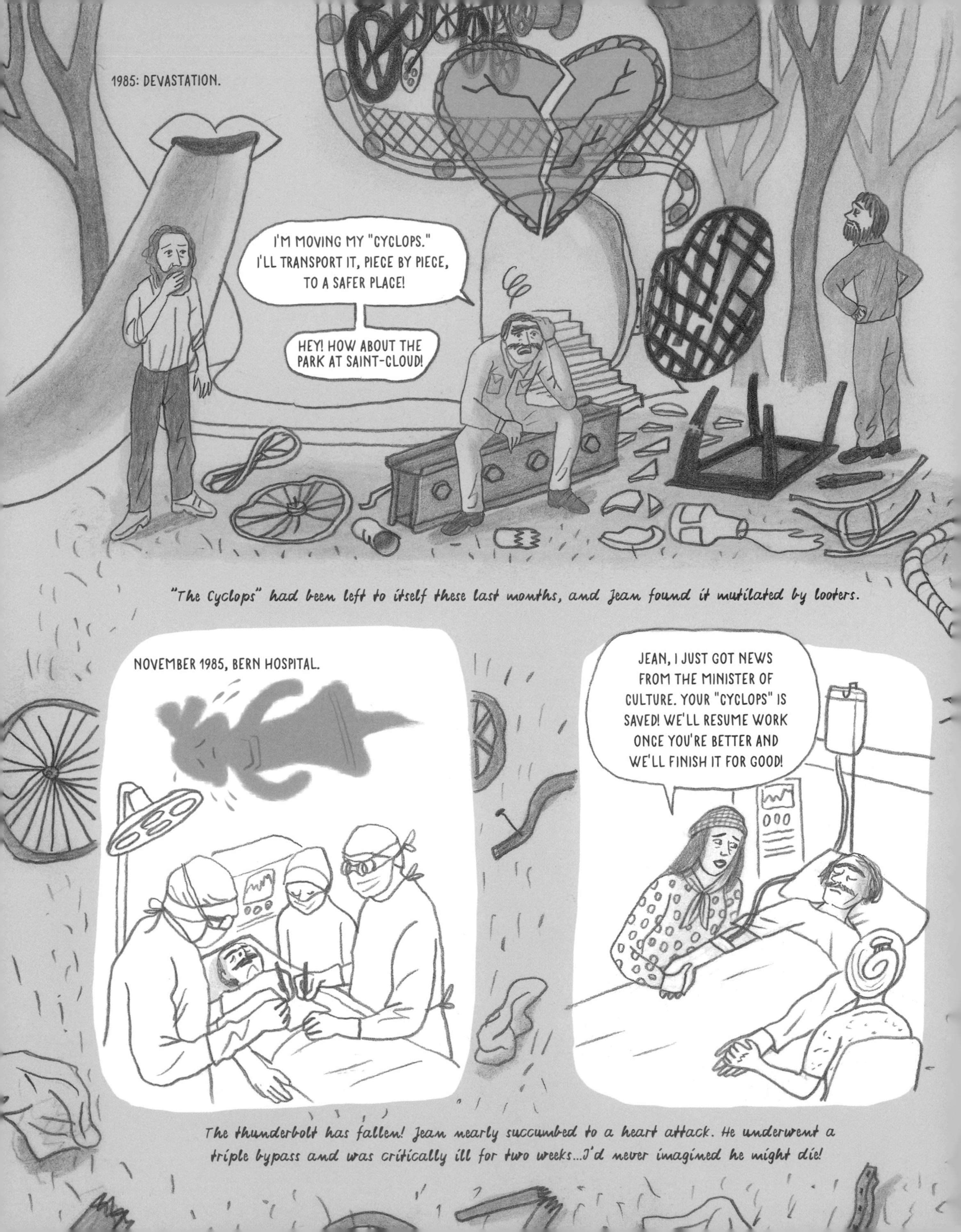
1985: DEVASTATION.
I'M MOVING MY "CYCLOPS." I'LL TRANSPORT IT, PIECE BY PIECE, TO A SAFER PLACE!
HEY! HOW ABOUT THE PARK AT SAINT-CLOUD!
"The Cyclops" had been left to itself these last months, and Jean found it mutilated by looters.
NOVEMBER 1985, BERN HOSPITAL.
JEAN, I JUST GOT NEWS FROM THE MINISTER OF CULTURE. YOUR "CYCLOPS" IS SAVED! WE'LL RESUME WORK ONCE YOU'RE BETTER AND WE'LL FINISH IT FOR GOOD!
The thunderbolt has fallen! Jean nearly succumbed to a heart attack. He underwent a triple bypass and was critically ill for two weeks...I'd never imagined he might die!

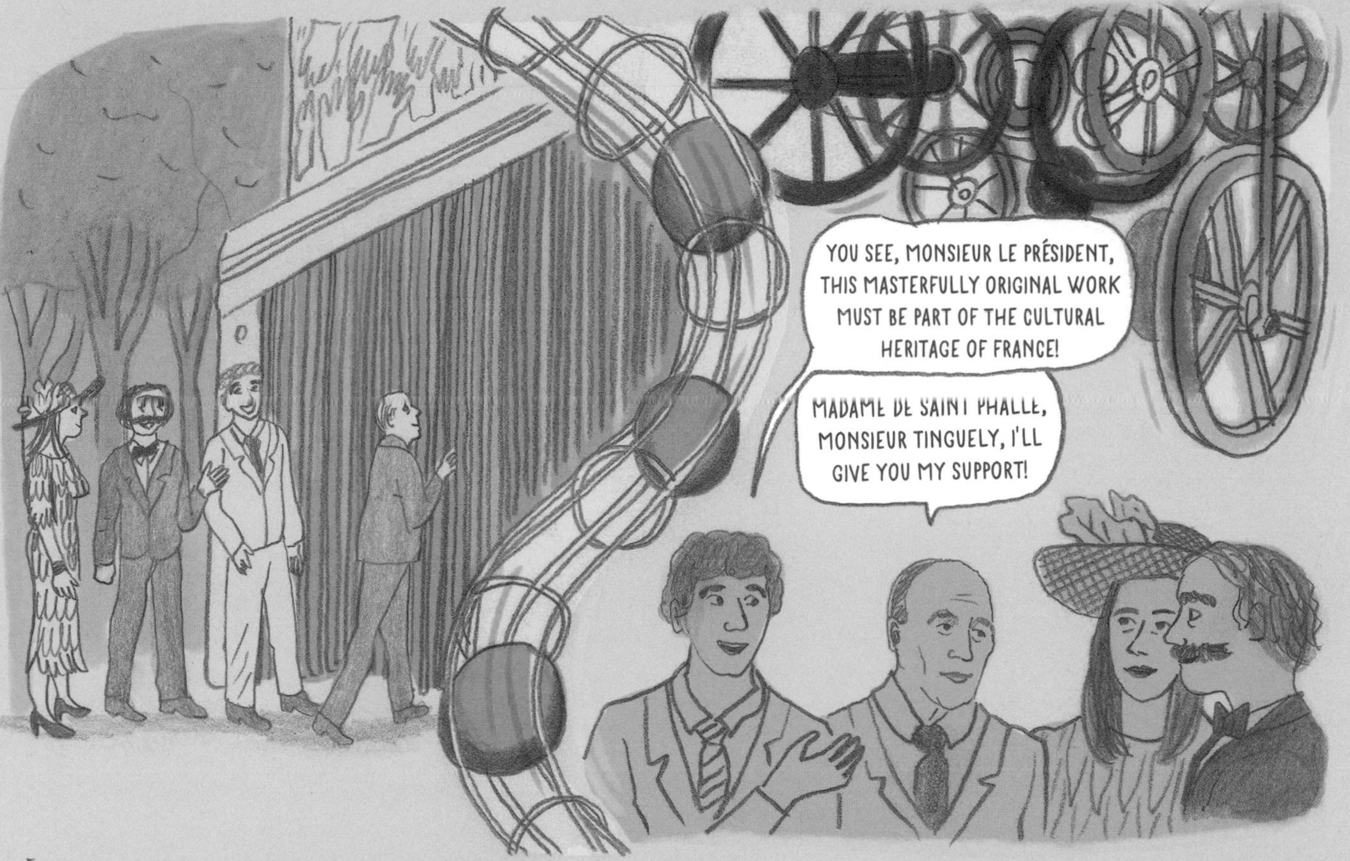
YOU SEE, MONSIEUR LE PRÉSIDENT, THIS MASTERFULLY ORIGINAL WORK MUST BE PART OF THE CULTURAL HERITAGE OF FRANCE!
MADAME DE SAINT PHALLE, MONSIEUR TINGUELY, I'LL GIVE YOU MY SUPPORT!

*We were successful in getting the French president and his minister of Culture to come to Milly-la-Forêt!*

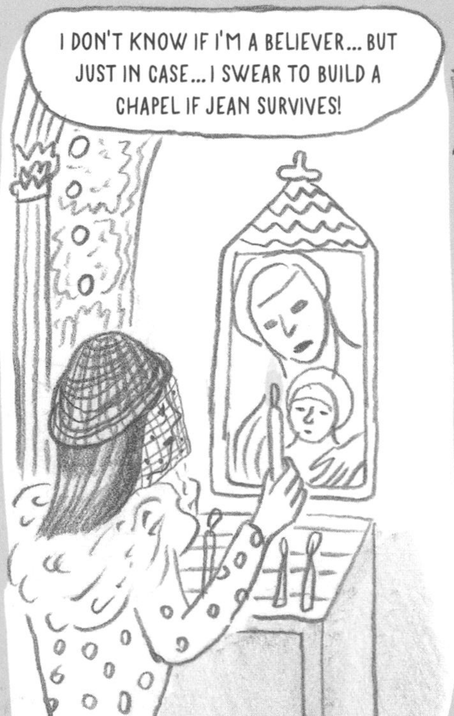
I DON'T KNOW IF I'M A BELIEVER... BUT JUST IN CASE... I SWEAR TO BUILD A CHAPEL IF JEAN SURVIVES!

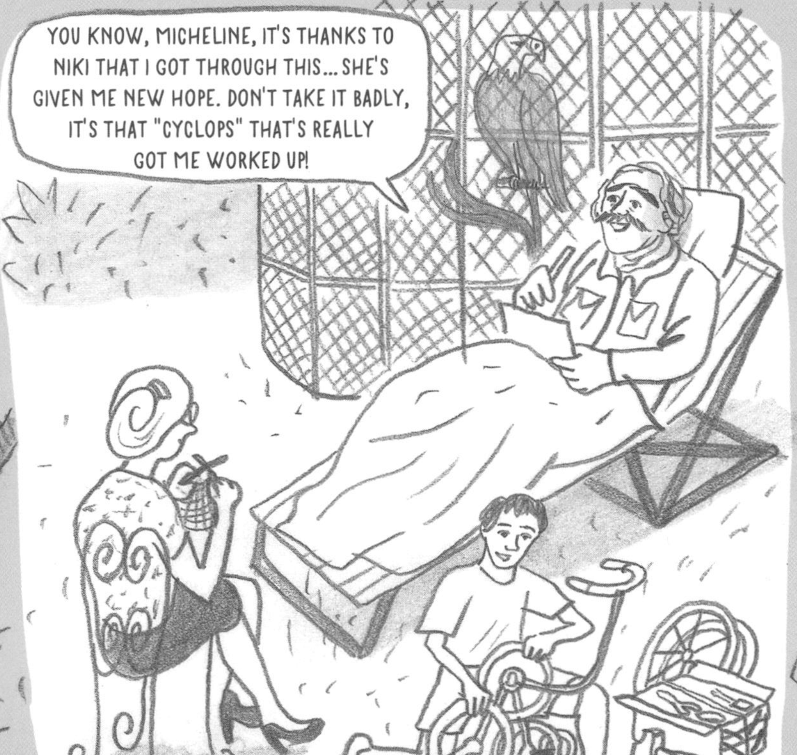
YOU KNOW, MICHELINE, IT'S THANKS TO NIKI THAT I GOT THROUGH THIS... SHE'S GIVEN ME NEW HOPE. DON'T TAKE IT BADLY, IT'S THAT "CYCLOPS" THAT'S REALLY GOT ME WORKED UP!

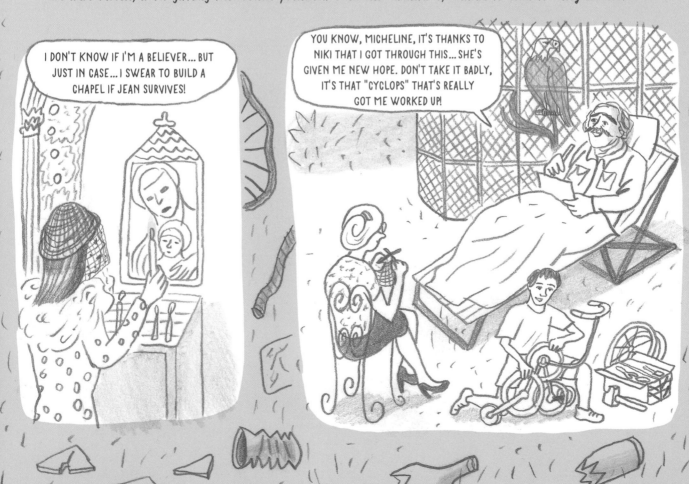

1986: A FACE FOR THE AWAKENED MONSTER.

*While Jean and I were making progress on a new fountain project at Château-Chinon, ordered by François Mitterrand, the construction of the "Cyclops" resumed with renewed intensity.*

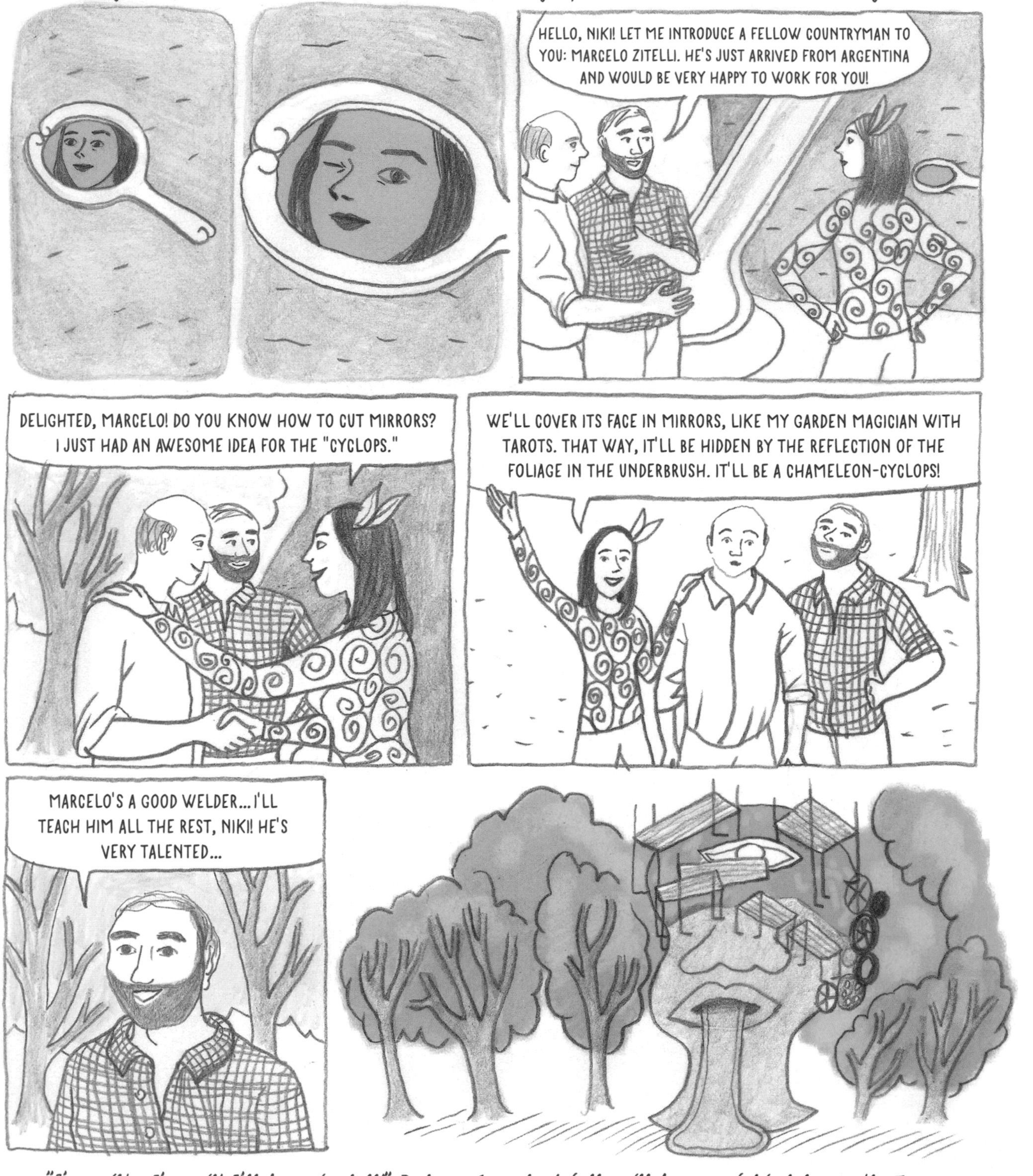

HELLO, NIKI! LET ME INTRODUCE A FELLOW COUNTRYMAN TO YOU: MARCELO ZITELLI. HE'S JUST ARRIVED FROM ARGENTINA AND WOULD BE VERY HAPPY TO WORK FOR YOU!
DELIGHTED, MARCELO! DO YOU KNOW HOW TO CUT MIRRORS? I JUST HAD AN AWESOME IDEA FOR THE "CYCLOPS."
WE'LL COVER ITS FACE IN MIRRORS, LIKE MY GARDEN MAGICIAN WITH TAROTS. THAT WAY, IT'LL BE HIDDEN BY THE REFLECTION OF THE FOLIAGE IN THE UNDERBRUSH. IT'LL BE A CHAMELEON-CYCLOPS!
MARCELO'S A GOOD WELDER... I'LL TEACH HIM ALL THE REST, NIKI! HE'S VERY TALENTED...


*"I'm guilty, I'm evil! I'll burn in hell!" Perhaps Jean had fallen ill because of his help on the Tower, and then I didn't understand Ricardo was already preparing his "departure" by introducing Marcelo to succeed him...*

# CHAPTER 16

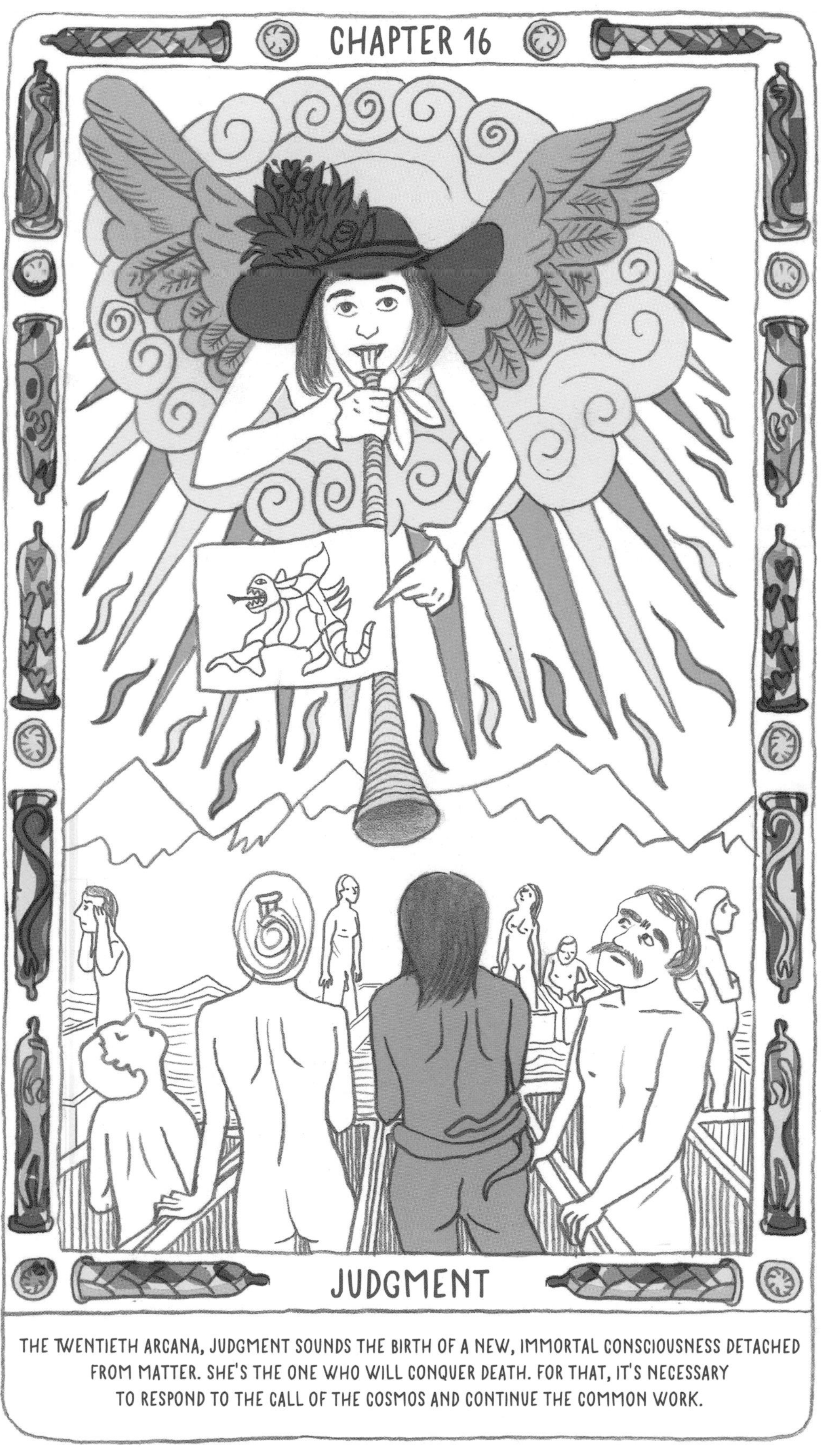

## JUDGMENT

THE TWENTIETH ARCANA, JUDGMENT SOUNDS THE BIRTH OF A NEW, IMMORTAL CONSCIOUSNESS DETACHED FROM MATTER. SHE'S THE ONE WHO WILL CONQUER DEATH. FOR THAT, IT'S NECESSARY TO RESPOND TO THE CALL OF THE COSMOS AND CONTINUE THE COMMON WORK.

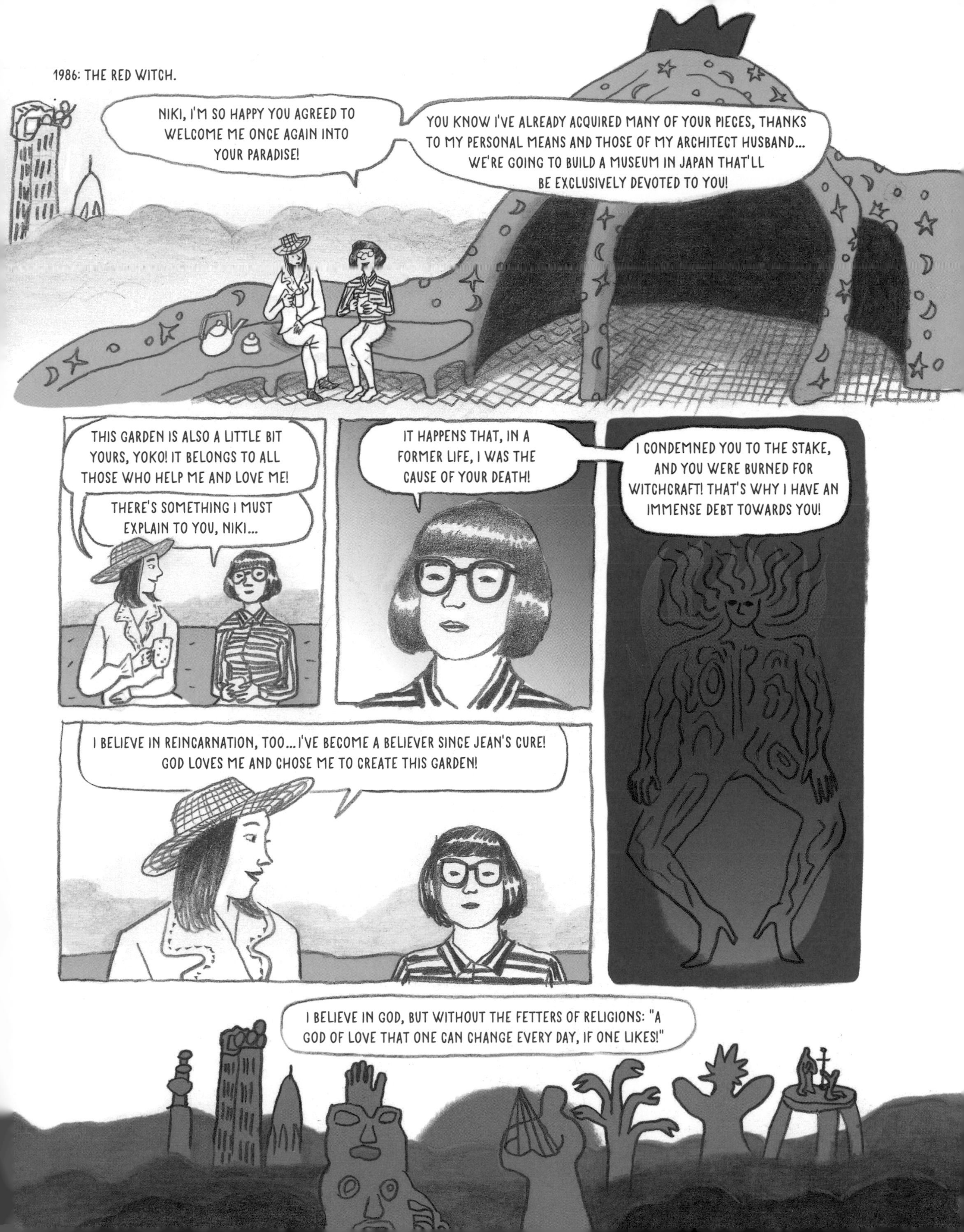
1986: THE RED WITCH.
NIKI, I'M SO HAPPY YOU AGREED TO WELCOME ME ONCE AGAIN INTO YOUR PARADISE!
YOU KNOW I'VE ALREADY ACQUIRED MANY OF YOUR PIECES, THANKS TO MY PERSONAL MEANS AND THOSE OF MY ARCHITECT HUSBAND... WE'RE GOING TO BUILD A MUSEUM IN JAPAN THAT'LL BE EXCLUSIVELY DEVOTED TO YOU!
THIS GARDEN IS ALSO A LITTLE BIT YOURS, YOKO! IT BELONGS TO ALL THOSE WHO HELP ME AND LOVE ME!
THERE'S SOMETHING I MUST EXPLAIN TO YOU, NIKI...
IT HAPPENS THAT, IN A FORMER LIFE, I WAS THE CAUSE OF YOUR DEATH!
I CONDEMNED YOU TO THE STAKE, AND YOU WERE BURNED FOR WITCHCRAFT! THAT'S WHY I HAVE AN IMMENSE DEBT TOWARDS YOU!
I BELIEVE IN REINCARNATION, TOO... I'VE BECOME A BELIEVER SINCE JEAN'S CURE! GOD LOVES ME AND CHOSE ME TO CREATE THIS GARDEN!
I BELIEVE IN GOD, BUT WITHOUT THE FETTERS OF RELIGIONS: "A GOD OF LOVE THAT ONE CAN CHANGE EVERY DAY, IF ONE LIKES!"

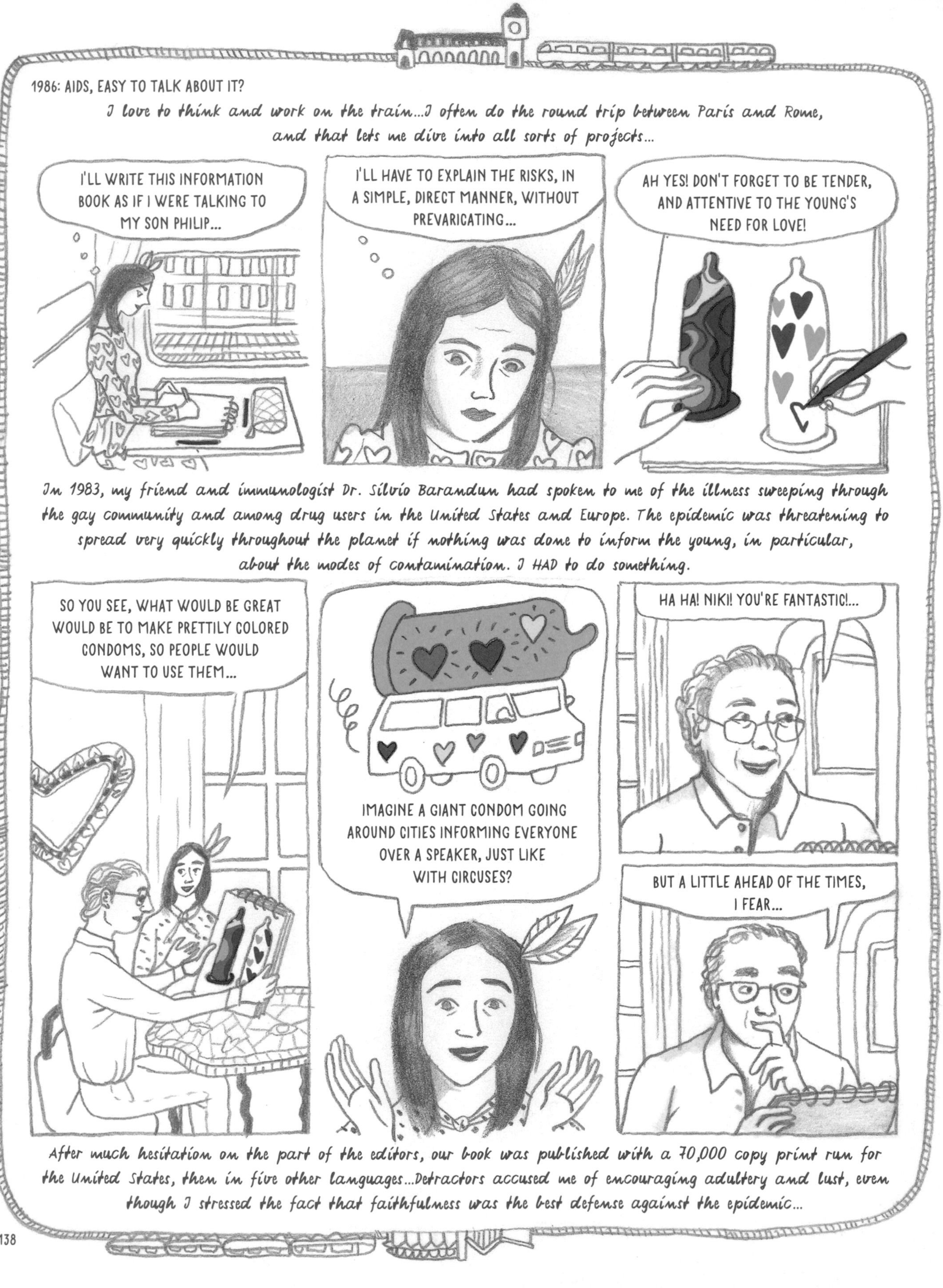
1986: AIDS, EASY TO TALK ABOUT IT?
I love to think and work on the train...I often do the round trip between Paris and Rome, and that lets me dive into all sorts of projects...
I'LL WRITE THIS INFORMATION BOOK AS IF I WERE TALKING TO MY SON PHILIP...
I'LL HAVE TO EXPLAIN THE RISKS, IN A SIMPLE, DIRECT MANNER, WITHOUT PREVARICATING...
AH YES! DON'T FORGET TO BE TENDER, AND ATTENTIVE TO THE YOUNG'S NEED FOR LOVE!
In 1983, my friend and immunologist Dr. Silvio Barandun had spoken to me of the illness sweeping through the gay community and among drug users in the United States and Europe. The epidemic was threatening to spread very quickly throughout the planet if nothing was done to inform the young, in particular, about the modes of contamination. I HAD to do something.
SO YOU SEE, WHAT WOULD BE GREAT WOULD BE TO MAKE PRETTILY COLORED CONDOMS, SO PEOPLE WOULD WANT TO USE THEM...
IMAGINE A GIANT CONDOM GOING AROUND CITIES INFORMING EVERYONE OVER A SPEAKER, JUST LIKE WITH CIRCUSES?
HA HA! NIKI! YOU'RE FANTASTIC!...
BUT A LITTLE AHEAD OF THE TIMES, I FEAR...
After much hesitation on the part of the editors, our book was published with a 70,000 copy print run for the United States, then in five other languages...Detractors accused me of encouraging adultery and lust, even though I stressed the fact that faithfulness was the best defense against the epidemic...

1987: THE NEW DEVOURING MOTHER

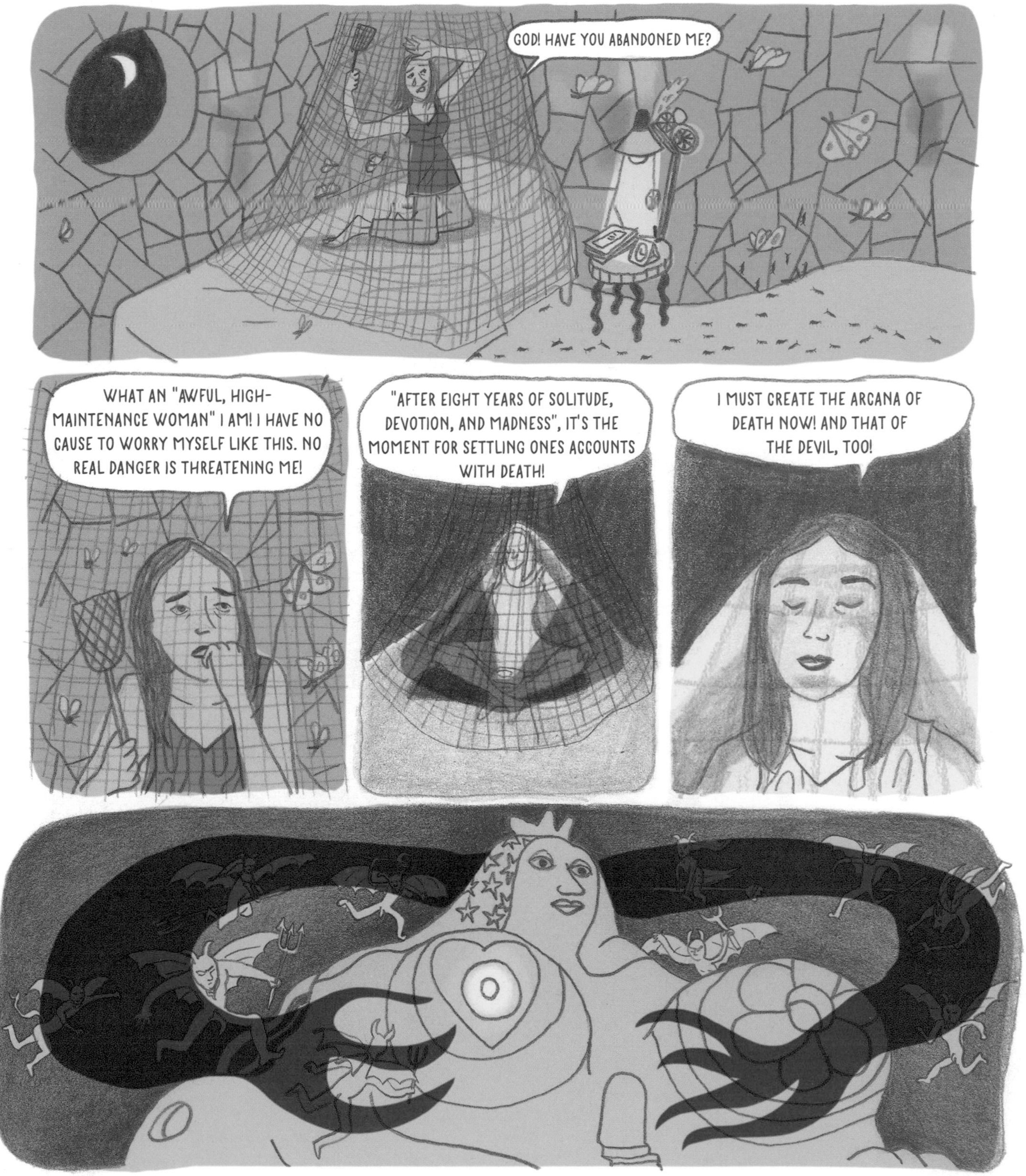
GOD! HAVE YOU ABANDONED ME?
WHAT AN "AWFUL, HIGH-MAINTENANCE WOMAN" I AM! I HAVE NO CAUSE TO WORRY MYSELF LIKE THIS. NO REAL DANGER IS THREATENING ME!
"AFTER EIGHT YEARS OF SOLITUDE, DEVOTION, AND MADNESS", IT'S THE MOMENT FOR SETTLING ONES ACCOUNTS WITH DEATH!
I MUST CREATE THE ARCANA OF DEATH NOW! AND THAT OF THE DEVIL, TOO!

I began to consult all manner of psychiatrists and hypnotists to try to conquer my growing anguish. One of them, a certain Jacques-Antoine, nearly entranced me for real! By chance, I always ended up prevailing, thanks to Art and my work.

AUGUST 1987: RETURN BY PLANE.

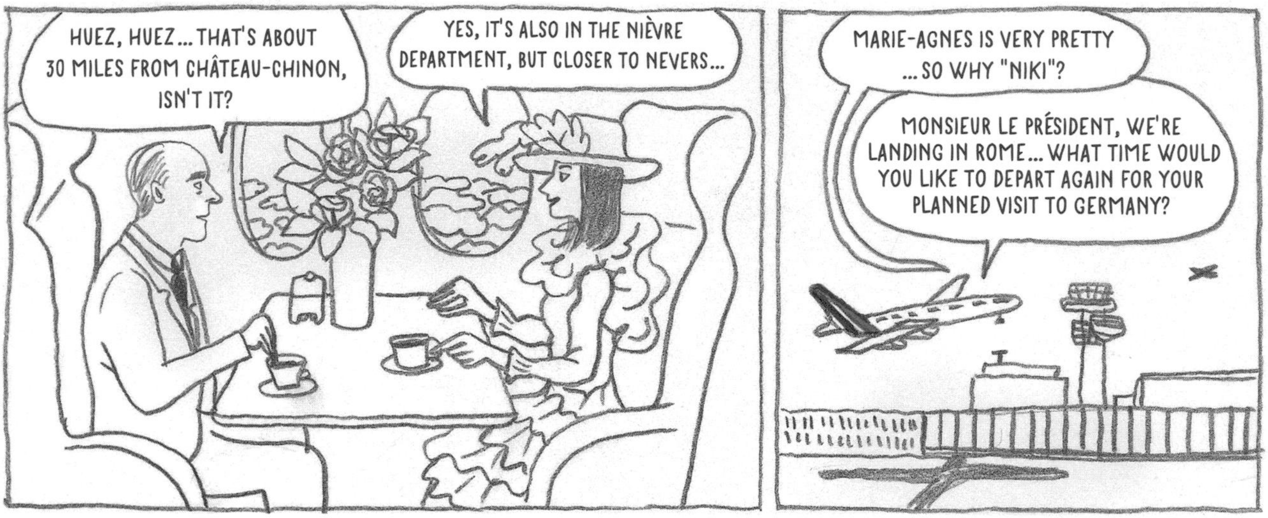
HUEZ, HUEZ... THAT'S ABOUT 30 MILES FROM CHÂTEAU-CHINON, ISN'T IT?
YES, IT'S ALSO IN THE NIÈVRE DEPARTMENT, BUT CLOSER TO NEVERS...
MARIE-AGNES IS VERY PRETTY ... SO WHY "NIKI"?
MONSIEUR LE PRÉSIDENT, WE'RE LANDING IN ROME... WHAT TIME WOULD YOU LIKE TO DEPART AGAIN FOR YOUR PLANNED VISIT TO GERMANY?

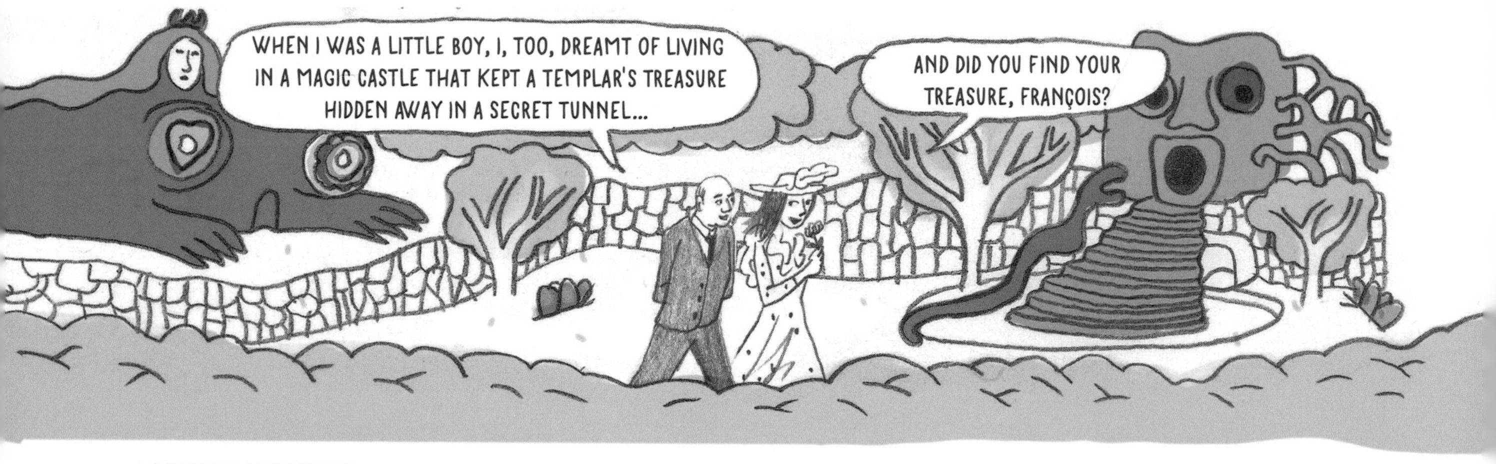
WHEN I WAS A LITTLE BOY, I, TOO, DREAMT OF LIVING IN A MAGIC CASTLE THAT KEPT A TEMPLAR'S TREASURE HIDDEN AWAY IN A SECRET TUNNEL...
AND DID YOU FIND YOUR TREASURE, FRANÇOIS?

A FOUNTAIN BETWEEN US.

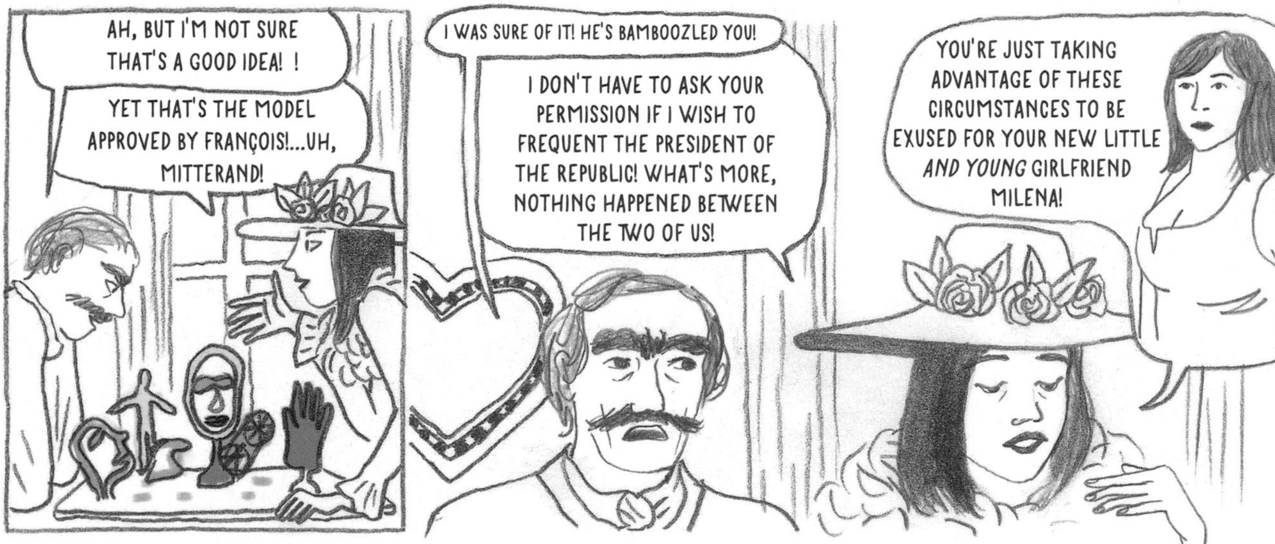
AH, BUT I'M NOT SURE THAT'S A GOOD IDEA! !
YET THAT'S THE MODEL APPROVED BY FRANÇOIS!...UH, MITTERAND!
I WAS SURE OF IT! HE'S BAMBOOZLED YOU!
I DON'T HAVE TO ASK YOUR PERMISSION IF I WISH TO FREQUENT THE PRESIDENT OF THE REPUBLIC! WHAT'S MORE, NOTHING HAPPENED BETWEEN THE TWO OF US!
YOU'RE JUST TAKING ADVANTAGE OF THESE CIRCUMSTANCES TO BE EXUSED FOR YOUR NEW LITTLE *AND YOUNG* GIRLFRIEND MILENA!

*It was I who introduced Milena Palakarkina, the Bulgarian painter, to Jean last year... Now, in the event of her own exhibition openings, he no longer wants to appear at the side of an "old lady" like me. He'd rather be strutting around with a sweet young thing! ...Macho pig!*

1988: THE GLASSWORKS.

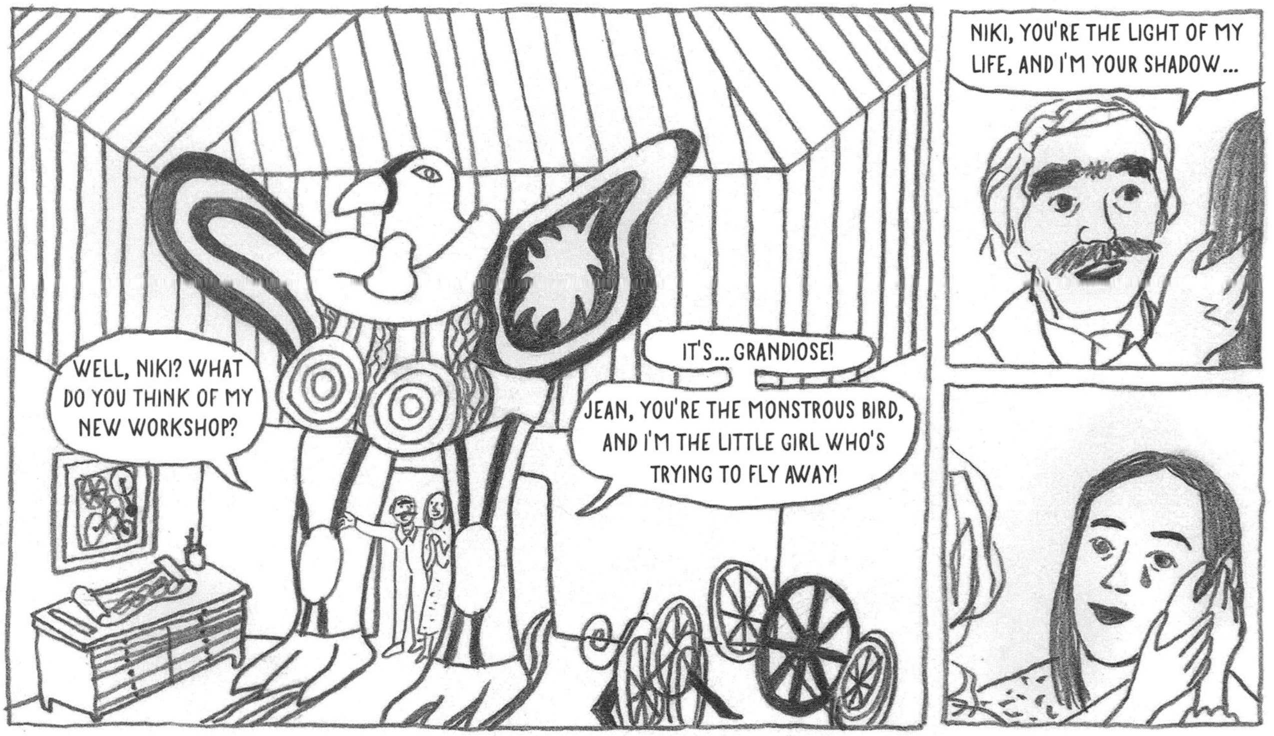
WELL, NIKI? WHAT DO YOU THINK OF MY NEW WORKSHOP?
IT'S... GRANDIOSE!
JEAN, YOU'RE THE MONSTROUS BIRD, AND I'M THE LITTLE GIRL WHO'S TRYING TO FLY AWAY!
NIKI, YOU'RE THE LIGHT OF MY LIFE, AND I'M YOUR SHADOW...

MAY 1989: DOUBLE EXHIBITION IN PARIS.

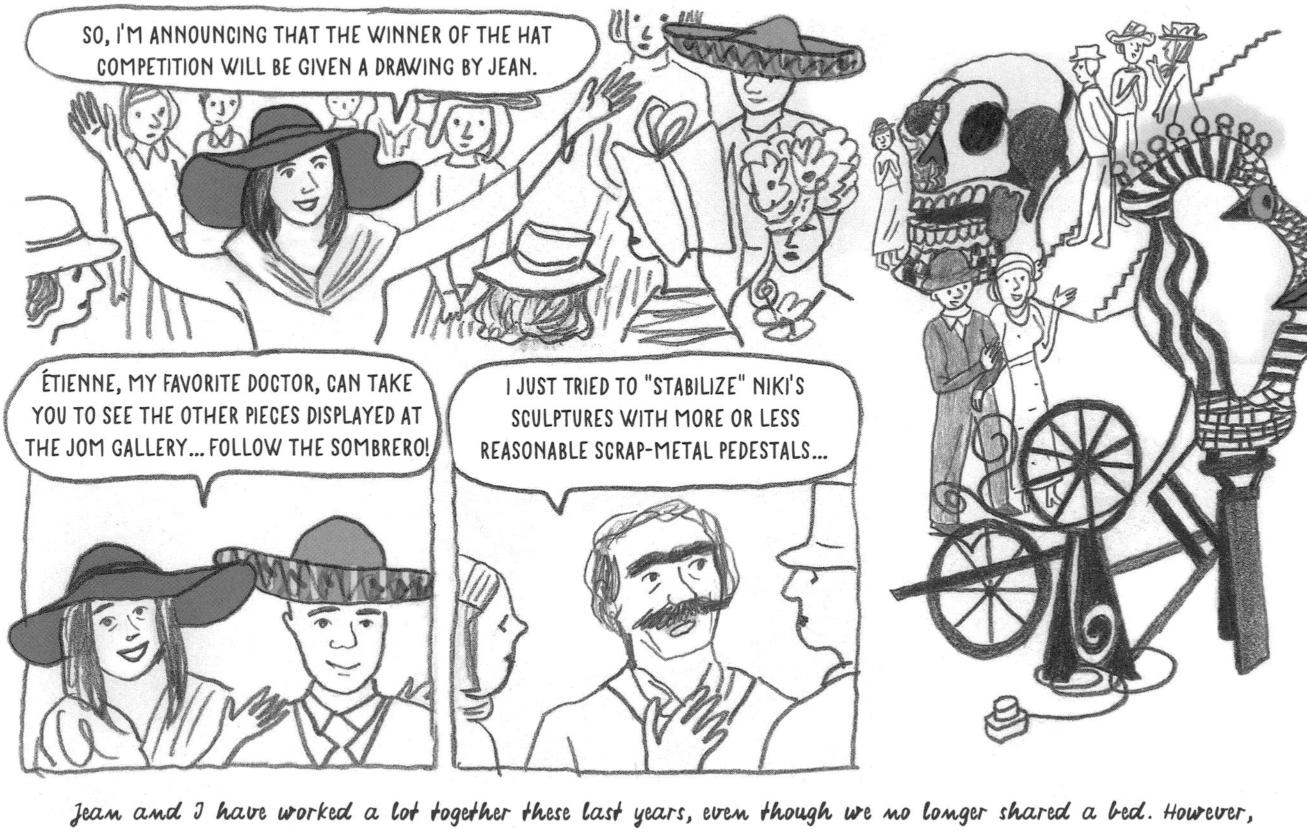
SO, I'M ANNOUNCING THAT THE WINNER OF THE HAT COMPETITION WILL BE GIVEN A DRAWING BY JEAN.
ÉTIENNE, MY FAVORITE DOCTOR, CAN TAKE YOU TO SEE THE OTHER PIECES DISPLAYED AT THE JOM GALLERY... FOLLOW THE SOMBRERO!
I JUST TRIED TO "STABILIZE" NIKI'S SCULPTURES WITH MORE OR LESS REASONABLE SCRAP-METAL PEDESTALS...

*Jean and I have worked a lot together these last years, even though we no longer shared a bed. However, our mutual love was growing, like the branches of an oak tree spreading above its unshakeable trunk.*

1989: AN IMAGINARY CAT IN A MAGIC GARDEN.

*Ricardo left us without fanfare. He left like he'd come, modestly. He was one of those silent and countless victims of AIDS...*

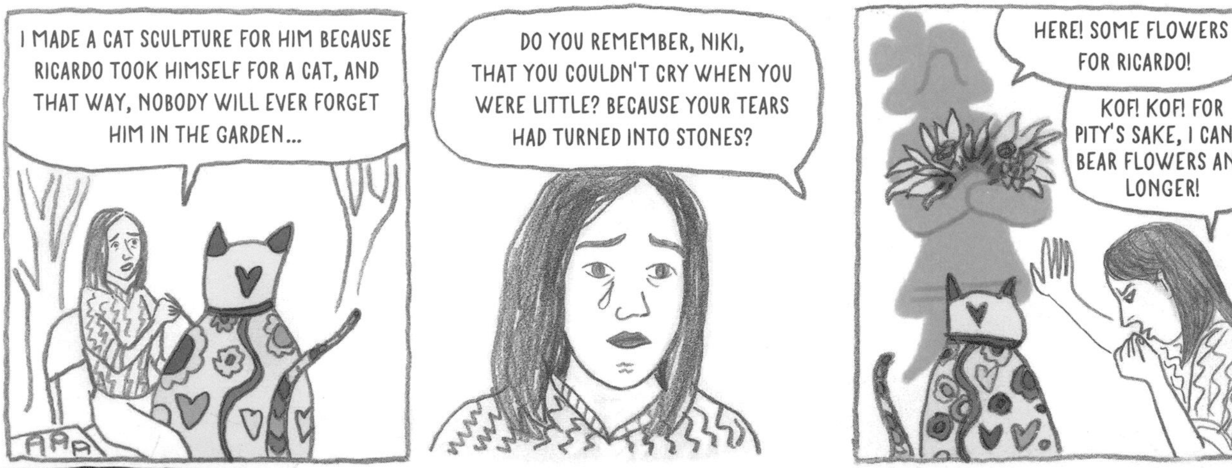

I MADE A CAT SCULPTURE FOR HIM BECAUSE RICARDO TOOK HIMSELF FOR A CAT, AND THAT WAY, NOBODY WILL EVER FORGET HIM IN THE GARDEN...
DO YOU REMEMBER, NIKI, THAT YOU COULDN'T CRY WHEN YOU WERE LITTLE? BECAUSE YOUR TEARS HAD TURNED INTO STONES?
HERE! SOME FLOWERS FOR RICARDO!
KOF! KOF! FOR PITY'S SAKE, I CAN'T BEAR FLOWERS ANY LONGER!


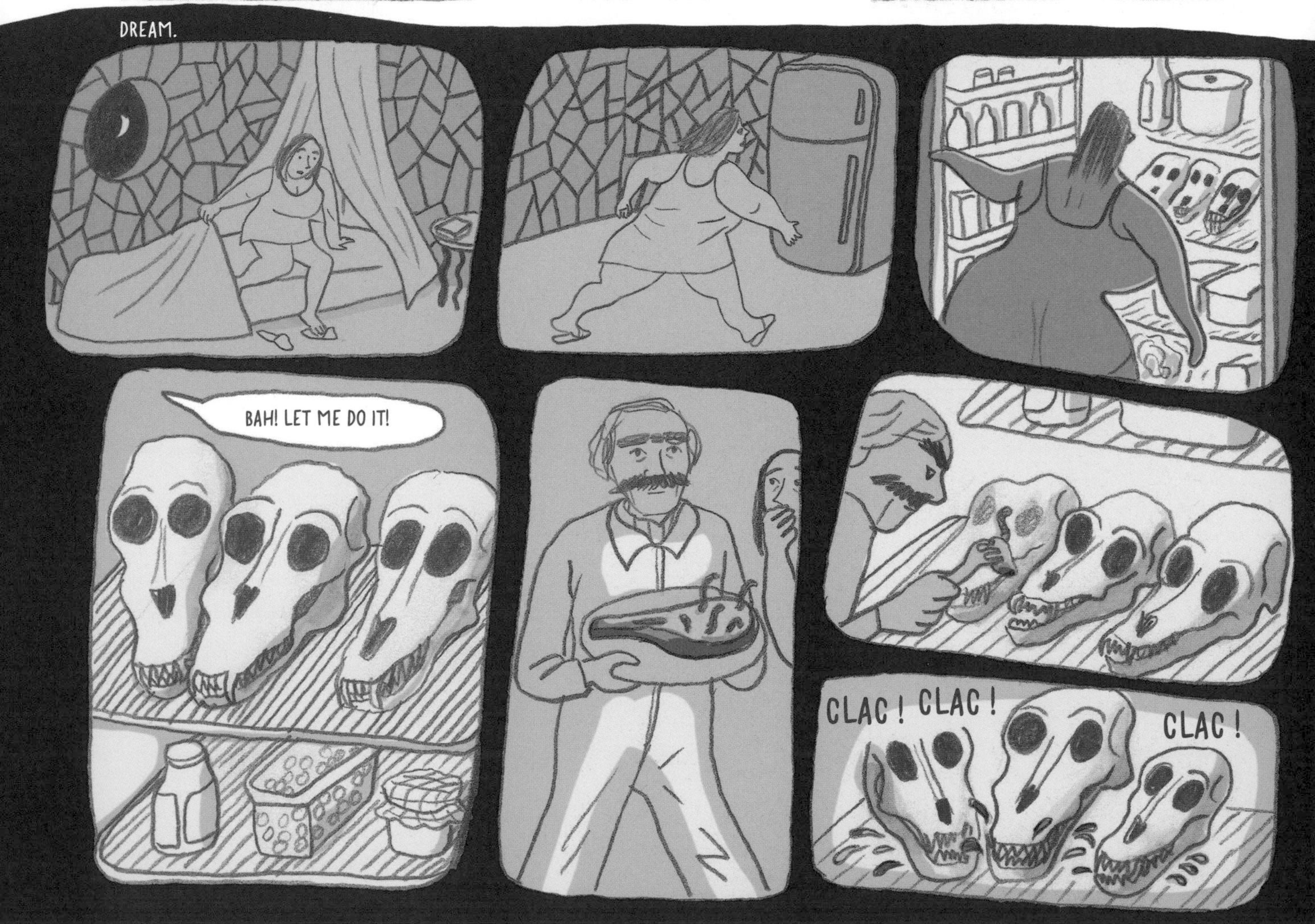

DREAM.
BAH! LET ME DO IT!
CLAC! CLAC!
CLAC!


*The death of my dearest friend and my condition of unbearable anguish were crystalizing in a new sculpture with open wounds, to which Jean offered a "stabilization" of his own invention. I called it "Wounded Mythology." It was the expression of innocent beauty facing the aggressive shock of pain.*

# CHAPTER 17

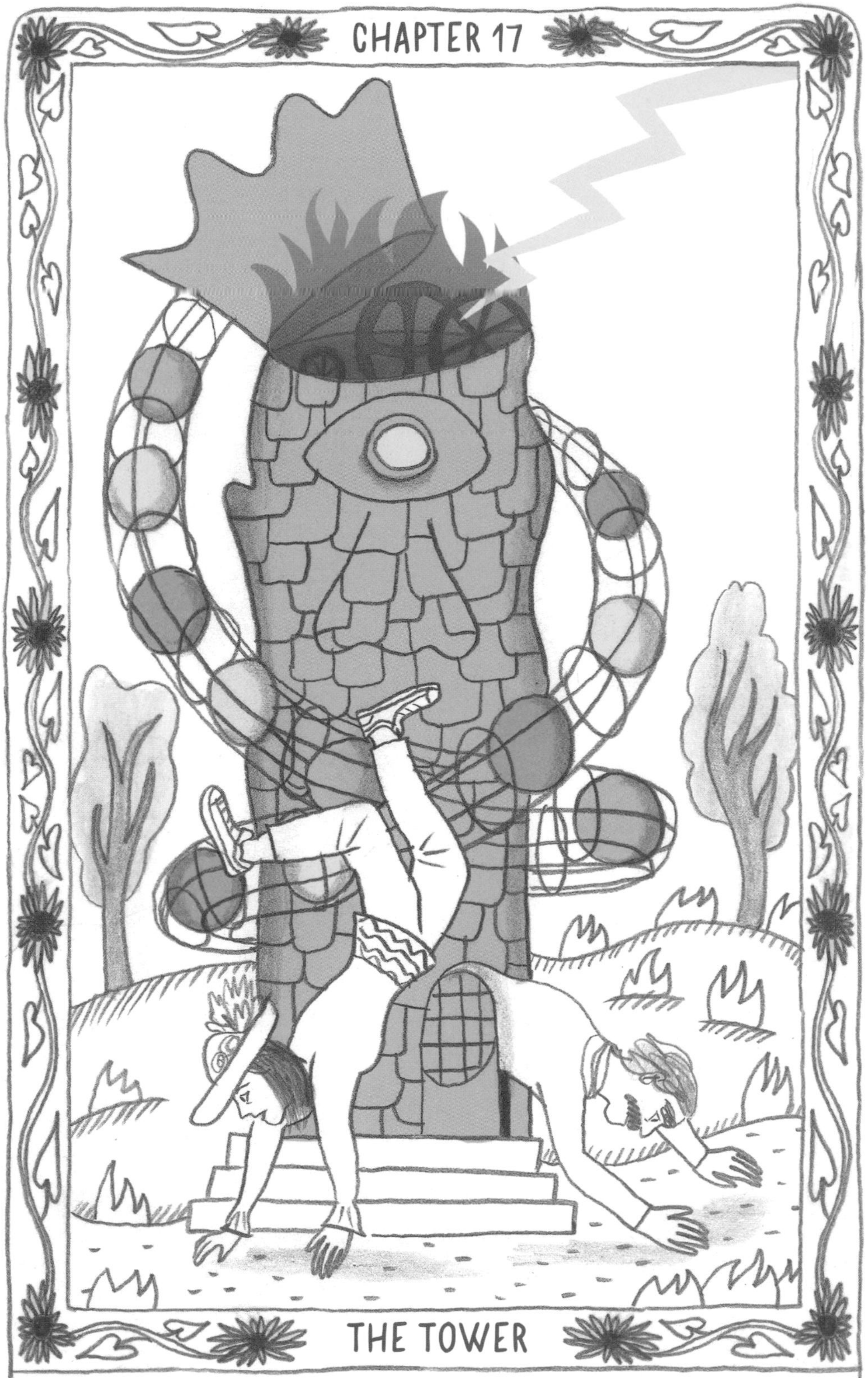

## THE TOWER

THE SIXTEENTH ARCANA, THE TOWER ANNOUNCES A RADICAL CHANGE, ALL WHILE BRING SPIRITUAL COMFORT. IT SYMBOLIZES THE BODY OF MAN, WHOSE HEAD IS STRUCK BY DIVINE LIGHTNING AND IS FILLED WITH LIGHT. THE CATASTROPHE PROVOKES THE SEPARATION OF THE PERFECT COUPLE.

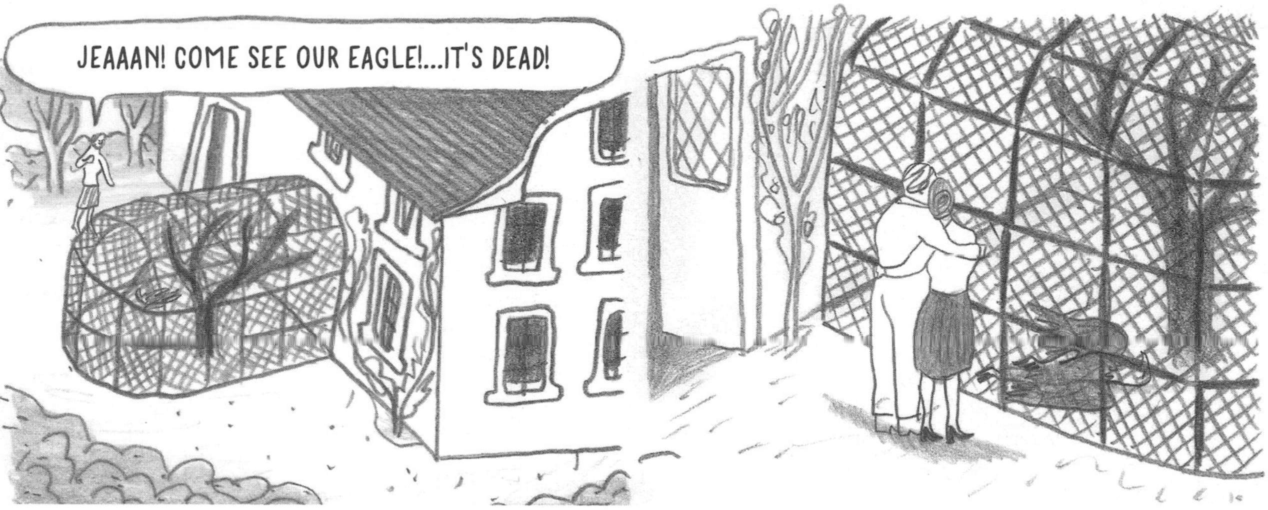
JEAAAN! COME SEE OUR EAGLE!...IT'S DEAD!

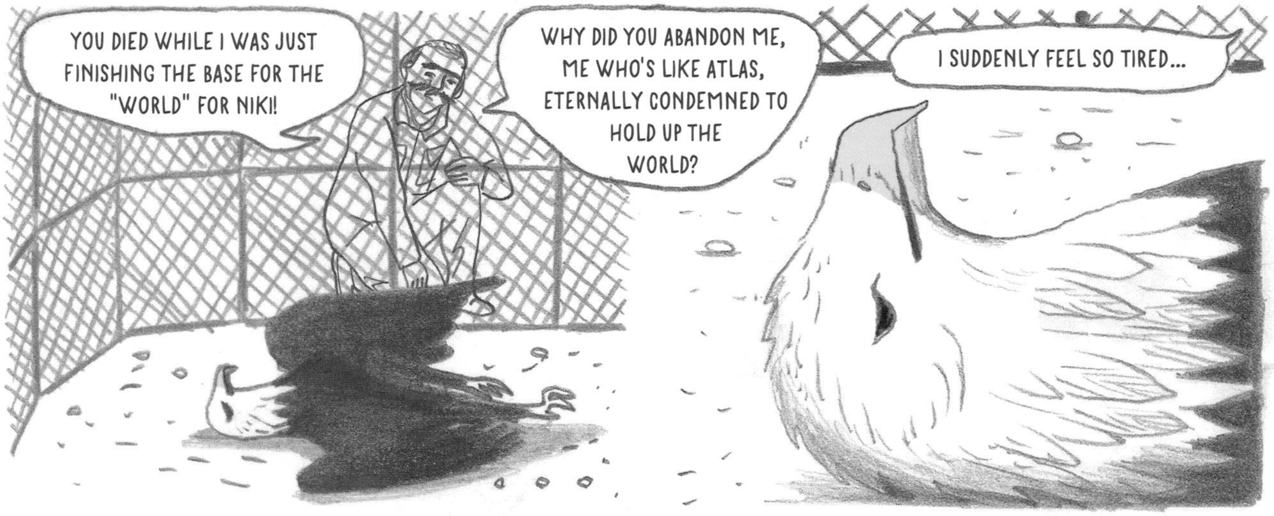
YOU DIED WHILE I WAS JUST FINISHING THE BASE FOR THE "WORLD" FOR NIKI!
WHY DID YOU ABANDON ME, ME WHO'S LIKE ATLAS, ETERNALLY CONDEMNED TO HOLD UP THE WORLD?
I SUDDENLY FEEL SO TIRED...

*In June 1991, Micheline Gygax suddenly left us. I was extremely saddened...Milan was only eighteen.*

AUGUST 18, 1991: PANIC

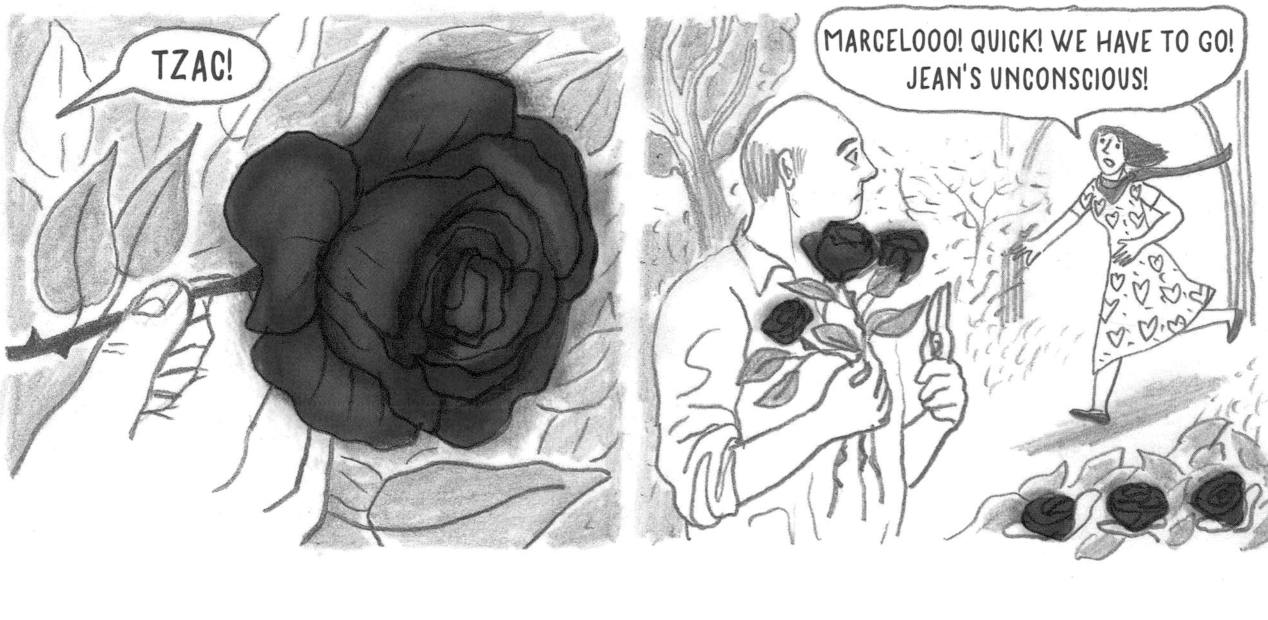
TZAC!
MARCELOOO! QUICK! WE HAVE TO GO! JEAN'S UNCONSCIOUS!

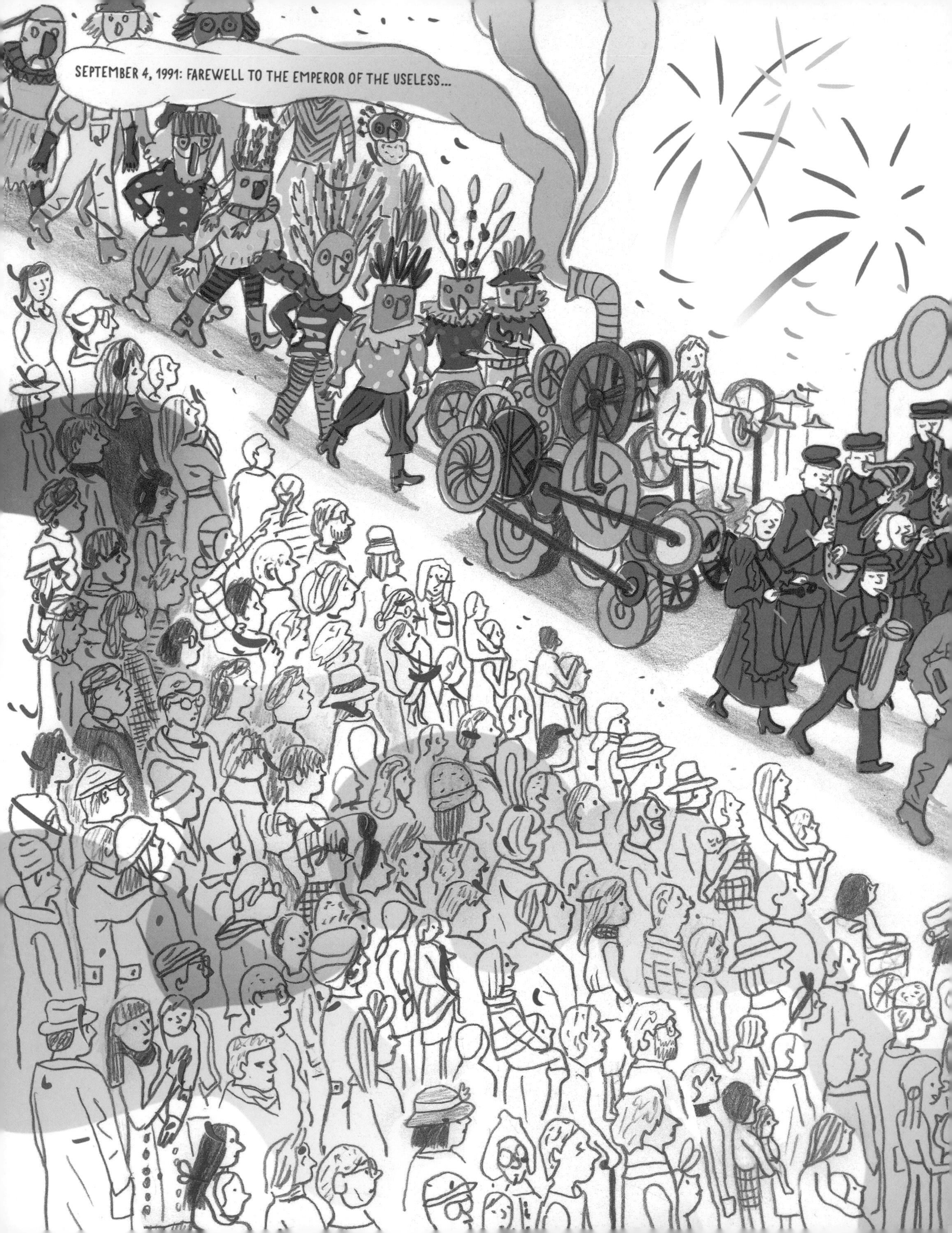
SEPTEMBER 4, 1991: FAREWELL TO THE EMPEROR OF THE USELESS...

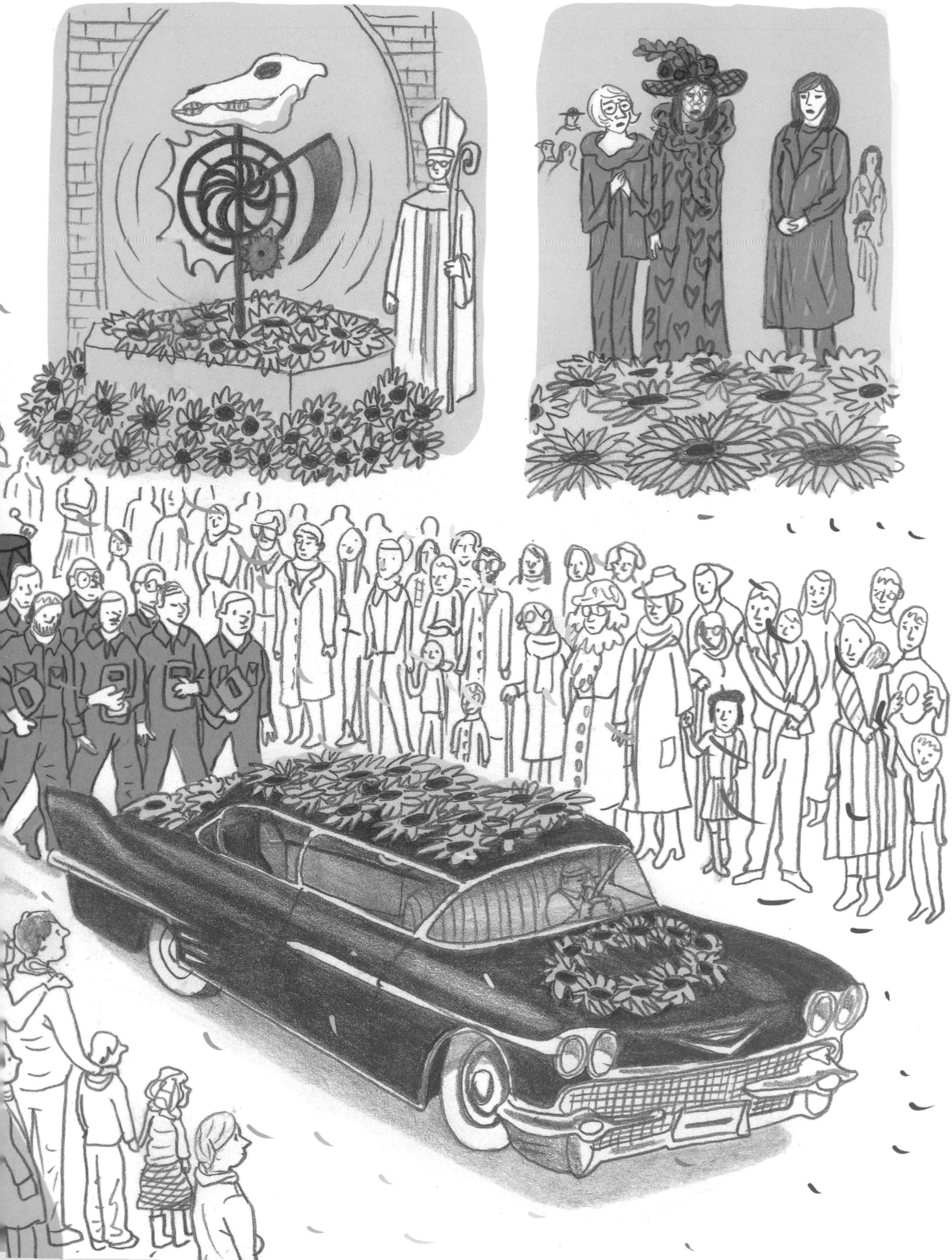

And that's it...IT HAPPENED.
The lightning fell...It struck
down our oak of love. How will I live now?

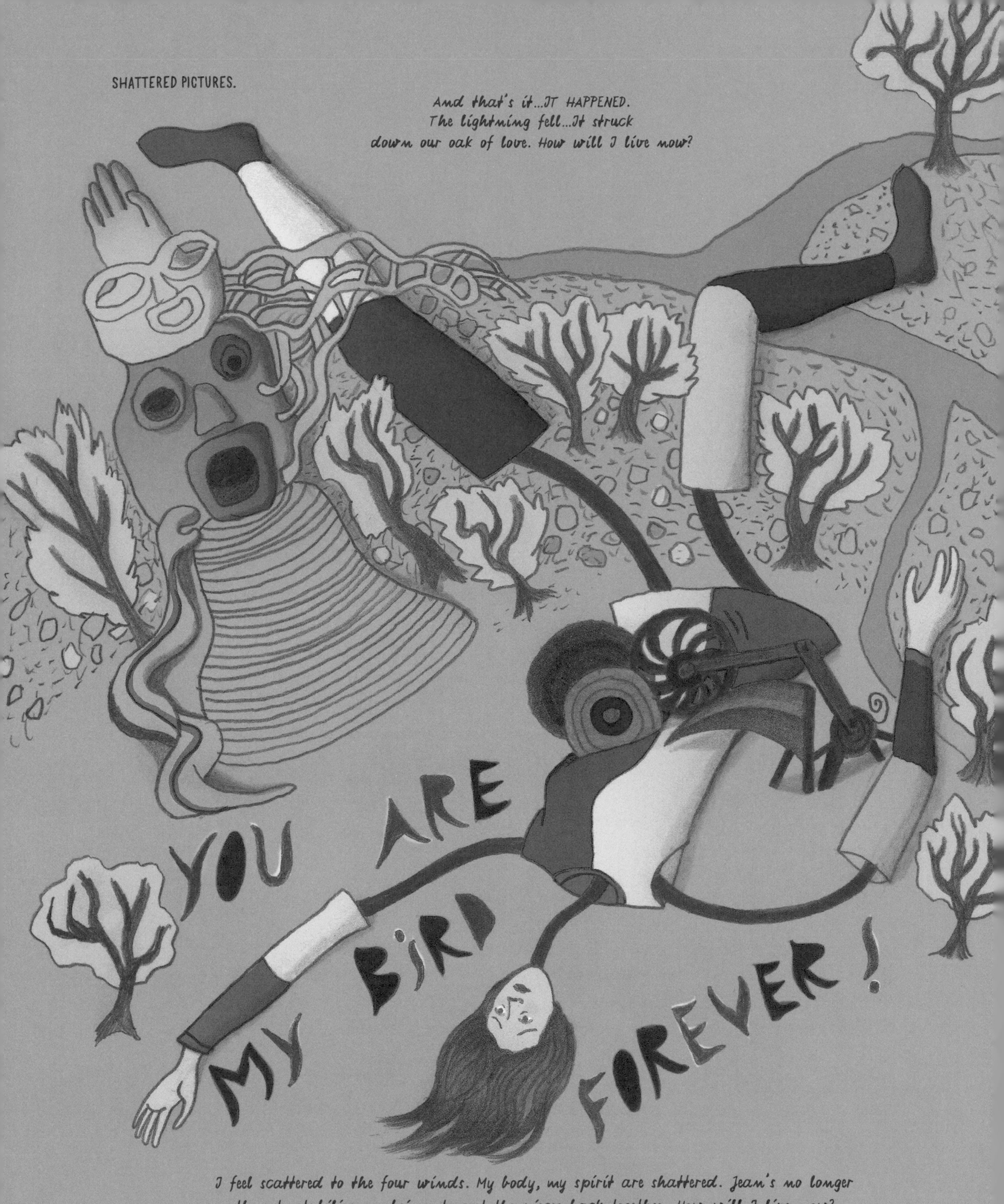
YOU ARE
MY BIRD
FOREVER!

I feel scattered to the four winds. My body, my spirit are shattered. Jean's no longer there to stabilize my being...to put the pieces back together. How will I live now?

# CHAPTER 18

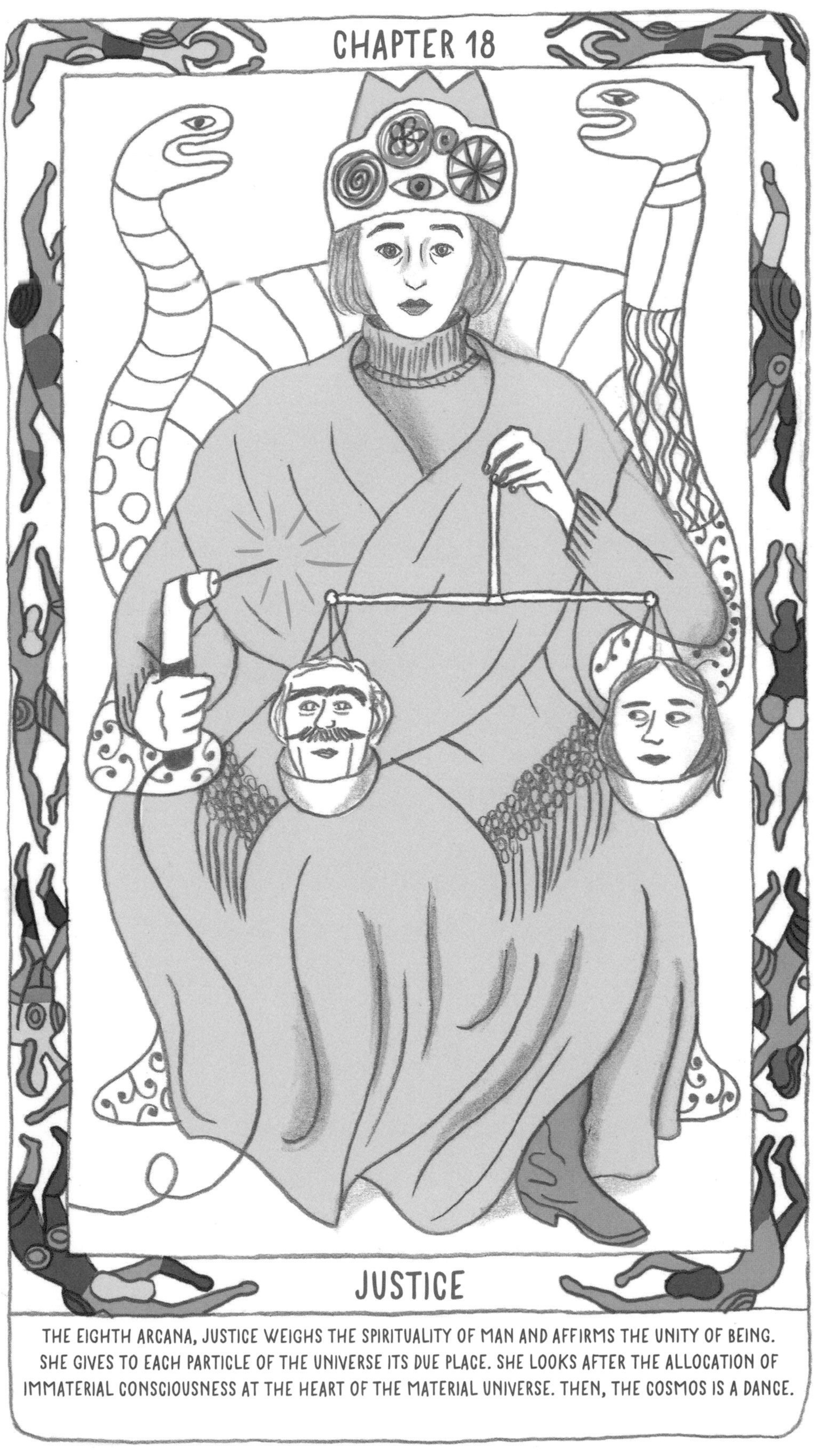

## JUSTICE

THE EIGHTH ARCANA, JUSTICE WEIGHS THE SPIRITUALITY OF MAN AND AFFIRMS THE UNITY OF BEING. SHE GIVES TO EACH PARTICLE OF THE UNIVERSE ITS DUE PLACE. SHE LOOKS AFTER THE ALLOCATION OF IMMATERIAL CONSCIOUSNESS AT THE HEART OF THE MATERIAL UNIVERSE. THEN, THE COSMOS IS A DANCE.

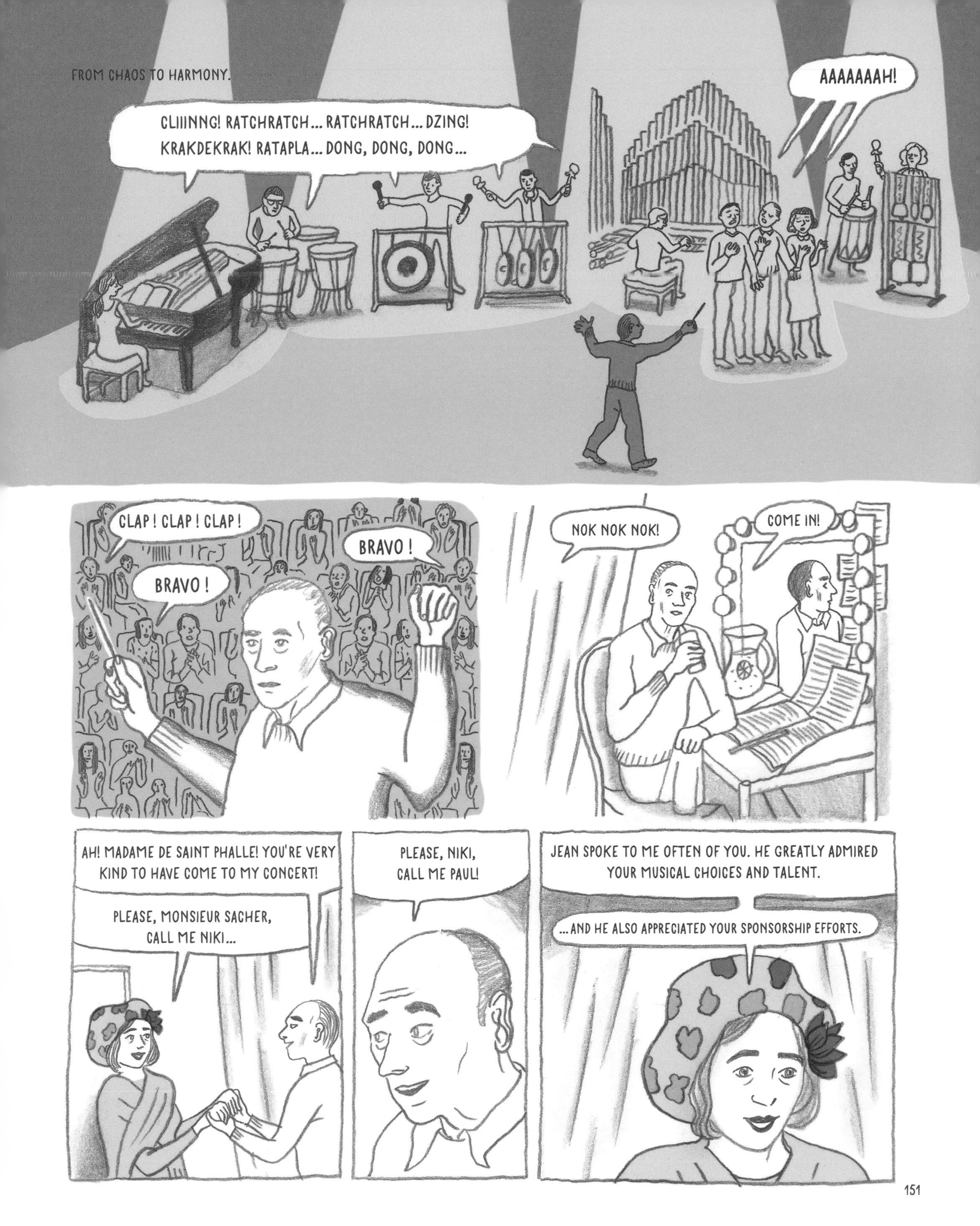
FROM CHAOS TO HARMONY.
CLIIINNG! RATCHRATCH... RATCHRATCH... DZING! KRAKDEKRAK! RATAPLA... DONG, DONG, DONG...
AAAAAAAH!
CLAP! CLAP! CLAP!
BRAVO!
BRAVO!
NOK NOK NOK!
COME IN!
AH! MADAME DE SAINT PHALLE! YOU'RE VERY KIND TO HAVE COME TO MY CONCERT!
PLEASE, MONSIEUR SACHER, CALL ME NIKI...
PLEASE, NIKI, CALL ME PAUL!
JEAN SPOKE TO ME OFTEN OF YOU. HE GREATLY ADMIRED YOUR MUSICAL CHOICES AND TALENT.
...AND HE ALSO APPRECIATED YOUR SPONSORSHIP EFFORTS.

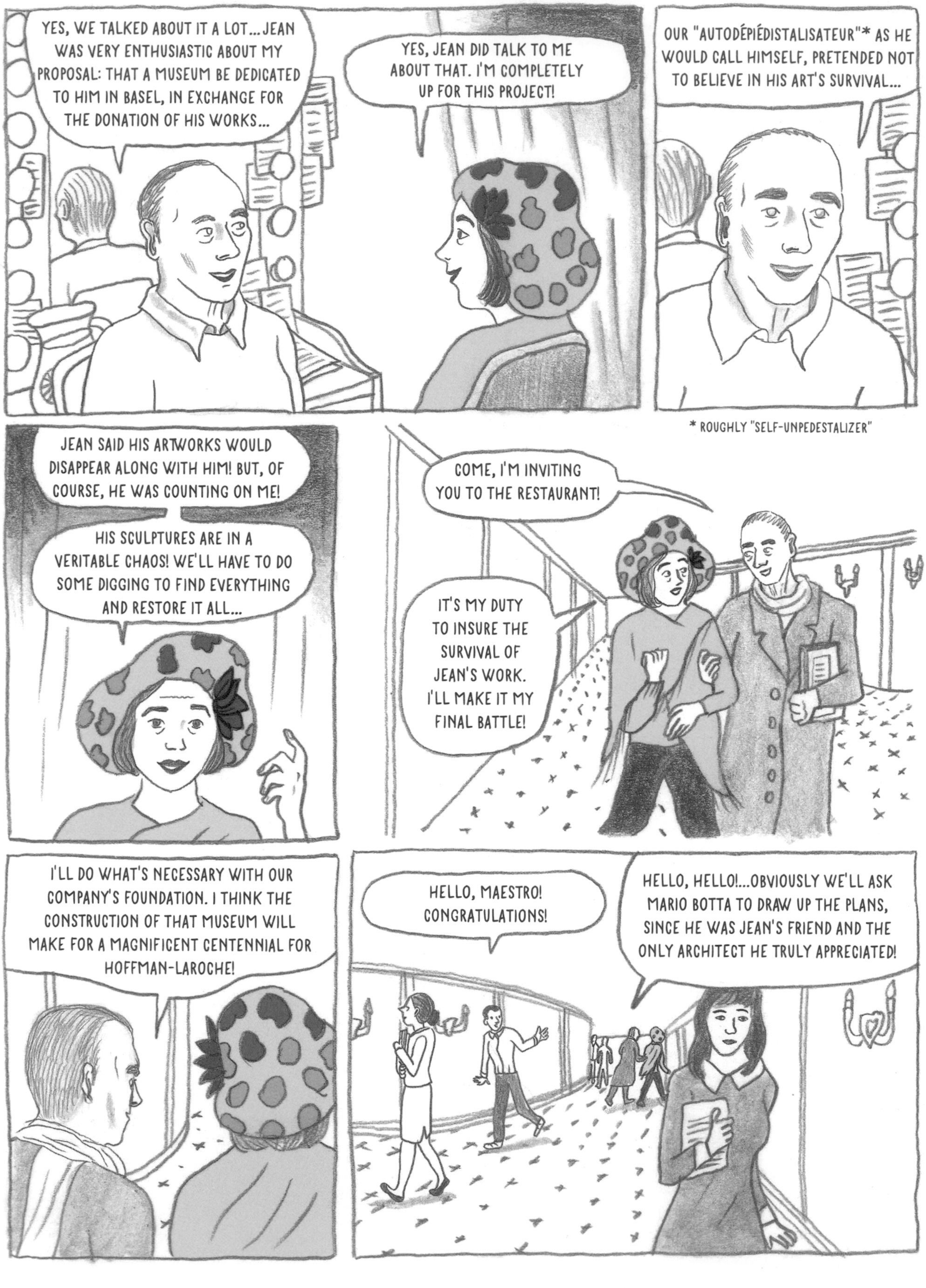
YES, WE TALKED ABOUT IT A LOT... JEAN WAS VERY ENTHUSIASTIC ABOUT MY PROPOSAL: THAT A MUSEUM BE DEDICATED TO HIM IN BASEL, IN EXCHANGE FOR THE DONATION OF HIS WORKS...
YES, JEAN DID TALK TO ME ABOUT THAT. I'M COMPLETELY UP FOR THIS PROJECT!
OUR "AUTODÉPIÉDISTALISATEUR"* AS HE WOULD CALL HIMSELF, PRETENDED NOT TO BELIEVE IN HIS ART'S SURVIVAL...
* ROUGHLY "SELF-UNPEDESTALIZER"
JEAN SAID HIS ARTWORKS WOULD DISAPPEAR ALONG WITH HIM! BUT, OF COURSE, HE WAS COUNTING ON ME!
HIS SCULPTURES ARE IN A VERITABLE CHAOS! WE'LL HAVE TO DO SOME DIGGING TO FIND EVERYTHING AND RESTORE IT ALL...
COME, I'M INVITING YOU TO THE RESTAURANT!
IT'S MY DUTY TO INSURE THE SURVIVAL OF JEAN'S WORK. I'LL MAKE IT MY FINAL BATTLE!
I'LL DO WHAT'S NECESSARY WITH OUR COMPANY'S FOUNDATION. I THINK THE CONSTRUCTION OF THAT MUSEUM WILL MAKE FOR A MAGNIFICENT CENTENNIAL FOR HOFFMAN-LAROCHE!
HELLO, MAESTRO! CONGRATULATIONS!
HELLO, HELLO!...OBVIOUSLY WE'LL ASK MARIO BOTTA TO DRAW UP THE PLANS, SINCE HE WAS JEAN'S FRIEND AND THE ONLY ARCHITECT HE TRULY APPRECIATED!

*How do I dispose the forces of the world in my favor?*

"JEAN, I'M EATING YOU. I'M TAKING YOUR STRENGTH. YOUR SOUL IS UNITING WITH MINE."

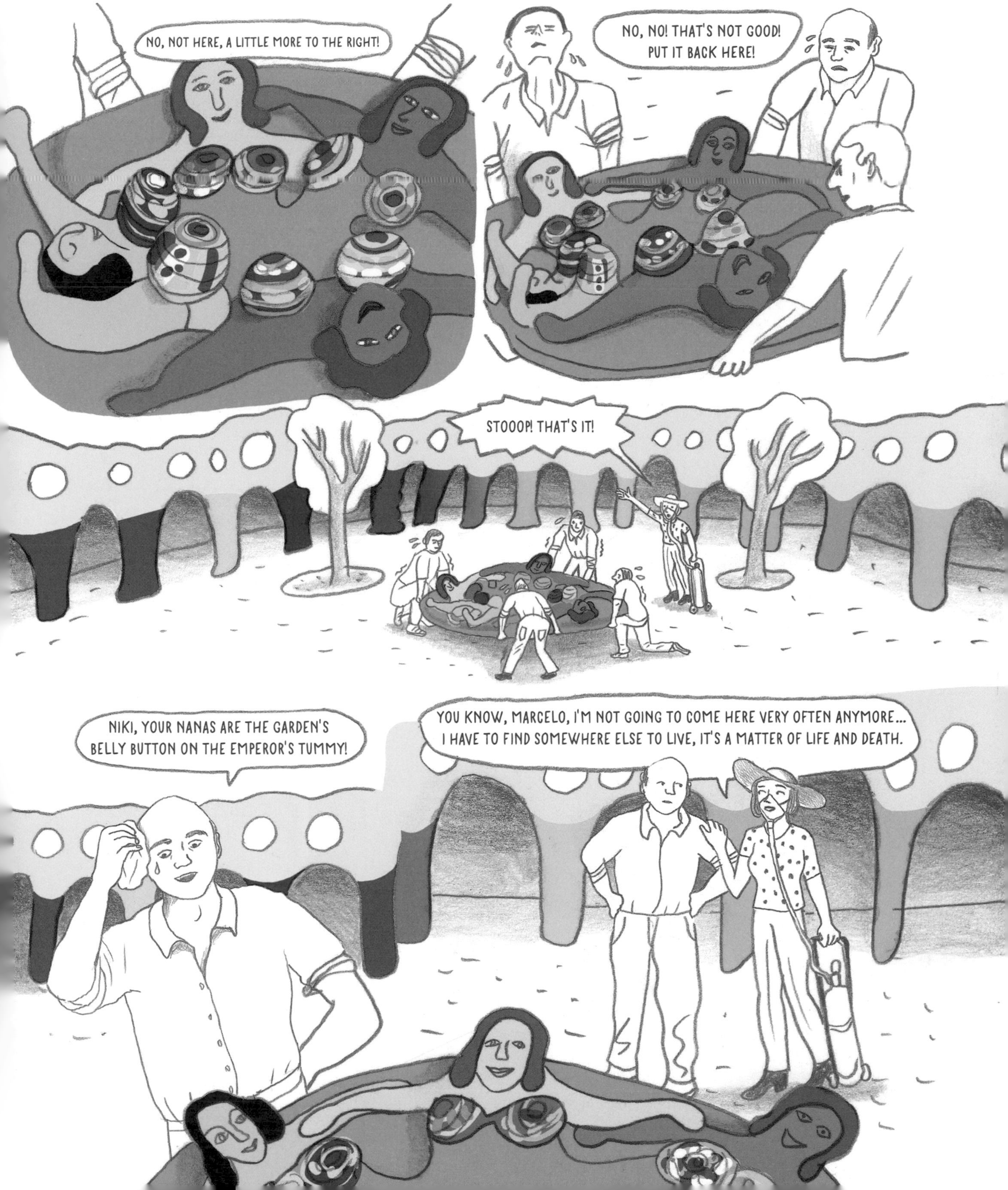
NO, NOT HERE, A LITTLE MORE TO THE RIGHT!
NO, NO! THAT'S NOT GOOD! PUT IT BACK HERE!
STOOOP! THAT'S IT!
NIKI, YOUR NANAS ARE THE GARDEN'S BELLY BUTTON ON THE EMPEROR'S TUMMY!
YOU KNOW, MARCELO, I'M NOT GOING TO COME HERE VERY OFTEN ANYMORE... I HAVE TO FIND SOMEWHERE ELSE TO LIVE, IT'S A MATTER OF LIFE AND DEATH.

FRIBOURG, SWITZERLAND: FROM THE DEPOT TO THE EXPO!

*My dear friend Pontus Hultén, named director of the brand-new Kunsthalle in Bonn, offered me a magnificent retrospective in 1992, which then toured in 1993 to Glasgow, Paris, and finished in Fribourg.*

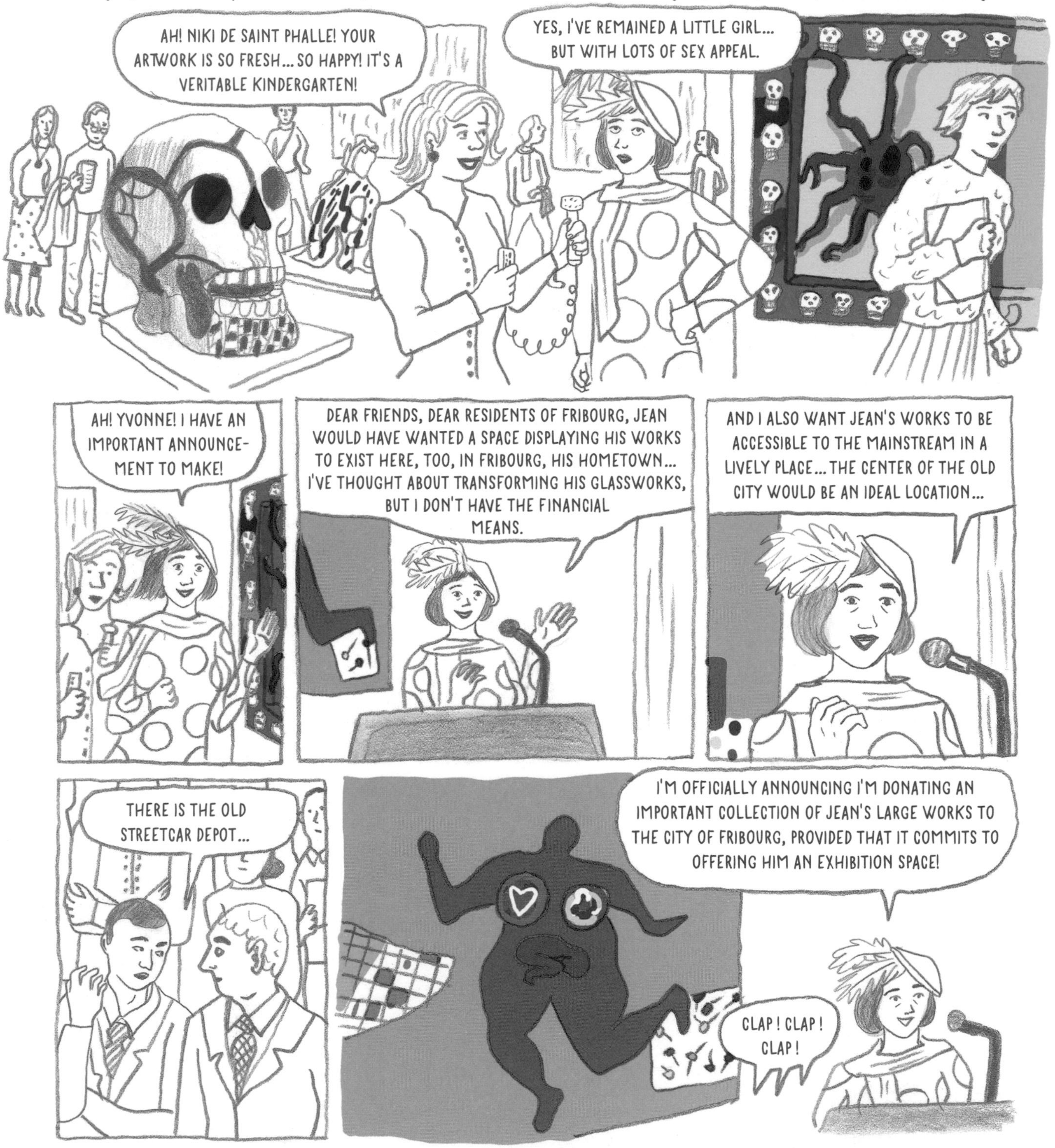
AH! NIKI DE SAINT PHALLE! YOUR ARTWORK IS SO FRESH... SO HAPPY! IT'S A VERITABLE KINDERGARTEN!
YES, I'VE REMAINED A LITTLE GIRL... BUT WITH LOTS OF SEX APPEAL.
AH! YVONNE! I HAVE AN IMPORTANT ANNOUNCE-MENT TO MAKE!
DEAR FRIENDS, DEAR RESIDENTS OF FRIBOURG, JEAN WOULD HAVE WANTED A SPACE DISPLAYING HIS WORKS TO EXIST HERE, TOO, IN FRIBOURG, HIS HOMETOWN... I'VE THOUGHT ABOUT TRANSFORMING HIS GLASSWORKS, BUT I DON'T HAVE THE FINANCIAL MEANS.
AND I ALSO WANT JEAN'S WORKS TO BE ACCESSIBLE TO THE MAINSTREAM IN A LIVELY PLACE... THE CENTER OF THE OLD CITY WOULD BE AN IDEAL LOCATION...
THERE IS THE OLD STREETCAR DEPOT...
I'M OFFICIALLY ANNOUNCING I'M DONATING AN IMPORTANT COLLECTION OF JEAN'S LARGE WORKS TO THE CITY OF FRIBOURG, PROVIDED THAT IT COMMITS TO OFFERING HIM AN EXHIBITION SPACE!
CLAP! CLAP! CLAP!

*Here I am a great-grandmother! My little Bloum brings me great joy: a baby of mixed race! When I think of my childhood of being fed by the "colored" wet-nurse: Nana! How I loved you... And what a lovely revenge on my family of white aristocrats!*

# CHAPTER 19

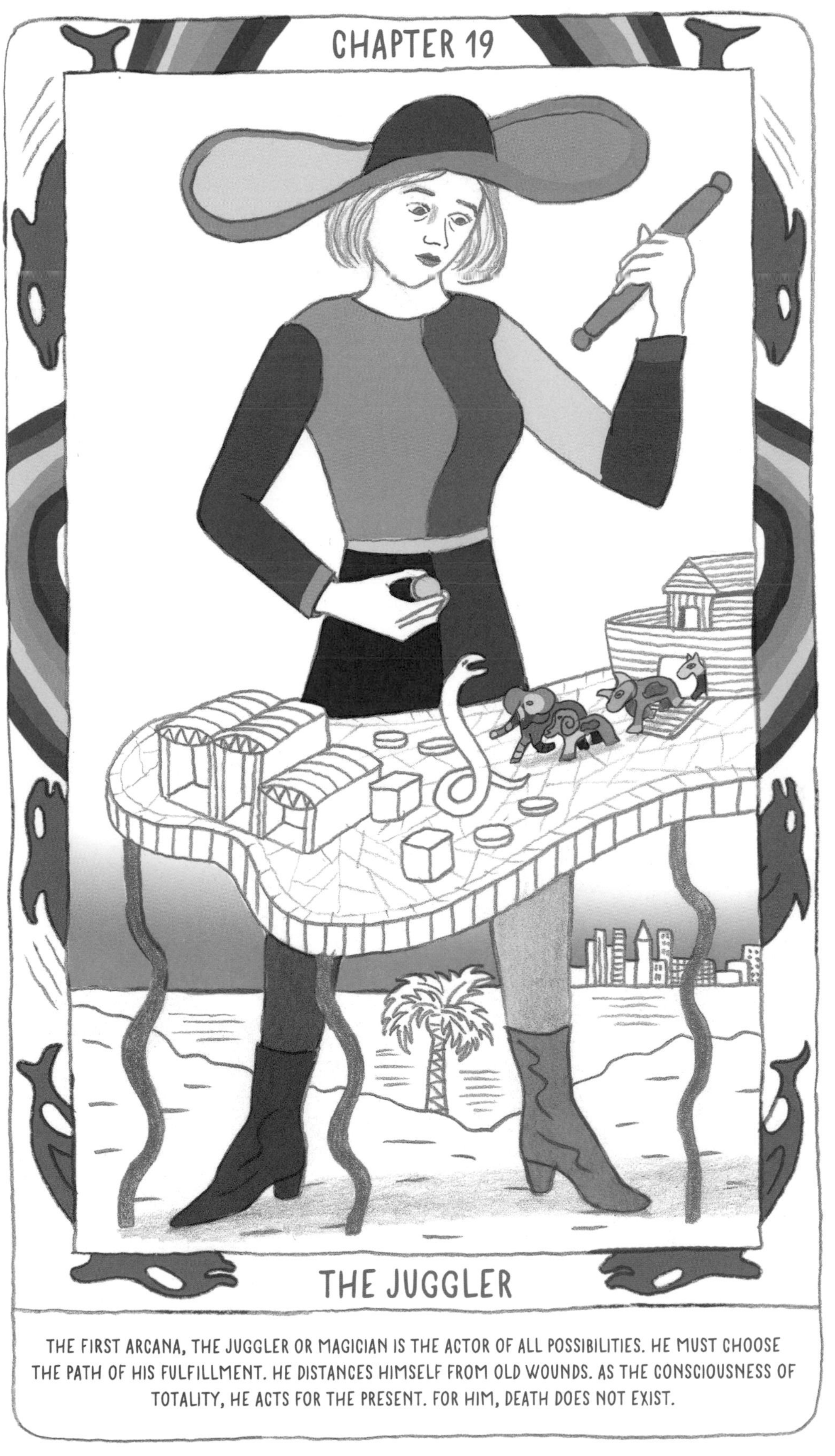

## THE JUGGLER

THE FIRST ARCANA, THE JUGGLER OR MAGICIAN IS THE ACTOR OF ALL POSSIBILITIES. HE MUST CHOOSE THE PATH OF HIS FULFILLMENT. HE DISTANCES HIMSELF FROM OLD WOUNDS. AS THE CONSCIOUSNESS OF TOTALITY, HE ACTS FOR THE PRESENT. FOR HIM, DEATH DOES NOT EXIST.

1994, SAN DIEGO, CALIFORNIA.

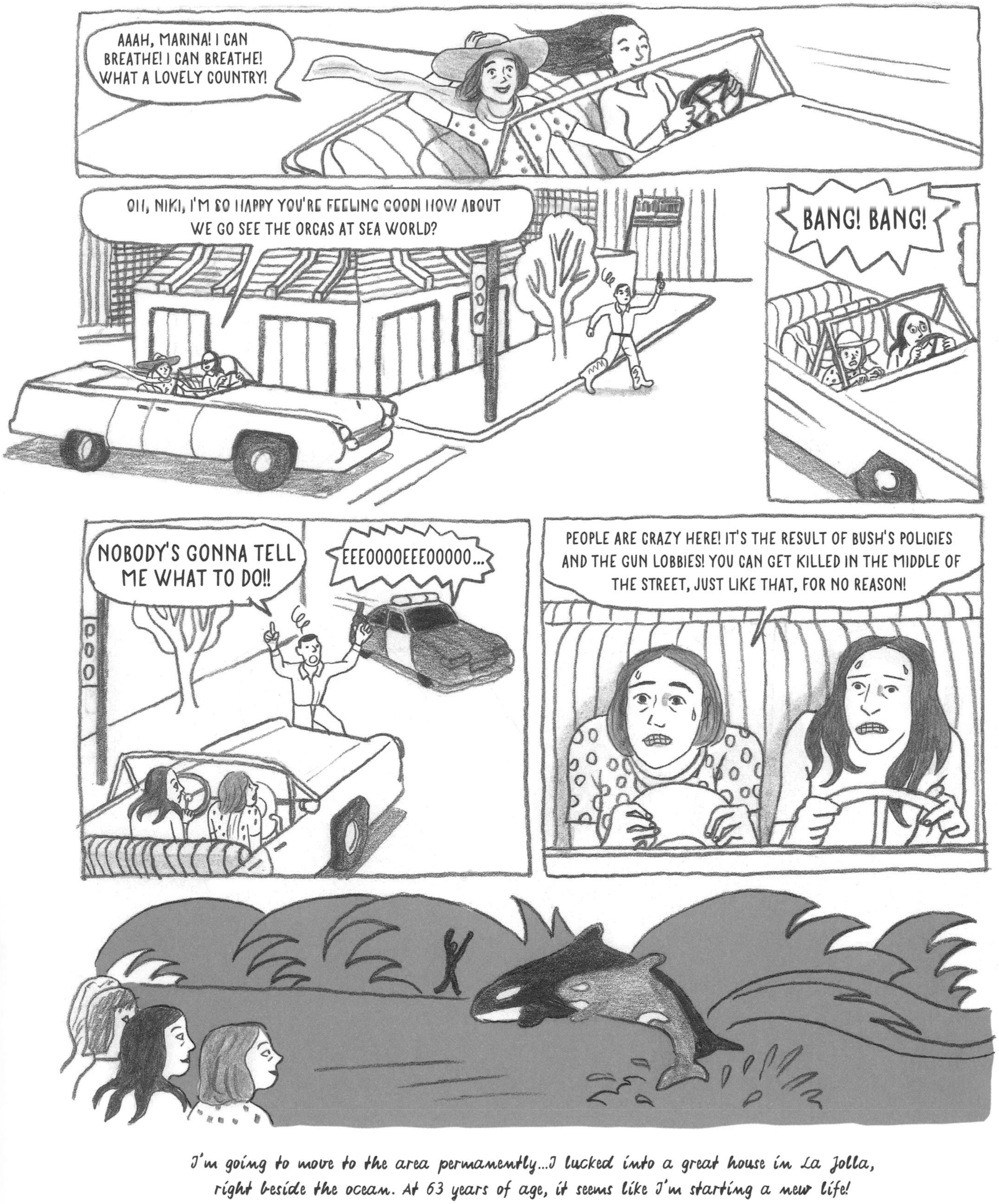
AAAH, MARINA! I CAN BREATHE! I CAN BREATHE! WHAT A LOVELY COUNTRY!
OH, NIKI, I'M SO HAPPY YOU'RE FEELING GOOD! HOW ABOUT WE GO SEE THE ORCAS AT SEA WORLD?
BANG! BANG!
NOBODY'S GONNA TELL ME WHAT TO DO!!
EEEOOOOEEEOOOOO...
PEOPLE ARE CRAZY HERE! IT'S THE RESULT OF BUSH'S POLICIES AND THE GUN LOBBIES! YOU CAN GET KILLED IN THE MIDDLE OF THE STREET, JUST LIKE THAT, FOR NO REASON!

*I'm going to move to the area permanently...I lucked into a great house in La Jolla, right beside the ocean. At 63 years of age, it seems like I'm starting a new life!*

LA JOLLA, 7907 PRINCESS STREET...

*I feel so good again in this American setting! My great-grandson Djamal is my new sun, and I'm reinventing the animals of creation for him. They'll go join my great project of Noah's Ark, which I began with Mario Botta, at Teddy Kollek's request.*

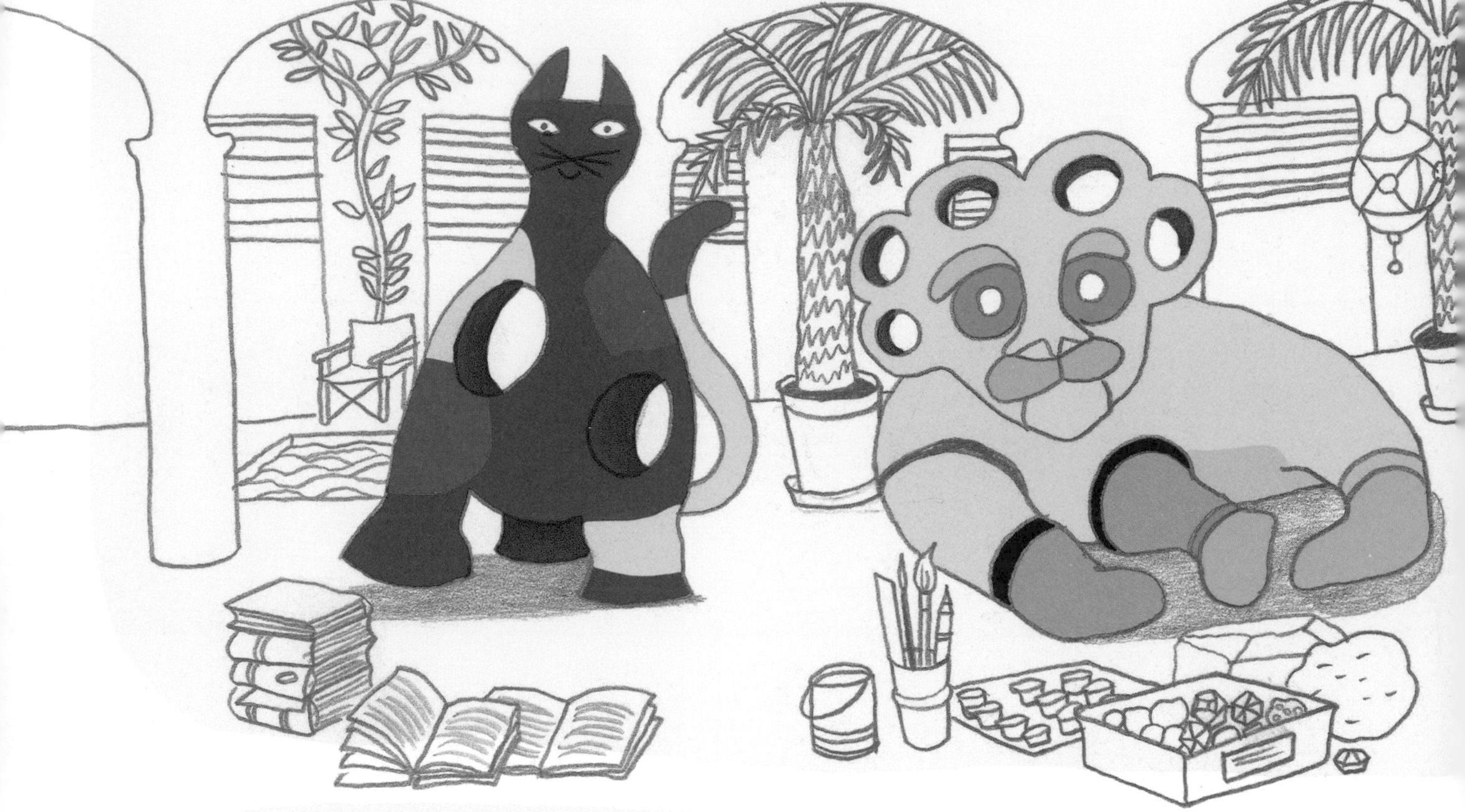

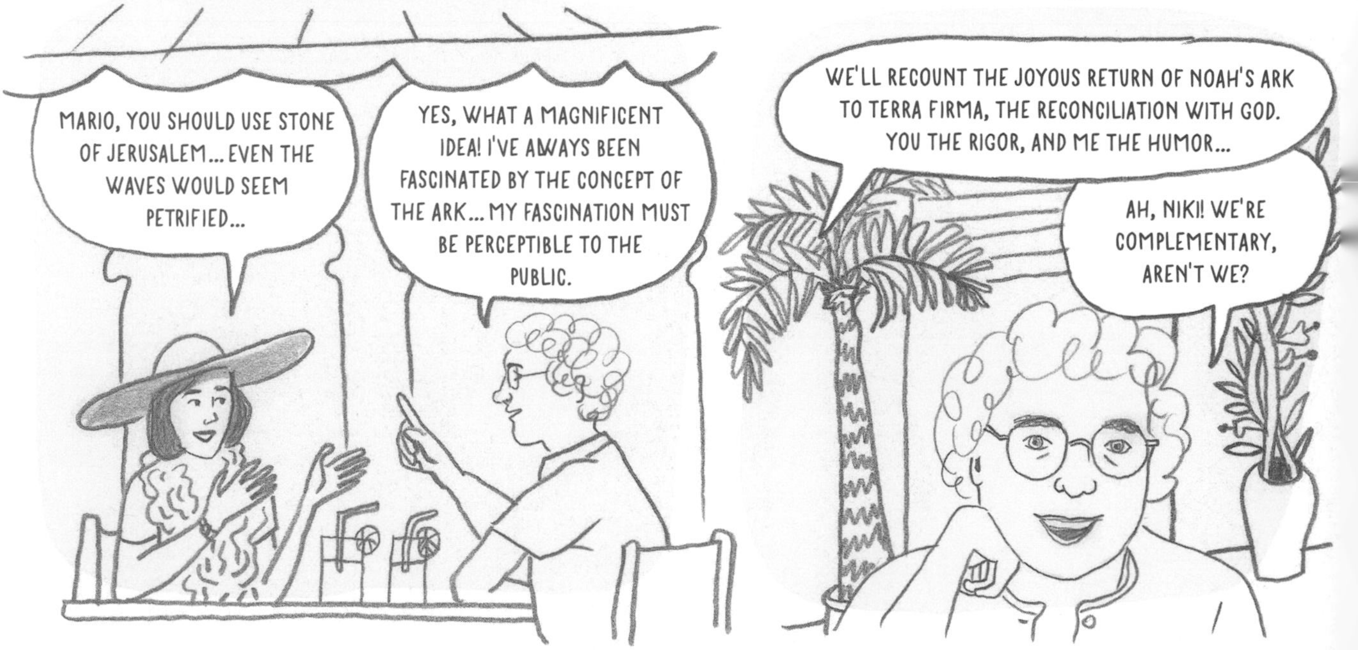
MARIO, YOU SHOULD USE STONE OF JERUSALEM... EVEN THE WAVES WOULD SEEM PETRIFIED...
YES, WHAT A MAGNIFICENT IDEA! I'VE ALWAYS BEEN FASCINATED BY THE CONCEPT OF THE ARK... MY FASCINATION MUST BE PERCEPTIBLE TO THE PUBLIC.
WE'LL RECOUNT THE JOYOUS RETURN OF NOAH'S ARK TO TERRA FIRMA, THE RECONCILIATION WITH GOD. YOU THE RIGOR, AND ME THE HUMOR...
AH, NIKI! WE'RE COMPLEMENTARY, AREN'T WE?

*Mario is my brother. We're bound by a sort of loving friendship and by our mutual passion for art. There's something like an electrical current that stimulates us...*

Teddy is my friend and the former mayor of Jerusalem, the one who'd once ordered the Golem from me, so long ago...He's also renowned for being the greatest builder in Jerusalem since King Herod!

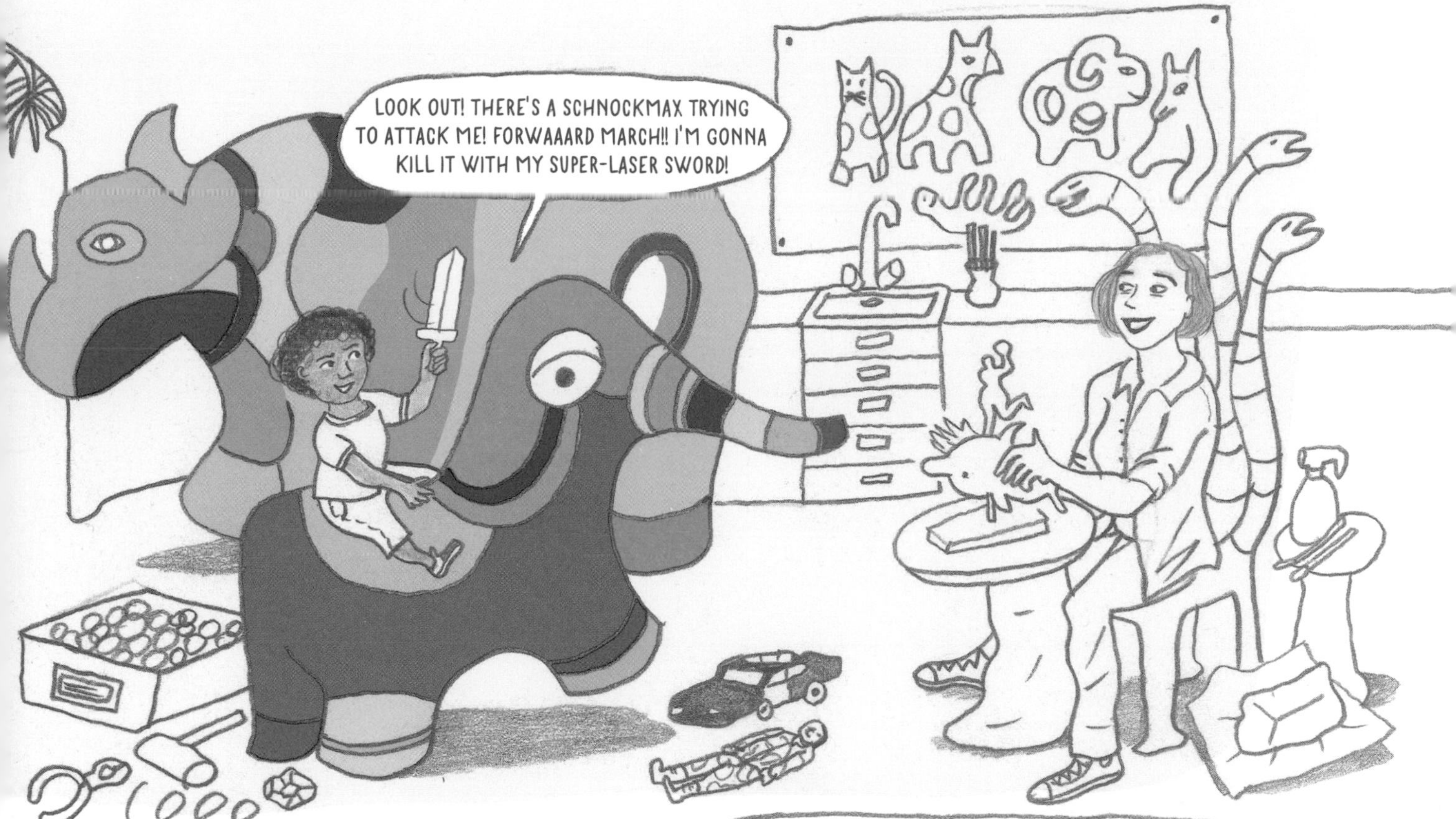
LOOK OUT! THERE'S A SCHNOCKMAX TRYING TO ATTACK ME! FORWAAARD MARCH!! I'M GONNA KILL IT WITH MY SUPER-LASER SWORD!

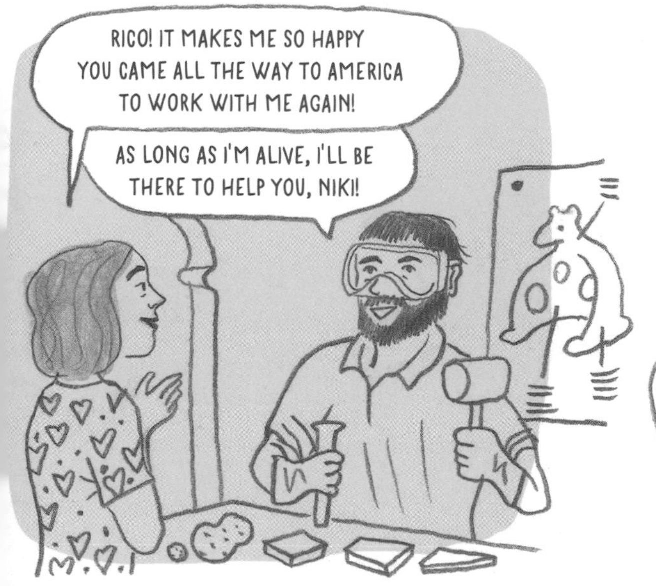
RICO! IT MAKES ME SO HAPPY YOU CAME ALL THE WAY TO AMERICA TO WORK WITH ME AGAIN!
AS LONG AS I'M ALIVE, I'LL BE THERE TO HELP YOU, NIKI!
M.V.I

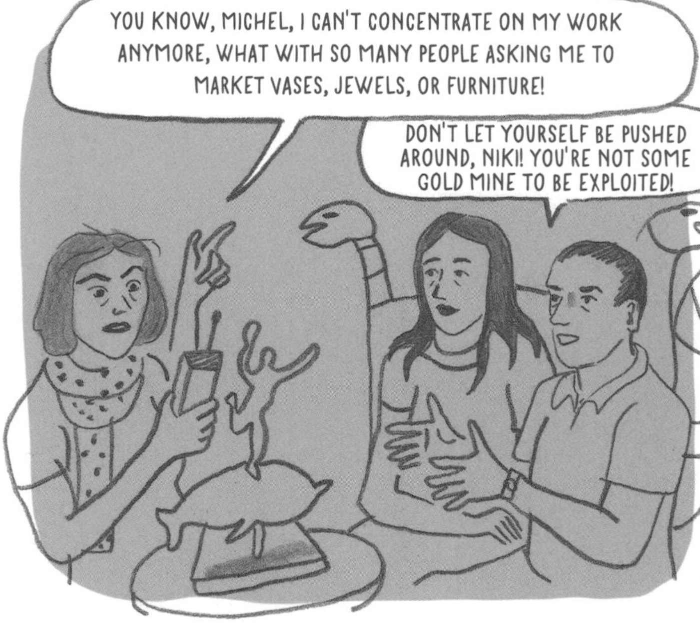
YOU KNOW, MICHEL, I CAN'T CONCENTRATE ON MY WORK ANYMORE, WHAT WITH SO MANY PEOPLE ASKING ME TO MARKET VASES, JEWELS, OR FURNITURE!
DON'T LET YOURSELF BE PUSHED AROUND, NIKI! YOU'RE NOT SOME GOLD MINE TO BE EXPLOITED!

My long-time friends come to visit and support me. They understand I have no intention of locking myself into the image of the mystic couple "Jean-Niki." Other people want me just to sign on the dotted line without doing anything else...But "I'm not Adam's rib"!

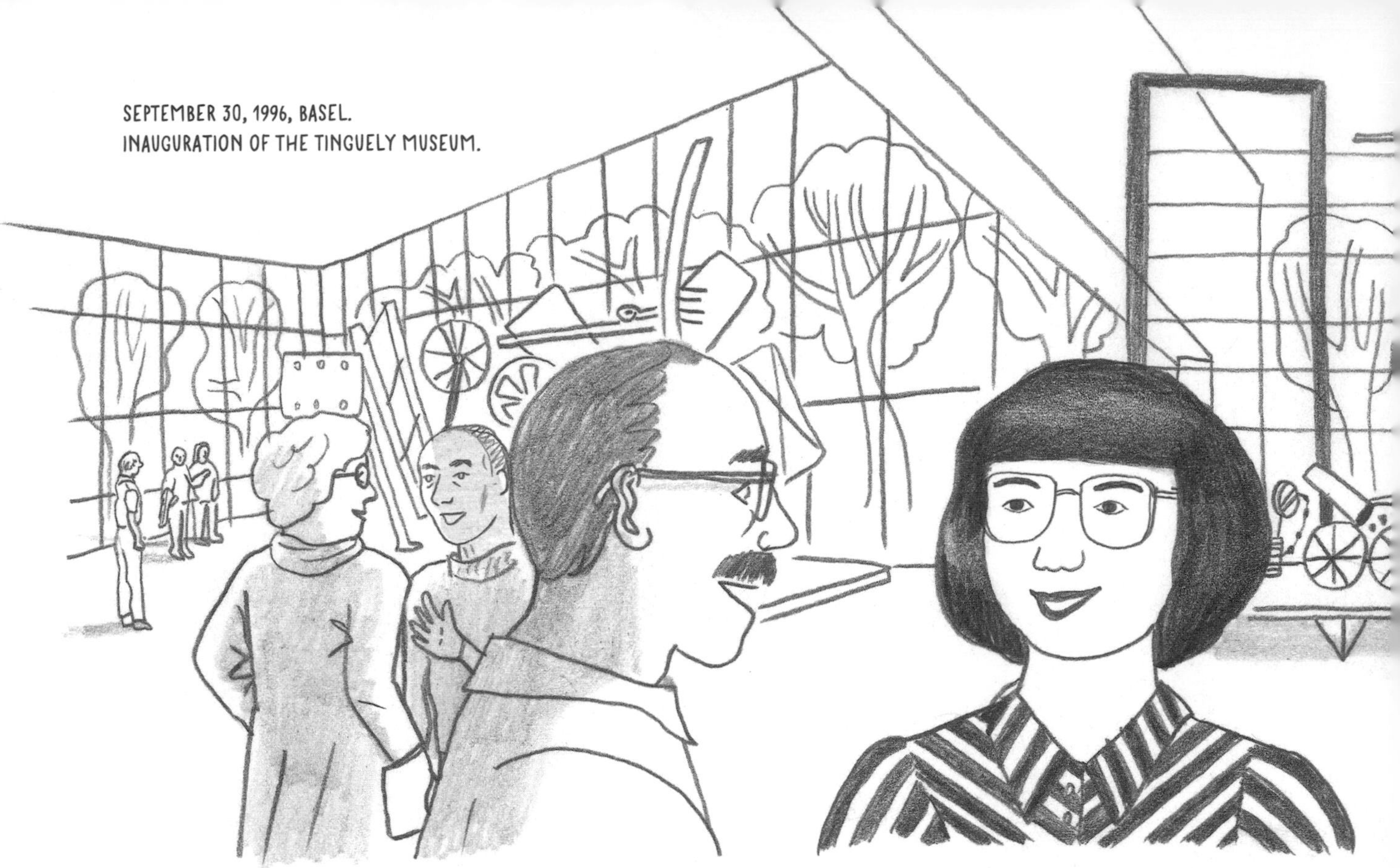
SEPTEMBER 30, 1996, BASEL.
INAUGURATION OF THE TINGUELY MUSEUM.

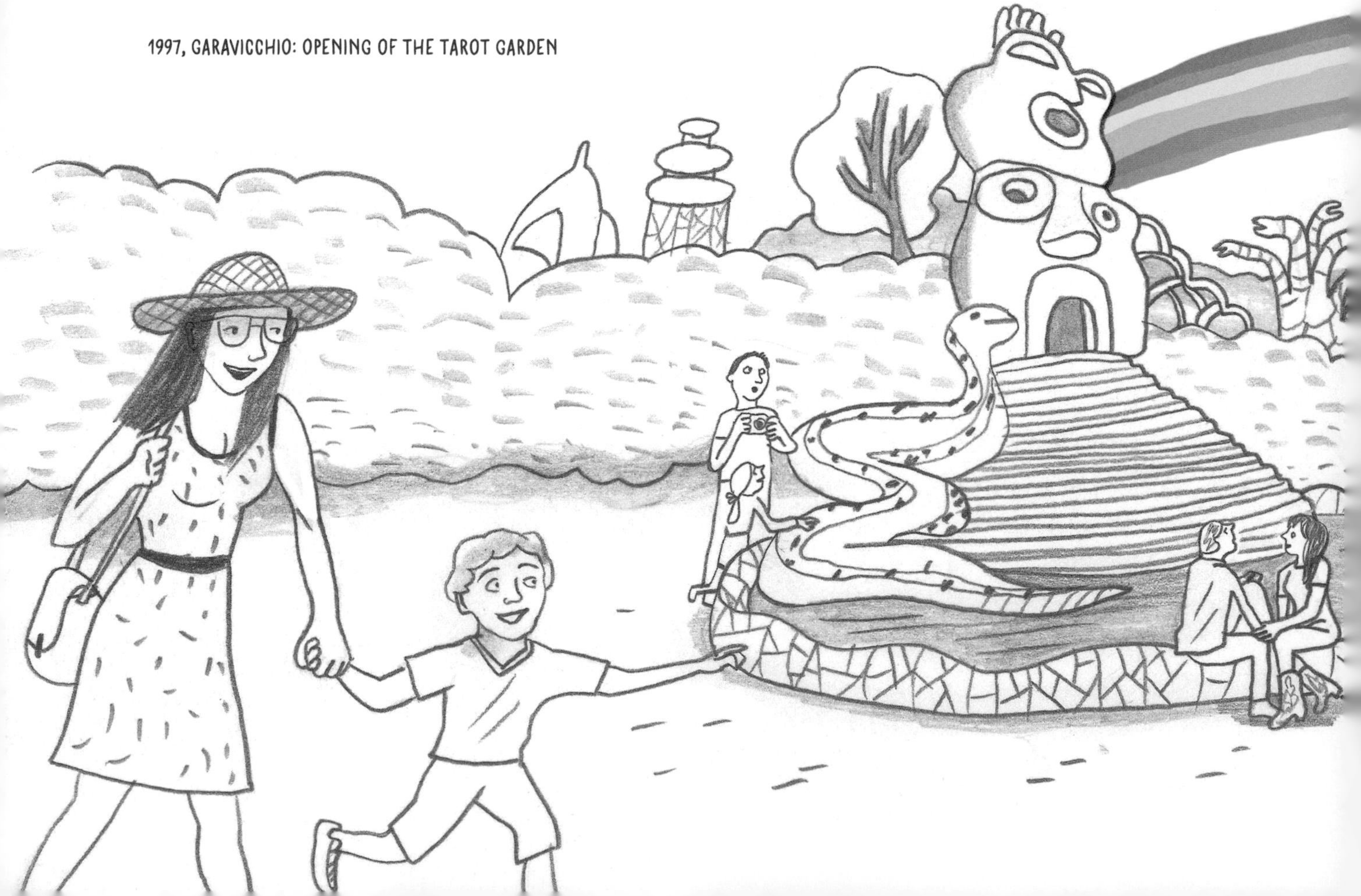
1997, GARAVICCHIO: OPENING OF THE TAROT GARDEN

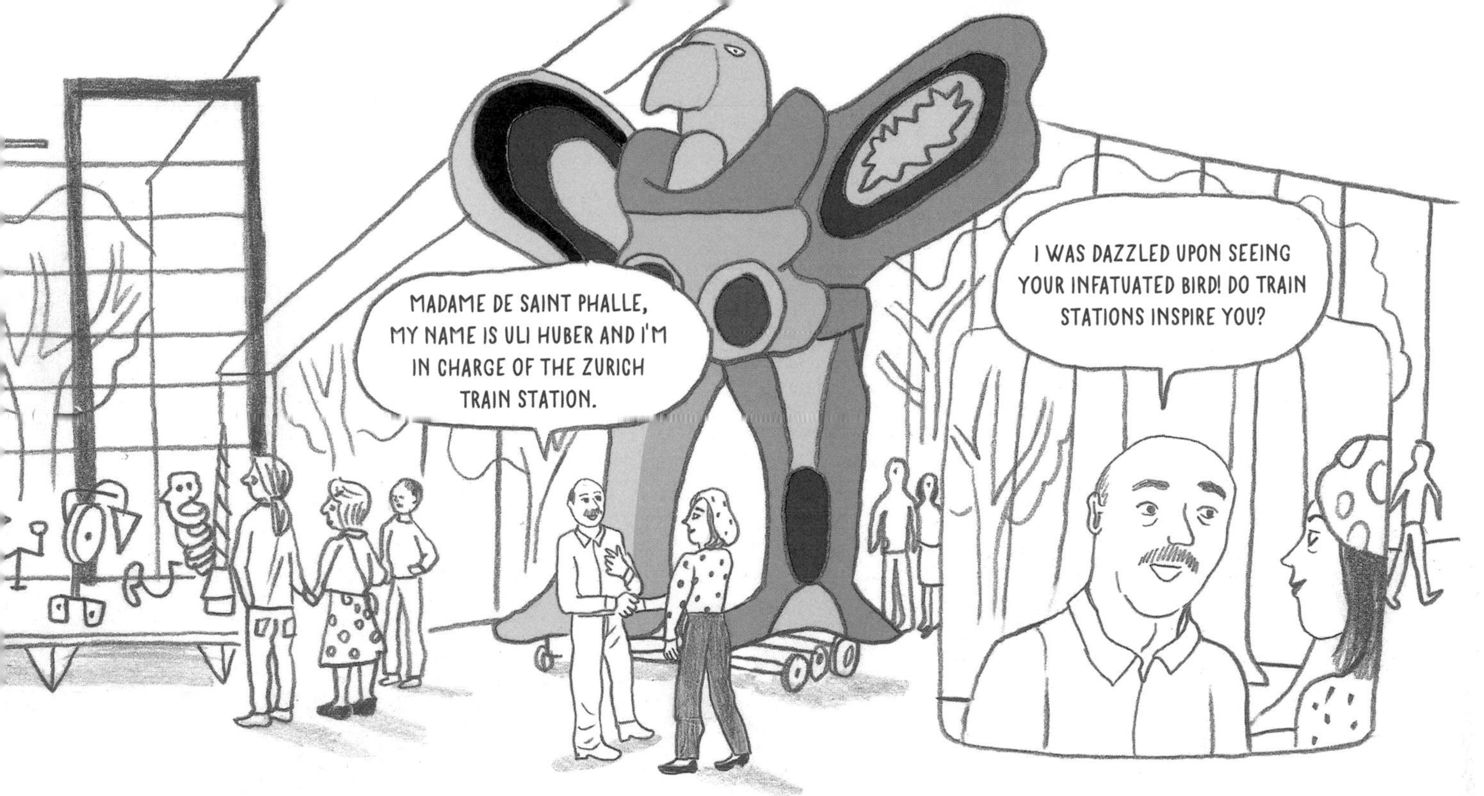
MADAME DE SAINT PHALLE, MY NAME IS ULI HUBER AND I'M IN CHARGE OF THE ZURICH TRAIN STATION.
I WAS DAZZLED UPON SEEING YOUR INFATUATED BIRD! DO TRAIN STATIONS INSPIRE YOU?

*I'm so comforted and proud of having succeeded in saving Jean's sculptures! They're now in good hands for generations to come... Now I can go on with my own life!*

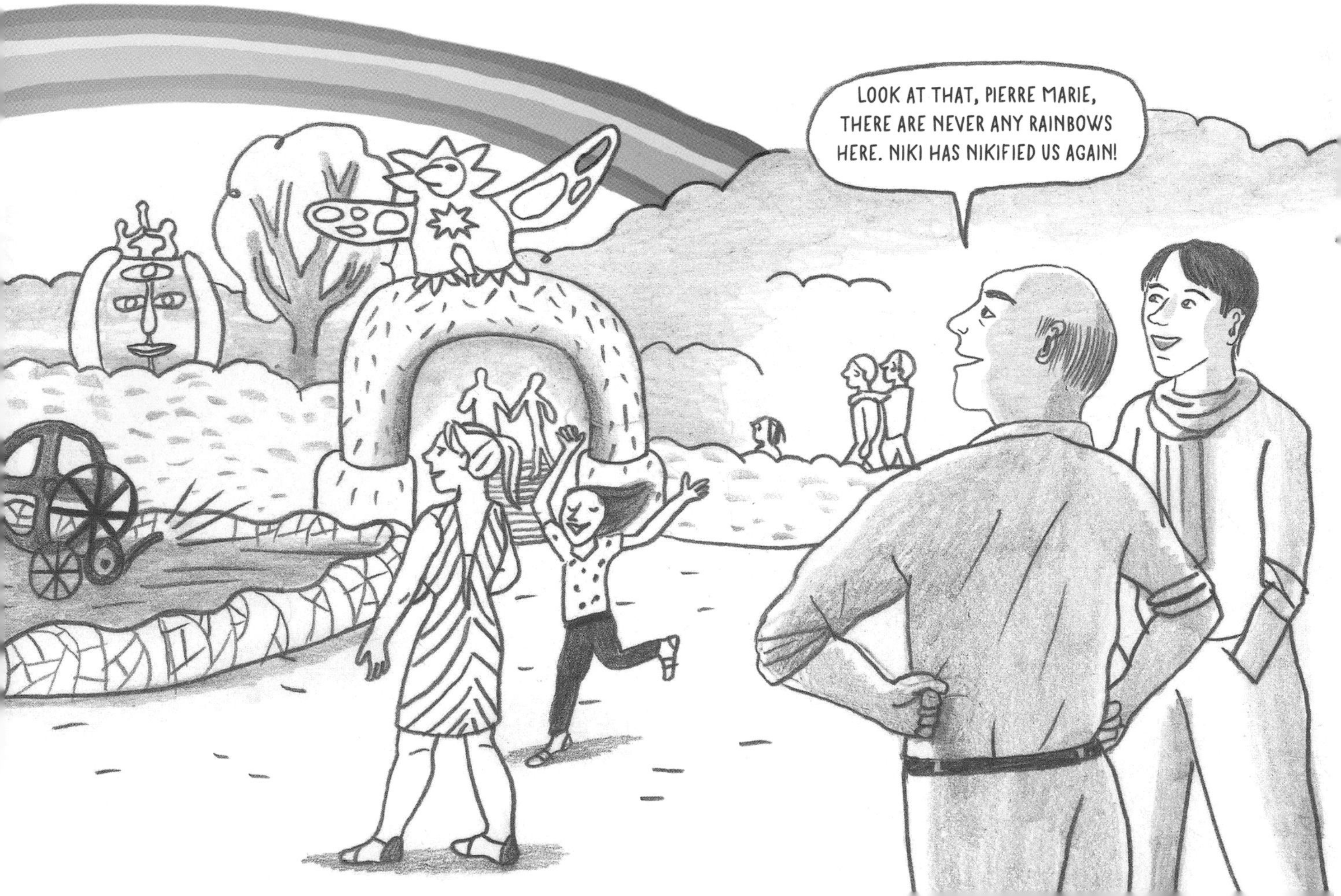
LOOK AT THAT, PIERRE MARIE, THERE ARE NEVER ANY RAINBOWS HERE. NIKI HAS NIKIFIED US AGAIN!

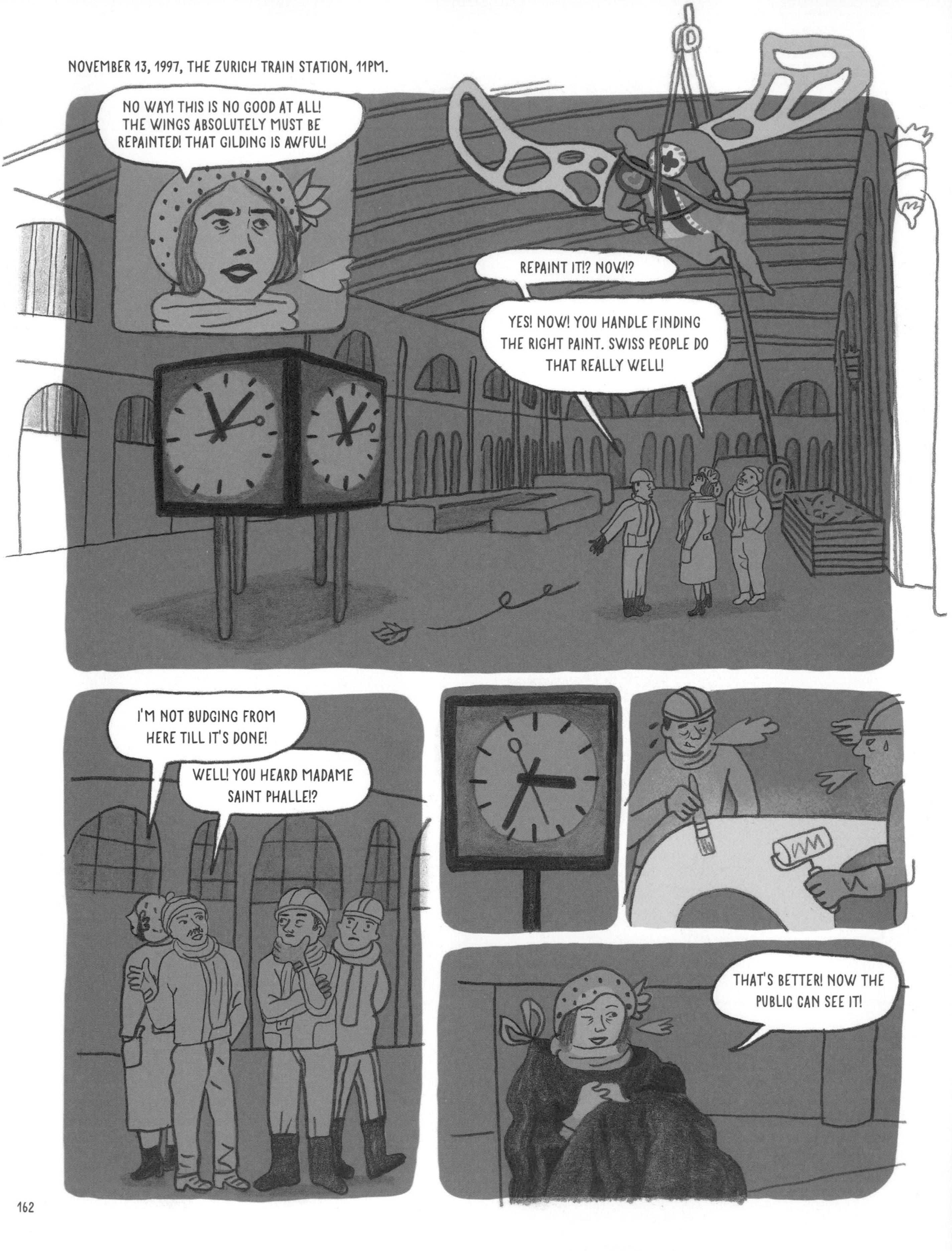
NOVEMBER 13, 1997, THE ZURICH TRAIN STATION, 11PM.
NO WAY! THIS IS NO GOOD AT ALL! THE WINGS ABSOLUTELY MUST BE REPAINTED! THAT GILDING IS AWFUL!
REPAINT IT!? NOW!?
YES! NOW! YOU HANDLE FINDING THE RIGHT PAINT. SWISS PEOPLE DO THAT REALLY WELL!
I'M NOT BUDGING FROM HERE TILL IT'S DONE!
WELL! YOU HEARD MADAME SAINT PHALLE!?
THAT'S BETTER! NOW THE PUBLIC CAN SEE IT!

# CHAPTER 20

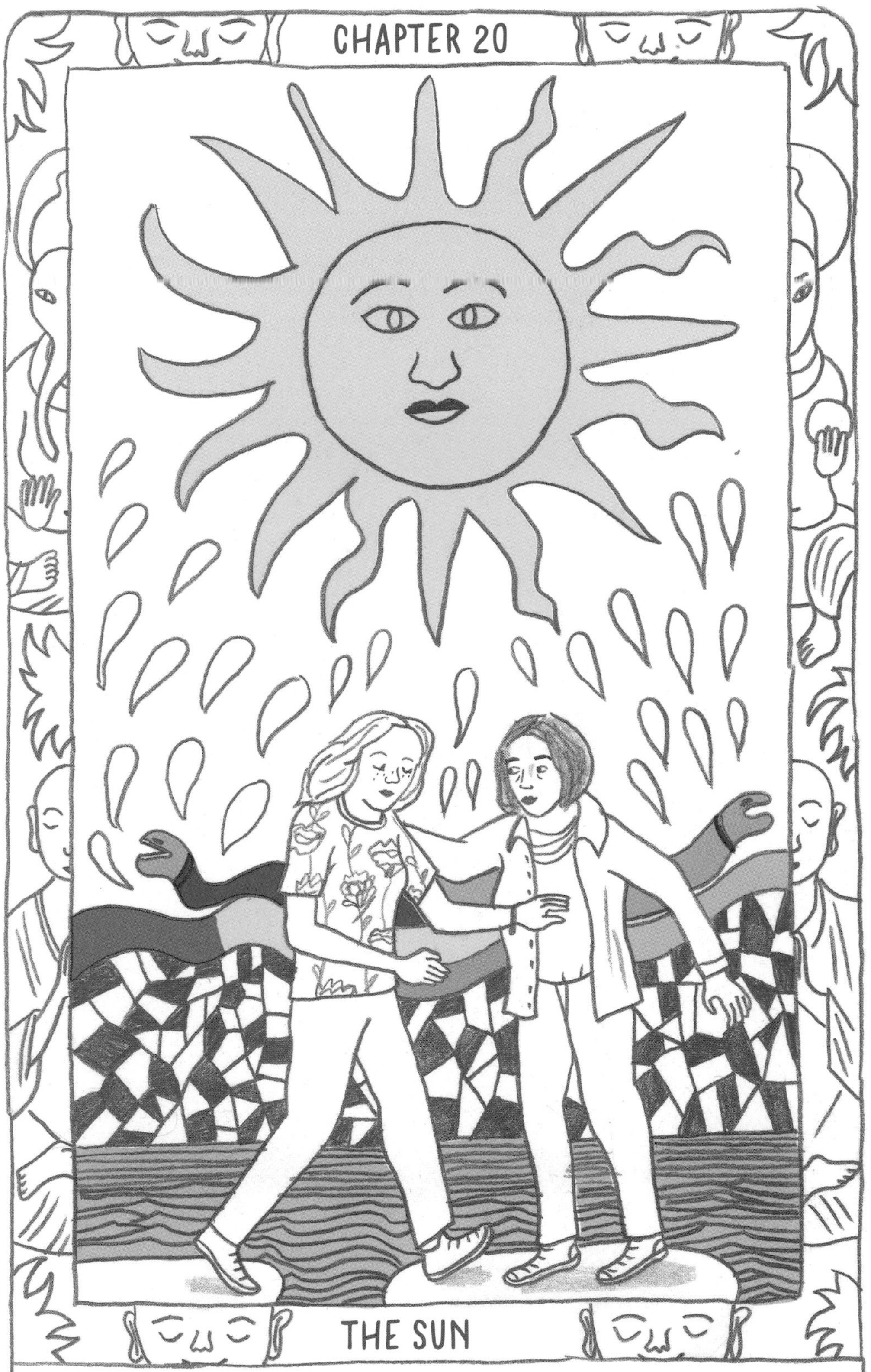

## THE SUN

THE NINETEENTH ARCANA, THE SUN MARKS ACHIEVEMENT AND SUCCESS, THE BEGINNING OF A NEW LIFE CASTING ASIDE THE DIFFICULTIES OF THE PAST. IT BRIGHTENS THE BEINGS WHO EXCHANGE THEIR AFFECTION. ITS LOVE IS THE EXPRESSION OF THE NEED OF OTHERS.

A SAVAGE QUEEN.

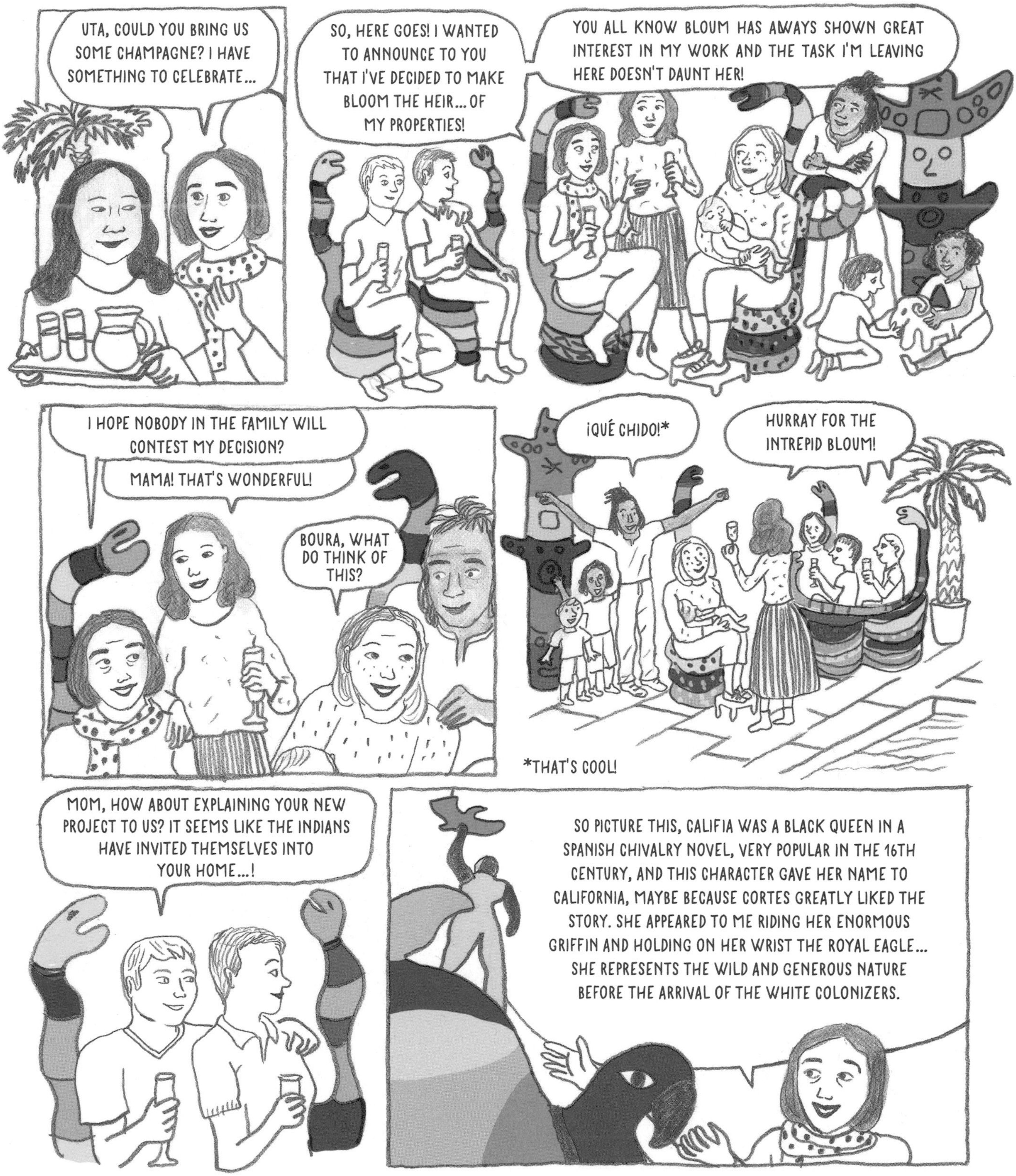
UTA, COULD YOU BRING US SOME CHAMPAGNE? I HAVE SOMETHING TO CELEBRATE...
SO, HERE GOES! I WANTED TO ANNOUNCE TO YOU THAT I'VE DECIDED TO MAKE BLOOM THE HEIR... OF MY PROPERTIES!
YOU ALL KNOW BLOUM HAS ALWAYS SHOWN GREAT INTEREST IN MY WORK AND THE TASK I'M LEAVING HERE DOESN'T DAUNT HER!
I HOPE NOBODY IN THE FAMILY WILL CONTEST MY DECISION?
MAMA! THAT'S WONDERFUL!
BOURA, WHAT DO THINK OF THIS?
¡QUÉ CHIDO!*
HURRAY FOR THE INTREPID BLOUM!
*THAT'S COOL!
MOM, HOW ABOUT EXPLAINING YOUR NEW PROJECT TO US? IT SEEMS LIKE THE INDIANS HAVE INVITED THEMSELVES INTO YOUR HOME...!
SO PICTURE THIS, CALIFIA WAS A BLACK QUEEN IN A SPANISH CHIVALRY NOVEL, VERY POPULAR IN THE 16TH CENTURY, AND THIS CHARACTER GAVE HER NAME TO CALIFORNIA, MAYBE BECAUSE CORTES GREATLY LIKED THE STORY. SHE APPEARED TO ME RIDING HER ENORMOUS GRIFFIN AND HOLDING ON HER WRIST THE ROYAL EAGLE... SHE REPRESENTS THE WILD AND GENEROUS NATURE BEFORE THE ARRIVAL OF THE WHITE COLONIZERS.

*Who is the savage queen? Califia, me Niki, or my little Bloum? I'm so happy she accepted the weight of my creations! I could no longer support that whole mountain on my own.*

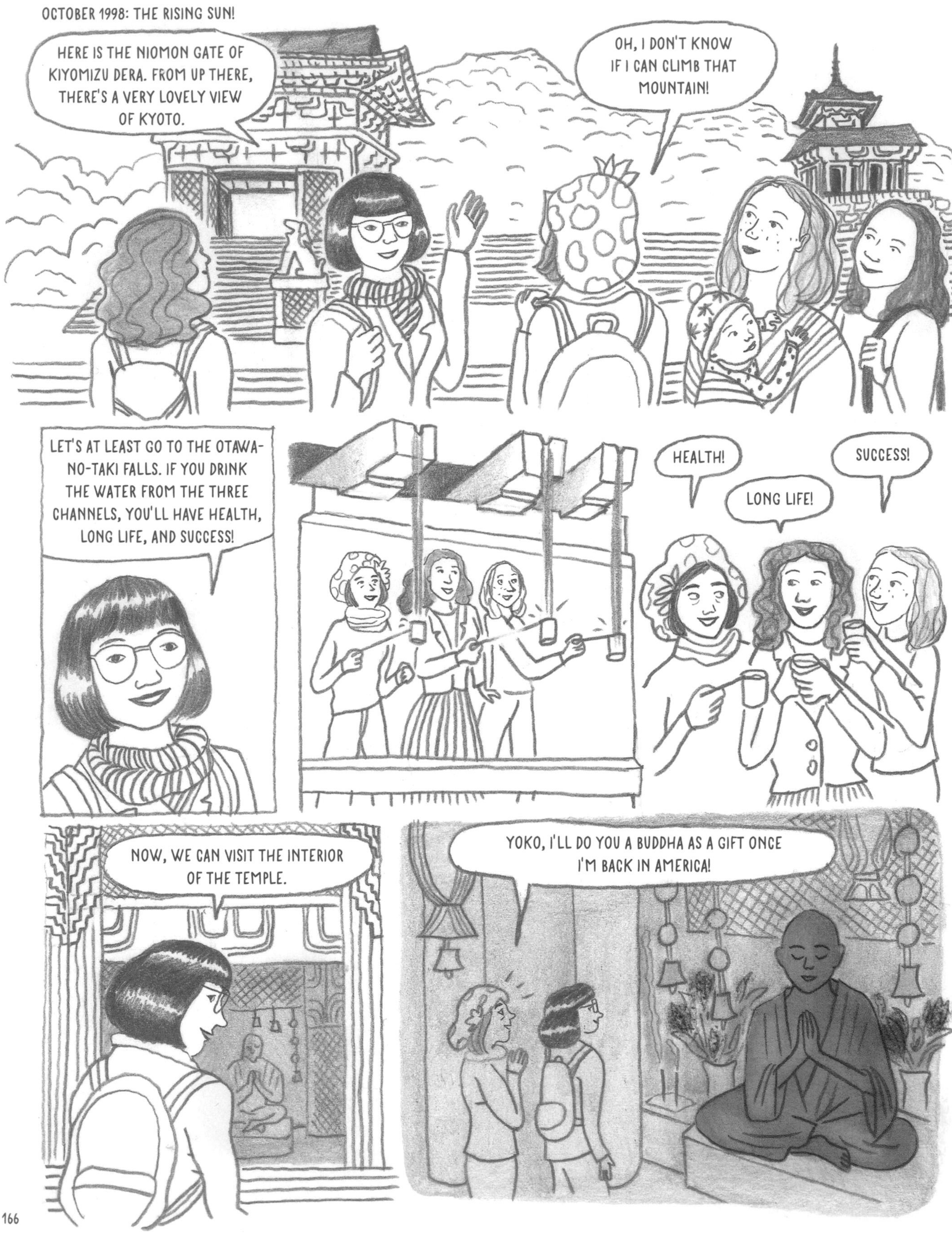
OCTOBER 1998: THE RISING SUN!
HERE IS THE NIOMON GATE OF KIYOMIZU DERA. FROM UP THERE, THERE'S A VERY LOVELY VIEW OF KYOTO.
OH, I DON'T KNOW IF I CAN CLIMB THAT MOUNTAIN!
LET'S AT LEAST GO TO THE OTAWA-NO-TAKI FALLS. IF YOU DRINK THE WATER FROM THE THREE CHANNELS, YOU'LL HAVE HEALTH, LONG LIFE, AND SUCCESS!
HEALTH!
LONG LIFE!
SUCCESS!
NOW, WE CAN VISIT THE INTERIOR OF THE TEMPLE.
YOKO, I'LL DO YOU A BUDDHA AS A GIFT ONCE I'M BACK IN AMERICA!

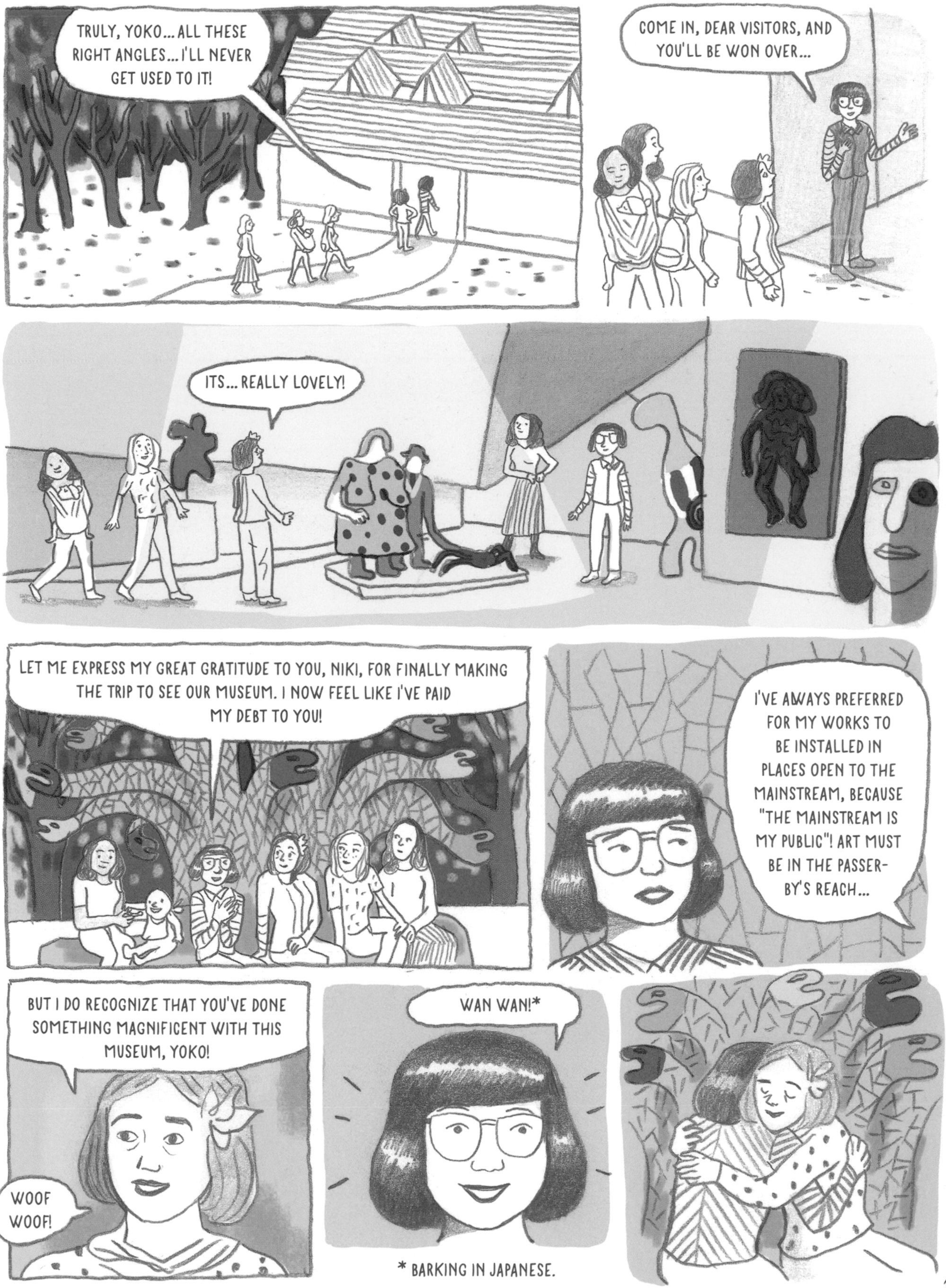
TRULY, YOKO... ALL THESE RIGHT ANGLES... I'LL NEVER GET USED TO IT!
COME IN, DEAR VISITORS, AND YOU'LL BE WON OVER...
ITS... REALLY LOVELY!
LET ME EXPRESS MY GREAT GRATITUDE TO YOU, NIKI, FOR FINALLY MAKING THE TRIP TO SEE OUR MUSEUM. I NOW FEEL LIKE I'VE PAID MY DEBT TO YOU!
I'VE ALWAYS PREFERRED FOR MY WORKS TO BE INSTALLED IN PLACES OPEN TO THE MAINSTREAM, BECAUSE "THE MAINSTREAM IS MY PUBLIC"! ART MUST BE IN THE PASSER-BY'S REACH...
BUT I DO RECOGNIZE THAT YOU'VE DONE SOMETHING MAGNIFICENT WITH THIS MUSEUM, YOKO!
WOOF WOOF!
WAN WAN!*
* BARKING IN JAPANESE.

1999, HANOVER: A LITTLE HELLO TO SOPHIE, CHARLOTTE, AND CAROLINE...

*In 1974, Michel Gehrke, the director of cultural affairs in the city of Hanover, gave me an order from me for three large Nanas that became the emblems of the city. And now some twenty years later, he proposes to me to develop the caves of the royal gardens, the magnificent Herrenhäuser Gärten. Caves! How could I resist?!*

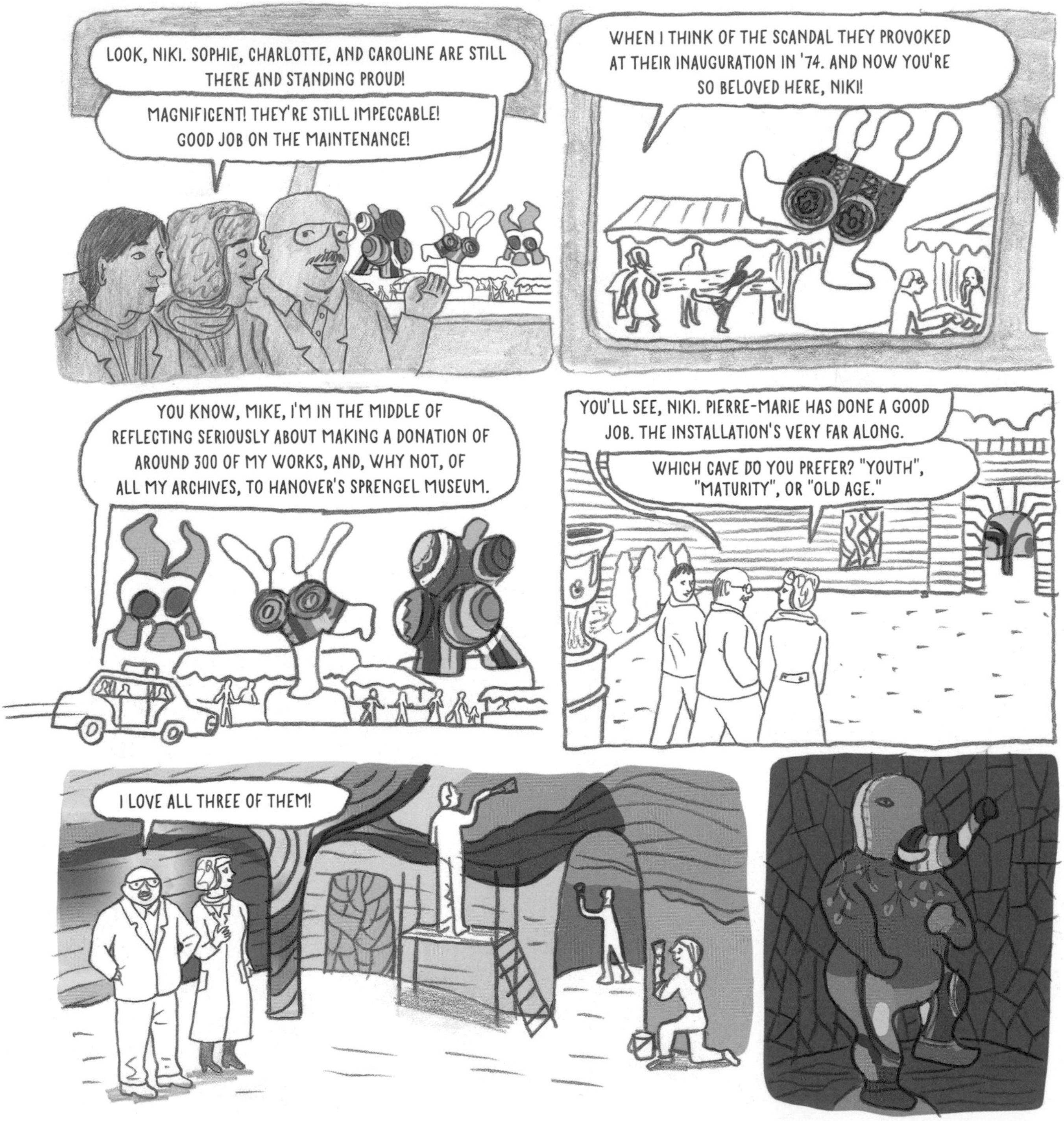
LOOK, NIKI. SOPHIE, CHARLOTTE, AND CAROLINE ARE STILL THERE AND STANDING PROUD!
MAGNIFICENT! THEY'RE STILL IMPECCABLE! GOOD JOB ON THE MAINTENANCE!
WHEN I THINK OF THE SCANDAL THEY PROVOKED AT THEIR INAUGURATION IN '74. AND NOW YOU'RE SO BELOVED HERE, NIKI!
YOU KNOW, MIKE, I'M IN THE MIDDLE OF REFLECTING SERIOUSLY ABOUT MAKING A DONATION OF AROUND 300 OF MY WORKS, AND, WHY NOT, OF ALL MY ARCHIVES, TO HANOVER'S SPRENGEL MUSEUM.
YOU'LL SEE, NIKI. PIERRE-MARIE HAS DONE A GOOD JOB. THE INSTALLATION'S VERY FAR ALONG.
WHICH CAVE DO YOU PREFER? "YOUTH", "MATURITY", OR "OLD AGE."
I LOVE ALL THREE OF THEM!

*All the sacred traditions of the world attract me more than ever, I've always dreamt of creating a temple open to all religions...Ganesh is my darling, with his child's body and his both human and divine nature. He masters the world thanks to his wisdom, he's in harmony with the universe... Other gods are calling to me, too, from the other side of the Atlantic...*

# CHAPTER 21

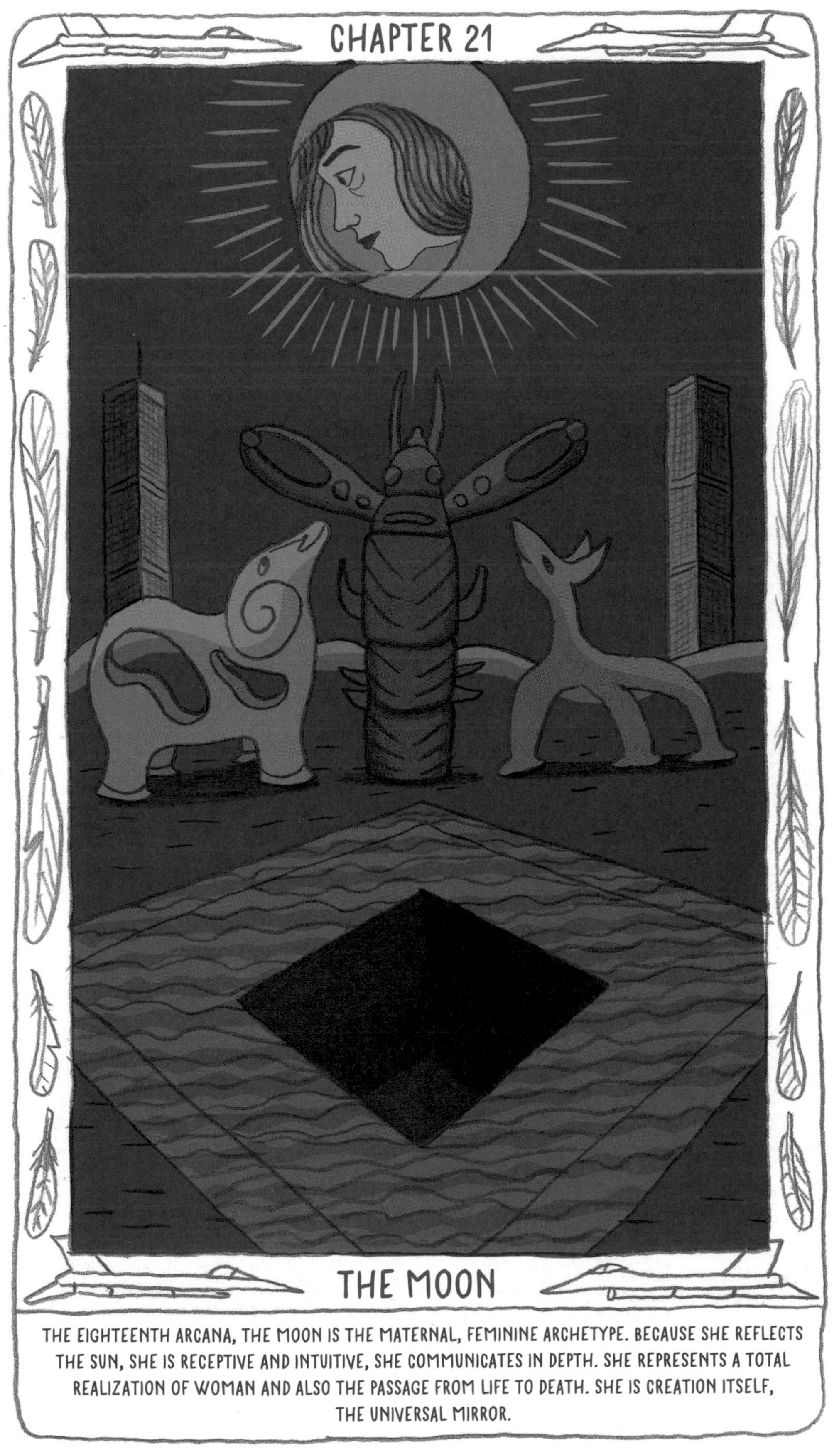

## THE MOON

THE EIGHTEENTH ARCANA, THE MOON IS THE MATERNAL, FEMININE ARCHETYPE. BECAUSE SHE REFLECTS THE SUN, SHE IS RECEPTIVE AND INTUITIVE, SHE COMMUNICATES IN DEPTH. SHE REPRESENTS A TOTAL REALIZATION OF WOMAN AND ALSO THE PASSAGE FROM LIFE TO DEATH. SHE IS CREATION ITSELF, THE UNIVERSAL MIRROR.

JANUARY 2000: A SETTING FOR THE MAGIC CIRCLE

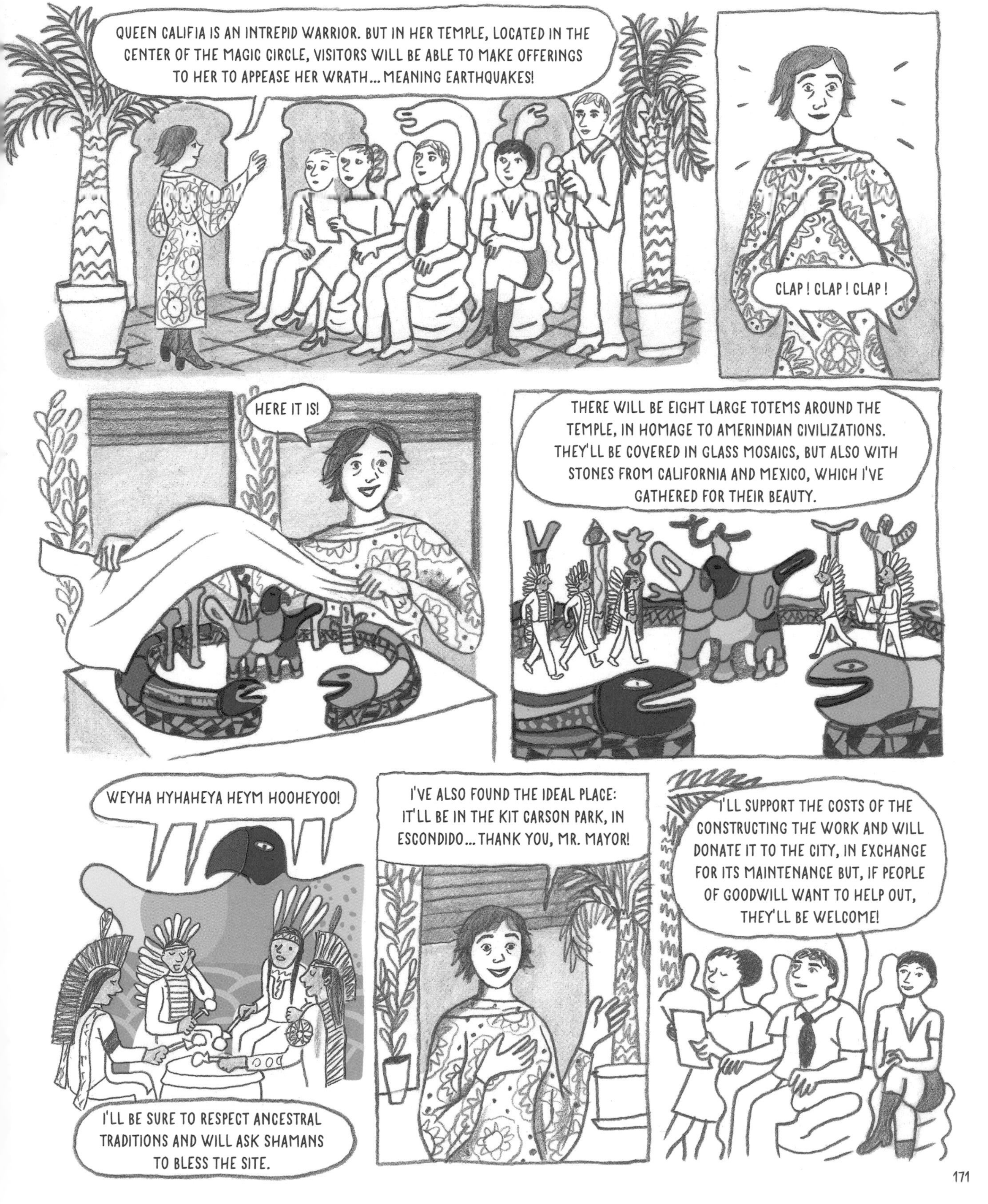
QUEEN CALIFIA IS AN INTREPID WARRIOR. BUT IN HER TEMPLE, LOCATED IN THE CENTER OF THE MAGIC CIRCLE, VISITORS WILL BE ABLE TO MAKE OFFERINGS TO HER TO APPEASE HER WRATH... MEANING EARTHQUAKES!
CLAP ! CLAP ! CLAP !
HERE IT IS!
THERE WILL BE EIGHT LARGE TOTEMS AROUND THE TEMPLE, IN HOMAGE TO AMERINDIAN CIVILIZATIONS. THEY'LL BE COVERED IN GLASS MOSAICS, BUT ALSO WITH STONES FROM CALIFORNIA AND MEXICO, WHICH I'VE GATHERED FOR THEIR BEAUTY.
WEYHA HYHAHEYA HEYM HOOHEYOO!
I'LL BE SURE TO RESPECT ANCESTRAL TRADITIONS AND WILL ASK SHAMANS TO BLESS THE SITE.
I'VE ALSO FOUND THE IDEAL PLACE: IT'LL BE IN THE KIT CARSON PARK, IN ESCONDIDO... THANK YOU, MR. MAYOR!
I'LL SUPPORT THE COSTS OF THE CONSTRUCTING THE WORK AND WILL DONATE IT TO THE CITY, IN EXCHANGE FOR ITS MAINTENANCE BUT, IF PEOPLE OF GOODWILL WANT TO HELP OUT, THEY'LL BE WELCOME!

SPRING 2001: A HOBBLED MESSAGE OF PEACE.

*The animals have departed for the Jerusalem Biblical Zoo, while the Ark will be built on site.*

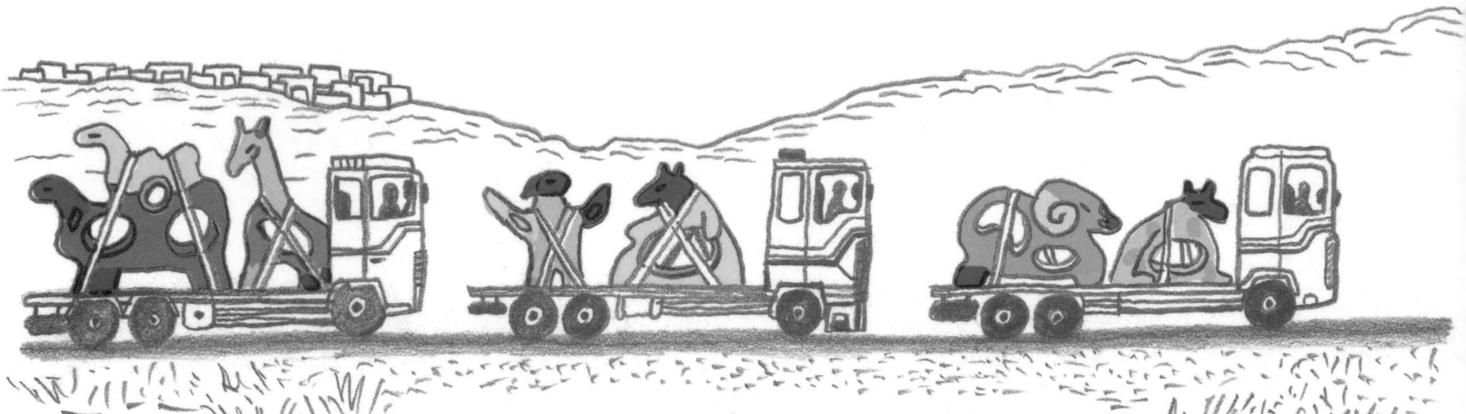

"DEAR TEDDY, WE WERE SO HAPPY AND PROUD, MARIO AND I,
TO OFFER YOU THE THE ARK AND ITS ANIMALS FOR YOUR 90TH BIRDTHDAY."

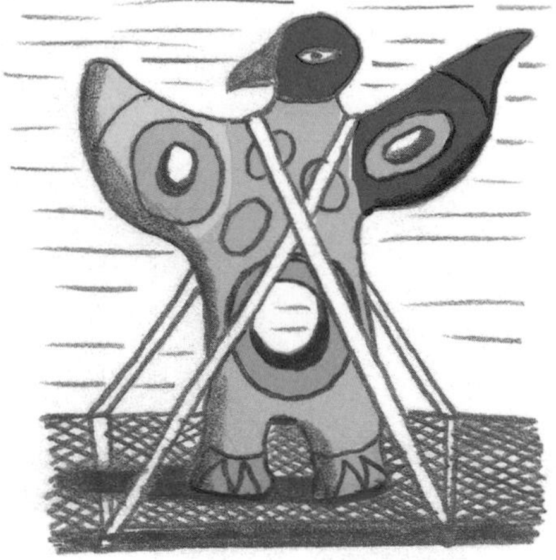

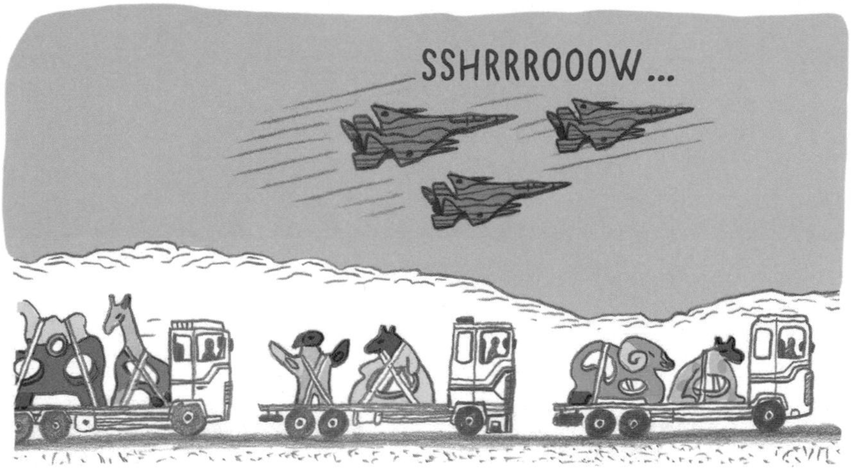
SSHRRROOOW...

"THE ANIMALS WERE SENT TO THE PROMISED LAND LIKE THE DOVE OF PEACE."

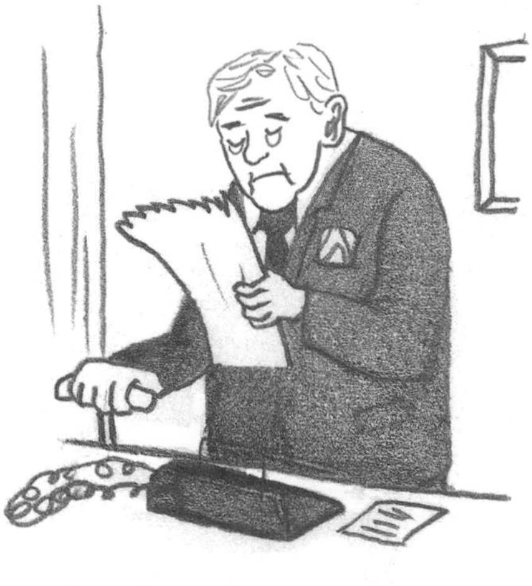

"WE REGRET TO ANNOUNCE THAT WE
WON'T BE ATTENDING THE INAUGURATION."

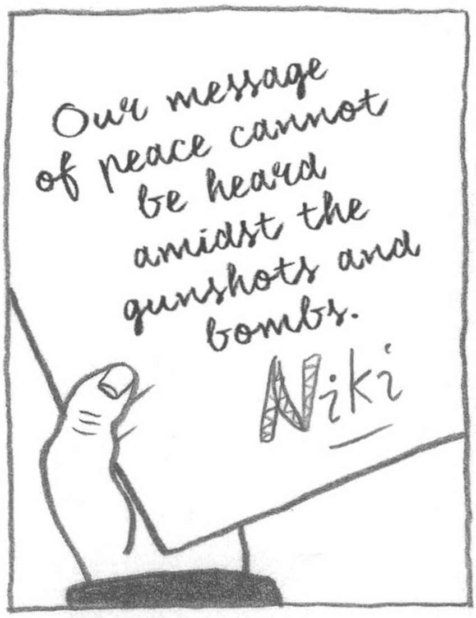
Our message
of peace cannot
be heard
amidst the
gunshots and
bombs.
Niki

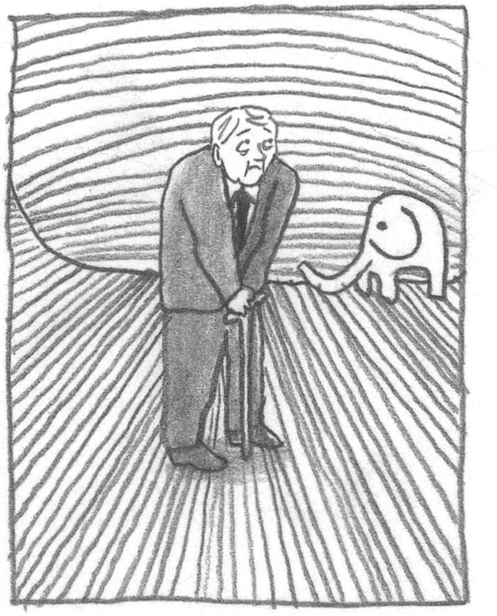

*The second Intifada began at the end of September 2000. Since the beginning of 2001, the new government of Ariel Sharon has been carrying out intensive repression of the Palestinians...I'm extremely sad.*

BLUE CLOUD.

*I stupidly broke my foot and haven't been able to walk in several months. Stormy weather is brewing. I feel it climbing in my throat like a bitter stone. The antidepressants are of no use to me. To help me, my niece Gisele gets me a very reputable Ojibwa shaman.*

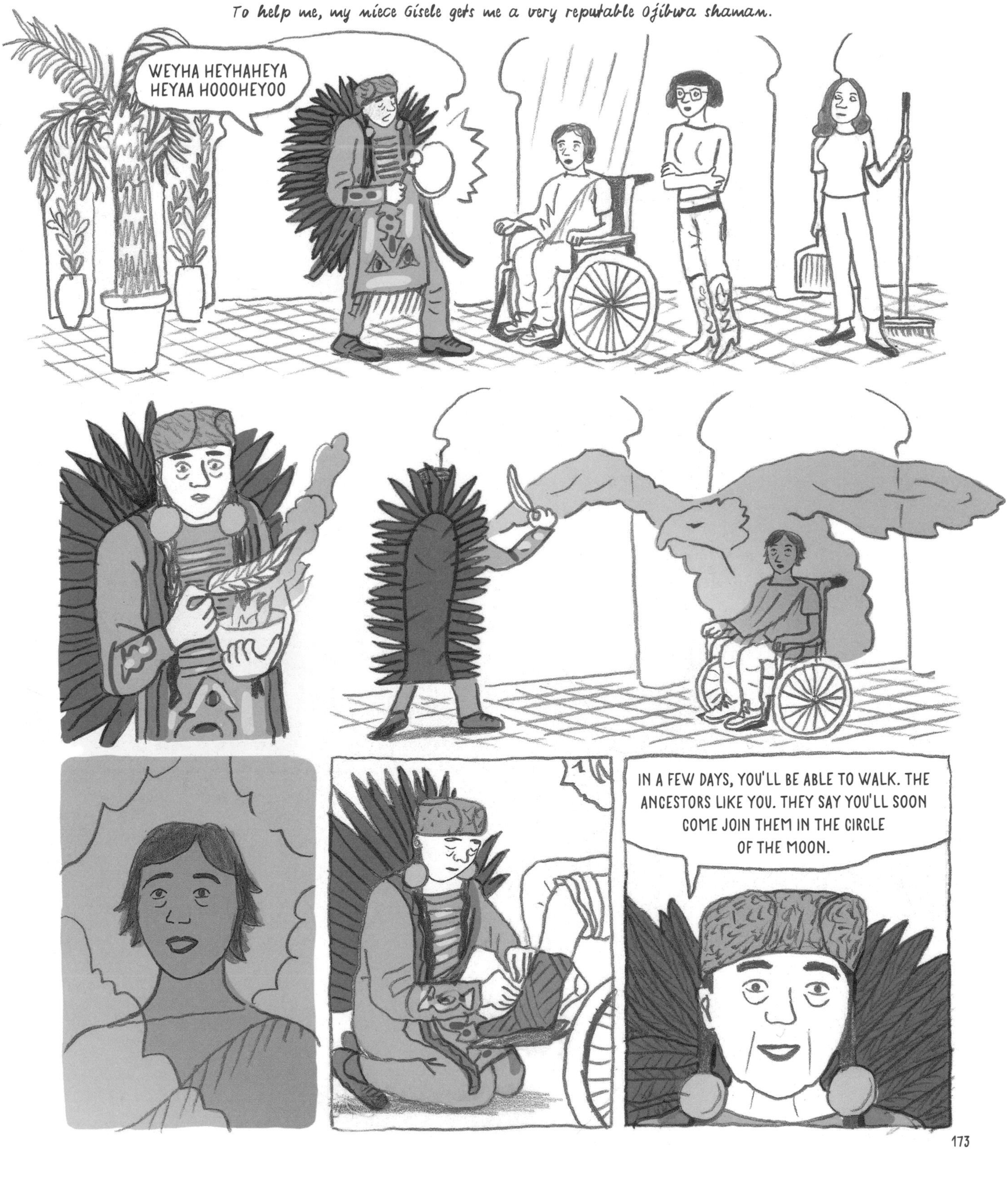
WEYHA HEYHAHEYA HEYAA HOOOHEYOO
IN A FEW DAYS, YOU'LL BE ABLE TO WALK. THE ANCESTORS LIKE YOU. THEY SAY YOU'LL SOON COME JOIN THEM IN THE CIRCLE OF THE MOON.

1962: THE CREATION OF THE SHOOTING PAINTING "KING KONG."

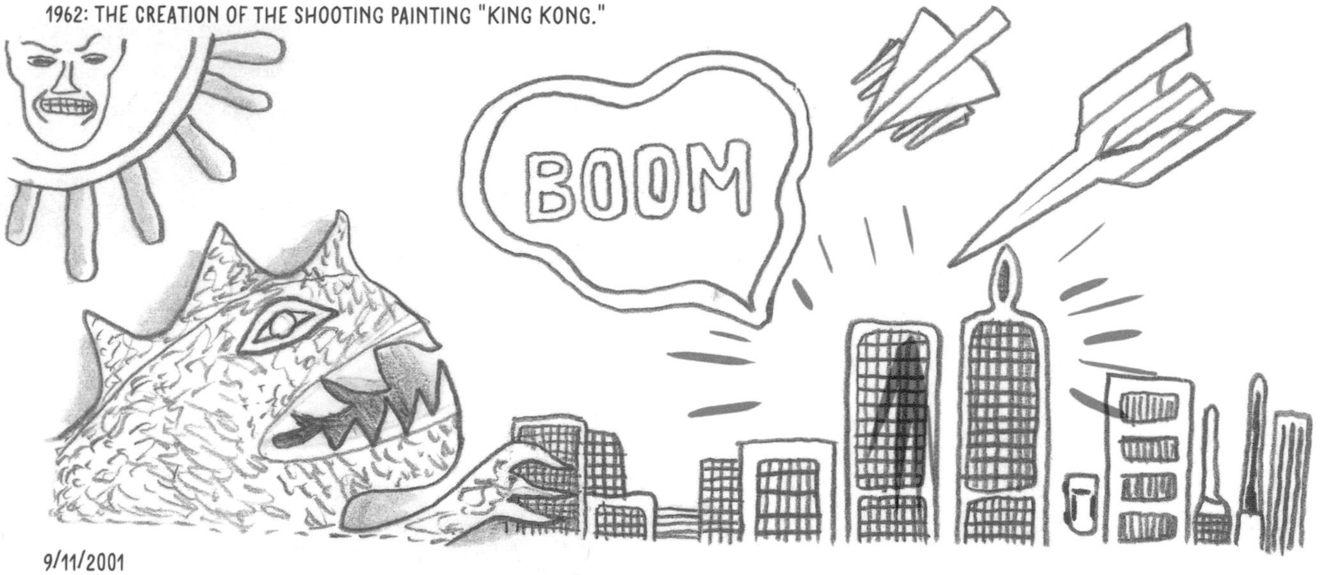
BOOM

9/11/2001

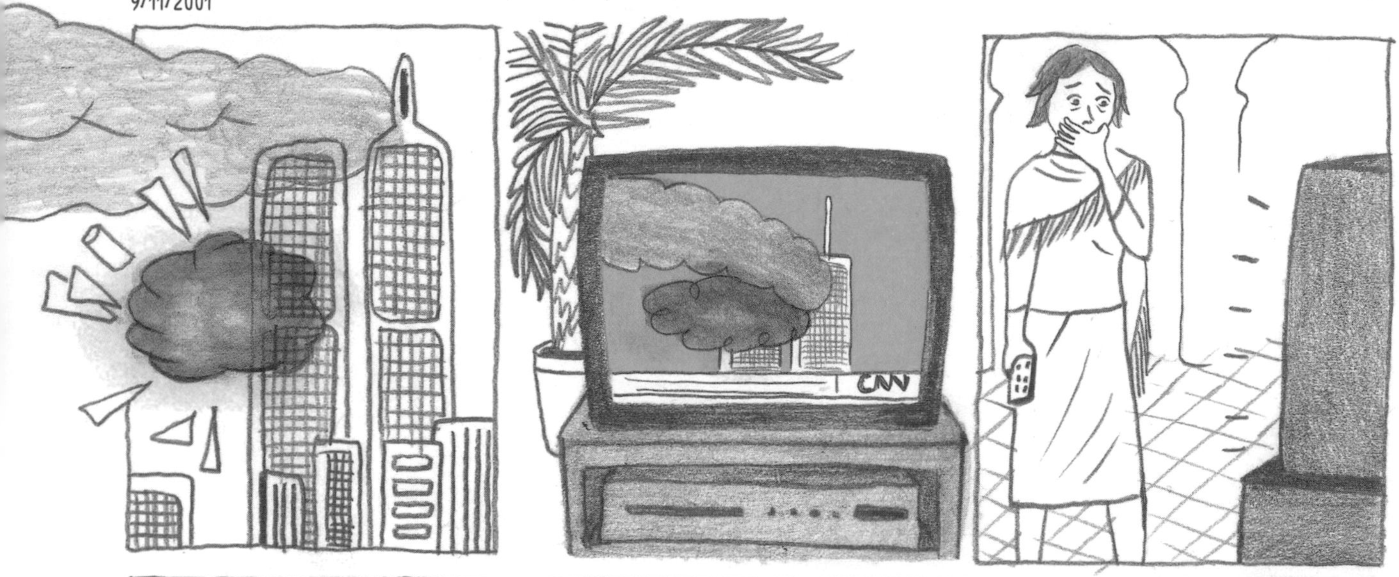
CNN

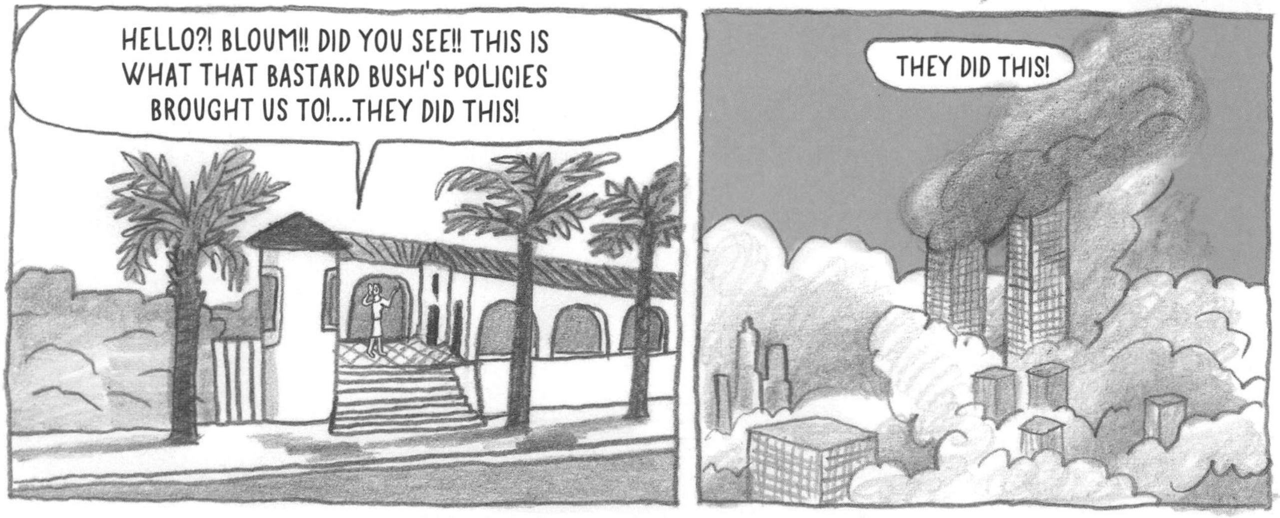
HELLO?! BLOUM!! DID YOU SEE!! THIS IS WHAT THAT BASTARD BUSH'S POLICIES BROUGHT US TO!...THEY DID THIS!
THEY DID THIS!

*How can I explain this feeling of absolute terror that's come over me?*
*Do I have gifts of premonition? Are we heading towards the end of the world?*

# CHAPTER 22

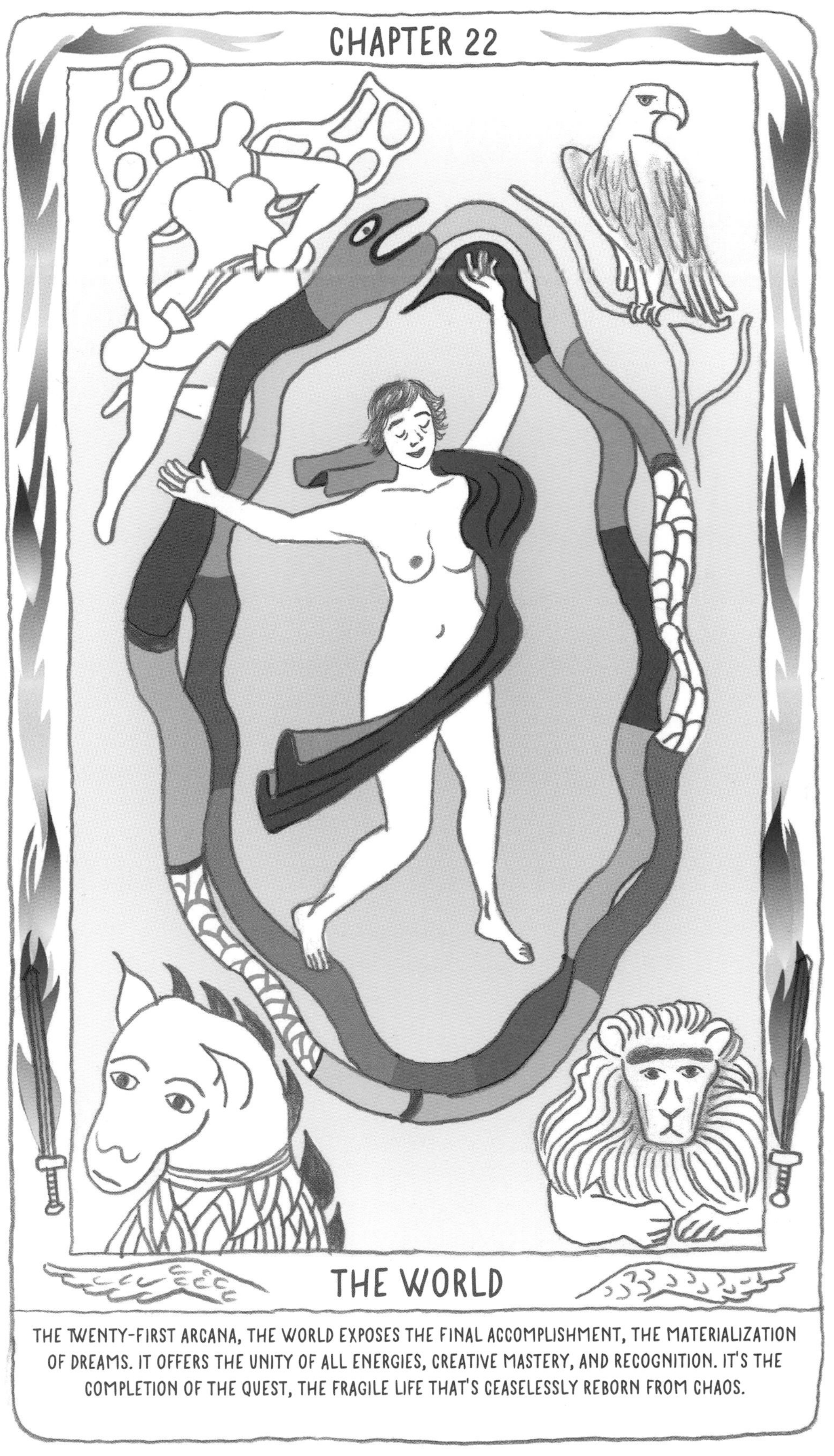

## THE WORLD

THE TWENTY-FIRST ARCANA, THE WORLD EXPOSES THE FINAL ACCOMPLISHMENT, THE MATERIALIZATION OF DREAMS. IT OFFERS THE UNITY OF ALL ENERGIES, CREATIVE MASTERY, AND RECOGNITION. IT'S THE COMPLETION OF THE QUEST, THE FRAGILE LIFE THAT'S CEASELESSLY REBORN FROM CHAOS.

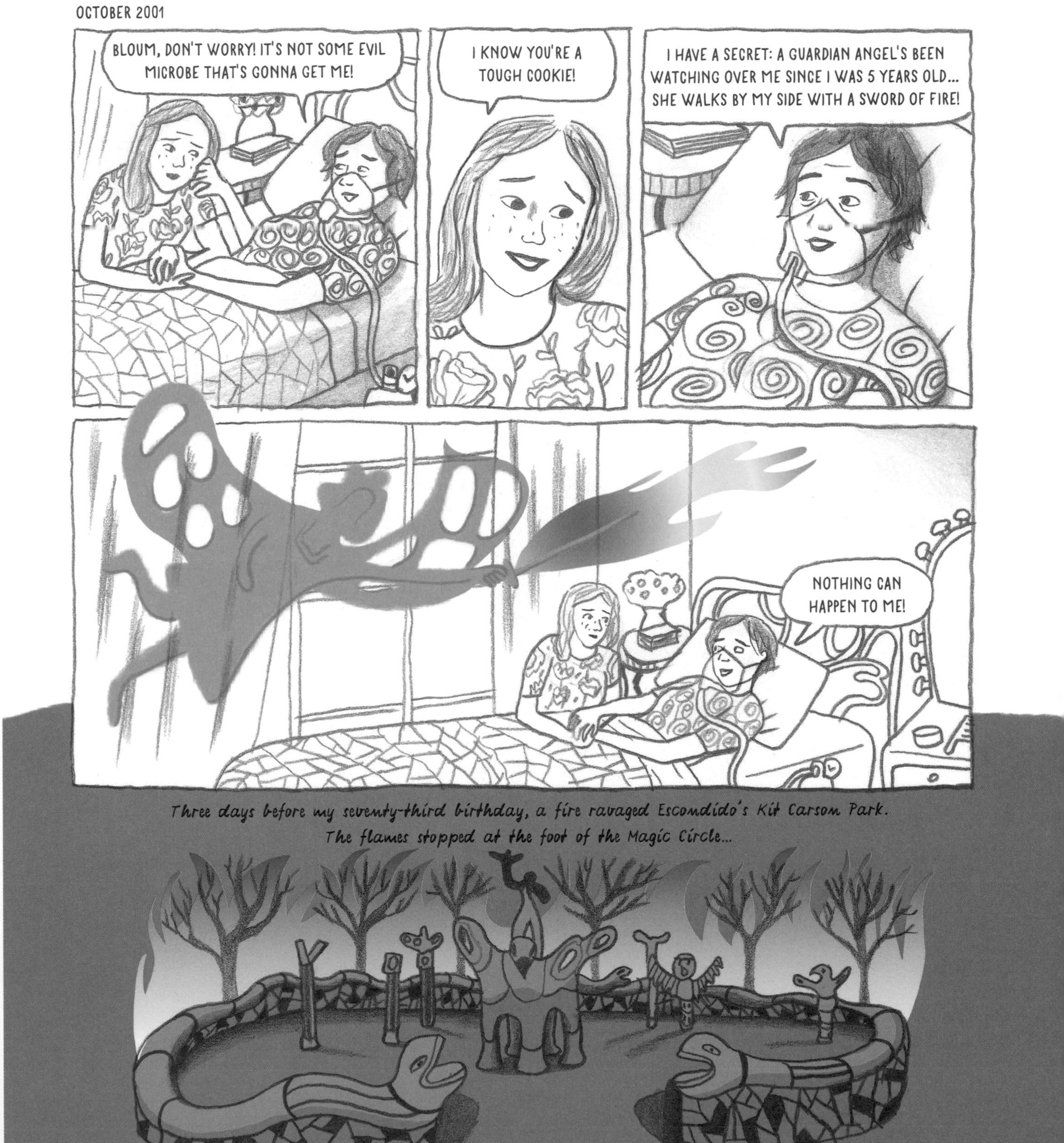
OCTOBER 2001
BLOUM, DON'T WORRY! IT'S NOT SOME EVIL MICROBE THAT'S GONNA GET ME!
I KNOW YOU'RE A TOUGH COOKIE!
I HAVE A SECRET: A GUARDIAN ANGEL'S BEEN WATCHING OVER ME SINCE I WAS 5 YEARS OLD... SHE WALKS BY MY SIDE WITH A SWORD OF FIRE!
NOTHING CAN HAPPEN TO ME!
Three days before my seventy-third birthday, a fire ravaged Escondido's Kit Carson Park. The flames stopped at the foot of the Magic Circle...
My works are part of the cosmos. They are its cherished infants, and the cosmos protects them... I feel the world entering me, I AM the world!

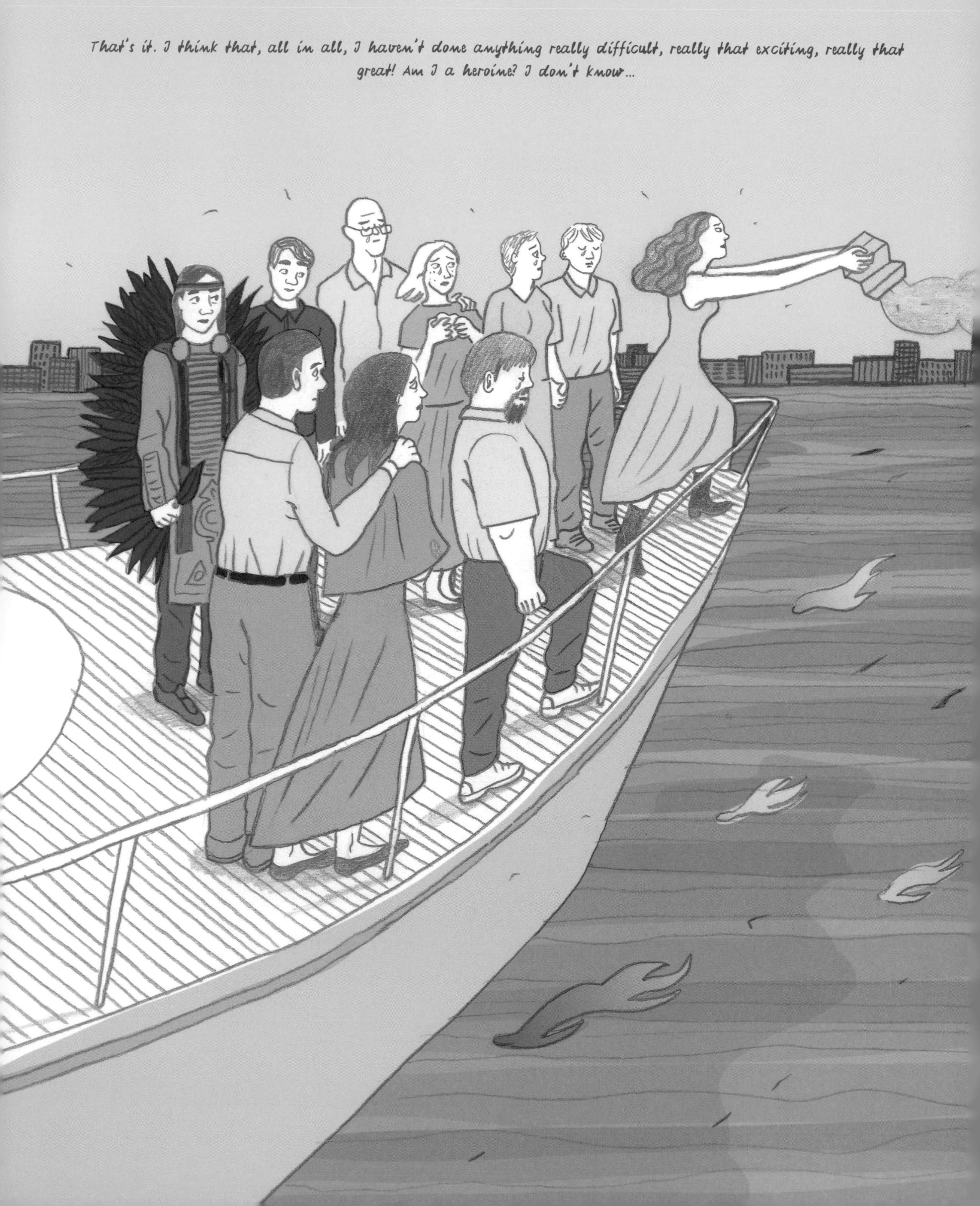
That's it. I think that, all in all, I haven't done anything really difficult, really that exciting, really that great! Am I a heroine? I don't know...

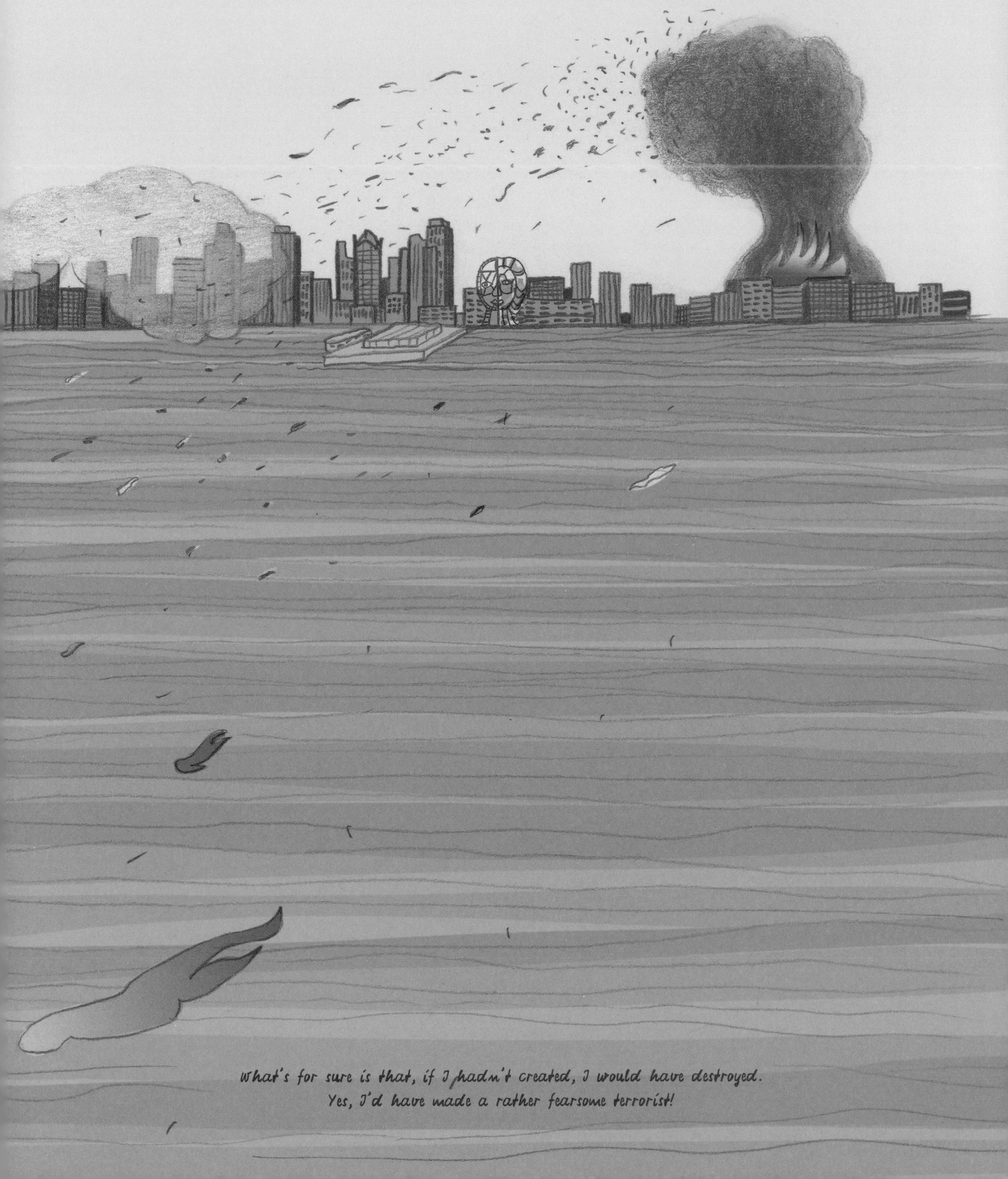
What's for sure is that, if I hadn't created, I would have destroyed.
Yes, I'd have made a rather fearsome terrorist!

**1930** The birth of Catherine Marie Agnes Fal de Saint Phalle, at Neuilly-sur-Seine, France, on October 29th. For astronomy lovers, her theme is "Scorpio ascendant Scorpio." For those keen on history, her entry into the world one year after the October 1929 stock market crash will turn Agnes into an abruptly penniless aristocrat, the family bank having been ruined as a result of this event. Her mother, Jeanne Jacqueline Harper, is an upper class American. Her father, André Marie, is French, of noble descent, related to the Montespans, a largely unacknowledged ancestry, all the same…

Their elder son, John, displays a mildly domineering character. The family will subsequently grow larger with the birth of two other daughters, Claire and Elizabeth, and a second son, Richard, in 1943. The youngsters are often taken across the Atlantic, dividing their lives with their parents in Connecticut or New York and with stays in the castles of their respective grandparents in France, in the Nièvre (Huez) and in the Oise (Fillerval). Deprived of her mother's presence for her three first years—unlike her big brother—Agnes will have painful memories of her premature separation from her mother.

**1937-1947** Agnes, or "Niki," drifts through several American schools, including private religious schools that her rebellious character has trouble tolerating. The Second World War stops the family's trips to France. Her paternal grandmother perishes during a fire at her Huez castle occupied by German troops.
After leaving the Brearly School of New York prematurely for having committed her first act of artistic revolt, Niki is placed in a convent school in Suffern, NY…where she loses her faith!
She earns her high school diploma at the Oldfield School in Maryland in 1947 and plans to go off to study art history and literature in Paris.

**1948-1949** "Narcissistic and vain," in her own words, Niki begins a career as a fashion model. She poses for several magazines, such as Vogue and Life. By happenstance, she

# CHRONOLOGY

runs into a childhood acquaintance in the person of Harry Matthews, who is hardly any older than she and doing his military service in the U.S. Navy. Henry comes from a well-heeled, highly cultivated family. It's love at first sight, and the two young people decide to get married on June 6, 1949, in order to be shed of the constraints of their respective families' notions of proprieties.

**1950** After a church wedding insisted upon by Niki's mother, the young couple moves to Massachusetts where Harry is pursuing his musical studies at Harvard, with the goal of becoming an orchestra conductor. Niki starts painting. The couple adores movies, devours American, English, and French literature, frequents painting exhibitions, all while a happy event is in store, to the great displeasure of the future grandmothers…

**1951** Laura is born at the public hospital in Boston on April 23rd. The young mother refuses to be cooped up at home and registers for a painting class that she will attend only twice, before deciding to learn on her own. The "witch-hunt" politics led by Senator McCarthy convinces the couple to relocate to France.

**1951** The young family comes to live in Paris. Niki takes theater classes while still continuing photo shoots for *Elle* and *Vogue* with the American photographer Henry Clarke. Harry devotes himself to music. The post-war Parisian ambiance at Saint-Germain-des-Prés, with its jazz clubs and celebrities is so distant from that of the then-segregated America!

**1953** For the sake of its music festival, the Matthews move to Menton. But Niki is suffering from mental health problems and finds it difficult to tolerate Harry's infidelities. Following a serious crisis exacerbated by jealousy, she is admitted to the Nice psychiatric hospital. After a radical treatment of insulin and electroshock, Niki regains an unhoped-for equilibrium, thanks to the art of collage and a few tubes of paint…Thus

is her vocation born, which she will then pursue to the very end.

**1954** The family returns to Paris into a home on Rue Hallé. The American painter Hugh Weiss regularly comes by to give Niki advice, mainly that of keeping her freshness as a self-taught artist. Giving in to Niki's encouragement, Harry starts writing. At year's end, the couple moves to Deiá, Majorca, very near the home of Robert Graves, the English poet and novelist. Life is simple and rustic there.

**1955** While Niki is pregnant again, the small family undertakes a trip to Spain, visits the museums, arenas, and churches… The Güell de Gaudí Park will be a major revelation for Niki, who dreams of herself creating a fabulous garden "where people will be happy."
Philip is born prematurely in April. He will experience three very difficult first years, while suffering from convulsions. Niki recovers from her second pregnancy with difficulty and, once again, develops the symptoms of hyperthyroidism: depression, tachycardia…

**1956-1959** Back in Paris, now at the Impasse Ronsin, the couple makes the acquaintance of Swiss artists Jean Tinguely and his wife Eva Aeppli, accompanied by the young and seductive Romanian Daniel Spoerri, the dancer and future mixed media artist. Despite their meager resources, Henry buys a piece from Jean. And Niki asks him for help fashioning her first sculpture, a "fantasy tree." She undergoes a partial removal of her thyroid gland in 1958.
Harry buys a house at Lans-en-Vercors where the family moves, alternating with trips to Paris. Niki continues painting in oils and with her collages. Mosaic makes an appearance in her work. She discovers the works of Jasper Johns, Robert Rauschenberg, and Jackson Pollock…

**1960** Niki decides to leave Harry in order to devote herself entirely to art. He assumes custody of the children. She continues her assembly of objects, takes inspiration from Jasper Johns by creating painting targets at which the public can throw darts. She ends up moving in with Jean Tinguely, who is alone at the Impasse Ronsin, after the departure of Eva.

**1961** Niki invents the "Shooting Actions," on February 12th. Twelve sessions spread out through February 1963, including in Malibu and Los Angeles (*King Kong*). Viewers are invited to shoot at the white panels, stuffed with objects and pockets of paint inserted in plaster, with the goal of creating a participatory work. Her performances are well-noticed and the art critic Pierre Restany consecrates her as a member of and the only woman among the "New Realists," in the manner of Jean Tinguely, Arman, Yves Klein, Daniel Spoerri, Martia Raysse, César…

On June 20, 1961, Niki participates with Robert Rauschenberg, Jasper Johns, and Tinguely at a concert-performance of John Cage, played by David Tudor, at the American Embassy in Paris. To the boos of the scandalized audience, each artist takes part by creating a work live on stage: painting, shots, the construction of a wall… Marcel Duchamp introduces Niki and Jean to the larger-than-life Salvador Dalí, who invites them to construct a "bull of fire" for the bull fight in Figueras.

**1962** Niki and Jean visit California, where they admire Rodia's Watts Towers, and the Olmec colossal heads in Mexico. Some *Shootings* and *Altars* are presented at the Galerie Rive Droite in Paris. Alexandre Iolas proposes to Niki an exhibition in New York in October. Before that, she participates in a big installation, *Dylaby* (Dynamic Labyrinth) at Amsterdam's Stedelijk Museum with Rauschenberg, Raysse, Spoerri, Tinguely, and the Swede Per Olof Ultvedt.

**1963-1965** Jean and Niki move into an ancient inn at Soisy-sur-École. Niki works on some *Brides* in fabrics, women in labor, wool heads, and dragons. She starts a reflection on the condition and role of women. She creates her first *Nanas*, which will be exhibited at Alexandre Iolas' gallery in Paris.

**1966** Roland Petit's ballet *The Praise of Folly* is quite the success. Niki designed the sets and costumes, in collaboration with Jean Tinguely and Martial Raysse. Pontus Hultén, the director of Sotckholm's Moderna Museet, invites Niki and Jean to create a monumental, ephemeral work with Per Olof Ultvedt. It will be *Hon*, "She" in Swedish. On this occasion, the couple will meet the Swiss man Rico Weber, who will become their most faithful collaborator.

**1967** With great conviction, Niki and Jean promote their sculptures, the *Fantastic Paradise*, for the French pavilion at the Expo 67 in Montreal. The sculptures are next erected in Central Park in New York. They are then retrieved by Stockholm's Moderna Museet where they are still located today. On August 17th, Niki's father dies from a heart attack.

**1968** The theatrical piece *Ich, All About Me* is performed on the occasion of the fourth documenta at Kassel, Germany. Niki wrote and staged it with Rainer von Diez and designed the sets and costumes. Two exhibitions of her work take place in Düsseldorf and Hanover.
Niki suffers from recurring respiratory problems. Jean Tinguely buys another inn, in Switzerland, for his new lover, Micheline Gygax, with whom he will have a son in 1973.

**1969-1970** The first construction of inhabitable sculptures begins in the forest in the Var, on land belonging to Rainer von Diez. Niki and Jean work there for three years. *The Dream of the Bird*, which was built without any official permit, is now categorized as a historical monument.
Simultaneously, Jean starts work on his *Cyclops* in Milly-la-Forêt without a construction permit, either. His Swiss friends Berhard Luginbühl and Rico Weber assist him.

**1971** Niki agrees to marry Jean. Their union safeguards the future of their works. Bloum—Niki's granddaughter and daughter of Laura and Laurent Condominas—is born in Bali.

**1972** Niki imagines *The Golem* in Jerusalem. This monster with three tongue-slides is great for children, but is also a true bunker conceived by Jean to protect against bombardments… Will it be displaced to lengthen the tramline currently under construction? Niki rents the Beauregard castle near Grasse, France, to shoot her scandalous movie *Daddy* with Peter Whitehead, a film director from the London underground. A second version will be shot in 1973 at Soisy with Mia Martin and Clarice Rivers performing. She has the play *Dragon* built at Knokke-le-Zoute, Belgium, at the request of Fabienne and Roger Nellens for their children.

**1974** The city of Hanover commissions three large *Nanas*. They are called *Caroline*, *Charlotte*, and *Sophie*, the names of three of the city's queens. Elizabeth, Niki's sister, commits suicide. Niki suffers from a pulmonary abscess that nearly kills her. She has a stays at the Bern hospital.

**1975-1976** Niki goes to California to convalesce, then returns to the Swiss Alps at St. Moritz. There, she meets Marella Agnelli, née Carracciolo, a friend she'd not seen in some twenty years. Niki reveals to Marella her obsession with creating a garden of monumental sculptures. Marella speaks to her of her brothers Carlo and Nicola, who possess an extensive property in Tuscany. Niki writes the screenplay for *A Dream Longer than the Night*, which is filmed with the participation of many artists and leading figures in the austere setting of the Commanderie in Dannemois, France.

**1977-1979** Niki works and travels to Mexico with the poet Constantin Mulgrave. Ricardo Menon becomes her assistant. She creates the first models of the *Tarot Garden*. In May 1978. Jeanne Jacqueline de Saint Phalle dies from cancer. Work begins at Garavicchio in Tuscany, on the land graciously offered by the Caracciolo brothers. A first exhibition of Niki's works takes place at the Watari Gallery in Tokyo. In New York, Gimpel & Weitzenhoffer display *Monumental Projects*.

**1980** A big retrospective of Niki's work occurs at the Centre Georges Pompidou in Paris, then in Germany, at Duisbourg and Hanover. Yoko Masuda organizes a first exhibition of Niki's work that she had collected with her own yen at the Space Niki in Tokyo.

**1981-1984** Niki works most of the time at Garavicchio. After beginning work on the *Magician*, the *Empress*, and the *Sun*, for which the cement is finally poured, the *Pope*, the *Tower*, the *High Priestess*, and *Justice* follow.

To finance the *Garden* work, Niki agrees to market a perfume with her name. She also creates and unveils jewelry, small sculptures and chairs, vases and serpent lamps.

In 1983, Niki moves inside the Empress. Ricardo Menon unearths a formidable ceramicist, Venera Finocchiaro, who will make all the tesserae to cover the *Tarot Garden* sculptures. In the interim, the two of them create *The Stravinsky Fountain* at the Beaubourg Plateau, an order initially offered to Jean Tinguely. Pierre Marie Lejeune—fresh out of the school of Beaux-Arts—comes to lend them a hand and will remain a close collaborator forever after. Niki is suffering from a rheumatoid arthritis that will torture her for more than four years, until she reluctantly agrees to a cortisone treatment.

**1985** Somewhat neglected, the Cyclops at Milly-la-Forêt is vandalized. Niki manages to convince the French government to accept the donation of the sculpture in exchange for its protection and maintenance.

A short while after installing his sculpture Eos at the summit of the *Garden's Tower*, Jean Tinguely, the victim of a heart attack, has open-heart surgery.

**1986** With the help of Professor Silvio Barandun, the Swiss immunologist, Niki writes and designs an information booklet on AIDS: *You Can't Catch it Holding Hands*. It will be translated into five languages and have 70,000 copies printed and distributed in schools and clinics. Niki has mirrors placed on the large face of the *Cyclops*, which will accelerate its completion.

**1987-1990** Exhibitions take place in Munich, Geneva, and at Roslyn, Long Island in the United States. At Château-Chinon, François Mitterand inaugurates a new fountain signed by Jean and Niki. In Paris, JGM Galerie and the Galerie de France handle the simultaneous exhibition of collaborative works of Niki and Jean during the Eighties. Ricardo Menon dies from AIDS in 1989. In 1990, the French agency combatting AIDS publishes the French version of Niki's informational booklet: *Sida, tu ne l'attraperas pas*, and distributes it to every school in France.

**1991** After the sudden death of Micheline Gygax in June, and while his new girlfriend, the Bulgarian painter Milena Palakarkina, is pregnant, Jean Tinguely dies from a stroke on August 30th. Paul Sacher raises the possibility of creating a Tinguely museum in Basel.

**1992-1993** Niki ensures the longevity of Jean's works by donating sculptures she had inherited for the creation of the museum in Basel and that of an Espace Jean Tinguely-Niki de Saint Phalle in Fribourg, Jean's hometown. She invents the *Shattered Paintings*, kinetic panels in homage to Tinguely.

**1994-1996** Her breathing problems becoming more and more acute, Niki moves to California for its air quality and for the reassuring presence of eminent physicians. The Niki Museum is inaugurated in October at Nasu in Japan, but Niki refuses to make the trip.

Jean's architect friend, Mario Botta, builds the Tinguely Museum and soon will construct the outer wall of the *Tarot Garden*. He also works with Niki on a new project ordered by the Jerusalem Foundation: a *Noah's Ark*. On September 30, 1996, the Tinguely Museum is inaugurated in Basel. Niki creates a big American lizard named "Gila" for a private residence in San Diego. She uses stones from California juxtaposed with glass mosaic to cover the sculpture. These local stones will become her favorite material for works to come.

**1997** *The Tarot Garden* is finally opening its doors in bits and stages. The Garden Foundation is created on August 4, 1997. The official opening must wait, however, until May 15, 1998. The Swiss national rail service orders a monumental sculpture for the Zurich train station: it will be the *Protecting Angel*.

**1998** Niki reunites her childhood memories in a photo album that is both written and illustrated: *Traces*.

She finally makes the trip to the Land of the Rising Sun, accompanied by her daughter Laura, her granddaughter, and her great-granddaughter! Yoko Masuda welcomes her with a feeling of accomplishment.

**1999** Niki responds to the request of the city of Hanover by creating the decoration of the caves of the Royal Gardens, the Herrenäuser Gärten, with the help of Pierre Marie Lejeune.

**2000** Niki receives the Praemium Imperiale, a prize akin to a Nobel prize for the arts, awarded by the Japan Art Association.

She leads a major new project at the Kit Carson Park in Escondido, California, which will be inaugurated after her death, in 2003: *Queen Califia's Magical Circle*. The 22 sculptures of fantastical animals will depart for Jerusalem, to join the *Ark* constructed by Mario Botta. But the two artists refuse to attend the inauguration for ethical reasons. Niki makes a large donation of her works to Hanover's Sprengel Museum. She undertakes the continuation of her autobiography: 1950-1960, *Harry and Me, The Family Years*.

**2001** The attack on the Twin Towers affects Niki to the very core of her being. On October 11th, she signs over another donation, to the city of Nice this time, in memory of the place where art had fully devoted her to its vocation.

**2002** Niki dies on May 21st, because she can no longer breathe.

In nearly fifty years of creating, she gave the world more than 3500 artworks, more than 1 a week...

## FURTHER READING

Christiane Weidermann, *Niki de Saint Phalle*. Prestel, 2014. ISBN 9783791349756.

Bloum Cardenas and Camille Morineau, *Niki de Saint Phalle*. La Fábrica/
Guggenheim Museum Bilbao, 2015. ISBN 9788415691983.

Niki de Saint Phalle. *Insider-Outside. World Inspired Art*. Mingei
International Museum, 1998. ISBN 9780914155102.

Niki de Saint Phalle and Marella Carraciolo. *Niki de Saint Phalle and the Tarot Garden*.
Benteli, 2010. ISBN 9783716515372.

Carla Schulz-Hoffman, *Niki de Saint Phalle: My Art-My Dreams*.
Prestel, 2008. ISBN 9783791339849.

### DOMINIQUE OSUCH

Graduate of the school of graphic arts of Strasbourg, Dominique
Osuch has done illustrations for many children's books as well as
written scripts for various graphic novels.

### SANDRINE MARTIN

Sandrine Martin has done numerous illustrations for children's
books and press along with a growing number of graphic novels.

The authors would like to thank warmly Bloum Cardenas for her sunny welcome and enthusiasm, as well as Christine Cam and Nejib Belhadj Kacem for their kind attention, and Catherine Francblin for her openness and indispensable work as an art historian.

Sandrine Martin is particularly grateful to Fanis for listening and for technical support, and to the Atelier Marsopolis for its professionalism and conviviality.

The sentences within quotation marks in the captions and dialog balloons are citations of Niki.

MONET

THOREAU

Other biographies in comics from NBM:
Monet, Itinerant of Light
Thoreau, a Sublime Life
Billie Holiday
A Girl in Dior

See many more with previews
and over 200 graphic novels at
**NBMPUB.COM**

NBM
160 Broadway, Suite 700, East Wing,
New York, NY 10038
Catalog available upon request

Girl in
Dior

MUÑOZ & SAMPAYO
BILLIE HOLIDAY

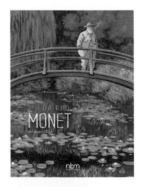

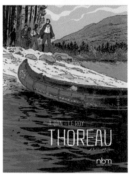

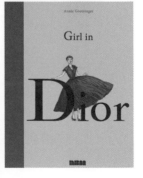

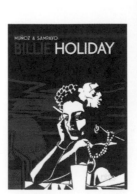